Multimodal Data Fusion for Bioinformatics Artificial Intelligence

Scrivener Publishing
100 Cummings Center, Suite 541J
Beverly, MA 01915-6106

Publishers at Scrivener
Martin Scrivener (martin@scrivenerpublishing.com)
Phillip Carmical (pcarmical@scrivenerpublishing.com)

Multimodal Data Fusion for Bioinformatics Artificial Intelligence

Edited by

Umesh Kumar Lilhore

Abhishek Kumar

Narayan Vyas

Sarita Simaiya

and

Vishal Dutt

Scrivener Publishing

WILEY

This edition first published 2025 by John Wiley & Sons, Inc., 111 River Street, Hoboken, NJ 07030, USA
and Scrivener Publishing LLC, 100 Cummings Center, Suite 541J, Beverly, MA 01915, USA

For more information about Scrivener publications please visit www.scrivenerpublishing.com.

Wiley Global Headquarters
111 River Street, Hoboken, NJ 07030, USA

For details of our global editorial offices, customer services, and more information about Wiley products visit us at www.wiley.com.

Library of Congress Cataloging-in-Publication Data

ISBN 9781394269938

Front cover images supplied by Pixabay.com
Cover design by Russell Richardson

Set in size of 11pt and Minion Pro by Manila Typesetting Company, Makati, Philippines

Printed in the USA

10 9 8 7 6 5 4 3 2 1

Contents

Preface

This book addresses the fascinating intersection of artificial intelligence (AI) and bioinformatics. This book, divided into 16 comprehensive chapters, delves into how AI technologies are revolutionizing the analysis and integration of diverse biological data. It provides a balanced perspective on the latest research, practical applications, and the challenges encountered in combining multiple types of data for bioinformatics research and healthcare innovation.

Chapter 1, "Advancements and Challenges in Multimodal Data Fusion for Bioinformatics AI," introduces how fusing various data types enhances research, yet poses significant challenges. Chapter 2 discusses the impact of Automated Machine Learning (AutoML) on bioinformatics, showcasing how automated processes simplify and accelerate research. Chapter 3 uncovers how AI-driven data analysis brings to light new biological insights, emphasizing its transformative potential.

Chapter 4 compares the effectiveness of Machine Learning and Deep Learning models, focusing on Parkinson's disease prediction. Chapter 5 outlines essential concepts of data fusion in AI, explaining how integrating diverse information sources enhances outcomes. Chapter 6 examines integrating emerging technologies such as IoT, Blockchain, and Quantum Machine Learning in healthcare and discusses associated ethical issues.

Chapter 7 provides a thorough review of data fusion techniques in biomedical research, using case studies to illustrate real-world applications. Chapter 8 explores machine learning methods that integrate imaging and molecular data, expanding the possibilities for bioinformatics research. Chapter 9 explains the methods used in time series analysis in genomics, offering insight into genetic changes and their link to diseases.

Chapter 10 explores various machine learning approaches to data fusion, covering their roles in fields like diagnostics and human-machine interactions. Chapter 11 presents recent AI advancements in bioinformatics, including novel algorithms for disease research and drug resistance analysis. Chapter 12 highlights future trends in AI and data fusion, focusing on privacy-preserving methods and cutting-edge technologies.

Chapter 13 addresses AI's role in precision medicine, demonstrating how integrating diverse medical data can enhance patient care. Chapter 14 discusses the Internet of Medicine, focusing on AI and Blockchain technologies and their potential to improve healthcare data security. Chapter 15 provides a simplified explanation of natural language processing (NLP) in analyzing biomedical literature, revealing how AI processes complex medical texts. Finally, Chapter 16 showcases how sentiment analysis in patient feedback can enrich medical research through advanced NLP techniques.

This book serves as a foundational guide for researchers, students, and professionals looking to understand and harness the power of AI-driven data fusion in bioinformatics, paving the way for future advancements in the field.

Dr. Umesh Kumar Lilhore
Galgotias University, Greater Noida, UP, India
Dr. Abhishek Kumar
Department of CSE, Chandigarh University, Mohali, India
Narayan Vyas
Department of Computer Science and Application, Vivekananda Global University, Jaipur, India
Dr. Sarita Simaiya
Galgotias University, Greater Noida, UP, India
Vishal Dutt
Department of CSE, Chandigarh University, Mohali, India

1

Advancements and Challenges in Multimodal Data Fusion for Bioinformatics AI

Priya Batta

Department of Computer Science and Engineering, Chandigarh University, Mohali, India

Abstract

An artificial intelligence technique used in bioinformatics integrates multiple biological data sources to understand complex biological processes. The research mainly focuses on the discovery of fusion technologies and their associated challenges. Despite the significant progress made in machine learning algorithms, various issues such as scalability, interpretability, and regulatory still exist. Drug discoveries, accurate medicine, and systems biology are the three main sectors of application. Future research should focus on increasing scalability, increasing interpretability, and promotion of data standardisation. Thus, it will make it easier to combine multimodal data in a more effective way, which will advance medical care and biological research.

Keywords: Artificial intelligence (AI), multimodal data fusion (MDF), bioinformatics, genomics, drug discovery

1.1 Introduction

There are many AI techniques which are used for combining various types of data from different biological sources; this is known as Multimodal data fusion (MDF) for AI [1]. Transcriptomics, proteomics, metabolomics, and medical data are only a few of the modalities that are used in this method

Email: priya.cse@cumail.in

Umesh Kumar Lilhore, Abhishek Kumar, Narayan Vyas, Sarita Simaiya and Vishal Dutt (eds.) Multimodal Data Fusion for Bioinformatics Artificial Intelligence, (1–12) © 2025 Scrivener Publishing LLC

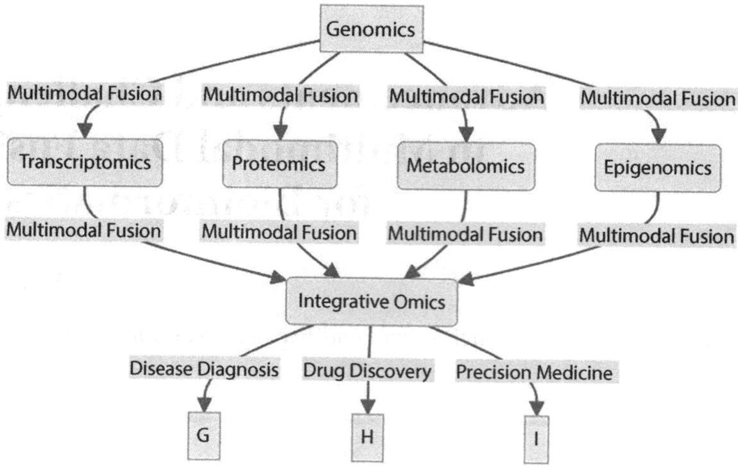

Figure 1.1 Multimodal data fusion for bioinformatics AI.

to improve biological understanding, disease diagnosis, and appropriate therapy [2, 3].

In bioinformatics AI, MDF (as shown in Figure 1.1) is used as follows:

- Integration of Various Features: Various AI methods are implemented to combine features that have been gathered from multiple data modalities. In some cases, combining gene expression data with protein interaction networks or DNA sequences with clinical characteristics may provide a more detailed knowledge of biological processes [4].
- Neural Network Architectures: Deep Neural Networks (DNNs), Neural Networks with Recurrent Connections (RNNs), and Deep Belief Networks (DBNs) are a few machine learning models that can handle difficult multimodal data. Such architectures are capable of capturing intricate relationships between different kinds of data and using those connections to create their own representations [3, 5].
- Multimodal Embeddings: Automatic Encoders (AE) and Variational Automatic Encoders (VAEs) are two kinds of AI techniques employed for creating low-dimensional representations for multimodal feedback. These connections keep significant characteristics throughout modalities, which simplifies later tasks like classification, categorising, and regression [2, 6].

- Grid-based Fusion: Grid neural networks (GNNs) and other grid-based AI models are used for combining diverse biological networks. As these models include both node features and network topology, they can be helpful for exactly simulating connections within complicated biological systems, such as networks of gene regulation or protein-protein interaction networks [7].
- Transferable Learning: The method of transferring knowledge from one activity or data source to another is made easier by transfer learning methods. For particular bioinformatics applications, pre-trained AI models developed on huge data sets can be augmented by utilising knowledge from multiple sources and disciplines [8].
- Medical Decision Assistance: AI in bioinformatics has been applied to systems that help clinical decision-making through multimodal data integration. These systems can assist healthcare providers in identifying disorders, determining the best course of therapy, and predicting projections by combining healthcare data with genetic identification, imaging results, and other relevant data [9].
- Medicinal Development and Recycling: AI-driven MDF expedites these processes by merging biological structure, medical records, response profiles to medication, and cellular information. With this method, potentially novel drugs can be found, drug efficacy can be anticipated, and therapeutic benefits can be maximised [10].
- Medical Care: MDF enables personalised medical care by enabling methods that are based on the genetic profiles, medical features, and treatment outcomes of specific patients. Based on their analysis of multiple modalities, AI systems classify patients, estimate the possibility of disease, and propose specific therapies for every individual [8]. Essentially, multimodal data fusion in bioinformatics AI makes use of artificial intelligence capacity to combine different biological types of information and results in advancement in the discovery of drugs, medical care, and medical research.
- Usage of Genomics Data: Genomics technology is used to generate very large data sets containing different biological components, such as proteins, DNA, and chemicals. Multimodal data fusion approaches enable the integration

of omics data from several platforms, providing a greater awareness of biological systems and functions [11, 12].

- Study of Biological Systems: MDF permits the development and analysis of biological networks, particularly genetic regulation systems, interaction between proteins networks, and biochemical networks. By combining various types of genomics data, researchers are able to determine complex connections and functional connections inside the biological systems [11, 13].
- Disease Biomarkers Recognition: Combining many genomic and imaging data sets enables researchers to identify valuable biomarkers and genetic fingerprints associated with diseases. This enables the development of individualised treatment plans and the early diagnosis of patient conditions [8, 14].

1.2 Literature Review

The state of MDF techniques has greatly advanced in the past few years. Deep Learning architectures have been used to improve traditional approaches such as Quantitative Fusion techniques [7, 10]. Combining data from various sources, including transcriptomics as well as these techniques, allows a more precise and deep knowledge of biological processes.

Various deep learning models [15] have shown remarkable capabilities in identifying various patterns from multimodal data. Graph-based fusion methods take advantage of the natural connections between biological components to model interactions, while ensemble learning techniques incorporate several models to improve the accuracy of predictions and standardisation.

Uses: MDF is used in various fields within bioinformatics AI. Personalised therapies are developed with the identification of disease subgroups and biomarkers in disease prognosis and diagnosis, which are made possible by the fusion of biological, transcriptomic, and imaging information. The creation of novel medicines is accelerated through the use of omics data integration in drug discovery, which makes target identification, drug repurposing, and drug response prediction easier [10]. Moreover, multimodal fusion is essential to precision medicine because it combines genetic profiles with patient-specific clinical data to customise therapy regimens and forecast treatment results. Reconstructing molecular pathways and regulatory mechanisms in systems biology allows for the integration of omics data with biological networks, revealing information on drug interactions and disease [13] processes.

Obstacles: Multimodal data fusion in bioinformatics AI has a number of obstacles in spite of its potential. Integrating heterogeneous data sources with different modalities, resolutions, and noise levels is a major problem. Maintaining compatibility and interoperability across various data types is still a crucial problem that calls for effective pre-processing and harmonisation methods [14].

Year-wise progress is shown as follows:

- 2018: The foundation for combining various data modalities in bioinformatics AI was established with the advent of fundamental fusion algorithms [5]. The restricted scalability of these strategies for huge datasets was one of the main obstacles faced, though.
- 2019: An important development was the use of machine learning for fusion activities. Nonetheless, problems with the models explainability and interpretability were apparent as significant holes.
- 2020: New potential for managing complicated biological data were presented by the development of graph-based fusion techniques. However, there were still issues in efficiently handling.
- 2021: Improving fusion performance through the use of ensemble learning approaches showed potential. Assessing the effectiveness of fusion models is still hampered by the absence of uniform evaluation metrics.
- 2022: While successfully merging temporal [11] and geographical data faced difficulties, the use of attention mechanisms in fusion algorithms was a noteworthy development.
- 2023: While fusion performance was enhanced by the incorporation of transfer learning techniques, permission and data privacy became more significant ethical problems.
- 2024: While new opportunities were created by the investigation of reinforcement learning in fusion tasks, interoperability between various data sources remained a major obstacle [4, 8].

Table 1.1 shows the year-wise progress of Multimodal data fusion in bioinformatics AI from 2018 to 2024 with methodology employed and gaps also.

Table 1.1 Year-wise progress of Multimodal data fusion in bioinformatics AI.

Year	Methodology used	Gaps
2018 [5]	Omics data integration for customised healthcare	Managing high-dimensional heterogeneous data
2019 [16, 17]	Developments in the architectures of deep learning	Fusion models' interpretability and explainability
2020 [7]	Emergence of techniques to graph-based fusion	Integration of temporal and spatial data
2021 [10, 12]	Use of multimodal fusion in the search for new drugs	Difficulties managing the heterogeneity and scalability of data, data privacy.
2022 [15]	Multimodal fusion algorithms advancements	Absence of uniform measures for evaluation
2023 [2]	Multimodal data integration in clinical contexts	Restricted compatibility between several data sources
2024 [3]	Multimodal fusion development for uncommon disorders	Pre-processing and data harmonisation challenges

Furthermore, there are difficulties with the interpretability and explainability of fusion models, especially in deep learning-based methods where the intricacy of neural networks makes it difficult to comprehend feature interactions and decision-making procedures. Furthermore, because biomedical data is sensitive, ethical concerns about data protection, privacy, and informed permission are critical.

Workflow of Multimodal Data Fusion in Bioinformatics

The process of multimodal data fusion in bioinformatics AI is depicted in this diagram (Figure 1.2), starting from the original data sources and ending with the creation of insights. This design can be expanded and altered to include certain data modalities, pre-processing procedures, AI models, and analysis methods that are applicable to your application are shown in Figure 1.2.

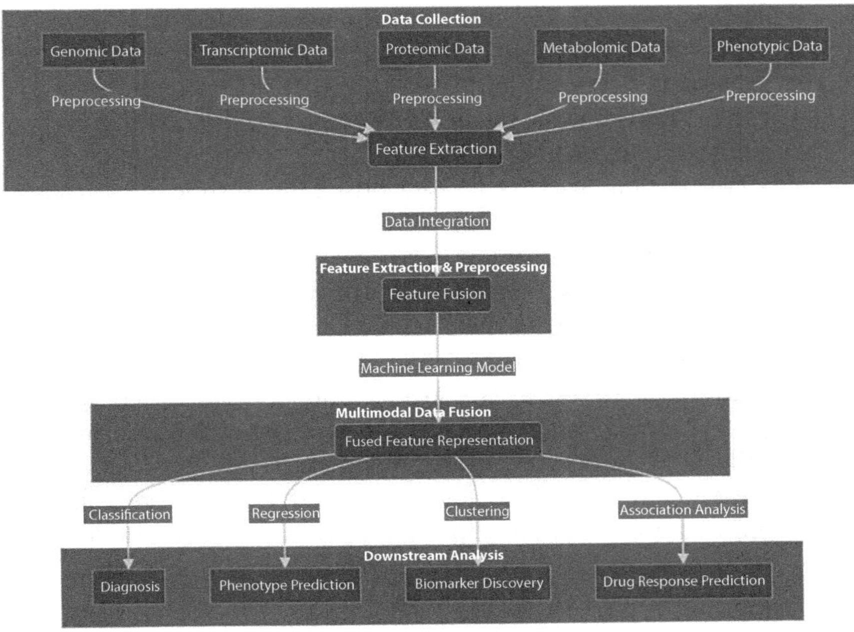

Figure 1.2 Workflow of multimodal data fusion in bioinformatics.

- Gathering of Data: Data are gathered on the genome, transcriptome, proteome, metabolome, and phenotype. These data types include a variety of biological informational components, including observable features (phenotypic), protein abundance (proteomic), RNA expression levels (transcriptomic), DNA sequences (genomic), and metabolite concentrations (metabolomics).
- Pattern Pre-processing & Extraction: Selection of features, standardisation, and reduction of noise are common methods of preprocessing that are used on many kinds of data. Following pre-processing, results are drawn from the raw data utilising feature extraction methods. These characteristics serve as input for the next fusion process.
- Integration of Multimodal Data: Methods for data fusion combine features that have been drawn from several data sources. During this fusion process, input from several sources gets combined to create one model that includes the supportive information accessible in each mode. Machine

learning models such as neural networks or combination methods are utilised for fusion tasks.

- Analysing downstream: Various downstream analysis tasks are carried out using the fused feature representation that is derived from the fusion process.
- Classification: Samples are categorised into distinct groups, such as disease vs. healthy or distinct disease subgroups, using the fused features.
- Regression: To estimate continuous variables, such as predicting the course of a disease based on biomarkers, predictive models are constructed.
- Clustering: To aid in the identification of biomarkers or patient stratification, unsupervised learning techniques are utilised to cluster samples that share comparable attributes.
- Association Analysis: Using statistical techniques, one can anticipate medication responses based on genetic profiles or find connections between molecular traits and clinical outcomes.

The above diagram (Figure 1.2) describes the various steps involved in multimodal data fusion in bioinformatics, following gathering information and pre-processing, such as extraction of features, fusion, and later analysis. For the integration of various biological data sources to support clinical decision-making, biomedical research, and the gathering of knowledge about complicated biological processes, each step of the workflow is important [18–21].

1.3 Results and Discussion

Researchers develop the foundation by looking into fundamental fusion methods including statistical techniques to integrate multiple information modalities in bioinformatics AI. Early studies focus on understanding the advantages and challenges of multimodal data fusion, such as variation in information as well as complexities.

As machine learning gains popularity, scientists are starting to look into how it might be used [5, 7, 15, 16, 19, 20, 22] in multimodal fusion for bioinformatics AI. Convolutional neural networks (CNNs) and recurrent neural networks (RNNs), two deep learning architectures, are studied for their capacity to process complex multimodal data and extract various as well as significant features of multimodal data.

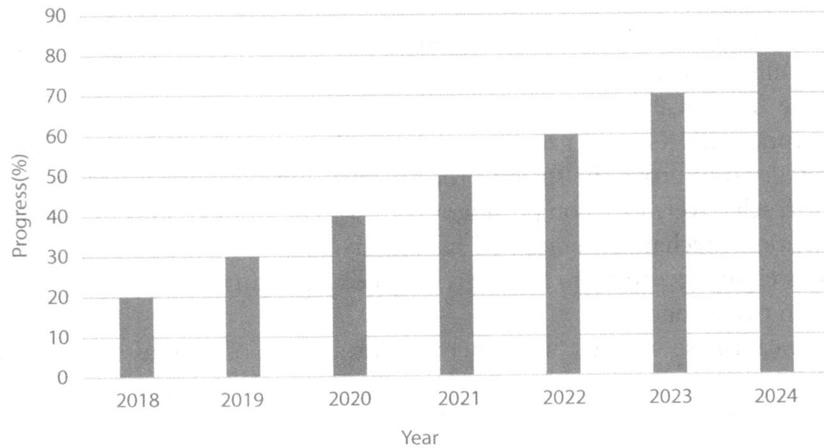

Figure 1.3 Year-wise progress in multimodal data fusion for bioinformatics AI.

The year-wise progress in multimodal data fusion for bioinformatics AI is shown in Figure 1.3. The advancement of bioinformatics multimodal data fusion techniques AI is an ongoing process characterised by small steps forward, cross-disciplinary cooperation, and the incorporation of state-of-the-art methods from machine learning and other related domains.

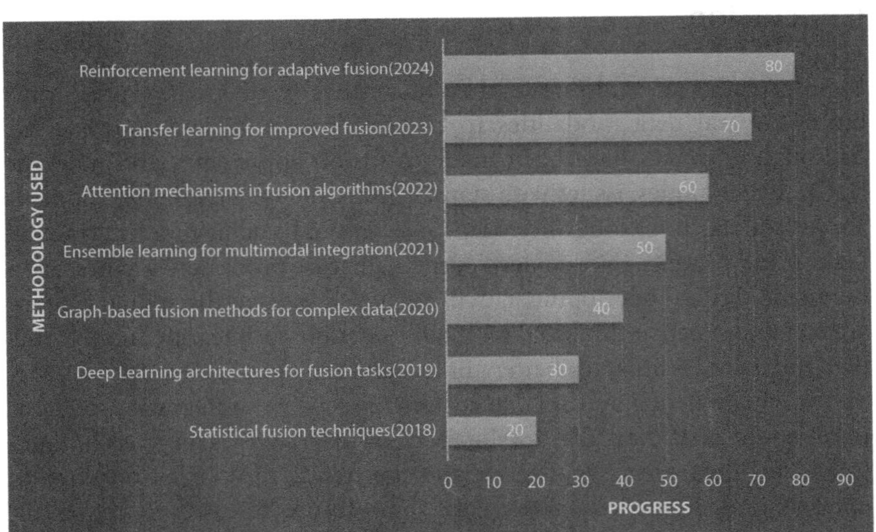

Figure 1.4 Various methodologies and their progress year-wise for multimodal data fusion for bioinformatics AI.

Graph-based fusion techniques as shown in Figure 1.4 are being used by researchers to take use of the interdependencies and linkages that are naturally present in biological entities. To capture intricate interactions inside biological networks and increase fusion accuracy, graph neural networks (GNNs) and graph convolutional networks (GCNs) are investigated. To improve the fusion process, attention mechanisms are added, which selectively focus on pertinent [17, 23] data from various modalities. Attention-mechanism-equipped models dynamically modify their attention weights according to feature relevance, improving interpretability and fusion performance.

To capitalise on the complementary advantages of various techniques, hybrid systems that integrate numerous fusion methodologies—for example, reinforcement learning with attention mechanisms or deep learning with graph-based methods—are being investigated. The creation of novel fusion approaches suited to the particular difficulties of bioinformatics AI is accelerated by interdisciplinary collaboration between academics in the domains of machine learning, bioinformatics, and other sciences.

In general, the development of multimodal data fusion strategies for bioinformatics AI is an ongoing process characterised by small steps forward, cross-disciplinary cooperation, and the incorporation of state-of-the-art methods from related domains such as machine learning.

Conclusion

Bioinformatics AI multimodal data fusion has made great strides, combining several data modalities to clarify intricate biological processes. Although advances have been made in fusion approaches and machine learning techniques, issues with standardisation, interpretability, and scalability still exist. Closing these gaps is essential to achieving multimodal fusion's full promise in drug development, disease processes, and precision medicine. Future developments will be fueled by interdisciplinary cooperation and creative thinking, making it possible to integrate multimodal data more successfully for better clinical and biological research.

The creation of interpretable fusion models, the integration of temporal and spatial data, the development of federated learning techniques to address data privacy concerns, and the standardisation of benchmark datasets and evaluation metrics are some future research directions in multimodal data fusion for bioinformatics AI. To overcome obstacles and realise the full promise of multimodal data fusion for advancing biomedical research and enhancing healthcare outcomes, researchers, clinicians, and policymakers must work together.

References

1. Acosta, J.N., Falcone, G.J., Rajpurkar, P., Topol, E.J., Multimodal biomedical AI. *Nat. Med.*, 28, 9, 1773–1784, 2022.
2. Jiang, Y., Li, W., Hossain, M.S., Chen, M., Alelaiwi, A., Al-Hammadi, M., A snapshot research and implementation of multimodal information fusion for data-driven emotion recognition. *Inf. Fusion*, 53, 209–221, 2020.
3. Cui, C., *et al.*, Deep multimodal fusion of image and non-image data in disease diagnosis and prognosis: a review. *Prog. Biomed. Eng.*, 5, 2, 022001, 2023.
4. Vyas, N., P., P.A., Das, P., Mahajan, Y., The Impact of Air Pollution on Respiratory Health Results: An Analysis of Asthma and COPD in a Population Study, in: *2023 International Conference on Computing, Communication, and Intelligent Systems (ICCCIS)*, Greater Noida, India, pp. 141–146, 2023, doi: 10.1109/ICCCIS60361.2023.10425187.
5. Punugoti, R., Duggar, R., Dhargalkar, R.R., Bhati, N., Intelligent Healthcare: Using NLP and ML to Power Chatbots for Improved Assistance, in: *2023 International Conference on IoT, Communication and Automation Technology (ICICAT)*, IEEE, Jun. 23, 2023, doi: 10.1109/icicat57735.2023.10263708.
6. Boehm, K.M., Khosravi, P., Vanguri, R., Gao, J., Shah, S.P., Harnessing multimodal data integration to advance precision oncology. *Nat. Rev. Cancer*, 22, 2, 114–126, 2022.
7. Burri, S.R., Agarwal, D.K., Vyas, N., Duggar, R., A Machine Learning Framework for Accurate Prediction of Parkinson's Disease from Speech Data, in: *2023 3rd International Conference on Innovative Sustainable Computational Technologies (CISCT)*, Dehradun, India, pp. 1–6, 2023, doi: 10.1109/CISCT57197.2023.10351422.
8. Steyaert, S., *et al.*, Multimodal data fusion for cancer biomarker discovery with deep learning. *Nat. Mach. Intell.*, 5, 4, 351–362, 2023.
9. Patil, R.R. and Kumar, S., Rice-fusion: A multimodality data fusion framework for rice disease diagnosis. *IEEE Access*, 10, 5207–5222, 2022.
10. Gan, Y., Liu, W., Xu, G., Yan, C., Zou, G., DMFDDI: deep multimodal fusion for drug–drug interaction prediction. *Briefings Bioinf.*, 24, 6, bbad397, 2023.
11. Punugoti, R., Dutt, V., Kumar, A., Bhati, N., Boosting the Accuracy of Cardiovascular Disease Prediction Through SMOTE, in: *2023 International Conference on IoT, Communication and Automation Technology (ICICAT)*, Gorakhpur, India, pp. 1–6, 2023, doi: 10.1109/ICICAT57735.2023.10263703.
12. Xu, C., *et al.*, AutoOmics: New multimodal approach for multi-omics research. *Artif. Intell. Life Sci.*, 1, 100012, 2021.

13. Das, S., Ghosh, S., Mallik, S., Qin, G., Feature Selection, Machine Learning and Deep Learning Algorithms on Multi-modal Omics Data, in: *Artificial Intelligence Technologies for Computational Biology*, pp. 305–322, CRC Press, 2022, Accessed: Apr. 02, 2024. [Online]. Available: https://www.taylorfrancis.com/chapters/edit/10.1201/9781003246688-14/feature-selection-machine-learning-deep-learning-algorithms-multi-modal-omics-data-supantha-das-soumadip-ghosh-saurav-mallik-guimin-qin.
14. Bhati, N., Duggar, R., Saber, A., Empowering Safety by Embracing IoT for Leak Detection Excellence, in: *Innovations in Machine Learning and IoT for Water Management*, pp. 231–251, IGI Global, Nov. 27, 2023, doi: 10.4018/979-8-3693-1194-3.ch 012.
15. Mylavarapu, R.T., Pokhriyal, A., Dhargalkar, R.R., Bhati, N., Empowering Healthcare with AI: Addressing Challenges and Envisioning the Future, in: *2023 4th International Conference on Electronics and Sustainable Communication Systems (ICESC)*, Coimbatore, India, pp. 1393–1398, 2023, doi: 10.1109/ICESC57686.2023.10193228.
16. Bhati, N., Duggar, R., Alzahrani, A., Exploring few-shot learning approaches for bioinformatics advancements, in: *Applying Machine Learning Techniques to Bioinformatics*, pp. 303–316, IGI Global, 2024.
17. Zulch, P., Distasio, M., Cushman, T., Wilson, B., Hart, B., Blasch, E., Escape data collection for multi-modal data fusion research, in: *2019 IEEE Aerospace Conference*, IEEE, pp. 1–10, 2019, Accessed: Apr. 02, 2024. [Online]. Available: https://ieeexplore.ieee.org/abstract/document/8742124/.
18. Shaik, T., Tao, X., Li, L., Xie, H., Velásquez, J.D., A survey of multimodal information fusion for smart healthcare: Mapping the journey from data to wisdom. *Inf. Fusion*, 102040, 2023.
19. Burugadda, V.R., Dutt, V., Mamta, Vyas, N., Personalized Cardiovascular Disease Risk Prediction Using Random Forest: An Optimized Approach, in: *2023 IEEE World Conference on Applied Intelligence and Computing (AIC)*, Sonbhadra, India, pp. 226–232, 2023, doi: 10.1109/AIC57670.2023.10263915.
20. Rahim, N., El-Sappagh, S., Ali, S., Muhammad, K., Del Ser, J., Abuhmed, T., Prediction of Alzheimer's progression based on multimodal deep-learning-based fusion and visual explainability of time-series data. *Inf. Fusion*, 92, 363–388, 2023.
21. Tan, W., Tiwari, P., Pandey, H.M., Moreira, C., Jaiswal, A.K., Multimodal medical image fusion algorithm in the era of big data. *Neural Comput. Applic.*, Jul. 2020. doi: 10.1007/s00521-020-05173-2.
22. Zhao, Y., *et al.*, A review of cancer data fusion methods based on deep learning. *Inf. Fusion*, 102361, 2024.
23. Burugadda, V.R., Mane, P.M., Kumar, A., Bhati, N., A Machine Learning-Based Algorithm for Early Detection of Sepsis in Hospitalized Patients: Development and Evaluation, in: *2023 1st International Conference on Circuits, Power and Intelligent Systems (CCPIS)*, Bhubaneswar, India, pp. 1–6, 2023, doi: 10.1109/CCPIS59145.2023.10291447.

2

Automated Machine Learning in Bioinformatics

Pushpendra Kumar[1]*, Gagan Thakral[1], Vivek Kumar[2] and Upendra Mishra[1]

[1]Department of Computer Science and Engineering, KIET Group of Institutions, Delhi-NCR, Ghaziabad, UP, India
[2]Department of Computer Science and Engineering, MIET, Meerut, UP, India

Abstract
The applications of machine learning are gaining popularity in various fields day by day. Bioinformatics is one of the fields in which automated machine learning, AutoML, has great potential in the future. AutoML can be used to create the predictive models and find certain patterns in biological data. Machine learning can be used as a tool for decision making and analysis of biological data. In this work, we have focused on how AutoML pipelines can be integrated into bioinformatics processes and emphasize how it can be used for tasks like drug discovery, protein structure prediction, and sequence analysis. Further, there are a few limitations associated with AutoML in bioinformatics, such as data scarcity, heterogeneous data, interpretability problems, and scalability problems. In conclusion, the future directions and possible developments in AutoML techniques for bioinformatics are discussed, highlighting how the field of artificial intelligence and machine learning can build sustainable technologies using machine learning for bioinformatics applications.

***Keywords*:** Automated machine learning, bio-informatics, genomics, proteomics, deep learning

**Corresponding author*: pushpendra.kumar@kiet.edu

Umesh Kumar Lilhore, Abhishek Kumar, Narayan Vyas, Sarita Simaiya and Vishal Dutt (eds.) Multimodal Data Fusion for Bioinformatics Artificial Intelligence, (13–32) © 2025 Scrivener Publishing LLC

2.1 Introduction

In recent years, advancements in technologies have allowed us to capture loads of complex data including the domains of proteomics, metabolomics, imaging, and genomics. To analyse this data and get insights from it is a challenging task. Even this data can be further used for intelligent predictions and decision-making. Conventional bioinformatics data processing techniques have their own limitations; they are labour intensive, require manual interference, and are biased. This huge data bring both challenges and opportunities for researchers. From the field of artificial intelligence, machine learning is such a useful tool to use this data constructively and make automated predictions in bio informatics as shown in Figure 2.1.

Automated machine learning, also coined as AutoML [1, 2] is a technique which requires no human intervention to process the bioinformatics data. We can derive useful insights and predictions for the bioinformatics applications with the help of AutoML. The entire machine learning pipeline starting from data cleaning, feature engineering, model selection, hyperparameter tuning, data preparation, processing, predictions, insights and decision-making can be made automated with AutoML applications.

This chapter explores various approaches in bioinformatics [3] benefited by AutoML. Further, various problems faced in the task of applying machine learning in bioinformatics, including noise, data scarcity, interpretability, and heterogeneity of data are explored. This chapter also discusses how AutoML techniques might help to counter these difficulties. This chapter explores the use of Big Data [4] with AutoML for various bioinformatics applications such as customized medicines, drug discovery,

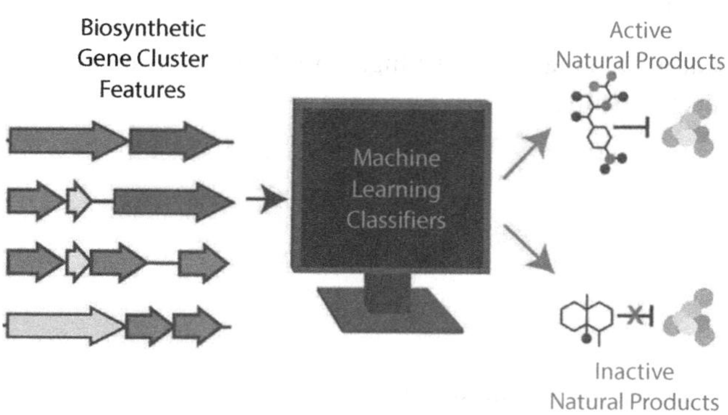

Figure 2.1 Machine learning in bioinformatics.

protein structure and sequence analysis. There are several new discoveries in the area of life sciences and bioinformatics that are accelerated with the advancements of the latest machine learning technologies. AutoML could help us in making more complex biological interpretations [5] and hypotheses by automating time-consuming and repetitive manual procedures.

A. Challenges of Automated Machine Learning Approaches in Bioinformatics

There are several challenges faced by Machine Learning (AutoML) in processing biological data. The data collected from biological activities has particular qualities. This data is generally very complex in nature, variable and inconsistent. This data may vary in a wide range such as protein structures, genome sequences and medical records. There can be noise and inconsistencies in the data which are very common to biological data. Such challenges can be an obstacle for conventional machine learning techniques. The second issue with AutoML in bioinformatics can be the selection of model. The model must be interpretable and self-explainable since full openness of decision-making processes and transparency is required. Huge and complex datasets require a lot of processing resources. Another requirement is scaling, since the amount of data could rise with time. Various computing parallelization and optimization techniques can be very useful.

B. Advantages of Automated Machine Learning Approaches in Bioinformatics

There are several benefits of applying AutoML in bioinformatics. Transparency and minimization of human intervention, simplified model-building process, powerful insights, interpretations, reproducibility and standardization are major benefits of Automated machine learning in bioinformatics. The capability of processing a huge amount data in minimal time [6], building automatic machine learning pipelines for interpretable and self-explainable models, and fetching insights for effective and efficient decision-making could be very useful. AutoML frameworks provide optimal model performance by managing the challenges of hyperparameter tuning and feature engineering, thereby relieving researchers of some of their workload. AutoML enhances the reproducibility and openness by standardizing [7] the documentation and machine learning workflow, encouraging open scientific principles, and making it easier to validate and replicate findings across other investigations.

C. Process of Automated Machine Learning

There is a basic difference between conventional machine learning and automated machine learning processes. There is an automatic algorithm selection step. This step automatically selects a model based on the optimal outcome. The following figure displays the process of automated machine learning.

2.2 Need of Automated Machine Learning

There are several reasons why Automated Machine Learning (AutoML) is necessary. These reasons all add to the need for automated solutions in the fields of data analysis and machine learning. The following salient points underscore the necessity of AutoML:

- **Complexity of Machine Learning Pipeline:** Numerous complex procedures [8], such as feature engineering, model selection, hyperparameter tweaking, and data preprocessing are involved in traditional machine learning workflows.

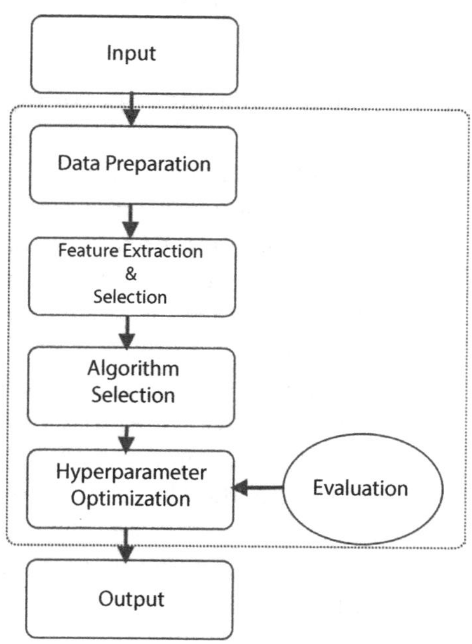

Figure 2.2 Automated machine learning process.

Model development takes less time and effort when these procedures are automated as shown in Figure 2.2.

- **Scarcity of Data Science Experts:** There is a dearth of qualified data scientists that are adept at machine learning methods as well as subject expertise. By making it possible for academics and subject matter experts with little experience with programming or statistics to efficiently use sophisticated analytical tools, AutoML democratizes machine learning.
- **Rapidly Growing Data Volumes:** Large datasets are becoming too enormous to handle by hand as big data spreads across many areas, including bioinformatics. Scalable solutions for effectively processing and analyzing large amounts of data are offered by AutoML as shown in Figure 2.3.

Table 2.1 summarizes the significance of AutoML in bioinformatics. We can summarize the significance of the automated machine learning as follows.

- **Rapid Model Deployment:** Rapid deployment of AutoML make them most suitable and viable. Organizations can quickly implement predictive analytics solutions because of AutoML's ability to speed up the model building process.
- **Reproducibility and Transparency:** AutoML frameworks standardize the model construction process and provide thorough documentation for each stage. This process helps

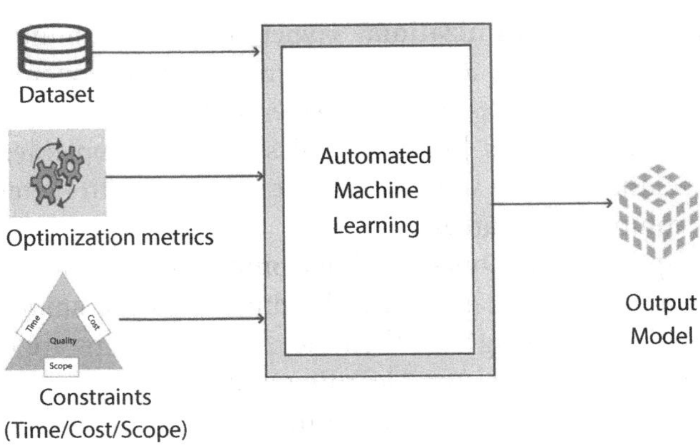

Figure 2.3 Automated machine learning.

Table 2.1 Significance of AutoML in bioinformatics.

	How AutoML addresses features in bioinformatics
Data Collection & Interpretation	AutoML streamlines data collection by automating data preprocessing, cleaning, and integration from diverse biological sources. Machine learning steps of data cleaning feature extraction and selection can be automated.
Economical & High Productivity	No or minimal human intervention helps in saving time and resources. Rapid model development, higher productivity can be achieved with AutoML.
Fair & Impartial Decision-Making	Fairness, Transparency, impartiality, standardization and reproducibility can be ensured by applying AutoML.
No Human Error & Risk	Minimizing human error, automating repetitive tasks, optimizing model performance. Eventually, a robust model.
Availability	High availability as open-source libraries and commercial products. Provides wide range of easy-to-use and efficient tools.

to enhance reproducibility and transparency. This ensures the validity of scientific results by guaranteeing that tests can be repeated and that the results can be understood.

- **Resources Optimization:** Hyperparameter tuning and model selection are two resource-intensive operations. AutoML automates these processes and maximizes computational resources [9]. Financial savings by implementing machine learning solutions can be achieved with better use of computer resources.
- **Adaptation to Dynamic Environments:** Manual model retraining and adaption can be difficult as the amount of data keep growing with the time. AutoML setups are capable to provide real-time learning and updating the model. This ensures the adaptation of machine learning models in dynamic environments.

2.3 Automated ML in Various Areas of Bioinformatics

The major areas in bioinformatics where AutoML can be applied are genomics, functional genomics, structural bioinformatics, computational biology, metabolomics, transcriptomics and pharmacogenomics as shown in Figure 2.4. AutoML can be applied to develop AI based Decision system in these areas as shown in Figure 2.5.

Genomics: Large genomic datasets can be processed and pipeline automatically with the help of automated machine learning. Automated Machine Learning (AutoML) has completely changed the field of genomics [10]. Identification of genetic variants and gene function prediction can be automated with machine learning. In the field of genomics the comprehension behind the complex genetic disorders and diseases can be made with AutoML. Significant and dynamic features in genomic data can be interpreted easily with these models. These models can continuously learn from the dynamic data generation. The models need to be adaptive, especially in the field of genomics.

Proteomics: The research related to protein structures in bioinformatics is known as proteomics. These structural data of proteins can be analyzed and modelled [11] easily with the help of AutoML. The integration of diverse data sources, the interpretation of sizable proteomic datasets, and the requirement for reliable algorithms can be achieved by this technology. Sparse and noisy data are some of the major challenges that still need to

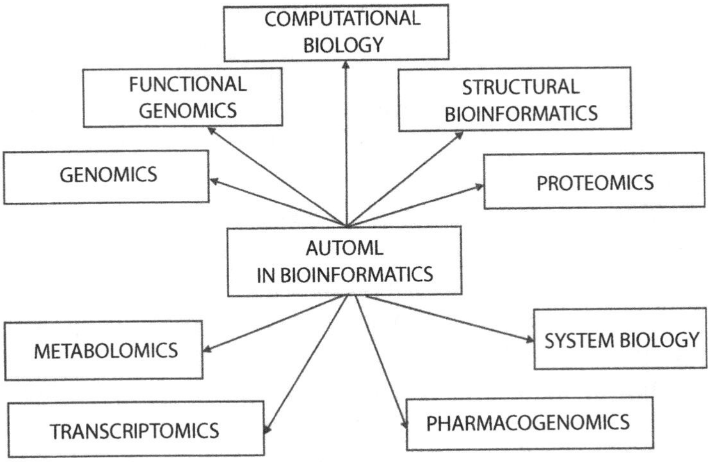

Figure 2.4 Automated ML in various areas of bioinformatics.

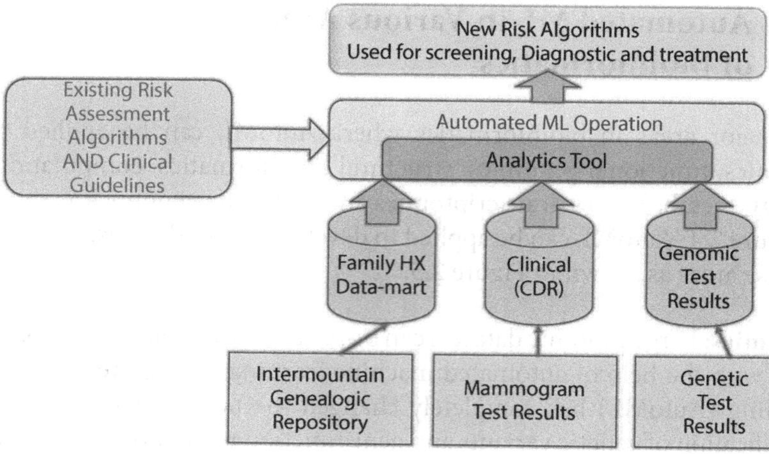

Figure 2.5 AI-based decision-making system.

be overcome in proteomics. However, machine learning can be applied for the creation of predictive models for the prediction of protein structure and function, the discovery of biomarkers for the diagnosis and prognosis of diseases. The investigation of protein-protein interactions and signaling pathways can be applied. Proteomics researchers can get new insights into the molecular pathways underlying health and illness. This can be used in personalized medicine and focused therapeutic interventions.

Transcriptomics: The study of an organism's transcriptome, which is the complete set of RNA transcripts, is known as Transcriptomics as described in Figure 2.6 [12]. It has become possible to analysis huge transcriptomics datasets with the advancements of computational technologies. We can bring valuable insights from this data. We can use AutoML to handle heterogeneous and noisy data for this purpose. The prediction of gene expressions patterns can be achieved. The identification of novel RNA biomarkers for the diagnosis and treatment of disease are some tasks that can be addressed with the help of AutoML.

Metabolomics: Analysis of complex metabolic patterns is known as Metabolomics [13]. Accurate and fast analysis of complex metabolic patterns can benefit from the addition of machine learning. Some challenges faced by applications in metabolomics are data preprocessing, metabolite identification, and handling the inherent unpredictability. Metabolomic data is related to the automation of machine learning processes in the metabolomics. The scope for machine learning is huge in metabolomics. We can perform identification of metabolic signatures linked to medication

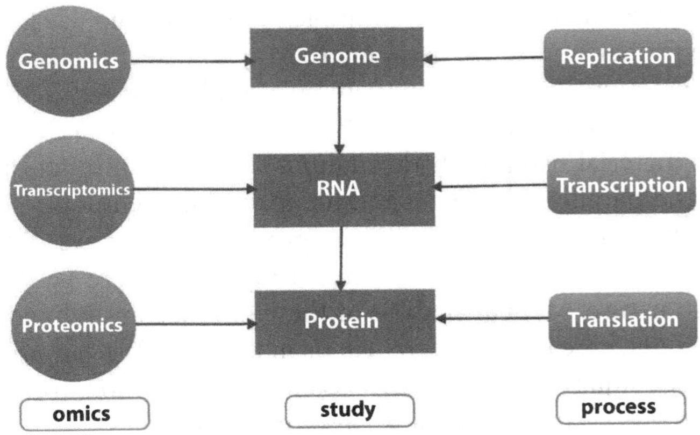

Figure 2.6 Transcriptomics.

response and toxicity. We can also get clarification of metabolic pathways, and the identification of biomarkers for illness diagnosis and prognosis. New insights can be gained into metabolic control and biomolecular interactions, and metabolic phenotypes.

Structural Bioinformatics: Structural bioinformatics [14] is another area in bioinformatics where machine learning can be applied. We can build more accurate and efficient protein structure analysis and prediction with AutoML. There are a few problems associated with data collection. The lack of good training data and computational complexity are common limitations. The interpretation of structural predictions is the main challenge faced. It can be used for drug design, protein-ligand interaction and protein structure prediction. New protein structures and interactions can be identified more quickly by utilizing machine learning techniques. The applications of these frameworks are medication development, protein engineering, and the comprehension of complicated biological systems.

Systems Biology: Machine learning can be applied in systems biology [14]. AutoML enables the integration and analysis of many biological data types such as proteomics, metabolomics, transcriptomics, and genomes. Systems biology can benefit greatly from machine learning. This potential includes developing predictive models for biological networks and recognizing emergent characteristics in intricate biological systems. The clarification of the connections between genotype and phenotype can be understood and better insights into living systems and developing applications for synthetic biology provided. Customized medicine and biotechnological process optimization by utilizing machine learning can be obtained.

Microarray: A microarray is a multiplex lab-on-a-chip [27]. These are two-dimensional arrays. We use a microarray to detect thousands of biological interactions. We can keep them on a solid substrate. Generally, it is a glass slide or silicon thin-film cell. We can assay and test large amounts of biological material using high-throughput screening, miniaturized, multiplexed, and parallel processing and identification techniques. There can be several types of microarrays such as protein microarrays, DNA, RNA, Microchip, cellular and antibody microarrays. These are very large and complex in nature. Manual analysis of these microarrays is a tedious task. Automated machine learning can help us in this task. We can use machine learning techniques like Bayesian classification, decision trees, random forests, and deep learning for the analysis of microarrays.

Computational Biology: As described in Figure 2.7, computational biology [15] has a great scope for AutoML, especially incorporating large datasets. The processing and interpretation of large, complicated biological data sets can be achieved with machine learning pipelines. Structural biology, statistics, biochemistry, physical chemistry, molecular biology and control theory are the main fields of computational biology where we can apply automated machine learning. This scope includes the ability to predict the structure and function of proteins, identify genetic variants linked to disease, and integrate multi-omics data to provide comprehensive biological insights.

Other areas: Other important areas in bioinformatics involving AutoML include functional genomics [16], evolutionary biology and pharmacogenomics. Functional genomics allows for very accurate predictions of gene functions and regulatory relationships. Evolutionary biology [17] is the study of evolutionary processes and patterns in a wide range of species. Pharmacogenomics [18] provides customized medication dosing based on genetic variables. All these areas can be applied with AutoML frameworks.

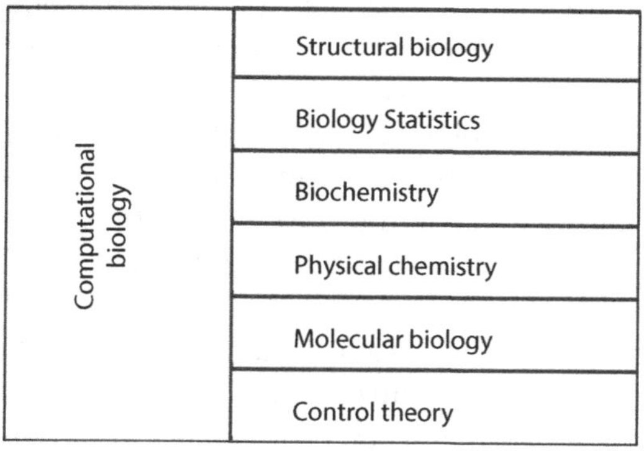

Figure 2.7 Computational biology.

2.4 Major Obstacles for Automated ML in Various Areas of Bioinformatics

The biological operations generate a vast amount of data. We need the help of automation and machine learning to process this much data. Not only the amount of the data but also the heterogeneity of the data is a challenge. Table 2.2 summarizes the various challenges faced by the AutoML.

Table 2.2 Major challenges faced by automated machine learning (AutoML).

Challenges	Details
Data Heterogeneity	Variety of data kinds, including protein structures, genetic sequences, and clinical information. Makes feature engineering and data preprocessing difficult.
Interpretability	Some AutoML models are not interpretable. Difficult to draw conclusions from intricate biological data. Lack transparency.
Scalability	Scalability problems. Not able to deal with large bioinformatics datasets.
Domain-specific Knowledge	Lack of domain-specific knowledge. Incorporating domain knowledge into AutoML Framework might be difficult.
Noise and Missing Data	Missing and null values. Noisy data. Ineffective handling of noise.
Processing Resources	High Computational demands. Effective use of resources (optimization, parallelization).
Ethics and Regulation	Sensitive data, including genetic information and medical records. Model creation and deployment are made more difficult by the need for AutoML algorithms to abide by legal and ethical constraints [19] for data protection and privacy.
Validation and Reproducibility	Ensuring the validity and reproducibility [20] of machine learning models.

This data is in unrefined form and needs further cleaning and preprocessing. Also, we need to choose the correct machine learning model automatically.

2.5 Applications of Automated ML in Various Areas of Bioinformatics

Several uses of Automated Machine Learning (AutoML) in diverse bioinformatics domains include (as summarized in Table 2.3):

Table 2.3 Applications of AutoML in bioinformatics.

AREA	Application
Genetics	Regulatory components and gene functions predicted through modelling.
	Studies on genotype-phenotype associations and variant calling.
	Analysis of gene expression and transcriptome profiling.
	Investigations of genome-wide associations (GWAS) [21] for the examination of complicated traits.
The proteomics	Predicting and folding the structure of proteins.
	Detection of protein-protein interactions and post-translational modifications (PTMs) [22].
	Proteome profiling and biomarker identification for prognosis and disease diagnosis.
	Functional annotation and subcellular localization of proteins predicted.

(Continued)

Table 2.3 Applications of AutoML in bioinformatics. (*Continued*)

AREA	**Application**
The study of transcriptomics	Differential gene expression profiling in response to various therapies or circumstances.
	Predicting isoforms and alternative splicing.
	Analysis of gene co-expression and inference from regulatory networks.
	Classification and functional annotation of long non-coding RNAs (lncRNAs).
The study of metabolism	Identification and annotation of metabolites.
	Flux analysis and reconstruction of metabolic pathways.
	Identification of biomarkers for metabolic profiling and illness diagnosis.
	Drug metabolism pathways and metabolic phenotype prediction.
Biology of Systems	Reconstruction of biological networks, including metabolic and gene regulatory networks.
	Modelling of system-level behavior and dynamic biological processes [23].
	Multi-omics data integration for a thorough systems-level investigation.
	Prediction of cellular responses to perturbations and interactions between drugs and targets.
Employing Functional Genomics	Gene and non-coding region functional annotation.
	Prediction of biological pathways and concepts from the Gene Ontology [24] (GO).
	Finding transcription factor binding sites and gene regulatory elements.
	Genetic variation annotation and implications for function.

(*Continued*)

Table 2.3 Applications of AutoML in bioinformatics. (*Continued*)

AREA	Application
Biology of Evolution	Evolutionary divergence study and reconstruction of phylogenetic trees.
	Identification of adaptive evolution and positive selection.
	Studies on molecular evolution and comparative genomics.
	Ecological connections and species distribution forecasts.
Pharma-cogenomics	Genetic variation-based personalized medication response prediction.
	Finding pharmacogenetic indicators for the toxicity and effectiveness of drugs.
	Predicting polypharmacology and repurposing drugs.
	Creation of personalized treatment plans using precision medicine techniques [25].

2.6 Case Study 1

Title: Automated Machine Learning for Predictive Modelling of Protein-Protein Interactions [26].

Problem Statement: Decoding physiological processes and creating innovative therapeutic interventions require a thorough understanding of protein-protein interactions (PPIs). The complexity of protein structures and functions along with large search space makes it difficult to analyse and predict. The aim is to create an automated machine learning process that uses structural characteristics and protein sequence to predict PPIs.

Method:

Data collection: We need to compile huge datasets available publicly. These datasets can be downloaded from platforms like BioGRID and STRING that include known protein-protein interactions.

Feature extraction is the process of identifying important characteristics. Examples of such features are makeup of amino acids, physicochemical characteristics, and structural motifs, from protein sequences and structural data.

Preprocessing: We need to divide the dataset into training, validation, and test sets. Then clean the data, handle missing values and normalize the features.
Model Choice: We need to select suitable ML algorithm and tune hyperparameters. Ultmately, AutoML framework like TPOT or Auto-Sklearn can be used.
Model Training: Cross-validation is applied to guarantee robustness and generalization, upon the chosen models on the training set.
Model Evaluation: Metrics like accuracy, precision, recall, and area under the receiver operating characteristic curve (AUC-ROC) to assess how well the trained models performed on the validation set can be used.
Model Testing: Evaluate the final model's performance. Use test dataset to measure its capacity for generalization and accuracy in prediction.
Interpretation: To determine the essential characteristics and trends influencing protein-protein interactions, interpret the trained models.
Results: The model's interpretability helped to generate new hypotheses. A highly accurate and predictive model for PPIs is successfully created using the automated machine learning pipeline. The model showed that it could generalize to previously untested data and outperform other approaches. The biological research can be enhanced by outlining the underlying mechanisms governing PPIs.

Case Study 2:
Title: Ribosomally synthesized and post-translationally modified peptides or RiPPMiner [28].
Problem Statement: Decoding of chemical structures. It contains more than 20 subclasses. A variety of organisms, including prokaryotes, eukaryotes, and archaea, produce RiPPs, which possess a wide range of biological functions.

Method:
Data collection: It has an inbuilt database RiPPDB database.
Components: This is a bioinformatics tool based on automated machine learning. You can use it for genome mining-based RiPP chemical structure

decoding. RiPP has two main components: the RiPPDB database and the RiPPMiner web server. RiPPMiner is a quary interface. RiPPMiner finds 12 subclasses of RiPPs by guessing where the leader peptide will cut and where the last cross-link will be in the RiPP chemical structure.
Results: With the help of genome sequences, RiPPMiner is a special tool that can predict the intricate chemical structures of several kinds of RiPPs. The model provides a simple, easy to understand and operate user interface. Complex analysis can be done very easily with the help of this tool.

2.7 Conclusion and Future Directions

Automated machine learning, or AutoML, has great potential to revolutionize bioinformatics research. AutoML expedites the analysis of extensive, intricate, and massive datasets. It makes it easier to discover new insights in the areas of transcriptomics, proteomics, genomics, and more by automating the model-development process. We can apply AutoML for predictive modeling, biomarker identification, and systems-level understanding of biological processes. AutoML's primary challenge is the scarcity of high-quality training data. There are challenges such as data heterogeneity, variability, data scarcity, missing values, and interpretability. AutoML has the potential to transform bioinformatics research. Interdisciplinary collaborations between artificial intelligence and bioinformatics innovations can transform the future. We can open new avenues for biotechnology applications that will significantly impact human health and the environment, including precision agriculture, personalized medicine, and sustainable biotechnological applications. AutoML in bioinformatics can help to develop specialized algorithms for specific biological domains. We can use AutoML to address the various problems faced by bioinformatics. High scalability and interoperability of machine learning algorithms are the most useful traits for bioinformatics. Artificial intelligence and machine learning are the most powerful technologies that will shape the future. Bioinformatics, being one of the most important verticals of biology, has to incorporate the goodness of machine learning and artificial intelligence. Automated machine learning can handle problems such as data heterogeneity, interpretability, and model transparency, integrating with emerging technologies for comprehensive understanding.

References

1. He, X., Zhao, K. and Chu, X., AutoML: A survey of the state-of-the-art. *Knowl.-Based Syst.*, 212, 106622, 2021.
2. Dutt, V., Sasubilli, S.M., Yerrapati, A.E., Dynamic Information Retrieval with Chatbots: A Review of Artificial Intelligence Methodology, in: *2020 4th International Conference on Electronics, Communication and Aerospace Technology (ICECA)*, Coimbatore, India, pp. 1299–1303, 2020, doi: 10.1109/ICECA49313.2020.9297533.
3. Swarna, S.R., Kumar, A., Dixit, P., Sairam, T.V.M., Parkinson's Disease Prediction Using Adaptive Quantum Computing, in: *2021 Third International Conference on Intelligent Communication Technologies and Virtual Mobile Networks (ICICV)*, Tirunelveli, India, pp. 1396–1401, 2021, doi: 10.1109/ICICV50876.2021.9388628.
4. Yang, Liu, Y., Yang, Y., Li, D., Wang, Z., InDEP: an interpretable machine learning approach to predict cancer driver genes from multi-omics data. *Brief. Bioinform.*, 24, 5, 2023.
5. Kashyap, H., Ahmed, H.A., Hoque, N., Roy, S., Bhattacharyya, D.K., *Big Data Analytics in Bioinformatics: A Machine Learning Perspective*, 2015, arXiv [cs.CE].
6. Auslander, N., Gussow, A.B., Koonin, E.V., Incorporating machine learning into established bioinformatics frameworks. *Int. J. Mol. Sci.*, 22, 6, 2903, 2021.
7. Sasubilli, S.M., Kumar, A., Dutt, V., Improving Health Care by Help of Internet of Things and Bigdata Analytics and Cloud Computing, in: *2020 International Conference on Advances in Computing and Communication Engineering (ICACCE)*, Las Vegas, NV, USA, pp. 1–4, 2020, doi: 10.1109/ICACCE49060.2020.9155042.
8. Wratten, L., Wilm, A., Göke, J., Reproducible, scalable, and shareable analysis pipelines with bioinformatics workflow managers. *Nat. Methods*, 18, 10, 1161–1168, 2021.
9. Du, H., *et al.*, *Beyond Deep Reinforcement Learning: A tutorial on generative Diffusion Models in network optimization*, 2023, arXiv [cs.NI].
10. Chandrasekaran, S., Dutt, V., Vyas, N., Kumar, R., Student Sentiment Analysis Using Various Machine Learning Techniques, in: *2023 International Conference on Artificial Intelligence and Smart Communication (AISC)*, Greater Noida, India, pp. 104–107, 2023, doi: 10.1109/AISC56616.2023.10085018.
11. Sekhar, U.S., Vyas, N., Dutt, V., Kumar, A., Multimodal Neuroimaging Data in Early Detection of Alzheimer's Disease: Exploring the Role of Ensemble Models and GAN Algorithm, in: *2023 International Conference on Circuit Power and Computing Technologies (ICCPCT)*, Kollam, India, pp. 1664–1669, 2023, doi: 10.1109/ICCPCT58313.2023.10245177.

12. Pais, R.J., Lopes, F., Parreira, I., Silva, M., Silva, M., Moutinho, M.G., Predicting Cancer Prognostics from Tumour Transcriptomics Using an Auto Machine Learning Approach. *Med. Sci. Forum*, 22, 6, 2023.
13. Kumar, S.A., Kumar, H., Dutt, V., Soni, H., Self-Health Analysis with Two Step Histogram based Procedure using Machine Learning, in: *2021 Third International Conference on Intelligent Communication Technologies and Virtual Mobile Networks (ICICV)*, Tirunelveli, India, pp. 794–799, 2021, doi: 10.1109/ICICV50876.2021.9388427.
14. Radivojević, T., Costello, Z., Workman, K., Garcia Martin, H., A machine learning Automated Recommendation Tool for synthetic biology. *Nat. Commun.*, 11, 1, 4879, 2020.
15. Waring, J., Lindvall, C., Umeton, R., Automated machine learning: Review of the state-of-the-art and opportunities for healthcare. *Artif. Intell. Med.*, 104, 101822, 2020.
16. Makrodimitris, S., Van Ham, R.C., Reinders, M.J.T., Automatic gene function prediction in the 2020's. *Genes*, 11, 11, 1264, 2020.
17. Lürig, M.D., Donoughe, S., Svensson, E., II, Porto, A., Tsuboi, M., Computer vision, machine learning, and the promise of phenomics in ecology and evolutionary biology. *Front. Ecol. Evol.*, 9, 642774, 2021.
18. Lin, E., Lin, C.-H., Lane, H.-Y., Precision psychiatry applications with pharmacogenomics: artificial intelligence and machine learning approaches. *Int. J. Mol. Sci.*, 21, 3, 969, 2020.
19. Punugoti, R., Dutt, V., Anand, A., Bhati, N., Exploring the Impact of Edge Intelligence and IoT on Healthcare: A Comprehensive Survey, in: *2023 International Conference on Sustainable Computing and Smart Systems (ICSCSS)*, Coimbatore, India, pp. 1108–1114, 2023, doi: 10.1109/ICSCSS57650.2023.10169733.
20. Boyapati, S., Swarna, S.R., Dutt, V., Vyas, N., Big Data Approach for Medical Data Classification: A Review Study, in: *2020 3rd International Conference on Intelligent Sustainable Systems (ICISS)*, Thoothukudi, India, pp. 762–766, 2020, doi: 10.1109/ICISS49785.2020.9315870.
21. Sun, S., Dong, B., Zou, Q., Revisiting genome-wide association studies from statistical modelling to machine learning. *Briefings Bioinf.*, 22, 4, bbaa263, 2021.
22. Shah, A.A., Ehsan, M.K., Sohail, A., Ilyas, S., Analysis of machine learning techniques for identification of post translation modification in protein sequencing: A review, in: *2021 International Conference on Innovative Computing (ICIC)*, pp. 1–6, 2021.
23. Su, W.-H., Chou, C.-S., Xiu, D., Deep learning of biological models from data: applications to ODE models. *Bull. Math. Biol.*, 83, 1–19, 2021.
24. Bourgeais, V., Zehraoui, F., Ben Hamdoune, M., Hanczar, B., Deep GONet: self-explainable deep neural network based on Gene Ontology for phenotype prediction from gene expression data. *BMC Bioinf.*, 22, 10, 1–25, 2021.

25. Burugadda, V.R., Jadhav, N., Vyas, N., Duggar, R., Exploring the Potential of Deep Reinforcement Learning for Autonomous Navigation in Complex Environments, in: *2023 7th International Conference On Computing, Communication, Control And Automation (ICCUBEA)*, Pune, India, pp. 1–6, 2023, doi: 10.1109/ICCUBEA58933.2023.10392109.
26. Kumar, A., Kumar, S.A., Dutt, V., Dubey, A.K., Narang, S., A Hybrid Secure Cloud Platform Maintenance Based on Improved Attribute-Based Encryption Strategies. *Int. J. Interact. Multimedia Artif. Intell.*, 8150, 2, 2023. Universidad Internacional de La Rioja, doi: 10.9781/ijimai.2021.11.004.
27. Casadio, R., Martelli, P.L., Savojardo, C., Machine learning solutions for predicting protein–protein interactions. *Wiley Interdiscip. Rev.: Comput. Mol. Sci.*, 12, 6, e1618, 2022.
28. Burugadda, V.R., Pawar, P.S., Kumar, A., Bhati, N., Predicting Hospital Readmission Risk for Heart Failure Patients Using Machine Learning Techniques: A Comparative Study of Classification Algorithms, in: *2023 Second International Conference on Trends in Electrical, Electronics, and Computer Engineering (TEECCON)*, Bangalore, India, pp. 223–228, 2023, doi: 10.1109/TEECCON59234.2023.10335817.

3

Data-Driven Discoveries: Unveiling Insights with Automated Methods

Rakhi Chauhan

Department of Computer Science and Engineering, Geeta University, Panipat, India

Abstract

Bioinformatics has been greatly influenced by the use of automated machine learning (AutoML) approaches, which have enhanced data analysis, feature extraction, and predictive model construction. This essay provides an in-depth review of the benefits and drawbacks of using AutoML in bioinformatics approaches. Model selection, hyperparameter tweaking, and feature engineering are just a few of the many processes that may be automated with the help of an AutoML framework. Because of this automation, human interaction is reduced and the development of predictive models is accelerated. Genome analysis, protein structure prediction, drug development, and illness detection are just a few of the many domains that have reaped the rewards of applying AutoML approaches to the massive and complicated datasets seen in bioinformatics. But there are also obstacles to using AutoML in bioinformatics, such as domain expertise, the ability to understand complicated models, and ethical concerns about bias and data privacy. It is also difficult to evaluate various autonomous machine learning methods due to the absence of shared datasets and benchmarks. To solve these problems, bioinformaticians, ML experts, and ethicists must work together to build transparent Auto ML frameworks that meet the specific need of bioinformatics applications. In spite of setbacks, Auto ML is showing great potential to improve our knowledge of biological systems and speed up bioinformatics discoveries.

***Keywords*:** AutoML-bioinformatics, computational biology automation, machine learning automation in biomedical data, AI-driven bioinformatics

Email: er.rakhichauhan@gmail.com

Umesh Kumar Lilhore, Abhishek Kumar, Narayan Vyas, Sarita Simaiya and Vishal Dutt (eds.) Multimodal Data Fusion for Bioinformatics Artificial Intelligence, (33–48) © 2025 Scrivener Publishing LLC

3.1 Introduction

The results of "wet-bench" examinations, which entail the analysis of gene products and the contents of the genome, are examples of the kinds of biological data that can be found [1]. One more category of biological data is contained inside the molecular sequence data. The goal of bioinformatics, which is a subfield of the life sciences that is interdisciplinary in nature, is to discover novel approaches to the storage, organisation, systematization, annotation, display, querying, mining, comprehending, and interpretation of huge amounts of biological data. Methodologies in the fields of mathematics and statistics, cloud computing, pattern recognition, machine learning, simulation, iterative approaches, reconstruction, molecular modelling, and folding are all included in this category [1, 2].

Cloud computing is also covered. Nevertheless, the creation of computer programmes and software is inextricably linked to the emergence of bioinformatics and the continuous advancement of this field. The reason for this is that bioinformatics is completely necessary for the management and analysis of these factors.

At the moment, bioinformatics encompasses a wider range of biological research, which includes the examination of various types of biological data, the organisation, classification, annotation, querying, mining, and visualization of accessible biological information, as well as the evaluation of a large number of biomedical text records [1–3]. The disciplines of genomics and genetics continue to perceive it as an essential component in their research. On the other hand, this should not result in any misunderstandings concerning the nature of bioinformatics and the goals that it strives to accomplish. It is becoming increasingly difficult to differentiate between bioinformatics and other subjects that are tied to it as a result of the increasing use of computers, statistics, and mathematics in the biological sciences. In addition to bioinformatics, there are a number of other fields that are different from it. These fields include biometry and biostatistics, the creation of computers that can analyse DNA, and the organisation and processing of picture data through the use of computers.

It is absolutely necessary to take this distinction into consideration in order to correctly identify bioinformatics from its sister areas, computational biology and biological computation [1, 2]. Utilizing the most recent developments in the domains of molecular cell biology, bioengineering, cybernetics, and robotics, the objective of the field of biological computation is to develop organic computers. This will be accomplished by utilizing the latest information available. The molecular sequences that are derived from the genome and their interactions are the foundation of the area of bioinformatics, which is concerned with the creation and use of computing algorithms for the goal of grasping and interpreting biological processes. Bioinformatics is a subfield of computer science. As a result of this, the goals of bioinformatics and computational biology in a variety of different domains appear to be rather related to one another. The field of bioinformatics is primarily concerned with the provision of practical tools for the organisation and analysis of fundamental "omics" data, which includes genomic, proteomic, and sequence data, as well as sequence analysis and visualization [1, 2]. On the other hand, computational biologists tend to concentrate their efforts on the development of theoretical models for the purpose of conducting analyses of biological data. It is without reasonable doubt that computational biologists and bioinformatics are interested in genomic data, such as that which is obtained through a variety of sequence alignments and methods for genome assembly. This is because genomic data may contain information about the genome. If the theoretical and practical aspects of these two domains are ignored, the different boundaries that separate them will, in consequence, become less visible [2]. Molecular sequence data that is obtained from the genome and the principles that control its organisation are the primary focus of bioinformatics, which is largely concerned with the management, analysis, and interpretation of this data. It makes no difference whether the data is seen from an evolutionary/phylogenetics, comparative, or simulation point of view; this is always the case. These technologies have the potential to be advantageous to a wide variety of businesses, and they can be employed to a large degree in each and every one of those fields [1]. The application of these technologies to various industries has the potential to be beneficial. This field encompasses a wide range of subjects, some of which are evolution, system biology, artificial intelligence, biochemistry, physiology, biophysics, and all of the natural sciences, including agriculture, medicine, and the environment.

In wet-bench experimental molecular biology, it is possible to obtain a more in-depth understanding of molecular and evolutionary processes [4] as well as interactions derived from vast quantities of raw data [1, 2]. This is made possible through the utilisation of bioinformatics techniques such as signal processing. The main benefit of this technology can be found in a wide range of fields, such as genome sequencing and annotation, pattern recognition, and mutation profiling [1, 2, 4]. These applications can be beneficial to the "omics" sectors. On account of the fact that it records and evaluates genetic and metabolic pathways and networks, bioinformatics is a tool that is absolutely necessary for system biology [2, 5]. This, in turn, helps in combining and investigations for building a model of biological processes that is more comprehensive. The application of bioinformatic techniques for molecular modelling, pattern recognition, simulation, folding, and reconstruction can result in the discovery of significant structural properties and interactions of molecular sequences [6, 7]. These techniques can be utilised for the purposes of structural biology and the design of medical drugs [1, 2]. It is physically difficult to manually evaluate all of these huge molecular sequence studies of raw "big data" that are obtained from the genome. This is because of the magnitude of the data, because of which, researchers in the field of biology began integrating cutting-edge computing knowledge with multidisciplinary approaches to analyse big data, which led to the establishment of a new field of study known as interdisciplinary bioinformatics. This new field of study was a result of the aforementioned. An examination of the evolution of the discipline of bioinformatics throughout the course of time is the first thing that has to be done.

It has been demonstrated that the data mining strategy, which is founded on a fundamental methodology known as machine learning, is an efficient method for transferring meaningful knowledge from the raw data that was first collected. Through the construction of models, the creation of predictions, the performance of classifications and grouping, the discovery of associated rules, and eventually the revelation of patterns that are wanted, this technique has been widely implemented. On the other hand, deep learning is a relatively new theoretical framework and concept that possesses a substantially better capacity for the encoding of information at an abstract level. Deep learning is more advanced than traditional machine learning.

It is very tough to merge data analysis with bio informatics in order to achieve the objective of successfully mining biological data and bridging the gap that exists between the two fields in a methodical manner. The main focus of the study is on data mining and deep learning techniques. This is the contribution that this study makes. These methods have been implemented in a wide variety of bioinformatics applications, thanks to their versatility.

3.2 Important Functions in Bioinformatics Include Data Mining and Analysis

Due to the fact that there are a great number of important aspects that influence incremental datasets, it is necessary to have big data storage systems and analysis tools. In order to meet technological requirements, a data mining or machine learning technique is required. In order for data mining to accomplish its goal of acquiring accurate and trustworthy performance, it is necessary for certain qualities of abstract data representations to be present. However, human analysis and abstraction are not well-suited to enormous datasets that have high-dimensional features and a high number of occurrences. These datasets are not ideal for human consideration.

Furthermore, it is noteworthy that the rate of data expansion surpasses the rate of increase observed in conventional manual analysis technology. Furthermore, the significance of existence becomes obscured when we encounter difficulties in converting information into a more comprehensible representation, so hindering our ability to provide people with timely data. The establishment of a methodical technique for the automated analysis of data is therefore of the utmost importance in order to make effective use of this type of data for clinical diagnosis and to evaluate the therapeutic implications of drugs on experimental data. In the field of bio informatics, there have been tremendous efforts made in research and development, which has led to the creation of a wide variety of machine learning approaches. It is possible to trace the current predominance of adopting these tactics for data exploration and analysis to the advancements that have been made in these strategies. Within the realm of biomedical research, data mining is something that is utilised extensively across a variety of domains. The fields mentioned above include biological electronics and the nervous system, bioinformatics and computational biology, biological materials, biomedical imaging, image processing and visualisation, biomedical modelling, gene engineering, medical cell biology, nano biological analysis, nuclear magnetic resonance/CT/ECG, physiological signal processing, and various other domains.

Data preparation is the term used to describe the practice of handling data prior to the commencement of the primary operation. In the context of the real world, there exist specific categories of data that are commonly characterised by their unprocessed nature, presence of noise, incompleteness, and lack of consistency. These data types are not suitable for direct data mining, and the results obtained from mining them are insufficient on their own. Incorporating a preprocessing stage into the entire process is done with the aim of enhancing the efficiency of data mining. In the majority of instances, the required steps encompass data purification, integration, transformation, reduction, and other related activities [8]. To implement these preprocessing techniques before data mining leads to a substantial enhancement in pattern quality and a decrease in the time required for the actual mining procedure. Another name for data mining is Knowledge Discovery in Databases (KDD), which is an abbreviation. It has been effectively utilized by bioinformatics, a subject that deals with large volumes of data and necessitates important discoveries like gene expression, protein modelling, biomarker identification, drug development, and so forth. This holds true for the bioinformatics domain. Data mining can be used to derive a wide range of useful applications in the field of bioinformatics.

The numerous different data mining methodologies that are utilised in bioinformatics are presented in Table 3.1.

In the field of data mining, the processing of data includes the management of data prior to its use in the primary activity; this is referred to as the process of data preparation.

In practice, certain types of data frequently exhibit characteristics such as rawness, noise, incompleteness, and inconsistency, making them unsuitable for direct use in data mining. Furthermore, the results of such data mining efforts may prove unsatisfactory. Additionally, a preprocessing step is incorporated into the overall process as an essential component in order to enhance the effectiveness of the data mining algorithm. The purification of data, integration of data, transformation of data, reduction

Table 3.1 An examination of the many data mining approaches that are utilized in the field of biomedical analysis.

Technique	Purpose	Data source
KNN	Detecting hypertension risk	Cardiovascular disease dataset
NN	Identifying diseases without specific algorithms	Chest CT scans
EM	Diagnosing cardiovascular diseases	Aptamer chips data
SVM	Assigning entities to semantic classes	Protein, DNA, and RNA subclasses
NB	Predicting breast cancer recurrence	Breast cancer dataset
DT	Assisting in cancer classification decisions	Magnetic resonance imaging data
HC	Analyzing gene conversion	Archeal chaperonin sequences

of data, and other related operations are often included in this process [8]. The utilisation of preprocessing techniques prior to data mining results in an improvement in pattern quality and a reduction in the amount of time necessary for the specific mining operation.

3.3 Deep Learning in Bioinformatics

Throughout the course of the last few decades, data mining techniques have been mostly utilised for the purpose of discovering traditional knowledge within relational databases that are well-structured and primarily comprised of numerical data. This was done in order to fulfil the requirements of industrial company. The data analysis techniques were controlled by techniques like statistics. In the most recent decades, data mining approaches have been mostly utilised for the aim of unearthing conventional information within well-organized relational databases, with numerical data being the primary focus of this endeavour. For the purpose of catering to the particular requirements of industrial businesses, this strategy has been implemented. The methods of data analysis that were utilised most frequently in this investigation included methodologies such as statistical analysis and straightforward logical reasoning. In data mining there is a phase where it encompasses the study of various forms of data, such as structured, semi-structured, and unstructured data. Machine learning, pattern recognition, and artificial intelligence are some of the key concepts and processing methods that are utilised in order to accomplish this goal. In a manner analogous to that of human beings, the purpose is to utilise more advanced learning procedures and discover knowledge and information that had not been studied before. When it comes to the future course of the data mining industry, it is anticipated that in addition to addressing concerns regarding data structure, there will be an increased focus on the management of complex data objects. The complex data entities consist of huge datasets that are characterised by similar types, significant noise, various representations, large amounts, and fast streams. The complexity of a given task can be evaluated using advanced technologies such as metaheuristics, deep neural networks (DNN), fuzzy logic, parallel and distributed computing, and cloud computing. It is imperative to take into account the enormity of the challenge, while concurrently assessing the scope of the issue. The propensity for data mining is not surprising, since it serves as a powerful tool for processing large volumes of data and enabling the extraction of useful insights in various scientific and academic fields.

The acquisition and development of biomedical data have reached a level of breadth and depth that has never been seen before. Consequently, there has been a substantial increase in the number of machine learning algorithms that are intended to derive extremely useful insights from the field of bioinformatics. From the perspective of practical applications, there is a diverse range of situations that can be found in the actual world. One example of such a scenario is the management of enormous amounts of data, which poses a number of challenges. These challenges include the demand for greater processing capability in order to manage heterogeneous data, as well as the need for enhanced learning flexibility in order to manage high dimensions and big amounts of data. Traditional neural networks (NNs) have given way to a newer form of learning. The implementation of neural processors and the incorporation of a large number of processing layers are the distinguishing characteristics of this technique. To facilitate the transmission of non-linear interactions through the responses that are generated by each layer, these layers have been purposefully constructed in order to facilitate this process [9]. Technology enables the development of primary and efficient applications in a wide range of domains, such as natural language processing, biological research, image and speech recognition, and more. These applications can be used in a variety of contexts. The implementation of complicated learning mechanisms that eliminate the need for costly manual interventions, the ability to enable distributed and parallel computing, and the extraction of sophisticated abstractions from huge volumes of raw data are all areas in which it shines.

In order to enable more advanced learning strategies and unearth undiscovered knowledge, machine learning, pattern recognition, artificial intelligence, and other related methodologies are applied when studying both heterogeneous and homogeneous data in formats that are structured, semi-structured, or unstructured. This is done in a manner that is similar to how human cognitive processes operate. In terms of how the field of data mining will evolve in the future, it will deal with increasingly intricate data items in addition to the problem of data structures. This will be discussed further below. A lot of characteristics, including but not limited to large numbers, high-speed streams, diverse types, significant noise, and many representations, are only some of the characteristics that constitute big data. Taking into consideration the ideas of vastness and profoundness is another thing that needs to be involved. Cloud computing, fuzzy logic, metaheuristics, deep neural networks (DNN), parallel and distributed computing, and other related methodologies are some examples of the modern technologies that can be utilised to accomplish these goals. Not only does data mining serve as a dependable processing method for enormous datasets, but it also offers a deeper comprehension of information extraction in a wide range of academic and scientific fields. This is something that should not come as a surprise to anyone.

Since the beginning of the modern age, the quantity of data that is generated and collected for biological applications has reached a level of magnitude and comprehensiveness that was inconceivable before. In addition to this, it makes it easier to construct a comprehensive collection of machine learning algorithms, which is a step towards the goal of gleaning usable information from the field of bioinformatics. At the moment, the extensive range of practical applications encompasses a wide variety of circumstances that occur in the actual world. There are a number of challenges that come along with massive amounts of data, some of which include the capacity to learn and adapt to vast volumes and dimensions, increased processing capabilities for a variety of data, and other concerns. There has been a shift away from traditional neural networks (NNs) towards deep learning, which has become the new standard in machine learning techniques. The foundation of this concept is comprised of the fundamental conceptualization of neuron processors as well as the fundamental design of various processing levels. When it comes to deep learning, the objective is to transmit non-linear connections by utilising the responses of each layer [9]. In a wide range of fields, including as natural language processing, biomedical research, speech and picture recognition, and others, the technology makes it simpler to develop primary applications that are both successful and efficient. Through the utilisation of advanced learning techniques, the facilitation of distributed and parallel computation, and the provision of high-level abstractions of qualities that are present in enormous volumes of raw data, it performs remarkably well. It is interesting to note that these attributes can be achieved without a significant amount of strenuous manual work. Following the presentation of a comprehensive theoretical explanation of the various frameworks and architectures, it becomes apparent that deep learning is utilised in two primary fields of bioinformatics. Biological applications that require data analysis in the fields of genomics, transcriptomics, and proteomics are included in the domains that have been mentioned above. Additionally, medicinal applications, such as disease diagnosis, clinical decision making, medical image processing, drug development, and repurposing, are included in these domains.

Table 3.2 presents a thorough examination of the accomplishments attained by deep learning applications in real-world scenarios.

Table 3.2 An examination of a number of different deep learning approaches in the context of the science of biological analysis.

Application aim	Application aim	Technique
Techniques for the classification and detection of cancer [10]	The data on gene expression	Deep Belief Networks
Cancer that clusters together [11]	As well as ovarian and breast cancer	Support vector machine and convolution neural network
Cataracts score of thirteen [12]	Information pertaining to cataracts	convolution neural network
The automatic segmentation of medical images [13]	CT and MRI	Recurrent neural network
The prediction of the map of protein contacts [14]	A database of ASTRAL	Recurrent neural network and Deep Belief Networks
[15] A classification of the field of meta genomics	Data on the succession of microbiomes	Sparse autoencoder
Image reconstruction for medical purposes [16]	The MRI	Recurrent neural network
Analysis of the potential for drug-induced liver damage [17]	Data on drugs	-

3.4 Challenges and Issues

The utilisation of machine learning and deep learning methodologies in the analysis of bioinformatics data has been shown to possess significant capabilities and advantages across various domains, including preprocessing, feature extraction, feature selection, classification, and clustering. This phenomenon has been substantiated by several methodologies. However, it is crucial to acknowledge that these methodologies still encounter inherent challenges and give rise to new issues that require further investigation. This is a matter that requires recognition.

Data imbalance and data preprocessing: Conversely, the issue of imbalanced data and the challenge of data preparation have been examined in the pertinent part pertaining to this subject matter. The conversation has addressed both of these topics. The attributes of bioinformatics data, such as intricate and multi-dimensional properties, a substantial quantity of samples, and diversity originating from multiple sources, pose substantial challenges to the technique as time progresses and novel issues arise [18]. Nevertheless, the methodology persists in encountering an increasing array of obstacles. One illustration of this phenomenon can be observed in the amalgamation of valuable biological data with conventional computerised records pertaining to patients, medical imaging, or other forms of data. The restricted data fusion capabilities within a commercial information system pose a significant obstacle. More precisely, this is because the system was designed to handle a certain amount of data. The rationale for this assertion is that the integration of diverse data types may pose challenges in terms of implementation. When considering factors related to both the volume and precision of the data, it becomes evident how challenging it is to merge a substantial number of datasets. One further concern associated with managing vast quantities of biological data pertains to the inherent incompleteness of the data information. This barrier pertains to the management of biological data. The aforementioned scenario has transpired, notwithstanding the well-acknowledged occurrence of the curse of dimensionality. Insufficient data can be identified by the presence of missing values, inconsistent norms for identifying items, or the need to identify and remove duplicate entries. These are all instances of incompleteness. Each individual sort of incompleteness holds significance in its own regard. Some of these manifestations are described below.

We regret to inform you that the imbalanced data problem in bioinformatics [19] is a consequence of the expensive data gathering stage and the complex processing requirements, both of which restrict the amount of data that can be stored. As a consequence of this, there is a discernible inequality in the distribution of labels. In the database of an illness centre, for instance, there is a consistently lower number of healthy cases compared to sick ones. This is due to the fact that it is not necessary for a healthy individual to go to the hospital. Several academics have been working hard to find a solution to the issue of imbalanced data by employing a wide range of techniques. These techniques include sampling, per-training and cost-sensitive learning.

3.4.1 Data Requirements for Big Data Sets

There are five characteristics that set large volumes of data apart from other types of data: volume, variety, velocity, variability, and value. The three types of data are the volume, the diversity, and the reliability of the information. In this context, "volume" refers to the total amount of data, "variety" refers to the many kinds of data, and "veracity" suggests that the data are consistent with one another. Value is the final aim or objective. The modern means of producing and collecting data fast, continuously, and comprehensively are described by these features. This is also true for the bioinformatics field's real-world applications; it's a major source of frustration for those working in academia and industry alike. The five Vs of big data is easily shown in Figure 3.1.

The expansion of batch-based data analytics modes into distributed and parallel computing methodologies is a common practice that is used to circumvent the velocity problem [20–24]. The 5Vs of big data make real-time analytics significantly more challenging than it was in the past. This is the reason why this is the case. On the other hand, the data throughput of I/O operations is a barrier that precludes real-time analytics from being carried out [25]. There are a few frameworks that create deep learning on big data platforms; nevertheless, the great majority of artificial intelligence learning algorithms were not initially developed for distributed and parallel computation. This is despite the fact that there are still some frameworks that do so. Despite the fact that there are a few frameworks that build deep learning, this demonstrates that it is possible.

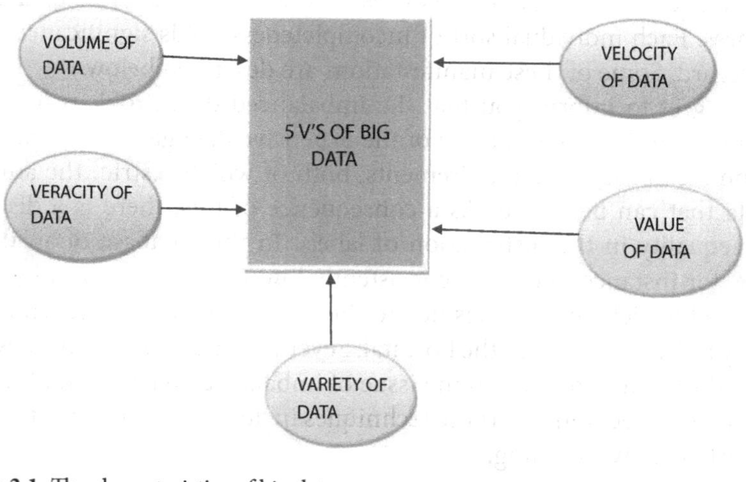

Figure 3.1 The characteristics of big data.

3.4.2 Model Selection and Learning Strategy

A number of obstacles have arisen in recent years for data mining algorithms. These include an overwhelming amount of data that is neither structured nor homogeneous, and data that contains enormous interconnected objects [18, 26–28]. Strategies for learning and model selection have become more difficult due to these challenges. So, in order to find new patterns, we need improved learning techniques. To begin, one of the most effective methods for creating maps of objects with interconnected structures is graph theory. The term "graph-based learning" refers to a composite methodology that incorporates a number of different methodologies, including topology, network analysis, and data conceptual representation, amongst others. Furthermore, the usage of topology-based learning offers tremendous potential in properly processing computational geometry data that includes an extended range of dimensions. The only use case for it thus far has been pattern recognition in the brain. When it comes to machine learning algorithms, the third entropy-based method usually has to deal with the justifiable problem of including more complicated information theories. No matter how good the results are, this means that the model's underlying and internal structure is still hard to explain and stays mysterious. Things are never better in a bioinformatics setting, by the way. The deep models used in bioinformatics aren't yet transparent enough to reveal complex structural relationships, despite visualization's attractiveness as a black-box solution.

3.5 Conclusion

The rapid expansion of bioinformatics has unleashed a plethora of opportunities in fields such as data analytics, biomedical research, knowledge discovery, and novel application development. One possible strategy for accomplishing these aims, both explicitly and implicitly, is data mining in the IT sector utilising elementary ML algorithms. The terrible truth is that performance bottlenecks might be deep, static, batch-oriented, and non-generalized. While traditional machine learning does have its limits, deep learning provides a more versatile toolkit for overcoming those restrictions. Biomedicine and bioinformatics are introduced as important topics in the article. Afterwards, the fundamentals of data mining and deep learning methods are discussed. Specifically addressed are methods for data preprocessing, categorization, and clustering as they pertain to machine learning. Finally, it uses a bioinformatics application to look at different deep frameworks. Many think that the bioinformatics and medical industries would greatly benefit from combining deep learning with machine learning because of this.

In addition, we are of the opinion that the methods of data fusion and the evaluation of the effectiveness of bioinformatics data will continue to have a good impact on applications that are already being utilised. Specifically, this is due to the fact that potential future research may involve the combination of intricate machine learning algorithms, which may result in new technological progression.

Automation of programme design and tool development is one approach to speeding up machine learning. An intriguing new development in machine learning is the practice of combining different deep architectures into one larger one in order to get higher performance and more integration. The utilization of huge data processing techniques has also increased interest in traditional deep learning extensions.

References

1. Mount, W.D., *Bioinformatics: Sequence and Genome Analysis*, 2nd, p. 692, Cold Spring Harbor Laboratory Press, New York, 2004, doi: 10.1086/431054.
2. *Bioinformatics*, [Online], Available: https://en.wikipedia.org/wiki/Bioinformatics. [Accessed: Mar. 10, 2016].
3. Sasubilli, S.M., Kumar, A., Dutt, V., Improving Health Care by Help of Internet of Things and Bigdata Analytics and Cloud Computing, in: *2020 International Conference on Advances in Computing and Communication Engineering (ICACCE)*, Las Vegas, NV, USA, pp. 1–4, 2020, doi: 10.1109/ICACCE49060.2020.9155042.
4. Punugoti, R., Duggar, R., Dhargalkar, R.R., Bhati, N., Intelligent Healthcare: Using NLP and ML to Power Chatbots for Improved Assistance, in: *2023 International Conference on IoT, Communication and Automation Technology (ICICAT)*, IEEE, Jun. 23, 2023, doi: 10.1109/icicat57735.2023.10263708.
5. Ma'ayan, A., Introduction to network analysis in systems biology. *Sci. Signaling*, 4, tr5, 2011. doi: 10.1126/scisignal.2001965.
6. *Molecular Modelling*, [Online], Available: https://en.wikipedia.org/wiki/Molecular_modelling. [Accessed: Mar. 10, 2016].
7. *Protein Folding*, [Online], Available: https://en.wikipedia.org/wiki/Protein_folding. [Accessed: Mar. 10, 2016].
8. Han, J., How can data mining help bio-data analysis?, in: *Proceedings of the 2nd International Conference on Data Mining in Bioinformatics*, pp. 1–2, 2002.

9. Han, J., How can data mining help bio-data analysis?, in: *Proceedings of the 2nd International Conference on Data Mining in Bioinformatics*, Springer Verlag, pp. 1–2, 2002.
10. Hinton, G.E. and Salakhutdinov, R.R., Reducing the dimensionality of data with neural networks. *Science*, 313, 5786, 504–507, 2006.
11. Kumar, S.A., Kumar, H., Dutt, V., Soni, H., Self-Health Analysis with Two Step Histogram based Procedure using Machine Learning, in: *2021 Third International Conference on Intelligent Communication Technologies and Virtual Mobile Networks (ICICV)*, Tirunelveli, India, pp. 794–799, 2021, doi: 10.1109/ICICV50876.2021.9388427.
12. Liang, M., Li, Z., Chen, T., Zeng, J., Integrative data analysis of multi-platform cancer data with a multimodal deep learning approach. *IEEE/ACM Trans. Comput. Biol. Bioinf. (TCBB)*, 12, 4, 928–937, 2015.
13. Gao, X., Lin, S., Wong, T.Y., Automatic feature learning to grade nuclear cataracts based on deep learning. *IEEE Trans. Biomed. Eng.*, 62, 11, 2693–2701, 2015.
14. Liao, S., Gao, Y., Oto, A., Shen, D., Representation learning: a unified deep learning framework for automatic prostate MR segmentation, in: *International Conference on Medical Image Computing and Computer-Assisted Intervention*, pp. 254–261, 2013.
15. Burri, S.R., Agarwal, D.K., Vyas, N., Duggar, R., A Machine Learning Framework for Accurate Prediction of Parkinson's Disease from Speech Data, in: *2023 3rd International Conference on Innovative Sustainable Computational Technologies (CISCT)*, Dehradun, India, pp. 1–6, 2023, doi: 10.1109/CISCT57197.2023.10351422.
16. Ditzler, G., Polikar, R., Rosen, G., Multi-layer and recursive neural networks for metagenomic classification. *IEEE Trans. Nanobiosci.*, 14, 6, 608–616, 2015.
17. Punugoti, R., Dutt, V., Anand, A., Bhati, N., Exploring the Impact of Edge Intelligence and IoT on Healthcare: A Comprehensive Survey, in: *2023 International Conference on Sustainable Computing and Smart Systems (ICSCSS)*, Coimbatore, India, pp. 1108–1114, 2023, doi: 10.1109/ICSCSS57650.2023.10169733.
18. Xu, Y., Dai, Z., Chen, F., Gao, S., Pei, J., Lai, L., Deep learning for drug-induced liver injury. *J. Chem. Inf. Model.*, 55, 10, 2085–209, 2015.
19. Holzinger, A., Dehmer, M., Jurisica, I., Knowledge discovery and interactive data mining in bioinformatics-state-of-the-art, future challenges and research directions. *BMC Bioinf.*, 15, 6, I1, 2014.
20. Kumar, A., Kumar, S.A., Dutt, V., Dubey, A.K., Narang, S., A Hybrid Secure Cloud Platform Maintenance Based on Improved Attribute-Based Encryption Strategies. *Int. J. Interact. Multimed. Artif. Intell.*, 8, 2. Universidad Internacional de La Rioja, 10.9781/ijimai.2021.11.004.

20. Kamal, M.S., Dey, N., Ashour, A.S., Large Scale Medical Data Mining for Accurate Diagnosis: A Blueprint, in: *Handbook of Large-Scale Distributed Computing in Smart Healthcare*, pp. 157–176, Springer, Cham, 2017.
21. Manogaran, G. and Lopez, D., Disease surveillance system for big climate data processing and dengue transmission. *Int. J. Ambient Comput. Intell. (IJACI)*, 8, 2, 88–105, 2017.
22. Burugadda, V.R., Jadhav, N., Vyas, N., Duggar, R., Exploring the Potential of Deep Reinforcement Learning for Autonomous Navigation in Complex Environments, in: *2023 7th International Conference on Computing, Communication, Control and Automation (ICCUBEA)*, Pune, India, pp. 1–6, 2023, doi: 10.1109/ICCUBEA58933.2023.10392109.
23. Swarna, S.R., Kumar, A., Dixit, P., Sairam, T.V.M., Parkinson's Disease Prediction using Adaptive Quantum Computing, in: *2021 Third International Conference on Intelligent Communication Technologies and Virtual Mobile Networks (ICICV)*, Tirunelveli, India, pp. 1396–1401, 2021, doi: 10.1109/ICICV50876.2021.9388628.
24. Vengadeswaran, S. and Balasundaram, S.R., An Optimal Data Placement Strategy for Improving System Performance of Massive Data Applications Using Graph Clustering. *Int. J. Ambient Comput. Intell. (IJACI)*, 9, 3, 15–30, 2018.
25. Burugadda, V.R., Pawar, P.S., Kumar, A., Bhati, N., Predicting Hospital Readmission Risk for Heart Failure Patients Using Machine Learning Techniques: A Comparative Study of Classification Algorithms, in: *2023 Second International Conference on Trends in Electrical, Electronics, and Computer Engineering (TEECCON)*, Bangalore, India, pp. 223–228, 2023, doi: 10.1109/TEECCON59234.2023.10335817.
26. Min, S., Lee, B., Yoon, S., Deep learning in bioinformatics. *Briefings Bioinf.*, 18, 5, 851–869, 2017.
27. Lan, K., Fong, S., Song, W., Vasilakos, A.V., Millham, R.C., Self-Adaptive Pre-Processing Methodology for Big Data Stream Mining in Internet of Things Environmental Sensor Monitoring. *Symmetry*, 9, 10, 244, 2017.
28. Vyas, N., P., P.A., Das, P., Mahajan, Y., The Impact of Air Pollution on Respiratory Health Results: An Analysis of Asthma and COPD in a Population Study, in: *2023 International Conference on Computing, Communication, and Intelligent Systems (ICCCIS)*, Greater Noida, India, pp. 141–146, 2023, doi: 10.1109/ICCCIS60361.2023.10425187.

4

Comparative Analysis of Conventional Machine Learning and Deep Learning Techniques for Predicting Parkinson's Disease

Monika Sethi* **and Vidhu Baggan**

Chitkara University Institute of Engineering and Technology, Chitkara University, Punjab, India

Abstract

A neurological disorder which gets worse as time progresses is Parkinson's disease (PD). Once dopaminergic generating neurons in certain regions of the cerebral cortex are weakened, individuals find it hard to express themselves, write, walk, or carry out essential responsibilities in their day-to-day life. Disruption of the dopamine-producing brain cells, which are triggering the condition, results in the inability of the neurons to connect with other cells in the brain. The brain cells that generate dopamine are those which provide movement control, flexibility, and mobility. The diagnosis/classification of PD is often determined on the basis of clinical evidence, including a listing of a variety of motor signs, and medical examinations. Conventional techniques for diagnosis, on the other hand, could be prone to subjectivity challenges since these depend on an analysis of movement which could be problematic to identify as they are sometimes imperceptible to the human eye. Additionally, initial non-motor signs of PD can appear minimal and are caused by a different illness. Thus, it could prove difficult to diagnose PD at the beginning since such signs are usually neglected. Nowadays, machine learning (ML) and deep learning (DL) methods are being utilized for the classification of individuals who are suffering from PD and healthy controls (HC) or even patients who have comparable clinical signs (such as disorders of movement or different Parkinsonian syndromes). In this chapter, the comparative analysis of various conventional ML methods, which includes SVM, K-NN, Multilayer Perceptron

**Corresponding author*: sethi.monika4@gmail.com

Umesh Kumar Lilhore, Abhishek Kumar, Narayan Vyas, Sarita Simaiya and Vishal Dutt (eds.) Multimodal Data Fusion for Bioinformatics Artificial Intelligence, (49–66) © 2025 Scrivener Publishing LLC

(MLP) and deep learning methods, is done along with the kind of data modalities that are being used nowadays for classification of PD.

Keywords: Deep learning, support vector machine, machine learning, convolutional neural network

4.1 Introduction

Parkinson's disease (PD) is a form of dementia which disrupts communication along with other motor functions of the brain. This illness was first identified by Dr. James Parkinson in 1817, who additionally gave it the name "Shaking Palsy." The term "neurodegenerative diseases" refers to inherited and sporadic disorders and has been defined by chronic neural impairment. PD is regarded as the second most prevalent neurodegenerative disease amongst many others, including Alzheimer's disease, brain cancer, degenerative nerve diseases, and epilepsy [1]. The movement control centre (MCC) of the nervous system, referred to as the substantia nigra, is the region of the middle brain wherein PD mainly comes due to a gradual depletion of neurons that produce dopamine. The nerve cells respond abruptly as a consequence of dopamine deficits leading to hypokinetic movement syndrome [2]. The root cause of PD remains unclear even after years of intensive research. Many scientists believe that PD is an amalgam of human cells and environmental elements, particularly contact with outdoor toxins, injury to the head, being raised in remote regions, manganese in the water we consume, and chemical contamination. Individuals could differ in several ways. Someone with PD might have a few particular indicators, and each PD sufferer may experience those signs in a distinctive manner. Vibration in the fingers, forearms, legs, jawline, and face are among the most prevalent motor symptoms of PD, as are bradykinesia, or delay in movement, tightness or hardness of the limbs and trunk, unstable posture, or poor coordination and sense of balance [3]. Along with the aforementioned signs, non-motor symptoms including sadness and decline in memory can appear as well while having an impact on quality life in general [4]. There is currently just one blood or laboratory examination which could be utilized to diagnose PD and monitor its progress over time. With the initial detection of PD, rating scales as the Hoehn and Yahr scale (1967), the Unified PD Rating Scale (UPDRS), and its refined form MDS-UPDRS [5] have been applied. Some challenges involved with such techniques are access to trained labour and interaction with the patient, which is required from time to time. Despite the fact that the disease is often observed while it is developed, appropriate treatments nevertheless are extremely hard to achieve. Additionally, there is no proven medicine or cure for PD yet. Furthermore, this disease is often diagnosed on the basis of signs that are clinical, which includes a listing of several kinds of movement signs, with medical examinations. Conventional techniques for diagnosis, on the contrary, might be susceptible to subjectivity problems since they rely on the decoding of gestures, which could prove challenging to identify since they can be oftentimes inconspicuous to the human eye. Furthermore, initial non-motor signs of PD may be slight and caused by a variety of different disorders. Thus, it could be problematic to diagnose PD at its earliest stages when those signs are often overlooked [6].

The field of healthcare continues to employ machine learning techniques extensively. Machine learning, as the term suggests, enables computer software to gain insight about facts and derive significant representations in a partially automatic mode. ML strategies are currently used in a wide range of data modalities, including writing movement sequences, neurological imaging, speech, cerebral spinal fluid (CSF), cardiac scintigraphy, and blood, to classify PD. ML models assist the incorporation of different modalities, including SPECT and MRI for the goal of diagnosing PD [7, 8]. Researchers are thus able to identify significant features which aren't usually applied to the clinical evaluation of PD via ML technologies and rely on these different approaches [6, 9]. In addition, by employing traditional feature extraction techniques for modeling destructive speech, methods based on deep learning have been effectively utilized in recent years for particular disease classification [10, 11], devanagari manuscripts recognition [12, 13], and assessing speech things, for instance the classification and diagnosis of PD. These techniques have enhanced the effectiveness of models in comparison to findings from conventional methods of ML. As an example, "2015 ComParE" offered a sub-task concerning automatic estimating the neurological disorder of PD sufferers based on the MDS-UPDRSIII rating. Gaussian processes along with DNN were used by the top performers for predicting clinical ratings, and the authors observed a correlation of 0.65 [14]. A DL algorithm to evaluate dysarthric speech has been suggested. The framework included an intermediate interpretable hidden layer which includes four perceptual dimensions—nasality, speech effectiveness, articulatory accuracy, and prosody—in order to estimate the extent of a condition known as dysarthria. The research team produced a concise result which had a strong connection to the subjective assessments given by speech-language pathology professionals [15]. The major impediment to finding the most effective method for classifying is how it is used on a specific sample. The authors of this chapter offered a comparative study of the ML and DL methods used in PD categorization.

4.2 Symptoms and Dataset for PD

A variety of computer-based techniques are currently being suggested for recognizing the preliminary signs of PD along with other neurodegenerative ailments, and numerous types of data, including voice, handwriting, and patterns of speech, have been utilized to recognize variations. Moreover, gadgets that track movement of muscles, such as wearable sensors, are being utilized to recognize PD. Tremors while still, rigidity, akinesia (or bradykinesia), and unstable posture are the four main symptoms of PD which are often known by the acronym TRAP. Furthermore, contracted posture and immobility (motor blocks) were also added to the group of traditional parkinsonism signs, with PD being the most prevalent kind. Motor/non-motor deficits must be assessed in conjunction with each patient's requirements and goals due to the varied histories and habits of PD individuals. Table 4.1 lists various signs of PD.

As indicated in Table 4.2, several datasets for the classification of PD based on the symptoms, including mobility data, handwriting patterns, voice recordings, etc., are publicly accessible.

Table 4.1 Symptoms for PD [16].

Motor symptoms	Non-motor symptoms
Tremor	Disturbances in the Sense of Smell
Bradykinesia	Sleep Problems
Postural Instability	Depression and Anxiety
Walking or Gait Difficulties	Psychosis
Vocal Symptoms	Cognitive Impairment
Decreased Arm Swing	
Difficulty in Daily Life Activities	

Table 4.2 Datasets available for PD classification

S. no.	Dataset name	Subjects	No. of subjects	Type of dataset
1	PaHaW	HC-38 PD-37	75	Handwritten Patterns
2	HandPD	HC-18 PD-74	92	Handwritten Patterns
3	NewHandPD	HC-35 PD-31	66	Handwritten Patterns
4	Parkinson's Drawings (10.3389/fneur.2017.00435)	HC-51 PD-51	102	Spirals Drawing and Waves
5	Parkinsons	HC-8 PD-23	31	Voice Measurements
6	Parkinson's Disease Classification	HC-64 PD-188	252	Voice Measurements
7	Parkinson's Telemonitoring	PD-42	-	Voice Measurements
8	Parkinson Speech Dataset	HC-20 PD-20	40	Sound Recordings
9	Parkinson Disease Spiral Drawings	HC-15 PD-62	77	Handwriting Database
10	Parkinson Dataset with replicated acoustic features	HC-20 PD-20	40	Voice Recordings

4.3 Parkinson's Disease Classification Using Machine Learning Methods

The primary objective of data mining alongside data analysis lies in extraction of relevant details that could be employed in various fields, along with several statistical frameworks, to increase learning and decision-making assistance over a specific process. The medical sector is using machine learning methods extensively. Machine learning, as the name states, permits computer software to gain insight on data as well as derive relevant interpretations in a semi-automatic fashion. An extensive variety of data modalities, among them penmanship trends, motion, neurological imaging, and communication are being subject to ML algorithms enabling the classification of PD. Thus, machine learning algorithms proved crucial for completing the data mining and analysis process effectively. Supervised Learning, Unsupervised Learning, and Reinforcement Learning constitute the three main categories of ML algorithms [17].

There have been more articles published over the past decade exploring the use of ML models in PD classification. While some past investigations have primarily examined the application of ML models in the diagnosis and assessment of PD, most have only looked at data from sensors worn by individuals, movement, and motor manifestations. Researchers can consequently utilize ML techniques for identifying appropriate features which are not often applied in the clinical evaluation of PD and focus on these other ways for identifying the disease when it is in preliminary phases or in unusual form. Table 4.3 illustrates the outcomes of researchers who employed a machine learning model to analyse a variety of factors, including voice recordings, motions, MRI data, handwriting patterns, PET, CSF, and combinations of different modalities to classify PD.

Table 4.3 Studies which utilized ML models to classify PD vs. healthy control (HC).

Ref. & year	Data source	Type of data	No. of subjects	ML model	Performance (accuracy/ sensitivity/ specificity)
[18] (2017)	UCI ML repository	Voice recordings	HC- 8 PD- 23	ECFA& SVM	Acc-98%, Sen-98%, Spec-97%
[19] (2017)	UCI ML repository	Voice recordings	HC- 8 PD- 23	Boosted Decision Tree	Acc-91.2%
[20] (2017)	Gathered from volunteers	Movement data	HC- 424 PD- 156	hidden Markov models (HMM)	Acc-85.51%
[21] (2017)	UCI ML repository	Speech recordings	HC-8 PD- 42	SVM	Acc-96.4%
[22] (2017)	Gathered from volunteers	Movement data	HC-12 PD-16	SVM	Acc-85.7%, Sen-83.5%, Spec-87.5%

(*Continued*)

Table 4.3 Studies which utilized ML models to classify PD vs. healthy control (HC). (*Continued*)

Ref. & year	Data source	Type of data	No. of subjects	ML model	Performance (accuracy/ sensitivity/ specificity)
[23] (2017)	Gathered from volunteers	Movement data	HC-26 PD-14	Random forest	Acc-94.6%, Sen-91.5%, Spec-97.2%
[24] (2017)	Gathered from volunteers	MRI	HC-21 PD-21	SVM	Acc-78, Precision -85%, AUC-85.3%, Recall-82%
[25] (2017)	Gathered from volunteers	MRI	HC-51 PD-50	SVM	Sen-92%, Spec-87%
[26] (2017)	UCI ML repository	Voice recordings	HC-22 PD-19	SVM	Acc-89%
[27] (2017)	PPMI Data	MRI	HC-18 PD-19	SVM	Acc-95%
[28] (2018)	UCI ML repository	Voice recordings	HC-20 PD-20	SVM	FNR-10%
[29] (2018)	UCI ML repository	Voice recordings	HC-8 PD-23	DNN	Acc-98%, Sen-99%, Spec-95%
[30] (2018)	Gathered from volunteers	Movement data	HC-12 PD-16	Naïve Bayes	Acc-81%, Sen-76%, Spec-86.5%
[31] (2018)	UCI ML repository	Voice recordings	HC-8 PD-23	FKNN	Acc-97.8%
[32] (2018)	PPMI Data	MRI	HC-169 PD-374	For features extraction-Random forest and SVM for classification	Acc-93%, Sen-93%, Spec-92%, AUC-97%
[33] (2019)	PPMI Data	MRI	HC-40 PD-40	SVM-RBF	Acc-87.5%, Sen-85%, Spec-90%, AUC-90%
[34] (2019)	PPMI Data	MRI	HC-169 PD-374	RFS-LDA	Acc-79.8%

(*Continued*)

Table 4.3 Studies which utilized ML models to classify PD vs. healthy control (HC). (*Continued*)

Ref. & year	Data source	Type of data	No. of subjects	ML model	Performance (accuracy/ sensitivity/ specificity)
[35] (2019)	PhysioNet	Movement data	HC-16 PD-15	SVM, Decision Tree, and KNN	Acc-96.8%
[36] (2019)	UCI ML repository	Voice recordings	HC- 20 PD-20	LDA-NN-GA	ACC-100%, Sen-100%
[37] (2019)	UCI ML repository	Voice recordings	HC- 20 PD-20	SVM-Linear	ACC-70%
[38] (2020)	UCI ML repository	Voice recordings	HC- 8 PD-23	SVM	Acc-93.84%
[39] (2020)	PPMI Data	MRI	HC- 183 PD-401	SVM	Acc-95.9%
[40] (2021)	UCI ML repository	Voice recordings	HC- 8 PD-23	Hybrid Model (Genetic + Random forest)	Acc-95.98%
[41] (2022)	Gathered from volunteers	Neurocognitive functional tests	HC- 25 PD-50	Decision tree	Acc-92.6%
[42] (2022)	PPMI Data and Parkinson's Disease Biomarker Program (PDBP)	MRI	-	Automated ML	AUC-89.72%
[43] (2022)	UCI ML repository	Voice recordings	HC- 8 PD-23	Random Forest	Acc-97%
[44] (2023)	Gathered from volunteers	Movement Data	HC- 6 PD-6	BLR, DT, RF, KNN, SVM, NB	BLR-90.5%, RF, KNN, SVM, NB Acc-100%
[45] (2023)	UCI ML repository	Voice recordings	HC- 48 PD-147	Ensemble model (Gradient boosting-GBC)	Acc-97.43%
[46] (2023)	UCI ML repository	Voice recordings	HC- 8 PD-23	Random Forest	Acc- 91.83% Sen-95%

4.4 Parkinson's Disease Classification Using DL Methods

Techniques based on deep learning have been effectively used in the past decade for analysing specific trends in language, especially the identification and tracking of PD, alongside conventional feature extraction techniques for predicting deteriorating speech. By employing these techniques, the effectiveness of the models has risen in comparison to the outcomes produced by using traditional ML techniques. For instance, a DL approach to evaluate dysarthria speech has been suggested in [47]. The design incorporates a partially interpretable hidden layer which includes four sensory dimensions in an attempt to estimate the degree of intensity of dysarthria. The research team provided a concise result which was closely associated with overall assessments conducted by speech-language pathology professionals. The structure of non-modal phonation in PD has been illustrated by the investigators in [48]. Deep neural networks were employed by the researchers to determine linguistic posteriors. Fifty PD and fifty HC individuals had their dysarthria levels predicted based on certain phonetic posteriors. With rate of accuracy varying from 70% to 89% depending on the spoken language, the investigators recognized PD and (Normal Control) NC participants utilizing speech samples in three different languages, SGC, where S is for Spanish, G for German, and C for Czech. Their results suggest that DL techniques offer potential when assessing speech recordings of PD sufferers. Researchers' results on classifying PD using DL models are shown in Table 4.4.

Table 4.4 Studies which utilized DL models to classify PD vs. healthy control (HC).

Ref. & year	Data source	Type of data	No. of subjects	ML model	Performance (accuracy/ sensitivity/ specificity)
[49] 2016	Gathered from volunteers	Movement Data	-	CNN	Acc-90.9%
[50] 2016	HandPD	Handwriting Patterns	HC- 18 PD-74	CNN	Acc-80.19%
[51] 2016	HandPD	Handwriting Patterns	HC- 18 PD-74	CNN	Acc-90.38%

(*Continued*)

Table 4.4 Studies which utilized DL models to classify PD vs. healthy control (HC). (*Continued*)

Ref. & year	Data source	Type of data	No. of subjects	ML model	Performance (accuracy/ sensitivity/ specificity)
[52] 2017	PPMI + SNUH	MRI	PPMI (HC- 193 PD-431) + SNUH (HC-72 PD-10)	CNN	Acc-90.7%
[53] 2018	HandPD	Handwriting Patterns	HC- 18 PD-74	CNN	Acc-93.5%
[54] 2019	HandPD	Handwriting Patterns	HC- 21 PD-14	CNN	Acc-87%
[55] 2019	UCI ML repository	Voice recordings	HC- 64 PD-188	CNN	Acc-81.3%
[56] 2019	PaHaW dataset	Handwriting Patterns	HC- 38 PD-37	CNN	Acc-98.28%
[57] 2020	Hospital Universiti Kebangsaan Malaysia Ethics Committee	EEG Signal	HC-20 PD-20	CNN	Acc-88.25% Sen-84.71% Spe-91.77%
[58] 2020	PPMI	MRI	HC-82 PD-100	CNN (AlexNet)	Acc-88.9%
[59] 2021	HandPD+ NewHandPD+ Parkinsons Drawings dataset	Handwriting Patterns	HC- 561 PD-973	CNN Model (AlexNet, VGGNet, resNet, GoogleNet)	Overall Acc-99.22%
[60] 2022	PhysioNet	Gait Signals	HC- 73 PD-93	Siamese Recurrent Network with Attention	Acc-81%
[61] 2022	Fujian Medical University Union Hospital	Movement Data	HC- 161 PD-296	CNN (ResNet)	Acc- 92.03%
[62] 2023	NewHandPD	Handwritten Specimens	HC- 315 PD-279	ResNet50, VGG19, Inception-V3	Acc-95%
[63] 2023	3-D Vector Data in Actual Time		-	CNN-BGRU	Acc- 8.73%, F1 score-98.40% Recall-98.33%, Precision-98.45%
[64] 2023	UCI ML repository	Voice recordings	HC- 10 PD-42	DL Model	R-squared-86%

4.5 Conclusion

PD is often diagnosed on the basis of symptomatic indications, such as an understanding of various kinds of motion/motor indicators, and medical investigations. Conventional methods for diagnosis, on the other hand, could be prone to subjectivity issues due to the fact that they depend on the interpretation of motions; this could prove hard to identify as these movements are usually imperceptible to the human eye. Furthermore, initial non-motor signs of PD might seem slight and caused by a variety of other illnesses. Consequently, it may prove difficult to diagnose PD at its earliest stages since such signs are often ignored. Computer-aided approaches including ML and DL are being developed for the classification of PD and HC or patients. The researchers have discussed the ML and DL techniques used for PD classification using a variety of datasets in this chapter. Researchers provided a variety of resources which include (a) ML and DL techniques which are being employed for the PD diagnosis along with results, (b) different kinds of clinical, behavioral, and biometric data which could potentially be applied for producing further precise diagnosis, and (c) possible biomarkers for assisting in making clinical decisions. In conclusion, while the adoption of novel biomarkers may result in improved utilization of PD diagnosis at the outset, the implementation of ML-DL assisted PD diagnosis produces tremendous results for an even more systematic clinical decision-making framework.

References

1. Pahuja, G. and Nagabhushan, T.N., A Comparative Study of Existing Machine Learning Approaches for Parkinson's Disease Detection. *IETE J. Res.*, 67, 1, 4–14, Jan. 2021. doi: 10.1080/03772063.2018.1531730.
2. Lang, A.E. and Lozano, A.M., Parkinson's Disease. *N. Engl. J. Med.*, 339, 16, 1130–1143, Oct. 1998. doi: 10.1056/NEJM199810153391607.
3. Morris, M.E., Movement Disorders in People with Parkinson Disease: A Model for Physical Therapy. *Phys. Ther.*, 80, 6, 578–597, Jun. 2000. doi: 10.1093/ptj/80.6.578.
4. Wu, S.-L., Liscic, R.M., Kim, S., Sorbi, S., Yang, Y.-H., Nonmotor Symptoms of Parkinson's Disease. *Parkinsons. Dis.*, 2017, 1–2, 2017. doi: 10.1155/2017/4382518.
5. Goetz, C.G., *et al.*, Movement Disorder Society-sponsored revision of the Unified Parkinson's Disease Rating Scale (MDS-UPDRS): Scale presentation and clinimetric testing results. *Mov. Disord.*, 23, 15, 2129–2170, Nov. 2008. doi: 10.1002/mds.22340.

6. Boyapati, S., Swarna, S.R., Dutt, V., Vyas, N., Big Data Approach for Medical Data Classification: A Review Study, in: *2020 3rd International Conference on Intelligent Sustainable Systems (ICISS)*, Thoothukudi, India, pp. 762–766, 2020, doi: 10.1109/ICISS49785.2020.9315870.
7. Sethi, M., Ahuja, S., Bawa, P., Classification of Alzheimer's disease using Neuroimaging Data by Convolution Neural Network, in: *2021 6th International Conference on Signal Processing, Computing and Control (ISPCC)*, pp. 402–406, Oct. 2021, doi: 10.1109/ISPCC53510.2021.9609431.
8. Sethi, M., Ahuja, S., Rani, S., Koundal, D., Zaguia, A., Enbeyle, W., An Exploration: Alzheimer's Disease Classification Based on Convolutional Neural Network. *Biomed Res. Int.*, 2022, 1–19, Jan. 2022. doi: 10.1155/2022/8739960.
9. Sethi, M., Ahuja, S., Rani, S., Bawa, P., Zaguia, A., Classification of Alzheimer's Disease Using Gaussian-Based Bayesian Parameter Optimization for Deep Convolutional LSTM Network. *Comput. Math. Methods Med.*, 2021, 1–16, Oct. 2021. doi: 10.1155/2021/4186666.
10. Trivedi, N.K., *et al.*, Early Detection and Classification of Tomato Leaf Disease Using High-Performance Deep Neural Network. *Sensors*, 21, 23, 7987, Nov. 2021. doi: 10.3390/s21237987.
11. Kukreja, V. and Dhiman, P., A Deep Neural Network based disease detection scheme for Citrus fruits, in: *2020 International Conference on Smart Electronics and Communication (ICOSEC)*, pp. 97–101, Sep. 2020, doi: 10.1109/ICOSEC49089.2020.9215359.
12. Moudgil, A., Singh, S., Sareen, B., CNN-LSTM Based Approach for Recognition of Devanagari Manuscripts, in: *2022 International Conference on Data Analytics for Business and Industry (ICDABI)*, pp. 1–5, Oct. 2022, doi: 10.1109/ICDABI56818.2022.10041262.
13. Arora, J., Sethi, M., Singh, S., Change Identification and Notification Framework for IoT Enabled Smart Security System, in: *2022 10th International Conference on Reliability, Infocom Technologies and Optimization (Trends and Future Directions) (ICRITO)*, pp. 1–6, Oct. 2022, doi: 10.1109/ICRITO56286.2022.9964542.
14. Punugoti, R., Dutt, V., Anand, A., Bhati, N., Exploring the Impact of Edge Intelligence and IoT on Healthcare: A Comprehensive Survey, in: *2023 International Conference on Sustainable Computing and Smart Systems (ICSCSS)*, Coimbatore, India, pp. 1108–1114, 2023, doi: 10.1109/ICSCSS57650.2023.10169733.
15. Tu, M., Berisha, V., Liss, J., Interpretable objective assessment of dysarthric speech based on deep neural networks. *Proc. Annu. Conf. Int. Speech Commun. Assoc. INTERSPEECH*, 2017-August, August, 1849–1853, 2017. doi: 10.21437/Interspeech.2017-1222.
16. Burugadda, V.R., Pawar, P.S., Kumar, A., Bhati, N., Predicting Hospital Readmission Risk for Heart Failure Patients Using Machine Learning Techniques: A Comparative Study of Classification Algorithms, in: *2023*

Second International Conference on Trends in Electrical, Electronics, and Computer Engineering (TEECCON), Bangalore, India, pp. 223–228, 2023, doi: 10.1109/TEECCON59234.2023.10335817.
17. Saxena, M. and Ahuja, S., Comparative Survey of Machine Learning Techniques for Prediction of Parkinson's Disease, in: *2020 Indo – Taiwan 2nd International Conference on Computing, Analytics and Networks (Indo-Taiwan ICAN)*, pp. 248–253, Feb. 2020, doi: 10.1109/Indo-TaiwanICAN48429.2020.9181368.
18. Dash, S., Thulasiram, R., Thulasiraman, P., An Enhanced Chaos-Based Firefly Model for Parkinson's Disease Diagnosis and Classification, in: *2017 International Conference on Information Technology (ICIT)*, pp. 159–164, Dec. 2017, doi: 10.1109/ICIT.2017.43.
19. Dinesh, A. and He, J., Using machine learning to diagnose Parkinson's disease from voice recordings, in: *2017 IEEE MIT Undergraduate Research Technology Conference (URTC)*, pp. 1–4, Nov. 2017, doi: 10.1109/URTC.2017.8284216.
20. Sekhar, U.S., Vyas, N., Dutt, V., Kumar, A., Multimodal Neuroimaging Data in Early Detection of Alzheimer's Disease: Exploring the Role of Ensemble Models and GAN Algorithm, in: *2023 International Conference on Circuit Power and Computing Technologies (ICCPCT)*, Kollam, India, pp. 1664–1669, 2023, doi: 10.1109/ICCPCT58313.2023.10245177.
21. Erdogdu Sakar, B., Serbes, G., Sakar, C.O., Analyzing the effectiveness of vocal features in early telediagnosis of Parkinson's disease. *PLoS One*, 12, 8, e0182428, Aug. 2017. doi: 10.1371/journal.pone.0182428.
22. Kumar, A., Kumar, S.A., Dutt, V., Dubey, A.K., Narang, S., A Hybrid Secure Cloud Platform Maintenance Based on Improved Attribute-Based Encryption Strategies. *Int. J. Interact. Multimed. Artif. Intell.*, 8, 2, 150, 2023. Universidad Internacional de La Rioja, doi: 10.9781/ijimai.2021.11.004.
23. Vyas, N., P., P.A., Das, P., Mahajan, Y., The Impact of Air Pollution on Respiratory Health Results: An Analysis of Asthma and COPD in a Population Study, in: *2023 International Conference on Computing, Communication, and Intelligent Systems (ICCCIS)*, Greater Noida, India, pp. 141–146, 2023, doi: 10.1109/ICCCIS60361.2023.10425187.
24. Kamagata, K., *et al.*, Connectome analysis with diffusion MRI in idiopathic Parkinson's disease: Evaluation using multi-shell, multi-tissue, constrained spherical deconvolution. *NeuroImage Clin.*, 17, 518–529, 2018. doi: 10.1016/j.nicl.2017.11.007.
25. Chandrasekaran, S., Dutt, V., Vyas, N., Kumar, R., Student Sentiment Analysis Using Various Machine Learning Techniques, in: *2023 International Conference on Artificial Intelligence and Smart Communication (AISC)*, Greater Noida, India, pp. 104–107, 2023, doi: 10.1109/AISC56616.2023.10085018.
26. Burugadda, V.R., Jadhav, N., Vyas, N., Duggar, R., Exploring the Potential of Deep Reinforcement Learning for Autonomous Navigation in Complex Environments, in: *2023 7th International Conference on Computing, Communication, Control and Automation (ICCUBEA)*, Pune, India, pp. 1–6, 2023, doi: 10.1109/ICCUBEA58933.2023.10392109.

27. Kazeminejad, A., Golbabaei, S., Soltanian-Zadeh, H., Graph theoretical metrics and machine learning for diagnosis of Parkinson's disease using rs-fMRI, in: *2017 Artificial Intelligence and Signal Processing Conference (AISP)*, pp. 134–139, Oct. 2017, doi: 10.1109/AISP.2017.8324124.
28. Punugoti, R., Duggar, R., Dhargalkar, R.R., Bhati, N., Intelligent Healthcare: Using NLP and ML to Power Chatbots for Improved Assistance, in: *2023 International Conference on IoT, Communication and Automation Technology (ICICAT)*, IEEE, Jun. 23, 2023, doi: 10.1109/icicat57735.2023.10263708.
29. Burri, S.R., Agarwal, D.K., Vyas, N., Duggar, R., A Machine Learning Framework for Accurate Prediction of Parkinson's Disease from Speech Data, in: *2023 3rd International Conference on Innovative Sustainable Computational Technologies (CISCT)*, Dehradun, India, pp. 1–6, 2023, doi: 10.1109/CISCT57197.2023.10351422.
30. Butt, A.H., *et al.*, Objective and automatic classification of Parkinson disease with Leap Motion controller. *Biomed. Eng. Online*, 17, 1, 168, Dec. 2018. doi: 10.1186/s12938-018-0600-7.
31. Cai, Z., *et al.*, An Intelligent Parkinson's Disease Diagnostic System Based on a Chaotic Bacterial Foraging Optimization Enhanced Fuzzy KNN Approach. *Comput. Math. Methods Med.*, 2018, 1–24, Jun. 2018. doi: 10.1155/2018/2396952.
32. Amoroso, N., La Rocca, M., Monaco, A., Bellotti, R., Tangaro, S., Complex networks reveal early MRI markers of Parkinson's disease. *Med. Image Anal.*, 48, 12–24, Aug. 2018. doi: 10.1016/j.media.2018.05.004.
33. Cigdem, O., Demirel, H., Unay, D., The Performance of Local-Learning Based Clustering Feature Selection Method on the Diagnosis of Parkinson's Disease Using Structural MRI, in: *2019 IEEE International Conference on Systems, Man and Cybernetics (SMC)*, pp. 1286–1291, Oct. 2019, doi: 10.1109/SMC.2019.8914611.
34. Adeli, E., *et al.*, Semi-Supervised Discriminative Classification Robust to Sample-Outliers and Feature-Noises. *IEEE Trans. Pattern Anal. Mach. Intell.*, 41, 2, 515–522, Feb. 2019. doi: 10.1109/TPAMI.2018.2794470.
35. Felix, J.P., *et al.*, A Parkinson's Disease Classification Method: An Approach Using Gait Dynamics and Detrended Fluctuation Analysis, in: *2019 IEEE Canadian Conference of Electrical and Computer Engineering (CCECE)*, pp. 1–4, May 2019, doi: 10.1109/CCECE.2019.8861759.
36. Ali, L., Zhu, C., Zhang, Z., Liu, Y., Automated Detection of Parkinson's Disease Based on Multiple Types of Sustained Phonations Using Linear Discriminant Analysis and Genetically Optimized Neural Network. *IEEE J. Transl. Eng. Heal. Med.*, 7, 1–10, 2019. doi: 10.1109/JTEHM.2019.2940900.
37. Ali, L., Khan, S.U., Arshad, M., Ali, S., Anwar, M., A Multi-model Framework for Evaluating Type of Speech Samples having Complementary Information about Parkinson's Disease, in: *2019 International Conference on Electrical, Communication, and Computer Engineering (ICECCE)*, pp. 1–5, Jul. 2019, doi: 10.1109/ICECCE47252.2019.8940696.

38. Karapinar Senturk, Z., Early diagnosis of Parkinson's disease using machine learning algorithms. *Med. Hypotheses*, 138, 109603, May 2020. doi: 10.1016/j.mehy.2020.109603.
39. Wang, W., Lee, J., Harrou, F., Sun, Y., Early Detection of Parkinson's Disease Using Deep Learning and Machine Learning. *IEEE Access*, 8, 147635–147646, 2020. doi: 10.1109/ACCESS.2020.3016062.
40. Lamba, R., Gulati, T., Alharbi, H.F., Jain, A., A hybrid system for Parkinson's disease diagnosis using machine learning techniques. *Int. J. Speech Technol.*, 25, 3, 583–593, Sep. 2022. doi: 10.1007/s10772-021-09837-9.
41. Templeton, J.M., Poellabauer, C., Schneider, S., Classification of Parkinson's disease and its stages using machine learning. *Sci. Rep.*, 12, 1, 14036, Aug. 2022. doi: 10.1038/s41598-022-18015-z.
42. Kumar, S.A., Kumar, H., Dutt, V., Soni, H., Self-Health Analysis with Two Step Histogram based Procedure using Machine Learning, in: *2021 Third International Conference on Intelligent Communication Technologies and Virtual Mobile Networks (ICICV)*, Tirunelveli, India, pp. 794–799, 2021, doi: 10.1109/ICICV50876.2021.9388427.
43. Ahmed, I., Aljahdali, S., Shakeel Khan, M., Kaddoura, S., Classification of Parkinson Disease Based on Patient's Voice Signal Using Machine Learning. *Intell. Autom. Soft Comput.*, 32, 2, 705–722, 2022. doi: 10.32604/iasc.2022.022037.
44. Bhati, N., Duggar, R., Alzahrani, A., Exploring few-shot learning approaches for bioinformatics advancements, in: *Applying Machine Learning Techniques to Bioinformatics*, pp. 303–316, IGI Global, 2024.
45. Chaurasia, V. and Chaurasia, A., Detection of Parkinson's Disease by Using Machine Learning Stacking and Ensemble Method. *Biomed. Mater. Devices*, Apr. 2023. doi: 10.1007/s44174-023-00079-8.
46. Govindu, A. and Palwe, S., Early detection of Parkinson's disease using machine learning. *Procedia Comput. Sci.*, 218, 249–261, 2023. doi: 10.1016/j.procs.2023.01.007.
47. Burugadda, V.R., Mane, P.M., Kumar, A., Bhati, N., A Machine Learning-Based Algorithm for Early Detection of Sepsis in Hospitalized Patients: Development and Evaluation, in: *2023 1st International Conference on Circuits, Power and Intelligent Systems (CCPIS)*, Bhubaneswar, India, pp. 1–6, 2023, doi: 10.1109/CCPIS59145.2023.10291447.
48. Cernak, M., Orozco-Arroyave, J.R., Rudzicz, F., Christensen, H., Vásquez-Correa, J.C., Nöth, E., Characterisation of voice quality of Parkinson's disease using differential phonological posterior features. *Comput. Speech Lang.*, 46, 196–208, Nov. 2017. doi: 10.1016/j.csl.2017.06.004.
49. Eskofier, B.M., *et al.*, Recent machine learning advancements in sensor-based mobility analysis: Deep learning for Parkinson's disease assessment, in: *2016 38th Annual International Conference of the IEEE Engineering in Medicine and Biology Society (EMBC)*, pp. 655–658, Aug. 2016, doi: 10.1109/EMBC.2016.7590787.

50. Pereira, C.R., Weber, S.A.T., Hook, C., Rosa, G.H., Papa, J.P., Deep Learning-Aided Parkinson's Disease Diagnosis from Handwritten Dynamics, in: *2016 29th SIBGRAPI Conference on Graphics, Patterns and Images (SIBGRAPI)*, pp. 340–346, Oct. 2016, doi: 10.1109/SIBGRAPI.2016.054.
51. Pereira, C.R., Pereira, D.R., Papa, J.P., Rosa, G.H., Yang, X.-S., Convolutional Neural Networks Applied for Parkinson's Disease Identification. 377–390, 2016.
52. Swarna, S.R., Boyapati, S., Dutt, V., Bajaj, K., Deep Learning in Dynamic Modeling of Medical Imaging: A Review Study, in: *2020 3rd International Conference on Intelligent Sustainable Systems (ICISS)*, Thoothukudi, India, pp. 745–749, 2020, doi: 10.1109/ICISS49785.2020.9315990.
53. Mylavarapu, R.T., Pokhriyal, A., Dhargalkar, R.R., Bhati, N., Empowering Healthcare with AI: Addressing Challenges and Envisioning the Future, in: *2023 4th International Conference on Electronics and Sustainable Communication Systems (ICESC)*, Coimbatore, India, pp. 1393–1398, 2023, doi: 10.1109/ICESC57686.2023.10193228.
54. Dutt, V., Sasubilli, S.M., Yerrapati, A.E., Dynamic Information Retrieval With Chatbots: A Review of Artificial Intelligence Methodology, in: *2020 4th International Conference on Electronics, Communication and Aerospace Technology (ICECA)*, Coimbatore, India, pp. 1299–1303, 2020, doi: 10.1109/ICECA49313.2020.9297533.
55. Gunduz, H., Deep Learning-Based Parkinson's Disease Classification Using Vocal Feature Sets. *IEEE Access*, 7, 115540–115551, 2019. doi: 10.1109/ACCESS.2019.2936564.
56. Naseer, A., Rani, M., Naz, S., Razzak, M., II, Imran, M., Xu, G., Refining Parkinson's neurological disorder identification through deep transfer learning. *Neural Comput. Appl.*, 32, 3, 839–854, Feb. 2020. doi: 10.1007/s00521-019-04069-0.
57. Punugoti, R., Dutt, V., Kumar, A., Bhati, N., Boosting the Accuracy of Cardiovascular Disease Prediction Through SMOTE, in: *2023 International Conference on IoT, Communication and Automation Technology (ICICAT)*, Gorakhpur, India, pp. 1–6, 2023, doi: 10.1109/ICICAT57735.2023.10263703.
58. Sivaranjini, S. and Sujatha, C.M., Deep learning based diagnosis of Parkinson's disease using convolutional neural network. *Multimed. Tools Appl.*, 79, 21–22, 15467–15479, Jun. 2020. doi: 10.1007/s11042-019-7469-8.
59. Kamran, I., Naz, S., Razzak, I., Imran, M., Handwriting dynamics assessment using deep neural network for early identification of Parkinson's disease. *Futur. Gener. Comput. Syst.*, 117, 234–244, Apr. 2021. doi: 10.1016/j.future.2020.11.020.
60. Ogul, B.B. and Ozdemir, S., A Pairwise Deep Ranking Model for Relative Assessment of Parkinson's Disease Patients from Gait Signals. *IEEE Access*, 10, 6676–6683, 2022. doi: 10.1109/ACCESS.2021.3136724.
61. Sasubilli, S.M., Kumar, A., Dutt, V., Improving Health Care by Help of Internet of Things and Bigdata Analytics and Cloud Computing, in: *2020*

International Conference on Advances in Computing and Communication Engineering (ICACCE), Las Vegas, NV, USA, pp. 1–4, 2020, doi: 10.1109/ICACCE49060.2020.9155042.
62. Abdullah, S.M., *et al.*, Deep Transfer Learning Based Parkinson's Disease Detection Using Optimized Feature Selection. *IEEE Access*, 11, 3511–3524, 2023. doi: 10.1109/ACCESS.2023.3233969.
63. Swarna, S.R., Kumar, A., Dixit, P., Sairam, T.V.M., Parkinson's Disease Prediction using Adaptive Quantum Computing, in: *2021 Third International Conference on Intelligent Communication Technologies and Virtual Mobile Networks (ICICV)*, Tirunelveli, India, pp. 1396–1401, 2021, doi: 10.1109/ICICV50876.2021.9388628.
64. Mahmood, A., Mehroz Khan, M., Imran, M., Alhajlah, O., Dhahri, H., Karamat, T., End-to-End Deep Learning Method for Detection of Invasive Parkinson's Disease. *Diagnostics*, 13, 6, 1088, Mar. 2023. doi: 10.3390/diagnostics13061088.

5

Foundations of Multimodal Data Fusion

Srinivas Kumar Palvadi[1]* and G. Kadiravan[2]

[1]*Department of Computer Science and Engineering, SRK Institute of Technology, Vijayawada, Andhra Pradesh, India*
[2]*Department of Computer Science and Engineering, Koneru Lakshmaiah Education Foundation, Vaddeswaram, Guntur, Andhra Pradesh, India*

Abstract
Multi-modal data fusion is an essential area of study that aims to integrate information from various sources or modalities to enhance understanding and generate deeper insights. This paper examines the foundational concepts of multi-modal data fusion, emphasizing its relevance across diverse fields such as healthcare, remote sensing, robotics, and social media analysis. As the volume of data increases in various forms—including images, text, sensor data, and video streams—the demand for effective fusion methods becomes more pronounced.

The core components of multi-modal data fusion can be divided into three main phases: data alignment, feature extraction, and decision-level fusion. Data alignment is the initial step that involves synchronizing and harmonizing data from different sources to ensure they are compatible for analysis. Following this, feature extraction identifies the most significant characteristics of each modality, allowing for the retention of unique information while minimizing dimensional complexity. The final phase, decision-level fusion, integrates outputs from various modalities to yield a cohesive result, thereby improving accuracy and reliability.

One of the primary benefits of multi-modal data fusion is its capability to utilize complementary information, often leading to insights that are more robust than those derived from a single modality. For example, in healthcare, the combination of imaging data with electronic health records enables a comprehensive evaluation of patient conditions, thereby enhancing diagnostic precision and treatment strategies. In the realm of autonomous vehicles, fusing data from cameras, LiDAR, and radar significantly improves environmental perception and decision-making processes.

**Corresponding author*: srinivaskumarpalvadi@gmail.com

Umesh Kumar Lilhore, Abhishek Kumar, Narayan Vyas, Sarita Simaiya and Vishal Dutt (eds.) Multimodal Data Fusion for Bioinformatics Artificial Intelligence, (67–102) © 2025 Scrivener Publishing LLC

However, the field faces challenges such as data heterogeneity, inconsistent noise levels across modalities, and increased computational demands. Tackling these issues necessitates the creation of advanced algorithms and techniques that can adeptly manage and integrate varied data types. Recent progress in machine learning and deep learning has shown potential in enhancing the efficacy of fusion techniques, enabling more sophisticated analyses and real-time applications.

Overall, the foundations of multi-modal data fusion are crucial for leveraging diverse data sources to facilitate informed decision-making across multiple domains. As technology progresses, the need for innovative fusion methodologies will only intensify, making this area a vital focus for future research. This paper aims to provide an in-depth overview of the principles and methods underlying multi-modal data fusion, highlighting its significance in contemporary data analysis and applications.

Keywords: Multi-modal data fusion, data alignment, feature extraction, decision-level fusion, healthcare analytics, sensor integration, machine learning, real-time applications

Introduction

In the domain of bioinformatics and man-made consciousness (man-made intelligence), the reconciliation of multimodal information remains as a foundation in unwinding the intricacies of organic frameworks. Consolidating different kinds of information—from hereditary successions to clinical estimations—offers a far-reaching perspective on organic peculiarities, giving exceptional open doors to disclosure and development. Fundamental to this combination is the idea of multimodal information incorporation—a cycle that amalgamates data from different sources to extricate further bits of knowledge and work with a more thorough comprehension of organic cycles.

This chapter fills in a crucial passage point in this expanding field, laying the foundation for grasping the standards, methods, and uses of multimodal information joining in bioinformatics and simulated intelligence. By digging into the crucial ideas supporting information mix, this segment prepares for investigating progressed systems and state-of-the-art applications that harness coordinated information to address pressing difficulties in biomedical exploration and medical care.

This presentation gives an outline of the critical topics and targets, offering a guide for exploring the complicated scene of multimodal information combination. From explaining the meaning of coordinating different information types to illustrating the systemic methodologies and functional ramifications, this chapter forms an essential guide for scientists, professionals, and understudies the same, looking to tackle the force of incorporated information in propelling comprehension about how we might interpret science and work on human well-being.

What is Multimodal Data Fusion in Bioinformatics AI?

Multimodal information combination in bioinformatics man-made intelligence alludes to the most common way of coordinating heterogeneous information types from different sources inside the organic area utilizing computerized reasoning methods [1]. It includes joining data from various modalities like genomics, proteomics, metabolomics, imaging information, clinical records, and more to acquire a thorough comprehension of natural frameworks and peculiarities [2].

1. Integration of Assorted Information Types
Bioinformatics man-made intelligence plans to coordinate information from various organic modalities, each offering extraordinary experiences into natural cycles [3]. This incorporates hereditary information, protein collaborations, metabolic pathways, clinical information, and imaging information, among others [4].

2. Harmonization of Heterogeneous Data
Multimodal information combination meets the test of information heterogeneity by creating procedures to blend and coordinate data from dissimilar sources. This includes pre-processing moves toward normalizing information designs, taking care of missing qualities, and tending to irregularities across modalities [5].

3. Extraction of More Profound Insights
By consolidating information from different modalities, multimodal information combination empowers the extraction of more profound bits of knowledge and the disclosure of stowed away examples inside organic datasets [6]. This can prompt novel revelations, for example, distinguishing biomarkers, explaining infection components, and anticipating treatment results.

4. Utilization of Man-Made Intelligence Techniques
Multimodal information combination uses computerized reasoning methods, including AI [7, 8], profound learning, factual demonstrating, and network investigation to coordinate and break down complex natural information.

5. Advancing Biomedical Exploration and Healthcare
The mix of multimodal information in bioinformatics and man-made reasoning holds a guarantee for progressing biomedical examination and further developing medical services results [9]. By offering a thorough perspective on natural frameworks [10], coordinated information can work with drug revelation, customized medication, sickness determination, and therapy improvement [11].

6. Significance and Challenges
The section highlights the meaning of coordinating multimodal information in the fields of bioinformatics and man-made intelligence, underscoring the potential for securing further experiences into mind-boggling natural cycles [12]. Moreover, it digs into the difficulties inherent in multimodal information combination, including issues connected with information heterogeneity, commotion, and adaptability [13].

7. Methodological Approaches
The section looks at the scope of systemic methods for multimodal information combination, including network-based, factual, and AI calculations. With regard to the combination and translation of assorted information sorts, every technique enjoys its own benefits [14].

8. Data Integration Frameworks
Inside the part, precise philosophies and systems for incorporating multimodal information are discussed. These systems might involve combination at either the component level or the choice level, offering organized ways to deal with separate significant experiences from coordinated information [15].

Types of Data Modalities in Bioinformatics

1. Genomics
Genomic data modalities incorporate information related with a creature's DNA grouping, including nucleotide arrangements, hereditary varieties (like single nucleotide polymorphisms or SNPs) [16], and underlying varieties (like additions, cancellations, and changes). Genomic information is key for grasping hereditary inclinations, quality articulation, and transformative connections [2, 17].

2. Transcriptomics

Transcriptomic data modalities include the assessment of a creature's transcriptome— the total arrangement of RNA records delivered by the genome under unambiguous circumstances or in unambiguous cell types [18]. This includes courier RNA (mRNA), non-coding RNA (like microRNA and long non-coding RNA), and other RNA particles. Transcriptomic information gives bits of knowledge into quality articulation designs, elective joining, and administrative organizations [19].

3. Proteomics

Proteomic data modalities centre around the examination of a life form's proteome— the total arrangement of proteins communicated by the genome. Proteomic methods examine protein structure, capability, post-translational alterations, collaborations, and overflows. Proteomic information is critical for grasping protein communications, flagging pathways, and protein elements in organic frameworks [20].

4. Metabolomics

Metabolomic information modalities include the investigation of a creature's metabolome—the total arrangement of little atoms (metabolites) present in cells, tissues, or natural liquids [21]. Metabolomic procedures investigate metabolite personalities, focuses, and metabolic pathways. Metabolomic information provides knowledge of cell digestion, biochemical cycles, and metabolic aggregates related to well-being and illness.

5. Epigenomics

Epigenomic information modalities investigate the epigenetic alterations and chromatin structure that control quality articulation and cell capability. This incorporates DNA methylation, histone changes, chromatin availability, and non-coding RNA-intervened guideline. Epigenomic information gives insight into quality guideline, cell separation, and sickness instruments [22].

6. Imaging Data

Imaging information modalities envelop different imaging methods, for example, microscopy, attractive reverberation imaging (X-ray), computed tomography (CT), positron emission tomography (PET), and single-photon emission computed tomography (SPECT). Imaging information permits representation and examination of cell structures, tissue morphology, physiological cycles, and infection states [23].

7. Clinical Data

Clinical information modalities incorporate patient socioeconomics, clinical chronicles, symptomatic tests, therapy results, and electronic health records (EHRs). Clinical information gives data about illness commonness, patient aggregates, treatment reactions, and medical care results [24], working with translational exploration and customized medication.

8. Phenotypic Data

Phenotypic data modalities capture observable traits or characteristics of organisms, such as morphological features, physiological measurements, behavior, and disease phenotypes. Phenotypic data provides insights into genotype-phenotype associations, gene function, and evolutionary relationships.

9. Environmental Data

Environmental data modalities encompass information about the external factors that influence biological systems, such as temperature, humidity, light exposure, nutrient availability, and pollutant concentrations. Environmental data facilitates studies on ecological interactions, adaptation mechanisms, and environmental impacts on organisms.

10. Spatial Data

Spatial data modalities involve the spatial distribution and organization of biological entities within tissues, organs, or ecosystems. This includes spatial transcriptomics, spatial proteomics, and spatial metabolomics techniques that enable the mapping of gene expression, protein localization, and metabolite concentrations within spatial contexts.

11. Temporal Data

Temporal data modalities capture changes in biological processes over time, such as gene expression dynamics, protein turnover rates, metabolic fluxes, and physiological responses to stimuli. This type of data gives us information in a day-to-day manner for developing as well as delivering the things [25].

12. Multi-omics Data

Multi-omics information modalities coordinate different omics layers, including genomics, transcriptomics, proteomics, and metabolomics, to offer an exhaustive perspective on natural frameworks. Utilizing multi-omics approaches considers the investigation of associations and crosstalk between various sub-atomic layers, in this way working with frameworks level examinations and applications in customized medication.

13. Single-cell Data

Single-cell information modalities include the profiling of individual cells inside heterogeneous populaces, empowering the portrayal of cell variety, genealogy directions, and useful states. Methods, for example, single-cell RNA sequencing (scRNA-seq) and single-cell proteomics give bits of knowledge into cell heterogeneity and elements being developed, illness, and tissue homeostasis [26].

14. Neuroimaging Data

Neuroimaging information modalities focus on the assessment of the cerebrum's construction, capability, and network using imaging methods, for example, functional magnetic resonance imaging (fMRI), diffusion tensor imaging (DTI), and electroencephalography (EEG). Neuroimaging information works with concentrates on mental health, neurological issues, mental capabilities, and mind conduct connections.

15. Phylogenomic Data

Phylogenomic information modalities involve the examination of developmental connections and hereditary variety across species utilizing genomic groupings and phylogenetic strategies. This information gives bits of knowledge into developmental cycles, speciation occasions, and the starting points of organic variety [27].

Challenges and Considerations in Multimodal Data Fusion

A few difficulties and contemplations in multimodal information mix are investigated, featuring the intricacies innate in organizing heterogeneous information sources. These difficulties shape the techniques and approaches utilized in multimodal information combination and impact its applications in bioinformatics and man-made brainpower. A few vital difficulties and contemplations include the following:

1. Information Heterogeneity

Multimodal information coordination frequently includes integrating information from different sources with changing configurations, scales, and levels of clamor. Tending to information heterogeneity requires creating vigorous preprocessing methods and normalization procedures to guarantee similarity and consistency across various modalities.

2. Highlight Choice and Dimensionality Decrease
Coordinating various information modalities can bring about high-layered include spaces, making investigation and translation computationally testing. Highlight choice and dimensionality decrease methods are expected to recognize pertinent elements, lessen excess data, and ease the scourge of dimensionality while saving fundamental data.

3. Information Reconciliation Strategies
Picking fitting information mix techniques is significant for actually joining data from various modalities. Strategies range from basic connection and early combination to additional perplexing methods like late combination, multimodal embeddings, and profound learning structures. Every strategy has its assets and restrictions, and the decision relies upon the attributes of the information and the particular exploration goals.

4. Semantic Arrangement and Interpretability
Incorporating information from various modalities requires adjusting their semantics to guarantee significant reconciliation and translation. This includes planning ideas, factors, and elements across modalities and explaining connections between them. Guaranteeing interpretability and straightforwardness in multimodal information joining results is fundamental for acquiring trust and understanding among analysts and partners.

5. Versatility and Computational Proficiency
As the size and intricacy of multimodal datasets keep on developing, adaptability and computational productivity become basic contemplations. Creating versatile calculations and equal registering procedures is important to deal with huge scope information joining undertakings effectively and empower constant or close ongoing examinations in bioinformatics and computerized reasoning applications.

6. Approval and Benchmarking
Assessing the presentation of multimodal information reconciliation strategies requires thorough approval and benchmarking against ground truth or highest quality level datasets. This includes surveying the precision, power, and generalizability of reconciliation models utilizing suitable measurements and approval conventions. Benchmarking systems and normalized assessment strategies assist with contrasting different reconciliation procedures and guide vital progressions.

7. Moral and Protection Concerns

Incorporating multimodal information raises moral and protection concerns connected with information sharing, informed assent, and information anonymization. Guaranteeing consistency with administrative structures and protecting sensitive data and people's security freedoms are central in directing mindful and moral examination in bioinformatics and man-made reasoning.

8. Space Explicit Difficulties

Different application spaces inside bioinformatics and man-made consciousness present novel difficulties and contemplations in multimodal information joining. For instance, clinical applications might require resolving issues, for example, patient heterogeneity, information predispositions, and puzzling variables, while ecological examinations might confront difficulties connected with natural fluctuation, inspecting inclinations, and information sparsity.

9. Data Quality and Reliability

The quality and dependability of information across various modalities can change fundamentally, prompting difficulties in information joining. Wellsprings of information changeability, like exploratory clamor, estimation blunders, and cluster impacts, should be addressed to guarantee the precision and consistency of coordinated information.

10. Temporal Misalignment

In longitudinal examinations or time-series information investigation, worldly misalignment between various modalities can happen because of contrasts in testing frequencies, time deferrals, or synchronization issues. Adjusting worldly profiles and tending to transient errors are fundamental for catching unique connections and fleeting conditions in multimodal information combination.

11. Biological Setting and Earlier Knowledge

Integrating organic setting and earlier information into multimodal information combination models upgrades interpretability and natural importance. Utilizing area explicit information, pathway data, and ontologies can direct element determination, model preparation, and speculation age, working on the organic interpretability of combination results.

12. Data Combination Predisposition and Overfitting
Information combination strategies might present inclinations or overfitting issues while perhaps not painstakingly executed. Predispositions might emerge from inconsistent commitments of various modalities or inborn predispositions in information assortment and pre-processing. Overfitting happens when models catch commotion or false relationships rather than genuine basic examples. Regularization procedures and cross-approval systems assist with alleviating these issues and work on the generalizability of combination models.

13. Dynamic Information Fusion
Numerous natural cycles show dynamic and setting subordinate way of behaving, requiring dynamic information combination moves toward that can adjust to changing circumstances and incorporate transient or spatial elements. Dynamic combination models, like recurrent neural networks (RNNs) or secret Markov models (Well), catch fleeting conditions and empower ongoing examination of dynamic natural frameworks.

14. Interdisciplinary Coordinated Effort and Information Sharing
Multimodal information combination frequently requires interdisciplinary cooperation between researcher, bioinformaticians, analysts, PC researchers, and area specialists. Viable correspondence, cooperation, and information-sharing practices are fundamental for coordinating aptitude from assorted teaches and utilizing reciprocal abilities and assets to address complex examination questions.

15. Robustness to Missing Information and Uncertainty
Multimodal datasets may contain missing qualities or vulnerability, which can influence the dependability and vigour of combination models. Dealing with missing information through ascription strategies or probabilistic displaying approaches mitigates predispositions and work on the culmination of coordinated datasets. Vulnerability evaluation techniques empower the appraisal of model vulnerability and give bits of knowledge into the dependability of combination forecasts.

By tending to these difficulties and contemplations, scientists can propel the field of multimodal information combination in bioinformatics and man-made intelligence, opening new insight into complex organic frameworks and driving advancements in biomedical examination, customized medication, and more. Cooperative endeavours, systemic progressions, and interdisciplinary methodologies assume key parts in defeating these difficulties and outfitting the maximum capacity of coordinated information for logical disclosure and information interpretation [28–30].

Foundational Principles of Data Fusion

A few fundamental standards of information combination are clarified, giving the premise to understanding the reconciliation of heterogeneous information sources in bioinformatics and computer-based intelligence. These fundamental standards envelop key ideas and systems that support multimodal information combination and guide its application in different areas. Some primary standards of information combination include the following:

1. Integration of Correlative Information
Information combination plans to join data from numerous sources or modalities to acquire a more exhaustive comprehension of perplexing peculiarities. By coordinating corresponding information modalities, like genomics, transcriptomics, proteomics, and metabolomics, specialists can uncover synergistic connections, recognize stowed away examples, and concentrate further experiences into organic frameworks [31].

2. Synergy and Redundancy
Multimodal information combination takes advantage of the collaboration between various information modalities while limiting overt repetitiveness. Cooperative energy alludes to the consolidated impact of coordinating assorted wellsprings of data, prompting upgraded prescient power and information disclosure.

3. Modelling Heterogeneity and Uncertainty
Information combination models ought to represent heterogeneity and vulnerability by integrating probabilistic structures, powerful measurable strategies, and vulnerability evaluation procedures. Demonstrating heterogeneity empowers the coordination of assorted information types, while taking care of vulnerability upgrades the dependability and heartiness of combination results [32].

4. Flexibility and Adaptability
Information combination strategies ought to be adaptable and versatile to oblige various information modalities, trial plans, and exploration targets. Adaptable combination designs, for example, measured structures or cross breed draws near, empower a consistent mix of assorted information sources and work with customization for explicit applications.

5. Interpretability and Transparency

Multimodal information combination ought to focus on interpretability and straightforwardness to work with understanding and trust among partners. Straightforward combination models give clear clarifications of how various information sources are coordinated, empowering analysts to decipher combination results and approve theories. Interpretable component portrayals and perception procedures assist with explaining basic examples and natural experiences got from incorporated information.

6. Scalability and Efficiency

Adaptability and proficiency are basic contemplations in multimodal information combination, especially with huge scope datasets or constant applications. Adaptable combination calculations influence equal figuring, appropriated handling, or enhancement procedures to deal with huge information challenges and empower effective combination of high-layered datasets. Proficiency advancements limit computational above and asset necessities, making combination techniques material to different examination settings and computational conditions.

7. Validation and Benchmarking

Thorough approval and benchmarking are fundamental for assessing the presentation and generalizability of multimodal information combination techniques. Approval conventions ought to incorporate cross-approval, holdout approval, or outside approval on autonomous datasets to survey combination model execution and power. Benchmarking against pattern techniques or highest quality level datasets helps analyze combination calculations and distinguish best practices for explicit applications [33].

8. Contextual Mindfulness and Semantics

Viable multimodal information combination requires context-oriented mindfulness and thought of the semantics innate in various information modalities. Figuring out the natural setting, exploratory circumstances, and connections between information sources is fundamental for significant joining and translation of combination results. Semantic arrangement procedures, ontologies, and semantic joining structures work with the planning of ideas and substances across modalities, upgrading the lucidness and organic importance of coordinated information.

9. Dynamic Transformation to Developing Information Dynamics

Multimodal information combination models ought to be able to progressively adjust to changing information elements, like changes in natural states, trial conditions, or mechanical headways. Versatile combination calculations, support learning procedures, and web-based gaining approaches empower combination models to gain from new information, update model boundaries, and advance combination methodologies progressively or close continuous settings. Dynamic variation guarantees that combination models stay receptive to arising designs, novel experiences, and developing examination needs in bioinformatics and simulated intelligence.

10. Interpretation and Explanation
Information combination models ought to focus on interpretability and clarification to work with understanding and trust among clients, partners, and chiefs. Giving interpretable combination yields, logical representations, and model-based clarifications explains the hidden systems, causal connections, and organic meaning of combination results. Straightforward combination models engage clients to approve theories, assess model choices, and pursue informed choices in light of combination experiences.

11. Robustness to Space Shift and Generalization
Multimodal information combination models ought to show heartiness to area shift and sum up well across various trial conditions, populaces, or natural settings. Strong combination procedures, move learning techniques, and area variation systems empower combination models to sum up information gained from one space to new, concealed areas while keeping up with execution and dependability. Power to space shift upgrades the pertinence and adaptability of combination models across different examination settings and true applications [34].

12. Feedback Circles and Iterative Improvement
Multimodal information combination includes iterative patterns of model refinement, approval, and input reconciliation to iteratively further develop combination execution and utility. Laying out input circles between information examination, model turn of events, and exploratory plan empowers analysts to iteratively refine combination models, approve speculations, and create new experiences. Iterative improvement encourages nonstop refinement of combination strategies, driving headways in bioinformatics, simulated intelligence, and translational exploration.

13. Collaborative Information Sharing and Open Science Practices
Advancing cooperative information sharing and open science rehearses works with information dispersal, reproducibility, and advancement in multimodal information combination research. Sharing information

assets, code storehouses, and benchmarking datasets cultivates straightforwardness, reproducibility, and coordinated effort across research networks. Open science drives, information vaults, and local area driven stages give foundation and motivations to sharing multimodal information, advancing interdisciplinary cooperation, and speeding up logical disclosure.

14. Ethical and Social Implications

Multimodal information combination exploration ought to think about the moral, social, and cultural ramifications of information coordination, examination, and translation. Tending to moral worries, protection dangers, and potential predispositions intrinsic in combination philosophies is fundamental for guaranteeing dependable information use and shielding people's privileges and interests [35]. Connecting with partners, policymakers, and the general population in conversations about the moral and social ramifications of information combination cultivates mindfulness, straightforwardness, and responsibility in bioinformatics, artificial intelligence, and medical services research.

Machine Learning and Deep Learning Techniques for Multimodal Data Fusion

The strategies influence progressed computational techniques to incorporate data from assorted information modalities and concentrate significant experiences from coordinated information. Some key AI and profound learning strategies for multimodal information combination include the following:

1. Early Fusion

Early combination procedures include linking highlights from various modalities into a solitary information portrayal prior to taking care of them into an AI model. Early combination improves on the combination cycle by consolidating all modalities forthright, taking into consideration joint learning of multimodal connections. Models incorporate linking quality articulation profiles with clinical highlights for illness characterization or coordinating imaging information with hereditary markers for aggregate expectation.

2. Late Fusion

Late combination methods join forecasts or portrayals from individual methodology explicit models at a later stage to pursue last choices or expectations. Late combination takes into account methodology explicit handling and component extraction prior to consolidating modalities, possibly catching correlative data from every methodology. Models incorporate joining expectations from individual classifiers prepared on various information modalities utilizing procedures, for example, choice combination, troupe learning, or stacking.

3. Multimodal Embeddings

Multimodal implanting methods gain joint portrayals of information from various modalities in a common inserting space [36]. These embeddings catch semantic connections and likenesses between modalities, empowering compelling reconciliation and examination of heterogeneous information. Models incorporate multimodal autoencoders, Siamese organizations, and cross-modular likeness learning approaches that learn embeddings for information modalities while saving their cross-modular connections.

4. Deep Canonical Correlation Analysis (CCA)

Deep Canonical Correlation Analysis (CCA) is a deep learning procedure that learns nonlinear changes of information modalities to boost their standard connections in a common idle space. Deep CCA empowers joint portrayal learning of multimodal information while catching complex connections and conditions between modalities. By amplifying connections in the idle space, Deep CCA works with viable coordination and combination of heterogeneous information.

5. Graph Neural Networks (GNNs)

Graph neural networks are deep learning models intended to work on chart organized information, making them appropriate for multimodal information combination undertakings where information connections are addressed as diagrams. GNNs can coordinate data from various modalities addressed as hubs or edges in a diagram, considering adaptable combination of heterogeneous information sources. Models incorporate utilizing GNNs to meld quality articulation networks with protein cooperation networks for drug target ID or infection quality prioritization.

6. Recurrent Neural Networks (RNNs)

Recurrent neural networks are deep learning structures intended to display successive or worldly information, making them appropriate for multimodal information combination undertakings including time-series or consecutive information modalities. RNNs can catch worldly conditions and elements in multimodal successions, working with mix and combination of heterogeneous transient information. Models incorporate utilizing RNNs to intertwine quality articulation time-series information with clinical time-series information for illness anticipation or treatment reaction expectation.

7. Attention Mechanisms

Consideration systems are parts generally utilized in deep learning models to zero in on significant pieces of information specifically. Consideration components can be applied to multimodal information combination errands to powerfully weight or join data from various modalities in light of their significance or significance. Models incorporate utilizing consideration systems to take care of striking highlights in multimodal pictures or to specifically meld enlightening locales in multimodal arrangements.

8. Generative Adversarial Networks (GANs)

Generative adversarial networks are profound learning designs made out of two brain organizations, a generator and a discriminator, prepared adversarially to produce sensible information tests. GANs can be utilized for multimodal information combination by learning joint circulations of information modalities and creating manufactured examples that catch the conveyance of coordinated information working closely together. Models incorporate utilizing GANs to produce engineered pictures from multimodal quality articulation and clinical information for information expansion or downstream examination undertakings.

9. Feature-level Fusion

Element-level combination includes joining highlights separated from various modalities into a solitary component portrayal prior to taking care of them into an AI or deep learning model. Methods like connection, expansion, or duplication of elements from various modalities empower the formation of a bound together component space that catches data from numerous sources all the while. Highlight-level combination saves the first modalities' attributes while working with joint learning and coordination inside the model [37].

10. Decision-level Fusion

Choice-level combination incorporates expectations or choices made by individual models prepared on various modalities to create a last melded yield. Outfit learning techniques, for example, larger part casting a ballot, averaging, or stacking, join expectations from numerous models to work on generally speaking execution and strength. Choice level combination use the integral qualities of individual models while alleviating their shortcomings, prompting more exact and dependable combination results.

11. Multimodal Embeddings

Multimodal embeddings address information from various modalities in a common idle space, where similitudes and connections between modalities are caught really. Procedures like joint embeddings, cross-modular hashing, or multimodal autoencoders learn shared portrayals that encode semantic connections and relationships across modalities. Multimodal embeddings work with data coordination, comparability estimation, and cross-modular recovery errands, empowering consistent combination of heterogeneous information sources in bioinformatics and man-made intelligence.

12. Graph-based Fusion

Chart-based combination models address connections and collaborations between various information modalities as a diagram structure, where hubs address elements or highlights, and edges address associations or connections. Graph neural networks (GNNs) and graph convolutional networks (GCNs) influence diagram portrayals to perform combination undertakings, like hub grouping, connect forecast, or diagram level expectation. Chart-based combination catches complex conditions and communications between modalities, empowering compelling coordination of organized and social information in bioinformatics and computer-based intelligence [38].

13. Attention Mechanisms

Consideration instruments center around significant data inside every methodology or across modalities, permitting combination models to specifically take care of instructive elements while smothering commotion or unimportant data. Consideration instruments, like self-consideration, cross-modular consideration, or multi-head consideration, empower combination models to adaptively weight inputs and progressively dispense consideration across modalities in light of their pertinence to the main job. Consideration-based combination upgrades model interpretability, strength, and execution, especially in situations with high-layered or boisterous information.

14. Adversarial Learning

Adversarial learning strategies, for example, generative adversarial networks (GANs) or adversarial preparation, figure out how to create engineered information portrayals that are vague from genuine information while saving their hidden construction and dissemination. Adversarial learning cultivates space transformation, information increase, and information amalgamation across modalities, empowering combination models to gain from restricted or imbalanced information sources successfully. Adversarial combination procedures improve model speculation, adaptability, and flexibility to space shifts, working with hearty multimodal information combination in bioinformatics and computer-based intelligence.

15. End-to-End Learning

End-to-end learning structures train combination models to straightforwardly upgrade task-explicit targets or execution measurements utilizing crude or transitional information portrayals from numerous modalities. End-to-end learning designs, for example, profound brain organizations or brain engineering search, mutually learn highlight extraction, combination, and expectation stages in a coordinated way, without express element designing or preprocessing steps. End-to-end learning smoothes out model turn of events, diminishes manual mediation, and empowers programmed disclosure of perplexing examples and portrayals across modalities.

16. Explainable Combination Models

Logical combination models give interpretable clarifications of combination choices, empowering clients to grasp the hidden elements, highlights, or collaborations driving model forecasts. Procedures, for example, consideration perception, include significance positioning, or saliency planning feature the commitments of individual modalities or highlights to the combined result, working with model translation and approval. Logical combination models upgrade straightforwardness, trust, and responsibility in multimodal information combination applications, especially in areas with rigid interpretability prerequisites or administrative imperatives [39].

Feature Representation and Fusion

1. Feature Representation

- Highlight portrayal includes changing crude information from various modalities into a typical element space reasonable for coordination.
- In bioinformatics, highlight portrayal procedures might incorporate removing quality articulation levels, protein

overflows, metabolite fixations, or imaging highlights from crude information.

- Include portrayal strategies frequently include dimensionality decrease methods like principal component analysis (PCA), singular value decompostion (SVD), or autoencoders to catch fundamental data while diminishing clamor and overt repetitiveness.
- Space explicit information and earlier data about organic cycles might direct the determination and extraction of important elements for mix.

2. Feature Fusion

- Highlight combination consolidates highlights extricated from various modalities into a solitary portrayal that catches corresponding data from numerous sources.
- Combination techniques might work at various levels, including early combination (joining highlights prior to demonstrating), late combination (consolidating forecasts from isolated models), or middle of the road combination (joining highlights at a moderate stage).
- Normal combination procedures incorporate link, summation, weighted averaging, or more complex techniques like canonical correlation analysis (CCA), multimodal autoencoders, or multimodal profound learning structures.
- Combination models ought to represent the heterogeneity and size of highlights from various modalities, as well as any semantic connections or conditions between them.

3. Semantic Integration

- Semantic reconciliation guarantees that highlights from various modalities are adjusted in view of their semantic importance or natural setting.
- Ontologies, information diagrams, or area explicit data sets might give semantic comments or mappings to work with the combination of heterogeneous highlights.
- Semantic mix empowers specialists to decipher combination brings about a naturally significant way, connecting subatomic elements, pathways, or organic capabilities across modalities.

4. Interpretability and Explainability

- Highlight portrayal and combination ought to focus on interpretability and reasonableness to work with understanding and confidence in combination models.
- Straightforward combination procedures give experiences into how highlights are joined and deciphered by the model, empowering specialists to approve speculations and get significant bits of knowledge from combination results.
- Perception procedures, including significance scores, or model clarifications assist with explaining the commitment of various modalities to combination results and feature pertinent natural examples or connections.

5. Scalability and Efficiency

- Adaptable component portrayal and combination techniques are fundamental for dealing with huge scope multimodal datasets productively.
- Procedures like equal handling, appropriated figuring, or equipment speed increase might be utilized to work on the adaptability and computational effectiveness of combination calculations.
- Effective combination models empower continuous or close ongoing examination of multimodal information, working with fast direction and disclosure in bioinformatics and artificial intelligence applications [40].

6. Dynamic Component Fusion

- Dynamic element combination strategies adaptively change the combination cycle in view of the qualities of the information or the main job.
- Dynamic combination methods might consolidate criticism components, consideration systems, or versatile weighting plans to powerfully balance the commitment of various modalities in view of their significance or significance in the ongoing setting.
- By progressively changing component combination methodologies, models can adjust to changing information

elements, handle information float, and streamline combination execution in true situations.

7. Hierarchical Combination Hierarchies

- Various leveled combination orders coordinate highlights from various modalities into progressive designs, catching multiscale portrayals of the information.
- Progressive combination empowers the combination of elements at various degrees of reflection, from low-level tactile information to significant level semantic portrayals.
- Progressive combination models might use profound brain organizations, convolutional structures, or recursive calculations to incorporate elements and catch complex connections across modalities progressively.

8. Cross-Modular Learning

- Cross-modular learning strategies expect to learn shared portrayals across various modalities, working with information move and cross-modular speculation.
- Cross-modular learning might include preparing joint inserting spaces, shared highlight encoders, or cross-modular comparability measurements that adjust portrayals from various modalities.
- By learning shared portrayals, cross-modular models empower successful combination of data across modalities, in any event, while preparing information is restricted or imbalanced across modalities.

9. Attention Mechanisms

- Consideration components specifically center around useful elements or modalities while stifling unessential or uproarious contributions during the combination cycle.
- Consideration systems might allocate consideration loads to elements or modalities in view of their significance or importance to the undertaking, empowering the model to take care of striking data progressively.
- Consideration-based combination improves the interpretability, power, and proficiency of combination models by

specifically incorporating applicable highlights and relieving the impact of boisterous or immaterial data sources.

10. Adversarial Learning

- Adversarial learning methods address area movements and dispersion criss-crosses between various modalities by learning space invariant portrayals or adjusting highlight appropriations.
- Adversarial learning structures, for example, generative adversarial networks (GANs) or space adversarial preparing, plan to limit the inconsistency between highlight disseminations across modalities while safeguarding discriminative data.
- Adversarial combination models upgrade the adaptability and generalizability of combination portrayals, empowering strong combination execution across different datasets or trial conditions [41].

Applications in Bioinformatics AI

1. Disease Analysis and Classification

- Multimodal information combination empowers the reconciliation of assorted patient information, including genomics, imaging, clinical records, and biomarker estimations, for more precise sickness finding and arrangement.
- Combination models join integral data from various modalities to work on symptomatic exactness, recognize infection subtypes, and define patient populaces in light of their atomic profiles and clinical attributes.

2. Drug Disclosure and Development

- Multimodal information combination works with the reconciliation of omics information, substance structures, drug-target connections, and clinical results to speed up drug revelation and advancement processes.
- Combination models anticipate drug viability, poisonousness, and pharmacokinetic properties by incorporating

atomic elements, cell reactions, and patient information, directing the determination and advancement of medication contender for clinical preliminaries.

3. Personalized Medication and Accuracy Healthcare

- Multimodal information combination empowers the reconciliation of patient-explicit information, including genomic profiles, biomarker estimations, imaging filters, and electronic health records, to tailor treatment procedures and enhance patient consideration.
- Combination models foresee individual treatment reactions, sickness movement directions, and problematic medication responses, empowering customized therapy suggestions and accuracy medical services intercessions.

4. Biological Pathway Investigation and Frameworks Biology

- Multimodal information combination coordinates omics information, pathway explanations, protein connections, and utilitarian comments to clarify natural pathways, subatomic instruments, and sickness etiologist.
- Combination models distinguish key administrative organizations, pathway crosstalk, and biomolecular communications fundamental complex natural cycles, giving experiences into sickness pathogenesis and possible helpful targets.

5. Biomedical Imaging Analysis

- Multimodal information combination joins imaging information from different modalities, like X-ray, CT, PET, and histopathology, to upgrade illness determination, treatment arranging, and checking.
- Combination models coordinate imaging highlights with genomic, clinical, and histopathological information to work on the exactness of illness portrayal, growth division, and treatment reaction evaluation in oncology and radiology.

6. Environmental and Microbiome Analysis

- Multimodal information combination incorporates natural information, microbiome profiles, have hereditary qualities, and well-being results to concentrate on the effect of ecological openings on human well-being and illness.
- Combination models reveal relationship between ecological variables, microbiome piece, and illness risk, giving experiences into the job of the microbiome-climate have cooperations in well-being and sickness.

7. Biomedical Text Mining and Information Discovery

- Multimodal information combination incorporates text information from logical writing, biomedical data sets, and electronic health records to remove information, find novel affiliations, and recognize arising research patterns.
- Combination models join text mining strategies with omics information investigation, network science, and AI ways to deal with focus on competitor qualities, foresee quality illness affiliations, and explain natural capabilities.

8. Clinical Choice Help Systems

- Multimodal information combination upgrades clinical choice emotionally supportive networks by coordinating patient information from different sources, including clinical imaging, electronic health records, research facility tests, and wearable gadgets.
- Combination models help clinicians in illness finding, treatment arranging, risk definition, and patient observing by giving thorough patient profiles and customized proposals in view of coordinated information examination.

9. Biomarker Revelation and Validation

- Multimodal information combination works with biomarker disclosure and approval by coordinating omics information, clinical information, and imaging information to distinguish atomic marks related with sickness determination, anticipation, and therapy reaction.

- Combination models consolidate sub-atomic elements, clinical aggregates, and imaging biomarkers to focus on up-and-comer biomarkers, approve their prescient utility, and make an interpretation of biomarker revelations into clinical applications.

10. Drug Reusing and Polypharmacology

- Multimodal information combination speeds up drug reusing endeavors by incorporating drug-related information, including compound designs, target profiles, quality articulation profiles, and clinical results, to recognize new remedial signs for existing medications.
- Combination models anticipate drug-illness relationship, off-target impacts, and medication blends by coordinating heterogeneous information sources and uncovering stowed away connections between medications, targets, and sicknesses.

11. Functional Genomics and Administrative Organization Inference

- Multimodal information combination empowers the joining of genomics information, epigenomics information, and transcriptomics information to induce quality administrative organizations, transcriptional administrative systems, and practical connections among qualities and non-coding components.
- Combination models incorporate multi-omics information with protein collaborations, record factor restricting themes, and pathway explanations to clarify the administrative scene of the genome and unwind the atomic premise of perplexing illnesses [42].

12. Predictive Demonstrating and Hazard Assessment

- Multimodal information combination upholds prescient displaying and risk appraisal by coordinating assorted information modalities, including segment information, clinical factors, ecological openings, and hereditary inclinations, to gauge sickness risk, therapy results, and populace well-being patterns.

- Combination models consolidate prescient elements from various sources to construct vigorous risk forecast models, delineate people in view of their vulnerability to illnesses, and illuminate preventive mediations and general well-being strategies.

13. Neuroinformatic and Cerebrum Availability Analysis

- Multimodal information combination coordinates neuroimaging information, hereditary information, and clinical information to concentrate on cerebrum availability, useful organizations, and neurological issues.
- Combination models consolidate primary and practical mind imaging information with hereditary markers, mental appraisals, and clinical aggregates to research the etiology of neurological illnesses, like Alzheimer's disease, Parkinson's disease, and schizophrenia.

14. Environmental Well-being and Openness Assessment

- Multimodal information combination upholds natural well-being research by incorporating ecological openness information, biomarker estimations, and well-being results to survey the effect of natural elements on human well-being.
- Combination models break down the relationship between ecological openings, organic reactions, and well-being results, empowering risk appraisal, natural checking, and strategy intercessions to relieve well-being risks related with natural poisons.

Evaluation Metrics and Validation Strategies

The assessment measurements and approval systems assume an essential part in evaluating the exhibition and power of multimodal information combination models in bioinformatics and simulated intelligence applications. Assessment measurements give quantitative measures to assess the precision, unwavering quality, and generalizability of combination models, while approval procedures guarantee the legitimacy and reproducibility of combination results. Normal assessment measurements for multimodal information combination incorporate measurements, for example, exactness, accuracy, review, F1-score, area under the receiver operating characteristic curve (AUC-ROC), and area under the precision recall curve (PR-AUC). These measurements evaluate the exhibition of combination models in different undertakings, including illness determination, drug reaction forecast, and biomarker disclosure. In addition, approval strategies like cross-approval, holdout approval, and outer approval are utilized to survey the heartiness and generalizability of joining models across different datasets, exploratory circumstances, and populaces. Thorough approval conventions assist with approving mix theories, distinguish model shortcomings, and guide upgrades in joining procedures. By using fitting assessment measurements and approval strategies, analysts can guarantee the unwavering quality and reproducibility of multimodal information reconciliation results, encouraging confidence in the utility and reasonableness of coordination models in bioinformatics, man-made brainpower, and biomedical examination [43].

Evaluation Metrics

Particularity and Responsiveness

Particularity checks the extent of genuine negatives precisely distinguished by the combination model, while awareness estimates the extent of genuine up-sides accurately recognized. These measurements are especially relevant in paired grouping errands, like sickness discovery or medication reaction forecast.

Mean Squared Error (MSE)

MSE measures the typical squared distinction among anticipated and noticed values in relapse assignments. It is important for surveying the precision of consistent result expectations, for example, quality articulation levels or clinical biomarker focuses.

Concordance Record (C-list)

The C-list assesses the unfair force of combination models in endurance examination or time-to-occasion expectation errands. It estimates the probability that the model accurately positions the endurance seasons of sets of people, with higher qualities demonstrating better prescient execution.

Data Gain and Entropy Decrease

Data gain measures the decrease in vulnerability accomplished by the combination model while foreseeing results. It estimates the improvement in prescient execution contrasted with a pattern model and offers experiences into the education of combination highlights.

Root Mean Squared Error (RMSE)

RMSE, likened to MSE, processes the square base of the typical squared contrasts among anticipated and noticed values. RMSE gives a more interpretable proportion of forecast precision, as it is communicated in similar units as the result variable.

Approval Techniques

Cross-Approval

Cross-approval parcels the dataset into different subsets (folds), iteratively preparing the combination model on a subset of the information and assessing its presentation on the leftover information. This approach offers an unprejudiced gauge of model execution and helps in evaluating its generalizability to concealed information.

Holdout Approval

Holdout approval haphazardly isolates the dataset into preparing and testing sets, using the preparation set for model preparation and the testing set for execution assessment. This technique is clear to execute and useful for surveying model execution on free information.

Outside Approval

Outside approval surveys the combination model's exhibition on a free dataset gathered from an alternate populace or exploratory condition. It guarantees the generalizability and vigor of combination models across different settings and upgrades trust in their utility and dependability.

Bootstrap Resampling

Bootstrap resampling produces different resamples of the dataset by arbitrarily testing with substitution, working with the assessment of certainty spans for assessment measurements. This procedure gives experiences into the changeability of model execution and helps in surveying its security and vigor.

Cross-Area Approval

Cross-space approval assesses combination models' exhibition across various areas or modalities, like approving a model prepared on quality articulation information against proteomics or imaging information. It empowers scientists to survey the adaptability and area versatility of combination models.

Ethical and Legal Considerations

Moral and legal considerations encompassing multimodal information combination in bioinformatics and computer-based intelligence are of most extreme significance. With the rising amount of information in biomedical exploration and medical care, it is critical to address the moral ramifications of consolidating assorted information modalities, including genomics, clinical records, imaging information, and patient socioeconomics.

Moral contemplations incorporate guaranteeing information security, privacy, and informed assent all through the information combination process, subsequently safeguarding people's privileges and independence. Specialists should likewise attempt to relieve the risk of information predispositions, separation, and abuse that might emerge from the combination and examination of heterogeneous information sources.

Legitimate contemplations include consistence with information security guidelines, like the General Data Protection Regulation (GDPR) in Europe or the Health Insurance Portability and Accountability Act (HIPAA) in the US, which administer the assortment, stockpiling, and sharing of sensitive health data. Scientists should comply with moral rules, institutional review board (IRB) conventions, and information access approaches to defend patient protection, keep up with information trustworthiness, and maintain moral principles in multimodal information combination research.

Besides, straightforwardness and responsibility in information taking care of, model turn of events, and result understanding are crucial for encouraging trust among partners, advance mindful information use, and alleviate moral and lawful dangers related to multimodal information combination. By tending to moral and legitimate contemplations proactively, analysts can guarantee the moral lead of multimodal information combination research, maintain information protection and privacy, and advance the mindful and impartial utilization of incorporated information for logical headway and cultural advantage [44].

Future Directions and Challenges

Future headings and tending to arising difficulties in multimodal information combination present energizing open doors for progressing bioinformatics and artificial intelligence. One critical future heading is the advancement of more complex combination procedures equipped for taking care of high-layered, heterogeneous information with expanded proficiency and versatility. Profound learning designs, like diagram brain organizations, consideration instruments, and generative models, hold guarantee for catching complex connections and inactive designs across numerous modalities, in this manner working with more complete and interpretable combination results.

Moreover, coordinating multimodal information with context-oriented data, like spatial and worldly elements, ecological variables, and patient aggregates, empowers analysts to reveal novel bits of knowledge into organic cycles, sickness components, and therapy reactions. Besides, addressing difficulties connected with information interoperability, normalization, and incorporation stays significant for empowering consistent information trade and coordinated effort across research spaces and establishments.

Moral and legitimate contemplations encompassing information security, assent, and reasonableness additionally present continuous difficulties that require cautious thought and administrative oversight. Also, encouraging interdisciplinary coordinated effort, local area commitment, and open science rehearses is fundamental for driving advancement, advancing straightforwardness, and boosting the cultural effect of multimodal information combination research.

By tending to these future headings and difficulties, specialists can open the maximum capacity of multimodal information combination in bioinformatics and artificial intelligence, preparing the way for extraordinary progress in customized medication, accuracy medical services, and biomedical exploration.

Conclusion

All in all, this chapter highlights the key standards, strategies, and applications that underlie the combination of heterogeneous information sources in bioinformatics and computer-based intelligence. By clarifying key ideas like component portrayal, combination methods, assessment measurements, and approval methodologies, this chapter gives a thorough system to understanding and carrying out multimodal information combination draws near.

The chapter features the flexibility and utility of multimodal information combination in tending to complex difficulties in biomedical exploration, medical care conveyance, and life sciences. Besides, it underscores the significance of moral and lawful contemplations in information combination research, supporting for capable information use, security assurance, and straightforwardness.

Looking forward, the chapter recognizes future bearings and arising difficulties in multimodal information combination, including the improvement of further developed combination strategies, tending to information interoperability issues, and exploring moral and administrative intricacies. By embracing interdisciplinary cooperation, development, and moral stewardship, analysts can outfit the force of multimodal information combination to drive extraordinary progress in grasping organic frameworks, diagnosing sicknesses, creating therapeutics, and working on persistent consideration.

Finally, the chapter highlights the vital job of multimodal information combination in moulding the future of bioinformatics, computer-based intelligence, and biomedical exploration, while upholding moral, straightforward, and dependable practices in information-driven science.

References

1. Belkin, M. and Niyogi, P., Laplacian eigenmaps for dimensionality reduction and data representation. *Neural Comput.*, 15, 6, 1373–1396, 2003.
2. Han, J., How can data mining help bio-data analysis?, in: *Proceedings of the 2nd International Conference on Data Mining in Bioinformatics*, Springer Verlag, pp. 1–2, 2002.
3. Burugadda, V.R., Pawar, P.S., Kumar, A., Bhati, N., Predicting Hospital Readmission Risk for Heart Failure Patients Using Machine Learning Techniques: A Comparative Study of Classification Algorithms, in: *2023 Second International Conference on Trends in Electrical, Electronics, and Computer Engineering (TEECCON)*, Bangalore, India, pp. 223–228, 2023, doi: 10.1109/TEECCON59234.2023.10335817.
4. Punugoti, R., Duggar, R., Dhargalkar, R.R., Bhati, N., Intelligent Healthcare: Using NLP and ML to Power Chatbots for Improved Assistance, in: *2023 International Conference on IoT, Communication and Automation Technology (ICICAT)*, IEEE, Jun. 23, 2023, doi: 10.1109/icicat57735.2023.10263708.
5. Ditzler, G., Polikar, R., Rosen, G., Multi-layer and recursive neural networks for metagenomic classification. *IEEE Trans. Nanobiosci.*, 14, 6, 608–616, 2015.
6. Burri, S.R., Agarwal, D.K., Vyas, N., Duggar, R., A Machine Learning Framework for Accurate Prediction of Parkinson's Disease from Speech Data, in: *2023 3rd International Conference on Innovative Sustainable Computational Technologies (CISCT)*, Dehradun, India, pp. 1–6, 2023, doi: 10.1109/CISCT57197.2023.10351422.

7. LeCun, Y., Bengio, Y., Hinton, G., Deep learning. *Nature*, 521, 7553, 436–444, 2015.
8. Holzinger, A., Dehmer, M., Jurisica, I., Knowledge discovery and interactive data mining in bioinformatics-state-of-the-art, future challenges and research directions. *BMC Bioinf.*, 15, 6, I1, 2014.
9. Burugadda, V.R., Jadhav, N., Vyas, N., Duggar, R., Exploring the Potential of Deep Reinforcement Learning for Autonomous Navigation in Complex Environments, in: *2023 7th International Conference on Computing, Communication, Control and Automation (ICCUBEA)*, Pune, India, pp. 1–6, 2023, doi: 10.1109/ICCUBEA58933.2023.10392109.
10. Peng, J., Xiang, S., Wang, Z., A review of multimodal data fusion for image-guided radiotherapy. *Engineering*, 4, 6, 841–848, 2018.
11. Burugadda, V.R., Dutt, V., Vyas, N., Personalized Cardiovascular Disease Risk Prediction Using Random Forest: An Optimized Approach, in: *2023 IEEE World Conference on Applied Intelligence and Computing (AIC)*, Sonbhadra, India, pp. 226–232, 2023, doi: 10.1109/AIC57670.2023.10263915.
12. Kumar, A., Kumar, S.A., Dutt, V., Dubey, A.K., Narang, S., A Hybrid Secure Cloud Platform Maintenance Based on Improved Attribute-Based Encryption Strategies. *Int. J. Interact. Multimed. Artif. Intell.*, 8, 2, 150, 2023. Universidad Internacional de La Rioja, doi: 10.9781/ijimai.2021.11.004.
13. Schölkopf, B. and Smola, A.J., *Learning with kernels: support vector machines, regularization, optimization, and beyond*, MIT press, 2002.
14. Swarna, S.R., Boyapati, S., Dutt, V., Bajaj, K., Deep Learning in Dynamic Modeling of Medical Imaging: A Review Study, in: *2020 3rd International Conference on Intelligent Sustainable Systems (ICISS)*, Thoothukudi, India, pp. 745–749, 2020, doi: 10.1109/ICISS49785.2020.9315990.
15. Cigdem, O., Demirel, H., Unay, D., The Performance of Local-Learning Based Clustering Feature Selection Method on the Diagnosis of Parkinson's Disease Using Structural MRI, in: *2019 IEEE International Conference on Systems, Man and Cybernetics (SMC)*, pp. 1286–1291, Oct. 2019, doi: 10.1109/SMC.2019.8914611.
16. Punugoti, R., Dutt, V., Anand, A., Bhati, N., Exploring the Impact of Edge Intelligence and IoT on Healthcare: A Comprehensive Survey, in: *2023 International Conference on Sustainable Computing and Smart Systems (ICSCSS)*, Coimbatore, India, pp. 1108–1114, 2023, doi: 10.1109/ICSCSS57650.2023.10169733.
17. Lan, K., Fong, S., Song, W., Vasilakos, A.V., Millham, R.C., Self-Adaptive Pre-Processing Methodology for Big Data Stream Mining in Internet of Things Environmental Sensor Monitoring. *Symmetry*, 9, 10, 244, 2017.
18. Punugoti, R., Dutt, V., Kumar, A., Bhati, N., Boosting the Accuracy of Cardiovascular Disease Prediction Through SMOTE, in: *2023 International Conference on IoT, Communication and Automation Technology (ICICAT)*, Gorakhpur, India, pp. 1–6, 2023, doi: 10.1109/ICICAT57735.2023.10263703.

19. Sutskever, I., Vinyals, O., Le, Q.V., Sequence to sequence learning with neural networks, in: *Advances in neural information processing systems*, pp. 3104–3112, 2014.
20. Vyas, N., P., P.A., Das, P., Mahajan, Y., The Impact of Air Pollution on Respiratory Health Results: An Analysis of Asthma and COPD in a Population Study, in: *2023 International Conference on Computing, Communication, and Intelligent Systems (ICCCIS)*, Greater Noida, India, pp. 141–146, 2023, doi: 10.1109/ICCCIS60361.2023.10425187.
21. Zhou, Z.H., A brief introduction to weakly supervised learning. *Natl. Sci. Rev.*, 5, 1, 44–53, 2017.
22. Mylavarapu, R.T., Pokhriyal, A., Dhargalkar, R.R., Bhati, N., Empowering Healthcare with AI: Addressing Challenges and Envisioning the Future, in: *2023 4th International Conference on Electronics and Sustainable Communication Systems (ICESC)*, Coimbatore, India, pp. 1393–1398, 2023, doi: 10.1109/ICESC57686.2023.10193228.
23. Dutt, V., Sasubilli, S.M., Yerrapati, A.E., Dynamic Information Retrieval With Chatbots: A Review of Artificial Intelligence Methodology, in: *2020 4th International Conference on Electronics, Communication and Aerospace Technology (ICECA)*, Coimbatore, India, pp. 1299–1303, 2020, doi: 10.1109/ICECA49313.2020.9297533.
24. Das, S., *et al.*, Multimodal Data Fusion: A Review of State-of-the-Art Methods. *Inf. Fusion*, 52, 44–60, 2019.
25. Wang, W., Lee, J., Harrou, F., Sun, Y., Early Detection of Parkinson's Disease Using Deep Learning and Machine Learning. *IEEE Access*, 8, 147635–147646, 2020. doi: 10.1109/ACCESS.2020.3016062.
26. Karapinar Senturk, Z., Early diagnosis of Parkinson's disease using machine learning algorithms. *Med. Hypotheses*, 138, 109603, 2020. doi: 10.1016/j.mehy.2020.109603.
27. Kumar, S.A., Kumar, H., Dutt, V., Soni, H., Self-Health Analysis with Two Step Histogram based Procedure using Machine Learning, in: *2021 Third International Conference on Intelligent Communication Technologies and Virtual Mobile Networks (ICICV)*, Tirunelveli, India, pp. 794–799, 2021, doi: 10.1109/ICICV50876.2021.9388427.
28. Liu, H., *et al.*, Deep Learning for Multi-Modal Medical Image Analysis. *Healthcare Inf. Res.*, 26, 3, 187–202, 2020.
29. Bhati, N., Duggar, R., Alzahrani, A., Exploring few-shot learning approaches for bioinformatics advancements, in: *Applying Machine Learning Techniques to Bioinformatics*, pp. 303–316, IGI Global, 2024.
30. Templeton, J.M., Poellabauer, C., Schneider, S., Classification of Parkinson's disease and its stages using machine learning. *Sci. Rep.*, 12, 1, 14036, Aug. 2022. doi: 10.1038/s41598-022-18015-z.
31. Zhang, J., *et al.*, Multi-Modal Data Fusion: A Comprehensive Review. *IEEE Trans. Knowl. Data Eng.*, 33, 6, 2345–2363, 2021.

32. Bhati, N., Duggar, R., Saber, A., Empowering Safety by Embracing IoT for Leak Detection Excellence, in: *Innovations in Machine Learning and IoT for Water Management*, pp. 231–251, IGI Global, Nov. 27, 2023, doi: 10.4018/979-8-3693-1194-3.ch012.
33. Burugadda, V.R., Mane, P.M., Kumar, A., Bhati, N., A Machine Learning-Based Algorithm for Early Detection of Sepsis in Hospitalized Patients: Development and Evaluation, in: *2023 1st International Conference on Circuits, Power and Intelligent Systems (CCPIS)*, Bhubaneswar, India, pp. 1–6, 2023, doi: 10.1109/CCPIS59145.2023.10291447.
34. Chandrasekaran, S., Dutt, V., Vyas, N., Kumar, R., Student Sentiment Analysis Using Various Machine Learning Techniques, in: *2023 International Conference on Artificial Intelligence and Smart Communication (AISC)*, Greater Noida, India, pp. 104–107, 2023, doi: 10.1109/AISC56616.2023.10085018.
35. Sasubilli, S.M., Kumar, A., Dutt, V., Improving Health Care by Help of Internet of Things and Bigdata Analytics and Cloud Computing, in: *2020 International Conference on Advances in Computing and Communication Engineering (ICACCE)*, Las Vegas, NV, USA, pp. 1–4, 2020, doi: 10.1109/ICACCE49060.2020.9155042.
36. Rahmani, A., *et al.*, A Review of Multi-Modal Data Fusion Methods in Remote Sensing: State-of-the-Art and Future Perspectives. *ISPRS J. Photogramm. Remote Sens.*, 153, 166–177, 2019.
37. Boyapati, S., Swarna, S.R., Dutt, V., Vyas, N., Big Data Approach for Medical Data Classification: A Review Study, in: *2020 3rd International Conference on Intelligent Sustainable Systems (ICISS)*, Thoothukudi, India, pp. 762–766, 2020, doi: 10.1109/ICISS49785.2020.9315870.
38. Yu, L., *et al.*, Multi-Modal Data Fusion for Improved Patient Diagnosis and Treatment: A Review. *J. Med. Syst.*, 43, 9, 1–14, 2019.
39. Liao, S., Gao, Y., Oto, A., Shen, D., Representation learning: a unified deep learning framework for automatic prostate MR segmentation, in: *International Conference on Medical Image Computing and Computer-Assisted Intervention*, pp. 254–261, 2013.
40. Swarna, S.R., Kumar, A., Dixit, P., Sairam, T.V.M., Parkinson's Disease Prediction using Adaptive Quantum Computing, in: *2021 Third International Conference on Intelligent Communication Technologies and Virtual Mobile Networks (ICICV)*, Tirunelveli, India, pp. 1396–1401, 2021, doi: 10.1109/ICICV50876.2021.9388628.
41. Ogul, B.B. and Ozdemir, S., A Pairwise Deep Ranking Model for Relative Assessment of Parkinson's Disease Patients From Gait Signals. *IEEE Access*, 10, 6676–6683, 2022. doi: 10.1109/ACCESS.2021.3136724.
42. Wang, R., *et al.*, Recent Advances in Multi-Modal Data Fusion for Remote Sensing Applications: A Review. *Remote Sens.*, 12, 20, 1–27, 2020.
43. Cernak, M., Orozco-Arroyave, J.R., Rudzicz, F., Christensen, H., Vásquez-Correa, J.C., Nöth, E., Characterisation of voice quality of Parkinson's disease

using differential phonological posterior features. *Comput. Speech Lang.*, 46, 196–208, Nov. 2017. doi: 10.1016/j.csl.2017.06.004.

44. Sekhar, U.S., Vyas, N., Dutt, V., Kumar, A., Multimodal Neuroimaging Data in Early Detection of Alzheimer's Disease: Exploring the Role of Ensemble Models and GAN Algorithm, in: *2023 International Conference on Circuit Power and Computing Technologies (ICCPCT)*, Kollam, India, pp. 1664–1669, 2023, doi: 10.1109/ICCPCT58313.2023.10245177.

6

Integrating IoT, Blockchain, and Quantum Machine Learning: Advancing Multimodal Data Fusion in Healthcare AI

Dankan Gowda V.[1]*, J. Rajalakshmi[2], Guruprakash B.[3], Venkatesan Hariram[4] and K. D. V. Prasad[5]

[1]*Department of Electronics and Communication Engineering, BMS Institute of Technology and Management, Bangalore, Karnataka, India*
[2]*Department of Electronics and Communication Engineering, Sethu Institute of Technology, Karriapatti, Virudhunagar, Tamil Nadu, India*
[3]*Department of CSE (AI&Ml), Sethu Institute of Technology, Kariapatti, India*
[4]*Department of Practice of Medicine, Vinayaka Mission's Homoeopathic Medical College and Hospital, A Constituent College of Vinayaka Mission's Research Foundation Deemed to be University, Salem, Tamil Nadu, India*
[5]*Symbiosis Institute of Business Management, Hyderabad and Symbiosis International (Deemed University), Pune, India*

Abstract
This chapter discusses the transformative nature by which IoT, blockchain and QML converge to address healthcare. With technological advancements being critical factors in defining a future medical practice, these three technologies make statements as pacesetters for better patient care record keeping and treatment procedures. The chapter starts with a discussion on singularities provided by IoT, blockchain and QML in the healthcare industry to increase patients' engagements in the safety of their medical information records as well optimize data-driven decision-making processes. It then analyzes the synergistic capability of these technologies when merged and proposes a new approach in health care which gives improved efficiency and unmatched security with personalized medicine breakthroughs. The discussion is also about practical cases as well as hypothetical situations, revealing the possibilities achieved with usage of IoT or

**Corresponding author*: dankan.v@bmsit.in

Umesh Kumar Lilhore, Abhishek Kumar, Narayan Vyas, Sarita Simaiya and Vishal Dutt (eds.) Multimodal Data Fusion for Bioinformatics Artificial Intelligence, (103–126) © 2025 Scrivener Publishing LLC

QML blockchain for treating chronic problems in healthcare including drug monitoring, remote consumer satisfaction and predictive analytics to disease management. The chapter also considers the ethical, regulatory and technical challenges that have been reported as a result of implementing these technologies to generate a more objective look at their feasibility in operation.

Keywords: Internet of things (IoT), blockchain, quantum machine learning (QML), medical data, healthcare innovation, predictive analytics, drug discovery

6.1 Introduction

In the field of healthcare, the use of the Internet of Things (IoT), blockchain and QML entails the change from a treatment-oriented to a health management paradigm. Separately as individual technologies, there is the potential to revolutionize how healthcare procedures are carried out. The Internet of Things, with its set up networked devices, brings new unprecedented levels of patient monitoring and personal data gathering [1, 2]. Blockchain technology provides a safe solution for the handling of sensitive health information with built-in trust, integrity, availability and confidentiality. One of the most promising fields for medical data processing today is quantum machine learning, which even at its earliest stages can already boast handling amounts bigger than any current standard could offer and therefore has every chance to transform such spheres as drug development or genetic research [3, 4]. It is a productive combination of these technologies that would offer us the synergistic framework through which some pressing healthcare issues, including data security, patient engagement and personalized medicine, could be tackled [5]. The main objective of this chapter is to investigate the movement towards amalgamating IoT, blockchain and QML that can potentially translate into a revolutionised vision for healthcare delivery with increased efficiency, security and patient orientation.

The introduction of the blockchain technology has revolutionized the way that data modeling and governance are understood in healthcare. This metamorphosis is largely attributed to its unprecedented morphological characteristics and ability to divide and protect, as well as provide the means by which healthcare prescription and services are shared in ways that have never been witnessed before [6, 7]. It has now become the pivotal reference point for several modern developments in healthcare. The emerging healthcare technologies based on blockchain can be conceptually

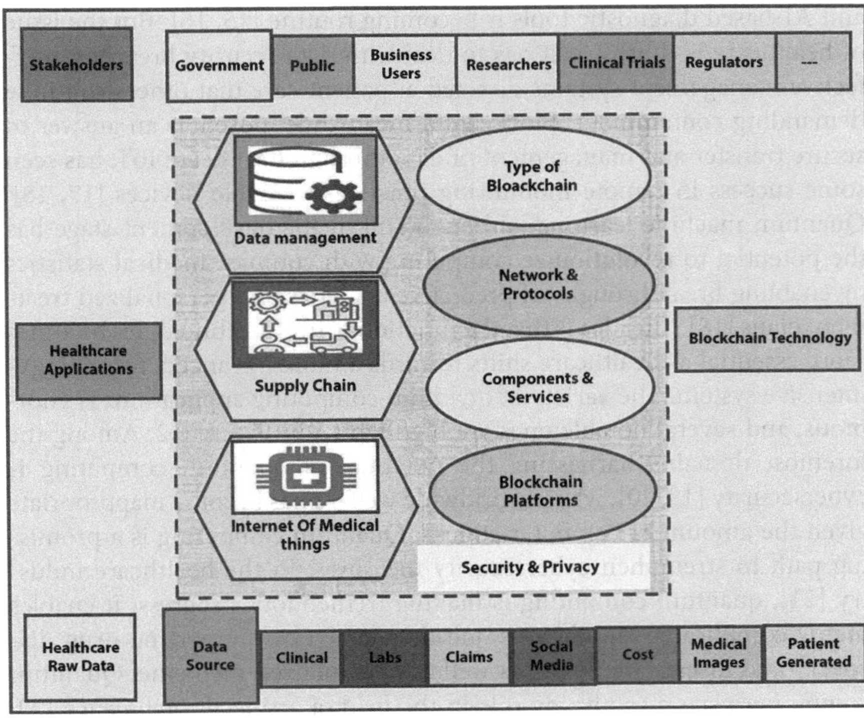

Figure 6.1 Sequence of operations in healthcare applications enhanced by blockchain.

categorized into four layers [8]: Data sets, blockchain technology applications for health care and the various stakeholders. Figure 6.1 shows blockchain-based healthcare application workflow [9, 10]. At the outset, all information obtained from various sources such as medical devices labs social media and others are incorporated to create raw data that further expands into a massive reservoir of big data [11, 12]. This information represents the basic underlying component that by all accounts helps to develop an entire blockchain-based healthcare ecosystem, which constitutes the first layer's foundation within a structure. On top of this rugged data bed lies blockchain technology, which serves as a core scaffolding designed to help build an impenetrable healthcare infrastructure with four unique parts [13, 14]. It is important to note, however, that various blockchain platforms have their own distinctive characteristics such as consensus algorithms and protocols which contribute in designing the overall architecture.

The fast-evolving environment in the world of healthcare technology proves this. The use of telemedicine, electronic health records (EHRs) and AI-based diagnostic tools is becoming routine [15, 16]. But the issue of healthcare is thorny as it has to deal with data security breaches, ineffective management systems directed at patient care that others continue demanding containment. Blockchain, meanwhile, posed as an answer to secure transfer and management of data through healthcare IoT, has seen some success in remote monitoring practices wearable devices [17, 18]. Quantum machine learning, although still in the development stage has the potential to revolutionize computing with complex medical statistics by enabling breakthroughs of predictive analytics and personalized treatment plans [18]. The idea is that the function of these technologies becomes more essential as healthcare shifts towards a more advanced, technology-intensive system. The variety of quantum computing applications is enormous, and several notable ones are highlighted in Figure 6.2. Among the foremost domains harnessing the potential of quantum computing is cybersecurity [19, 20], where worldwide welfare has become inappropriate given the amount of computer attacks. Quantum computing is a promising path to strengthen cybersecurity measures. In the healthcare industry [21], quantum computing is making tremendous progress. It enables highly complicated simulations and data analytics, supporting drug discovery and disease modeling as well as personalized medicine. Quantum computing plays a catalyzing role in the field of artificial intelligence [22, 23] by increasing speed and sophistication algorithms; thus, allowing for faster machine learning processes as well as real-time data analysis that can have revolutionary impacts on multiple industries. In financial modeling, quantum computing enables advanced and risk assessment to help change investment strategies as well as restructuring the response of risks. Quantum computing provides the high-performance capability required for logistics optimization through solving complex problems that can improve supply chain management and operations of logistics. In the field of weather forecasting, quantum computing provides considerable upgrades through fast simulations that lead to better and more timely predictions. With the rapidly increasing frequency of cyberattacks [24, 25] safety in internet environments has become more and more vulnerable. Although the security frameworks are vigorously implemented, traditional digital computers have set limits on making this process harder and less efficient. So quantum computing appears to be an important step in the fight against these challenges and strengthening cybersecurity for a modern world with constantly evolving threats [26].

This chapter is structured in a way that shows how IoT, blockchain and quantum machine learning revolutionize healthcare delivery [27, 28]. It begins with a detailed exploration of each technology: There will be a

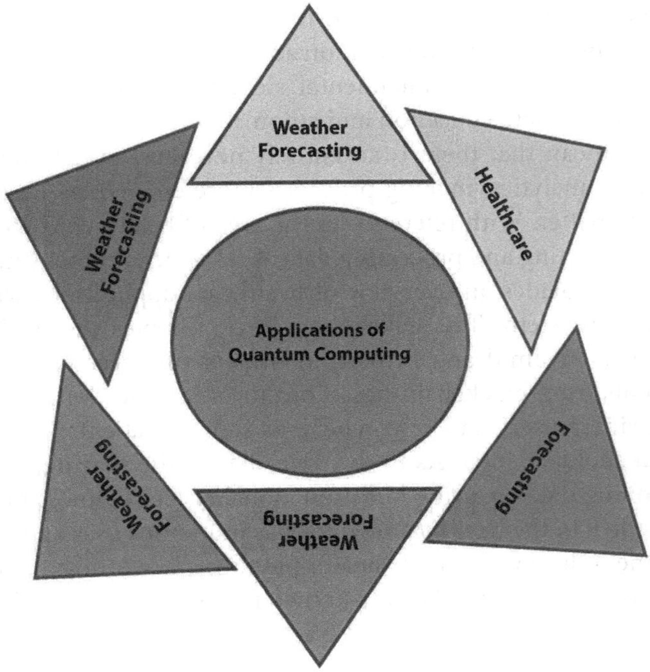

Figure 6.2 Real-world applications of quantum computing.

focus on IoT in healthcare and its implications for patient monitoring and data generation; the use of blockchain technology to secure medical information as well as simplifying clinical operations, with quantum machine learning leveraged against high level complicated health parameters. These sections discuss the integration of such technologies, focusing on how their joint use can provide novel approaches to healthcare services [29, 30]. These challenges include economic and ethical worries as well as regulatory and technical implications. The chapter concludes with a look ahead at the future implications of this integration and its prospective presence in the healthcare sector as another form showing that IoT, blockchains, QML is based on a new era in medical technology.

6.2 Internet of Things (IoT) in Healthcare

The Internet of Things (IoT) originally meant a web network formed by objects with embedded systems – sensing and algorithms, for interconnectivity between devices or exchanging data remotely over the internet.

Fundamentally, IoT is based on transforming objects into being "smart" through the ability to send information and use automation features without human support. The fundamental elements of IOT include device interconnectivity, data collection and automated functionality [31]. These connections mean that there is an entirely new level of data integration and real-time analytics, making processes more efficient as well as decision-making better. With reference to the area of health care, IoT's effectiveness in collecting and processing data as it happens comes into play.

Figure 6.3 provides an overview of healthcare applications within the blockchain ecosystem. The stakeholder level occupies the peak of this organizational pyramid and involves members who receive financial or other benefits from blockchain-based healthcare applications, which may include business users and researchers, as well as patients [32, 33]. The core of stakeholders' interests in this layer lies in the sharing, processing and controlling data ensuring both functionality (see below) and privacy safeguards. IoT in the health care sector has numerous uses and is revolutionizing the industry. Wearable health monitors, like fitness trackers and smartwatches, are possibly the best-known IoT technologies in this industry [34]. These devices measure and track a number of health biomarkers

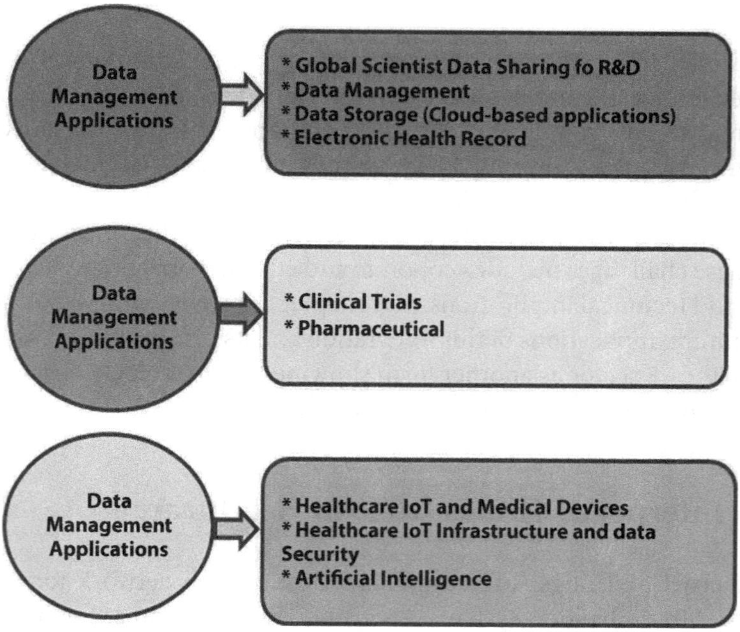

Figure 6.3 Integrating blockchain into healthcare.

continuously including heart rate and sleep patterns, as well as physical activity for personal use and sharing with medical practitioners in their quest for better customized care [35]. Wearables are only a subset of medical IoT solutions which include glucose monitors, blood pressure cuffs and even smart inhalers. Other areas of adoption include the utilization of IoT technologies for asset tracking, and temperature management in storage zones where drugs or blood are stored as well as to optimize a patient flow. This data also reflects this transition toward a more proactive, preventative health care industry that is very much dependent on continuous and accurate collection of information. With the constant development of electronic health-related data and prevalence besides cloud healthcare data storage products, patient information as well privacy regulations would have a huge breakthrough opportunity in their direction to tackle. These innovations not only improve data handling operations but patients' ability to access and share their health information [36]. Securing data, handling storage solutions, supporting secure payments and simplifying integration are the critical consumer demands in "data business," especially for healthcare. The blockchain technology can solve these important problems considerably. Figure 6.4 shows the seven-step workflow of healthcare data management within blockchain without mentioning more details about each step. This category of blockchain-based application includes data sharing, management, storage (both cloud and noncloud), and electronic health records. All such applications are overwhelmingly investigated to depict the essence and value they have in today's healthcare context. Integration of IoT in healthcare carries a number advantages. It improves the quality of care by providing continuous monitoring, which is particularly important for chronic conditions that necessitate constant surveillance. This constant data flow facilitates early detection of potential problems related to health, which enables timely interventions. IoT also has an important role to play when it comes to monitoring remotely based patients, thereby making healthcare more easily accessible even for those in remote places or who have mobility problems. Looking at the matter of data collection, IoT provides a clearer and more detailed picture about patient health over time that is necessary for making better decisions and in tune with specific treatment approaches.

But these developments are far from being perfected. The main security and privacy issues that arise in health data transmission and storage include breaches, unauthorized access, etc. Given that patient information is confidential, it is important to ensure integrity and preservation of data. Also, there is the problem of connecting IoT data with existing healthcare systems by maintaining compatibility between different devices and

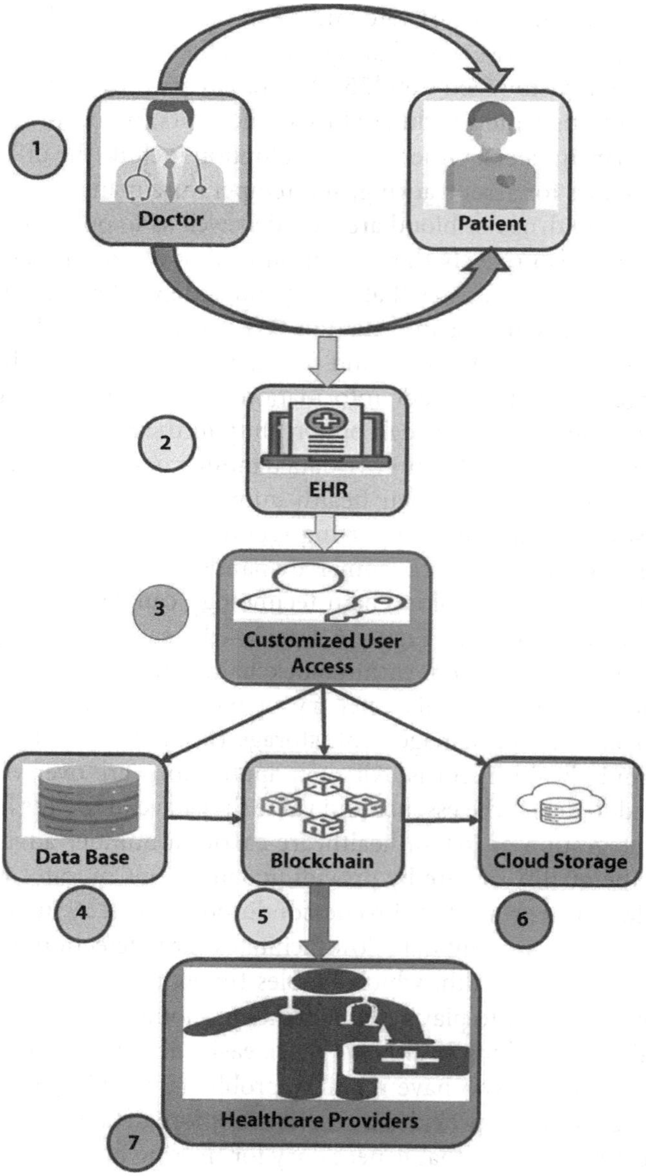

Figure 6.4 Blockchain-based healthcare data management.

platforms. Reliability and accuracy of IoT devices are also verified since fault or inaccuracy will lead to erroneous diagnosis, misdiagnosis, and mistake dosing, among other such errors. Solving them is also very important to achieving appropriate IoT implementation integration into the healthcare sphere and realizing all possible benefits in improved patient care and health outcomes.

6.3 Blockchain Technology in Healthcare

In essence, blockchain technology is a distributed digital database that stores transactions on numerous computers in such a way that previous recorded data cannot be altered retroactively. This technology lies at the fundamentals of cryptocurrencies, such as Bitcoin; however, it has much broader potential. A blockchain creates blocks of data that are chained together. Within each block, there is a cryptographic hash of the previous; this gives completeness and promotes immutability to the whole concept. It is also important in healthcare, where data integrity and security are of utmost significance. Ease of blockchain technology is decentralized; assuming that there can never be someone who will fail because failures cannot occur in distributed systems. Every transaction has the verification property as all parties are involved, ensuring transparency; alongside this they can ensure that their sensitive information remains private by anonymous. Blockchain is referenced to many different fields of applications and shows great potential in some healthcare industries. A major one is the development of secure and distributed patient records. In this system, medical records are weathered in a blockchain, thereby providing patients with their data access control. This not only increases privacy but also keeps data from being altered as well. Another example is drug supply chain management. With blockchain, pharmaceutical products are being tracked from production up to delivery, making counterfeit medication impossible and verifying the integrity of its original components. Secondly, blockchain can help simplify the insurance claims process by preventing fraud and maintaining transparency during transactions between patients, providers and insurers. This may result in improved claim processing, fewer mistakes, and increased trust from everyone.

The role of the Internet of Medical Things (IoMT) systems is crucial in developing health and medical information systems. IoMT allows healthcare equipment, such as heart monitors and body scanners that wearable

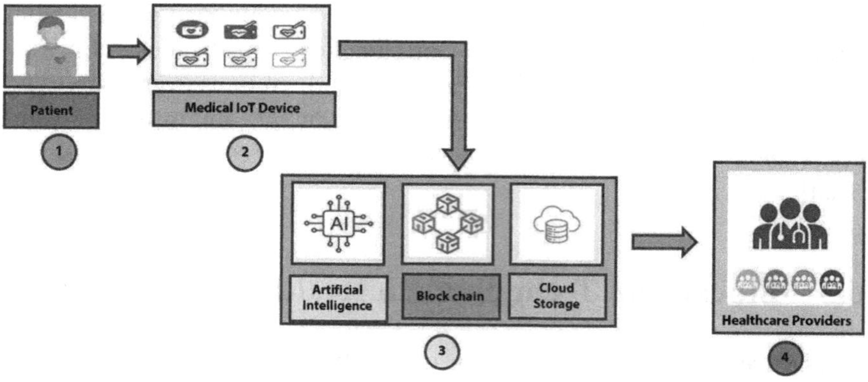

Figure 6.5 Blockchain's role in IoMT.

devices equip patients with, to collect, process and transmit data through the Internet in real time. A case in point, achieving integration of AI into health care using IoMT paradigm allows medical providers to record images that identify cancer or suspicious cells and quickly share this important information with authorized people. The rest of the sections dig deeper into spectacular improvement recorded in health IoT (Internet of Things) and smart medical devices under artificial intelligence. Figure 6.5 shows the form of IoMT in blockchain ecosystem showing how these revolutionary technologies meet and work together towards revolutionizing healthcare. Primarily the benefits of blockchain in healthcare are its attributes of transparency, security and immutability. Blockchain's transparency ensures that authorized users can access all the transactions for building trust and accountability. The security of blockchain results from the fact that it is decentralized and operates on cryptographic algorithms, which also makes its architecture almost impossible to hack or falsify information. In addition, immutable records imply that when a record is made true to form it cannot be changed, which stands very important for the credibility of medical documents. However, blockchain also faces limitations. One of the main challenges even now is scalability because as blockchain becomes big, it naturally results in longer transaction times and higher operational costs. Secondly, the criticality of carbon footprints relating to running a blockchain (especially for that using these PoW mechanisms) raises concerns and questions about environmental and sustainability issues. These limitations show that blockchain technology in health care needs constant innovation and optimization.

6.4 Quantum Machine Learning in Healthcare

Quantum computing refers to a paradigm shift from conventional computers that exploit the laws of quantum mechanics to achieve computation. But classic computing utilizes the number of bits as an essential unit of information, having either a 0 or 1 value while quantum systems use quantum bits that are referred to as qubits. Qubits are capable of having more than one state at the same time (superposition), so quantum computers can process many possible outcomes simultaneously. Entanglement is another inclusion which allows qubits that are entangled to be correlated with each other regardless of their separation. QML capitalizes on these functionalities, where quantum algorithms are used to enhance and speed-up machine learning jobs. In QML quantum computers perform calculations related to data processing, pattern recognition and optimization problems much faster than conventional computers. Determining the "excitement" level of a cluster state involves a two-step process: state preparation and quantum classifier training. Such complex cluster states can be used to interact with the traditional methods, which remain usable. These approaches modify the architectures of classical CNNs to work within quantum computational environments. In other words, when a quantum physics problem is converted to mainframe computer platforms from its position within a many-body Hilbert space, the level of data increases based on how much direct measurement one performs.

This may make traditional approaches inadequate to deliver satisfactory results. On the flip side, using qubits as data representations in a quantum domain provides an answer to this issue. With CCN structure implementation on a quantum computer, it is possible to solve and address such problems. To provide more details, the Q-deep CNN model involves a single quantum filter mixture model. After one layer of quantum convolution and all the bit-reading, a many feature neural network is used as Figure 6.6 shows. This holistic approach makes it possible for the issue at hand to be addressed in an appropriate manner. Quantum computing in healthcare holds vast potential and particularly revolutionary powers for drug discovery, genomics studies, and sophisticated data processing. Furthermore, the use of quantum computers facilitates significant speed-up in molecular simulations and drug candidate identification, a process that otherwise may include extensive time and high cost.

This may result in more effective responses to diseases and rapid development of new medications. In genomics, quantum computing enables

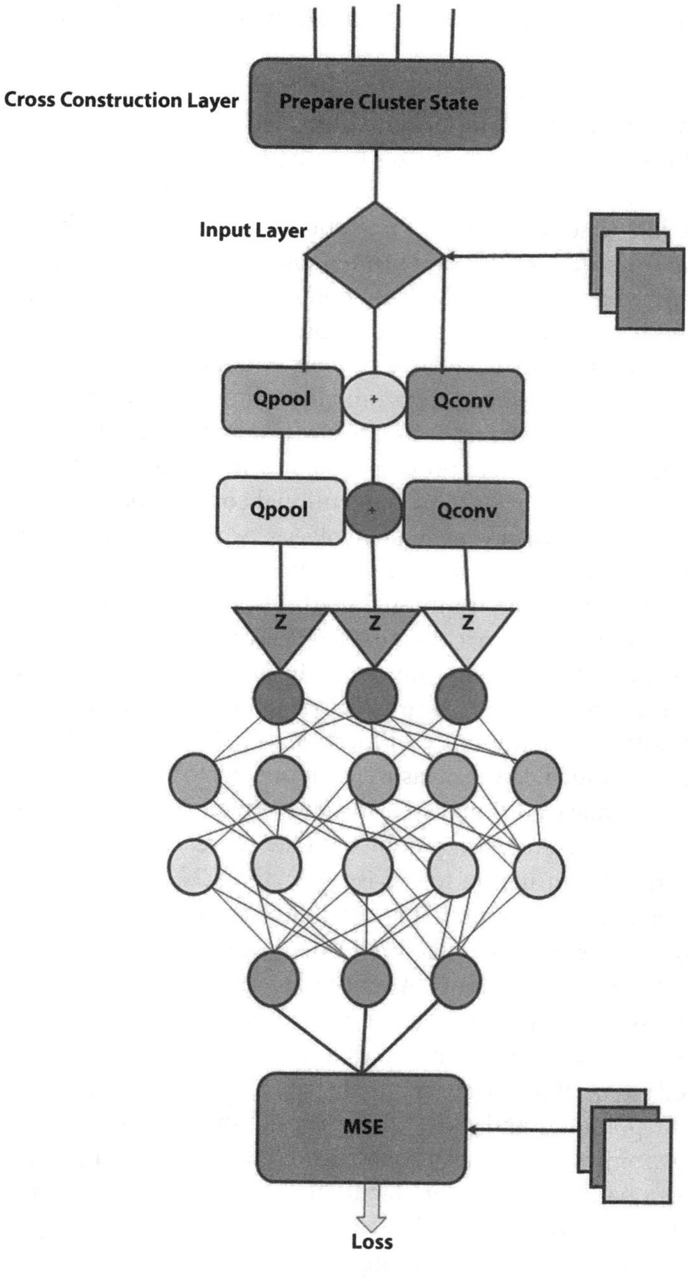

Figure 6.6 Use of multiple quantum filters in convolutional hybridization.

speedy analysis of genomic datasets which is unprecedented and results in discoveries of new genetic diseases, as well as personalized medicine. Quantum algorithms have the ability to process and analyze complicated biological information that is currently out of reach with classical computation, and as a result, breakthroughs in complex disease understanding using individualized patient treatment strategies may become possible. Precision medicine tends to distinguish and better understand the intricate networks of causality and treatments while predicting what will be the best course of action at an individual level. Traditional diagnosis, based on subjective reports of patients' symptoms, often leads to "umbrella" diagnoses that sometimes result in failed treatments. The implementation of quantum computing represents viable ways to exploit non-terminating data flows allowing personalized prediction of diseases and delivery the appropriate treatment if needed. Quantum enhanced predictive medicine emphasizes continuity care and seeks to favorably alter healthcare services for optimally structured personalization. On the individual patient level, quantum-enhanced modeling can be used to reinforce their adherence and engagement. A meaningful application of quantum-computing-driven precision medicine is presented in Figure 6.7, revealing the disruptive prospect that quantum technology brings to health with respect to the future intentions of personalized healthcare. It is still an infant stage in the phase of quantum machine learning, with most applications being research theory or early development. But fast changes in quantum computing technology predict a bright future. As quantum computers become more capable and available, their use for healthcare may change the way medical data is processed and how health resolutions are made. With regard to future findings, the development of personalized medicine will be attributed to further developments in quantum computing technology that will enhance treatments based on individual genetic profiles. In addition, quantum machine learning might have been a major actor in predictive health analytics which would help people to prevent or manage their disease better. Quantum machine learning in healthcare is set to bring groundbreaking changes by helping medical professionals comprehend, diagnose and treat illnesses like never before, positioning us firmly on the path towards a better future of quality health care provision.

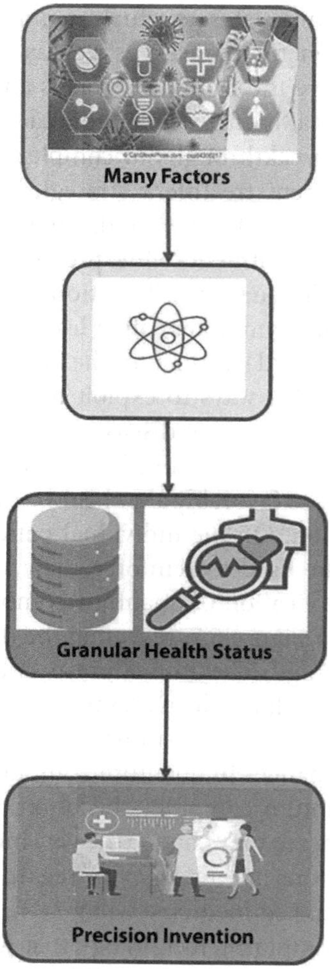

Figure 6.7 Quantum computing's role in advancing precision medicine with multimodal data.

6.5 Integration of IoT, Blockchain, and Quantum Machine Learning in Healthcare

The coexistence of IoT, blockchain, and QML pools together three complementary technologies nurturing invention with the possibility to create state-of-the art medical care and patient management. IoT may become an entirely new data collection and monitoring device, and considerably extend its capabilities evolving as a blockchain-based solution. This combination ensures not only the proper gathering of health information but also its safe, transparent and irreversible storage. Quantum machine learning can bring this symbiotic relationship one more notch higher by offering a wide range of powerful tools that facilitate analysis of massive data generated by IoT devices. Though IoT provides real-time data, the security of such data is ensured by blockchain while QML processes this data at unparalleled speed, facilitating more accurate, fast and personalized solutions in healthcare. Healthcare applications, which are of critical value for people's lives, need to be properly protected. But healthcare scientists are challenged by an important phenomenon, which is at the heart of the siloed nature of healthcare systems that stymies innovation and sharing as well as making systematic progress difficult. To advance appropriate actions to solve these challenges, Chuck Brooks, a leading cybersecurity professor and the chair of the Quantum Security Alliance stresses that partnership between academia, industry, researchers and government is necessary for provision of strong security. In the area of quantum-computing systems, security is also an important issue due to their ability to produce astronomical increases in computing capacity. This development creates a threat to the existing cryptographic-based techniques.

Although cryptography acts as the theoretical basis of security for healthcare information, the use of quantum computing in encryptology incorporates classical cryptography with quantum mechanics to offer unconditional security to both parties that are involved in the communication between a provider and an ultimate health service consumer. Significantly, quantum cryptography has been an emerging popular application of quantum computing with a commercial understanding that relies not on assumptions about the mathematics but on established facts about mechanics. Figure 6.8 proposes a taxonomy of vital security technologies that can greatly improve the information security aspect in healthcare, highlighting these essential measures for such an area as the system of healthcare. As an example of this integration, consider a patient with a long-term illness (for instance, diabetes). The human body is constantly tracked by the wearable IoT devices regarding blood sugar levels, physical activity and dietary intake pattern. This data can be transmitted and stored securely using the blockchain, guaranteeing data accuracy and medical patient confidentiality. Access to this blockchain publicly is only for healthcare providers with the patient's consent. Quantum machine learning algorithms are used to analyze these data, too; they analyzed other volumes of patients' data in order to find patterns and identify dangerous tendencies.

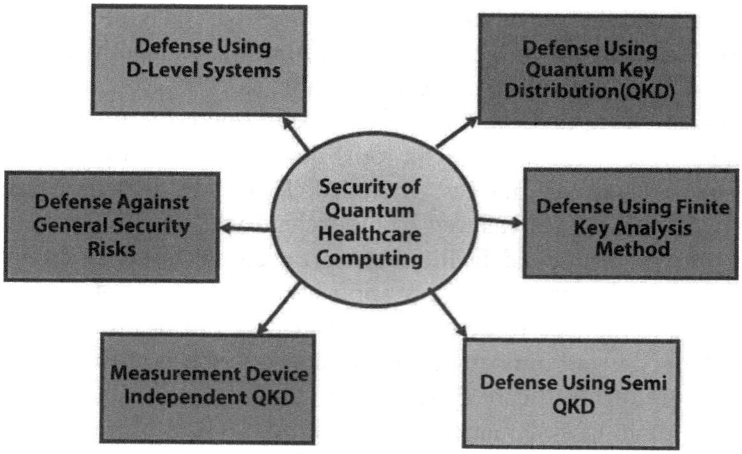

Figure 6.8 Categorization of essential eechnologies for securing healthcare information processing.

Such an analysis can, in turn, lead to specific treatment plans for the individual and proactive intervention strategies tailored to the patient's unique health profile. Alternatively the situation might be connected with the pharmaceutical supply chain management. Drug production, distribution and the conditions under which they are stored are all monitored in real time by IoT devices. All this data is written into a blockchain, providing an immutable open ledger tracking the drug from manufacturer to patient. Data generated from such devices can be run by quantum machine learning algorithms which will optimize supply chains, and even predict deficits while picking up abnormalities which may signify counterfeit products. In both cases, the implementation of IoT, blockchain and quantum machine learning not only improves health service efficiency and dependability but also dramatically boosts diabetes patients' outcomes by strengthening public trust in the healthcare system. This integrative nature of combined technologies shapes the evolution of healthcare technology to intelligent, agile and personalized care, facilitated via rapid secured platforms.

6.6 Ethical and Regulatory Considerations in Healthcare Technology

The acquisition of better technologies like IoT, blockchain, and quantum machine learning is accompanied by myriad ethical dilemmas that require consideration in healthcare. The privacy challenges are also key, especially with IoT medical devices that always collect confidential patient information. The line between obtaining data for better healthcare and safeguarding one's individual privacy rights is very thin. Lack of this aspect can lead to the unethical use of data in which for instance they will not be protected from misuse of ID; thus people may think their information will be misused. Another ethical issue is the discrimination through machine learning algorithms. Most of these biases are unintended but arise due to the fact that training data used is not accurate, or contain flaws resulting in producing imbalanced results for treated subjects. For instance, when addressing a model that is trained mainly on the datasets of a specific race or group of people, it can be of less use to other groups and make less accurate predictions. This necessitates doing away with these biases so that all patients receive fair healthcare results. The issue of regulatory frameworks regarding the introduction of technologies like IoT, blockchain, and quantum machine leaning into healthcare is rather complicated and soon to transition. It will have to strike a balance between patient safety and data protection with regard to advances in medical technological innovation. One of the problems is that there are no full-fledged standards and guidelines, which could evolve quite quickly relative to technological progress. Therefore, the authorities that regulate should be creative enough to come up with regulatory frameworks that can adjust to new technologies but still stringent enough to preserve patient safety and data credibility. In numerous areas, the already existing medical regulations may need to be altered or extended to encompass novel technological spheres, such as blockchain technology employed in registering patients' records, and quantum computing used in clinical diagnostics. Second of all, the fact that technology and health are applicable across borders makes another challenge: Because issues such as data sovereignty and cross-border sharing remain regulatorily unresolved, international cooperation in regulatory approaches is required. Innovations in technological development, by the healthcare industry players and regulators, requires use of collaborative approaches to bridge the gap between promising technologies and institutionalization of effective ethical practice.

6.7 Challenges and Future Directions in Healthcare Technology Integration

It is very challenging technically and practically to incorporate advanced technologies such as IoT, blockchain and QML into healthcare systems.

One of the main problems is interoperability, which entails communication and work alignment between various systems and devices. However, a major challenge is that there is a wide variety of IoT devices and platforms which makes having an established protocol for smooth data exchange and integration difficult. Furthermore, the technical complexities that come with these technologies cannot be overemphasized. Blockchain and QML, in particular, are highly specialized technologies that need specific infrastructure to be put into practice, thereby putting them outside the capabilities of most healthcare providers. Cost is another issue—setting up and continuing to use sophisticated technology systems may be costly, which could stymie wider adoption of these technological advances, especially in environment. This is especially important, as failure in the reliability and accuracy of these technologies could directly affect patient treatment. Secondly, ability to scale these solutions so that they can process large amounts of data produced in the healthcare environment while still preserving performance and safety is one more significant issue. In the future, a significant long-term influence will be seen when IoT, blockchain and QML are combined in healthcare. The evolution of these technologies will bring about revolutionary changes in how healthcare is given and managed. The technological improvements to IoT technology could, in turn lead to even smaller devices than exist today that would be extremely effective at providing deeper insights regarding patient health and truly individualized medicine. Blockchain may turn into a pillar in construction of the new healthcare data management system that is reliable, consistent and effective in making patients trust their own health information. Quantum machine learning, as it becomes more established, may go on to provide unprecedented powers in handling sophisticated medical data which could significantly translate into surprise findings relating to disease prediction, diagnosis and therapy. Combined, these technological innovations can contribute to a more proactive, predictive, and patient-centered method of healthcare. The future of healthcare technology integration is not just associated with technical developments but in fact the evolution of a fairer and more available health system. These technologies could prove to be solutions to the current challenges, which would help in narrowing gaps in health access and thus making advanced healthcare services available to nearly everyone. For the long term, IoT, blockchain and QML integration may underlie an era of healthcare where technology is an increasing means to better health outcomes, efficient delivery of care and a greater focus on prevention.

6.8 Results and Discussion

This chapter has focused in particular on the concept of merging IoT, blockchain and quantum machine learning (QML) for use in medicine imaging analysis study, revealing their individual peculiarities and conjugated synergies as well as abilities to transform healthcare. Our discussion touches on several important outcomes and provides a point in the dark for further deliberation. First of all, the individual attributes of IoT, blockchain and QML when applied in healthcare are very significant. IoT-based real-time data collection and patient monitoring improve the care and treatment accuracy for patients. It is in this aspect that blockchain has made a major contribution by providing security for sensitive medical information such as supply chain management and insurance claims. With QML being still at an early stage, it is possible to carry out complex data analysis tasks much more effectively compared with how such things were handled in the past, which has a lot of significance especially within drug discovery and genomic research.

Together, these technologies have the capacity to augment one another in such a way that their installation simultaneously can address some of healthcare's most severe issues. The integration assures a better and more secure healthcare system with some level of personalization, relative to patients. This integration of approaches used in the discussion about hypothetical situations, including chronic disease management and the pharmaceutical supply chain, shows how transformative this merger is. But the incorporation of these technologies does not come without its fair share of difficulties. Technical challenges such as interoperability, complexity and cost are formidable barriers. Ethical issues have always been a challenge to address, especially the persistent data privacy concerns alongside QML biases in ensuring an equitable and safe healthcare delivery. It is also established that various regulatory environments have been seen to be providing challenges which would therefore require a construct that allows quick technological advancements but protects the interests of patients as well.

Figure 6.9 illustrates the integration model of three cutting-edge technologies in healthcare: IoT, blockchain, and QML. It shows how these technologies integrate with each other in the healthcare ecosystem. Real-time patient data, securely stored and managed by blockchain technology was also generated using IoT devices. Quantum machine learning applies insights to this information to enhance patient care. The picture presents the information flow between these technologies indicating that they can work together. The prospects of IoT, blockchain, and QML in the healthcare

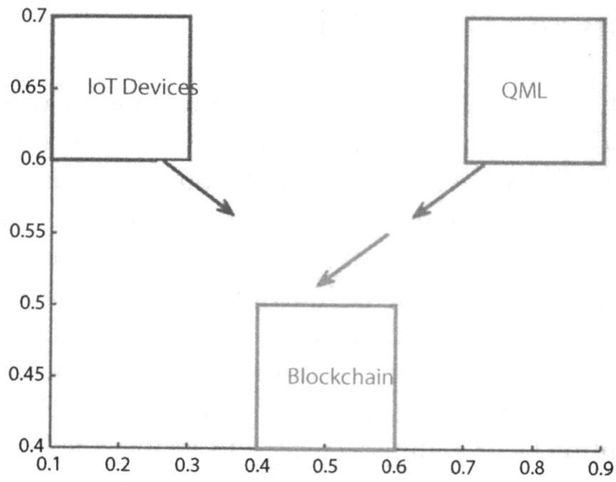

Figure 6.9 Integration model of IoT, blockchain, and QML in healthcare.

domain are bright but that endeavor should be adopted by all stakeholders (innovators, health professionals authorities and patients). Constant innovation accompanied by healthy ethical and regulatory watchfulness ensure that the full potential of these technologies is realized. As they progress, the tangible prospect of a more reactive, proactive disposition and effective healthcare system is closer. This integration might usher in the next major leap forward towards individualized treatment, whereby patients have improved outcomes and a new era of health care in which technology takes center stage to address global health concerns.

6.9 Conclusion

In this chapter, we presented a well-rounded study of the IoT, blockchain and QML integration in healthcare revealing their individual power and synergy effect. We started by discussing the fundamental aspects of IoT and its key importance in data acquisition and patient management, to be followed by blockchain technology as a device helping prescribe medical information while enhancing the efficiency of the healthcare processes. There were many findings from the exploration that QML can cope with increasingly advanced intricate health care data with such an unmatched pace. The focus moved towards the ability of such technologies to create synergy and a reflection on how the connected use of these technologies could usher in revolutionary improvements in healthcare delivery, particularly for chronic disease management, supply chain transparency and predictive health care analytic approaches. Finally, thinking about the ability of IoT, blockchain, and QML to revolutionize health care is crucial. These technologies either singularly or in combination rest on the cusp of ushering in a revolutionary transformation within the healthcare sector. Their integration does not promise just marginal gains but a radical transformation in the way that healthcare services could be administered and run. In such a world, healthcare will become more universal and efficient while at the same time becoming better matched to each patient's requirements.

References

1. Rani, S., Kumar Pareek, P., Kaur, J., Chauhan, M., Bhambri, P., Quantum Machine Learning in Healthcare: Developments and Challenges, in: *2023 IEEE International Conference on Integrated Circuits and Communication Systems (ICICACS)*, Raichur, India, pp. 1–7, 2023.
2. Kumar, S.A., Kumar, H., Dutt, V., Soni, H., Self-Health Analysis with Two Step Histogram based Procedure using Machine Learning, in: *2021 Third International Conference on Intelligent Communication Technologies and Virtual Mobile Networks (ICICV)*, Tirunelveli, India, pp. 794–799, 2021, doi: 10.1109/ICICV50876.2021.9388427.
3. Maheshwari, D., Garcia-Zapirain, B., Sierra-Sosa, D., Quantum Machine Learning Applications in the Biomedical Domain: A Systematic Review. *IEEE Access*, 10, 80463–80484, 2022.
4. Maheshwari, D., Garcia-Zapirain, B., Sierra-Soso, D., Machine learning applied to diabetes dataset using Quantum versus Classical computation, in: *2020 IEEE International Symposium on Signal Processing and Information Technology (ISSPIT)*, Louisville, KY, USA, pp. 1–6, 20202020.
5. Upama, P.B., *et al.*, Quantum Machine Learning in Disease Detection and Prediction: a survey of applications and future possibilities, in: *2023 IEEE 47th Annual Computers, Software, and Applications Conference (COMPSAC)*, Torino, Italy, pp. 1545–1551, 2023.
6. Kranthi, M. and Tanguturi, R.C., Design of Intelligent Medical Integrity Authentication and Secure Information for Public Cloud in Hospital Administration, in: *2023 2nd International Conference on Edge Computing and Applications (ICECAA)*, Namakkal, India, pp. 256–261, 2023.
7. Burugadda, V.R., Jadhav, N., Vyas, N., Duggar, R., Exploring the Potential of Deep Reinforcement Learning for Autonomous Navigation in Complex Environments, in: *2023 7th International Conference on Computing, Communication, Control and Automation (ICCUBEA)*, Pune, India, pp. 1–6, 2023, doi: 10.1109/ICCUBEA58933.2023.10392109.

8. Kavitha, R., Kumar, A., Kalpana, V., Hariram, V., Artificial Intelligence based Health Monitoring System on IoTH platform, in: *2023 Second International Conference on Augmented Intelligence and Sustainable Systems (ICAISS)*, Trichy, India, pp. 1458–1463, 2023.
9. Sasubilli, S.M., Kumar, A., Dutt, V., Improving Health Care by Help of Internet of Things and Bigdata Analytics and Cloud Computing, in: *2020 International Conference on Advances in Computing and Communication Engineering (ICACCE)*, Las Vegas, NV, USA, pp. 1–4, 2020, doi: 10.1109/ICACCE49060.2020.9155042.
10. Archana Shreee, S., Maheshwari, B., Jeevitha Sai, G., A Novel Method of Identification of Delirium in Patients from Electronic Health Records Using Machine Learning, in: *2023 World Conference on Communication & Computing (WCONF)*, RAIPUR, India, pp. 1–6, 2023.
11. Burugadda, V.R., Pawar, P.S., Kumar, A., Bhati, N., Predicting Hospital Readmission Risk for Heart Failure Patients Using Machine Learning Techniques: A Comparative Study of Classification Algorithms, in: *2023 Second International Conference on Trends in Electrical, Electronics, and Computer Engineering (TEECCON)*, Bangalore, India, pp. 223–228, 2023, doi: 10.1109/TEECCON59234.2023.10335817.
12. Mailapur, R.V. and K., M., Implementation of GUI based Vital Track Ambulance for Patient Health Monitoring, in: *2023 8th International Conference on Communication and Electronics Systems (ICCES)*, Coimbatore, India, pp. 1417–1424, 2023.
13. Kishore Kumar, R., Pandidurai, M., Senthil Kamalesh, M.S.C., Design of IoT based Rural Health Helper using Natural Language Processing, in: *2023 4th International Conference on Electronics and Sustainable Communication Systems (ICESC)*, Coimbatore, India, pp. 328–333, 2023.
14. Ram Vishal, B., Shankar, M.U., M, K.A., Cardiovascular Disease Prediction Using LSTM Algorithm Based on Cytokines, in: *2023 4th International Conference for Emerging Technology (INCET)*, Belgaum, India, pp. 1–5, 2023.
15. Swarna, S.R., Kumar, A., Dixit, P., Sairam, T.V.M., Parkinson's Disease Prediction using Adaptive Quantum Computing, in: *2021 Third International Conference on Intelligent Communication Technologies and Virtual Mobile Networks (ICICV)*, Tirunelveli, India, pp. 1396–1401, 2021, doi: 10.1109/ICICV50876.2021.9388628.
16. Burri, S.R., Agarwal, D.K., Vyas, N., Duggar, R., A Machine Learning Framework for Accurate Prediction of Parkinson's Disease from Speech Data, in: *2023 3rd International Conference on Innovative Sustainable Computational Technologies (CISCT)*, Dehradun, India, pp. 1–6, 2023, doi: 10.1109/CISCT57197.2023.10351422.
17. Prasad, K., Dekka, S., c. Tanguturi, R., Poornima, G., An Intelligent System for Remote Monitoring of Patients Health and the Early Detection of Coronary Artery Disease, in: *2022 International Conference on Smart Generation*

Computing, Communication and Networking (SMART GENCON), Bangalore, India, pp. 1–6, 2022.
18. Anandaram, H., B. A, N., Gupta, N., Verma, B.K., IoT Wearable Breast Temperature Assessment System, in: *2023 7th International Conference on Computing Methodologies and Communication (ICCMC)*, Erode, India, pp. 1236–1241, 2023.
19. Prasad, K., Anil Kumar, N., Reddy, N.S., Ashreetha, B., Technologies for Comprehensive Information Security in the IoT, in: *2023 International Conference for Advancement in Technology (ICONAT)*, Goa, India, pp. 1–5, 2023.
20. Venkatakiran, S., Ashreetha, B., Reddy, N.S., Implementation of a Machine Learning-based Model for Cardiovascular Disease Post Exposure prophylaxis, in: *2023 International Conference for Advancement in Technology (ICONAT)*, Goa, India, pp. 1–5, 2023.
21. Chakrasali, S.V., Kumar, C., Chaturvedi, A., Azhagu Jaisudhan Pazhani, A., Computer vision based healthcare system for identification of diabetes & its types using AI. *Meas.: Sens.*, 27, 10075, 2023.
22. Hombalimath, Palanikkumar, D., Patwari, N., Symmetrized Feature Selection with Stacked Generalization based Machine Learning Algorithm for the Early Diagnosis of Chronic Diseases, in: *2023 5th International Conference on Smart Systems and Inventive Technology (ICSSIT)*, Tirunelveli, India, pp. 838–844, 2023.
23. Kumar, A., Kumar, S.A., Dutt, V., Dubey, A.K., Narang, S., A Hybrid Secure Cloud Platform Maintenance Based on Improved Attribute-Based Encryption Strategies. *Int. J. Interact. Multimedia Artif. Intell.*, 8, 2, 150, 2023. Universidad Internacional de La Rioja, doi: 10.9781/ijimai.2021.11.004.
24. M. R., G. and Anandaram, H., Extraction of Fetal ECG Using ANFIS and the Undecimated-Wavelet Transform, in: *2022 IEEE 3rd Global Conference for Advancement in Technology (GCAT)*, pp. 1–5, 2022.
25. Vyas, N., P., P.A., Das, P., Mahajan, Y., The Impact of Air Pollution on Respiratory Health Results: An Analysis of Asthma and COPD in a Population Study, in: *2023 International Conference on Computing, Communication, and Intelligent Systems (ICCCIS)*, Greater Noida, India, pp. 141–146, 2023, doi: 10.1109/ICCCIS60361.2023.10425187.
26. Reddy P, S. and Patwal, P.S., Data Analytics and Cloud-Based Platform for Internet of Things Applications in Smart Cities, in: *2022 International Conference on Industry 4.0 Technology (I4Tech)*, pp. 1–6, 2022.
27. Kawale, S.R. and Diwan, S.P., Intelligent Breast Abnormality Framework for Detection and Evaluation of Breast Abnormal Parameters, in: *2022 International Conference on Edge Computing and Applications (ICECAA)*, pp. 1503–1508, 2022.
28. Kameswara Rao, B., Chaturvedi, A., Hussain, N., Industrial quality healthcare services using Internet of Things and fog computing approach. *Meas.: Sens.*, 24, 100517, 2022.

29. Namitha, A.R., Manu, Y.M., Rashmi, G.R., Chinamuttevi, V.S., IOT Based Smart Health Care System to Monitor Covid-19 Patients. *IJEER*, 10, 1, 36–40, 2022.
30. Ramesh Naidu, P. and Guruprasad, N., A High-Availability and Integrity Layer for Cloud Storage, Cloud Computing Security: From Single to Multi-Clouds. *J. Phys. Conf. Ser.*, 1921, 1, 012072, 2021.
31. Burugadda, V.R., Dutt, V., Mamta, Vyas, N., Personalized Cardiovascular Disease Risk Prediction Using Random Forest: An Optimized Approach, in: *2023 IEEE World Conference on Applied Intelligence and Computing (AIC)*, Sonbhadra, India, pp. 226–232, 2023, doi: 10.1109/AIC57670.2023.10263915.
32. Jeevan, K. and Sathisha, B.M., Implementation of IoT Based Wireless Electronic Stethoscope, in: *2020 Third International Conference on Multimedia Processing, Communication & Information Technology (MPCIT)*, pp. 103–106, 2020.
33. Swathi Pai, M., Shruthi, M., Naveen K, B., Internet of Things: A Survey on Devices, Ecosystem, Components and Communication Protocols, in: *2020 4th International Conference on Electronics, Communication and Aerospace Technology (ICECA)*, pp. 611–616, 2020.
34. Naveen, K.B., Ramesha, M., Pai, G.N., Internet of things: Internet revolution, impact, technology road map and features. *Adv. Math. Sci. J.*, 9, 7, 4405–4414, 2020.
35. Bhati, N., Duggar, R., Saber, A., Empowering Safety by Embracing IoT for Leak Detection Excellence, in: *Innovations in Machine Learning and IoT for Water Management*, pp. 231–251, IGI Global, Nov. 27, 2023, doi: 10.4018/979-8-3693-1194-3.ch012.
36. Punugoti, R., Dutt, V., Anand, A., Bhati, N., Exploring the Impact of Edge Intelligence and IoT on Healthcare: A Comprehensive Survey, in: *2023 International Conference on Sustainable Computing and Smart Systems (ICSCSS)*, Coimbatore, India, pp. 1108–1114, 2023, doi: 10.1109/ICSCSS57650.2023.10169733.

7

Integrating Multimodal Data Fusion for Advanced Biomedical Analysis: A Comprehensive Review

Umesh Kumar Lilhore* **and Sarita Simaiya**

Galgotias University, Greater Noida, UP, India

Abstract
The multimodality of biomedical data is on the rise, enabling the recording of intricate interactions between biological functions. Data fusion algorithms that utilize deep learning (DL) are often used to simulate these dynamic connections. Hence, we conduct a comprehensive examination of the existing cutting-edge techniques and put forth an elaborate classification system that enables a more knowledgeable selection of fusion approaches for biological purposes, along with an exploration of innovative methodologies. Through this process, we see that deep fusion techniques frequently surpass unimodal in nature and shallow techniques in terms of performance. Furthermore, the suggested subcategories of fusion techniques exhibit distinct benefits and limitations. The examination of existing methodologies has revealed that combined representation learning remains the favored strategy, particularly for intermediate merging methods, due to its ability to accurately capture the intricate relationships among many levels of biological organization. Ultimately, we acknowledge that the use of progressive fusion, which relies on existing biological understanding and search methodologies, holds great potential as a future avenue of study. Moreover, the application of transfer learning might potentially address the constraints imposed by a restricted number of samples with multimodal data collections. With the growing availability of large data sets, multimodal deep learning algorithms offer the chance to train comprehensive models capable of understanding the intricate regulatory dynamics associated with health and illness.

Keywords: Multimodal, data fusion, deep learning, AI, biomedical

**Corresponding author*: umeshlilhore@gmail.com

Umesh Kumar Lilhore, Abhishek Kumar, Narayan Vyas, Sarita Simaiya and Vishal Dutt (eds.) Multimodal Data Fusion for Bioinformatics Artificial Intelligence, (127–146) © 2025 Scrivener Publishing LLC

7.1 Introduction

Machine learning is commonly employed to address challenges in the healthcare industry, particularly in the context of clinical decision support. Traditionally, its application has concentrated chiefly on data with a single mode. The healthcare discipline of artificial intelligence (AI) has made efforts to enhance prediction and replicate the multimodal character of clinical expert decision-making by integrating diverse inputs (Vincenzo, 2024). The implementation of computational methods and machine learning techniques in the healthcare arena has been a goal for those involved in clinical decision support for quite some time. Computational decision supports encompass several data sources, such as laboratory test principles, methods of imaging and clinical (specifically, clinical scores).

Specific health diagnostics can be established based on a solitary laboratory value or a singular threshold, as exemplified by diabetes in elderly individuals. Diagnostic categories are determined by a combination of signs, symptoms, test results, and supported imaging. Frequently, medical diagnoses are established using additive scoring networks, which need the combination of both positive and negative characteristics before confirming the diagnosis (Jiao *et al.*, 2024).

The operational methodology employed in clinical diagnosis may overlook the significance of many data inputs and the probable existence of non-linear correlations, therefore underscoring the constraints of human decision-making abilities. One advantage of computational assistance with decision-making lies in its ability to delegate such responsibilities, hence potentially leading to a more favorable outcome. The potential of precision healthcare is evident. The objective of precision medicine/health is to develop a medical framework that customizes healthcare (including choices, treatments, and practices) to suit the specific characteristics of a person or patient. This encompasses the long-term tracking of individuals' health trajectories, frequently integrating genetics and DNA replication and employing mathematical modeling techniques to incorporate this distinctive information into diagnosis and therapies. In contrast, a one-drug-fits-all paradigm is characterized by the utilization of a singular medication for each illness (Liu *et al.*, 2024).

Data fusion refers to the integration of data from many different sources, which offer distinct perspectives on the same phenomena, in order to address an inference issue. This offers the potential to address such issues with a lower number of mistakes compared to unimodal methods. Data fusion offers multiple benefits, which may be classified as beneficial, redundant, and collaborative aspects. However, it is essential to note that the benefits mentioned above are not incompatible with one another (Kumar *et al.*, 2024). The multimodal examination of an individual with cancer serves as an illustrative example of the benefits associated with data fusion throughout the healthcare area. The utilization of the genomic information obtained from a tumor facilitates the discovery of genes that drive cancer, while whole-slide pictures (WSP) obtained from a biopsy offer insights into the anatomy and microenvironment of the tumor. These modalities are considered "complementary" as they offer insights into various aspects of the phenomena that would otherwise be unobservable (D'Souza, *et al.*, 2024).

The integration of transcriptional and chromatographic data is mutually reinforcing since not all mRNAs are translated into proteins, and it is unnecessary, as the presence of a protein validates the process of translation of a particular mRNA towards a protein. The presence of duplication is especially crucial in cases when the data exhibit noise or contain several missing values. The data collected through a combination of miRNA and mRNA scanning of the same tumor might be regarded as "cooperative" due to the enhanced complexity resulting from the integrated facts. The combination of both modalities offers a potential rationale for the varying levels of a protein, such as an ontogeny. This factor may have a significant impact on the prognostication of the patient's reaction to a particular therapeutic intervention. Figure 7.1 presents multimodal applications in smart healthcare (Nikolaou *et al.*, 2024).

The objective of fusion techniques is to efficiently leverage the shared, redundant, and collaborative characteristics of several channels. In order to effectively leverage these perspectives on the occurrence under investigation, it is imperative to employ machine learning (ML) techniques that can integrate data that is both structured and unstructured, characterized by distinct mathematical characteristics, non-biological explanations for variations, high-dimensionality, and varying occurrences of values that are missing. This chapter provides a review of Integrating Multimodal Data Fusion for Advanced Biomedical Analysis, its various methods, applications, and future directions. The chapter is organized in various sections. Section two covers multimodal genomics data, section three covers challenges in data fusion, section four covers neural network architectures for data fusion, section five covers case studies and applications, and finally, section six covers future directions.

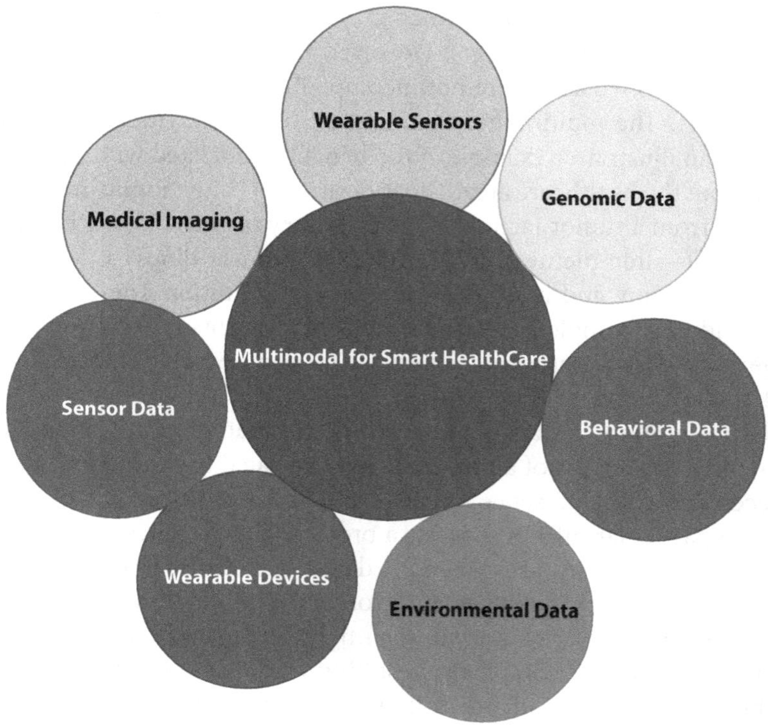

Figure 7.1 Multimodal applications in smart healthcare.

7.2 Multimodal Biomedical Analysis

Accurate diagnostic and curative choices rely on the knowledge gained by analyzing large-scale healthcare datasets using several modes of analysis. The progress in human genome sequencing, the processing of images, and the healthcare processing of data have facilitated the acquisition and organization of data inside medical establishments (Waqas *et al.*, 2023). The endeavors mentioned above have yielded extensive datasets and facilitated comprehensive exams that offer a more comprehensive understanding of the influence of a medical condition on the fundamental system. Integrating extensive biological data typically entails many intricate data transformation procedures, such as merging datasets to construct feature vectors for analytics. Affordable approaches to data integration are of paramount importance in shaping the future of focused treatment. While extensive data processing technologies are demonstrating encouraging performance in several fields, they are unable to facilitate the sustainable interpretation of intricate data types (Cui *et al.*, 2023).

Genetic data are becoming less expensive since they only need to be determined once in a person's lifetime. However, they also have little predictive capacity on an individual's behalf. The integration of genetic data statistics alongside additional omics data has the potential to present a more comprehensive and up-to-date understanding of the intricate interplay between genetic genealogy and exposure to environmental factors, hence enabling the quantification of the spectrum of medical conditions. For instance, Jiao *et al.* (2023), performed a study using whole-genome sequencing, also known as WGS, along with regular evaluations of other the use of omics multiple layers such as the transcriptomics, the proteome, metabolites, immunoglobulins, and clinical biological indicators. Table 7.1 presents a comparative analysis of various research studies in the field of multimodal biomedical analysis.

Table 7.1 Comparative analysis of various research in the field of multimodal biomedical analysis.

Reference	Dataset	Method used	Key points	Applications
Dalal *et al.* (2023).	TCGA	Deep learning approaches	Deep learning for cancer subtype classification and biomarker discovery	Cancer subtype classification, biomarker discovery
Liu, Q., *et al.* (2024).	ADNI	Multimodal data fusion	Identification of genetic markers in Alzheimer's disease using multimodal data fusion	Early detection of Alzheimer's disease, identification of therapeutic targets
Tang, *et al.* (2024).	METABRIC	Network-based analysis	Discovery of gene regulatory networks associated with breast cancer subtypes	Improved understanding of breast cancer biology, identification of potential therapeutic targets
Xie *et al.* (2020).	GDSC	Machine learning models	Predicting drug response in cancer patients using multimodal data fusion	Personalized medicine, identification of optimal treatment strategies

(*Continued*)

Table 7.1 Comparative analysis of various research in the field of multimodal biomedical analysis. (*Continued*)

Reference	Dataset	Method used	Key points	Applications
Srinivas *et al.* (2023).	TCGA GBM	Survival analysis methods	Predictive model for patient survival in glioblastoma based on integrated multimodal genomics data	Prognostic prediction, personalized treatment planning
Kumar *et al.* (2023).	PPMI	Machine learning algorithms	Identification of genetic markers associated with Parkinson's disease progression	Early diagnosis, disease progression prediction
Syeda-Mahmood, T. (2023)	TCGA PAAD	Clustering and network analysis	Molecular subtypes and driver genes of pancreatic ductal adenocarcinoma using integrated multimodal genomics data	Subtyping of pancreatic cancer, identification of therapeutic targets
Sabherwal, G. and Kaur, A. (2024).	TCGA LUAD	Integration of multiple omics data	Identification of novel molecular subtypes of lung cancer using integrated multi-modal genomics data	Improved subtyping of lung cancer, identification of potential therapeutic targets

7.3 Challenges in Data Fusion

Data fusion, the process of combining data from several sources to generate advanced models, offers substantial potential advantages for various businesses. This issue is a fundamental challenge in several fields when attempting to establish a data-driven economy. The process of integrating diverse datasets raises various conceptual and technological inquiries, especially when taking into account diverse analytical methodologies and formulating suitable assessment criteria. Comprehending these prospective obstacles, in conjunction with the intricacies associated with various forms of heterogeneity in the data, is crucial for the development of feasible data fusion methodologies. The delineation among generic and domain-dependent methodologies in the context of data fusion remains undefined Li *et al.* (2023). Table 7.2 presents a comparative analysis of various challenges in data fusion and possible solutions and approaches.

Table 7.2 Comparative analysis of various challenges in data fusion and possible solutions and approaches.

Challenge	Description	Solutions/approaches
Heterogeneity of Data Sources	Data comes from diverse sources with varying formats, structures, and semantics.	Standardization of data formats, use of ontologies for semantic integration, and data preprocessing.
Scalability	Handling large volumes of data from multiple sources while maintaining performance and efficiency.	Use of distributed computing frameworks (e.g., Hadoop, Spark), efficient data storage and retrieval.
Data Quality	Ensuring data accuracy, completeness, consistency, and reliability across different sources.	Data cleaning, validation, and normalization techniques, as well as quality metrics for evaluation, are also used.
Integration of Different Modalities	Integrating data from different modalities (e.g., imaging, genetic, clinical) to derive meaningful insights.	Development of multimodal fusion techniques, feature extraction, and selection methods.
Privacy and Security	Ensuring the privacy and security of sensitive data during integration and analysis.	Data anonymization, encryption, access control mechanisms, and compliance with data protection laws.
Interpretability and Transparency	Ensuring that the fusion process is interpretable and transparent to stakeholders.	Explainable AI (XAI) approaches visualizations of fusion results, and documentation of the fusion process.
Computational Complexity	Managing the computational complexity of integrating and analyzing large multi-modal datasets.	Optimization of algorithms, parallel processing, and utilization of specialized hardware (e.g., GPUs).
Knowledge and Expertise	Data fusion methodologies and their applications require domain-specific expertise as well as knowledge.	Domain specialists and data researchers collaborate, and there is continuous development and training.

7.4 Deep Learning Methods for Data Fusion

The methods based on deep learning to merging multiple omics information aim to obtain representations with low dimensions by mixing several kinds of statistics, which can subsequently be utilised for a variety of applications. The study we conducted has shown that numerous deep learning (DL), and machine learning, data integration algorithms can achieve this goal. These approaches involve the fully connected neural network (FCNN), convolutional neural network (CNN), autoencoder (AE), graph neural network (GNN), capsule network (CapsNet), generative adversarial network (GAN), and a mixture of DL-based algorithms for multi-omics information integration. Prior articles used a variety of techniques, including either late or early fusion, that made use of the majority of these theoretical structures developed by D'Souza *et al.* (2023). Early fusion is the technique of merging separate information from omics before feeding them to deep learning algorithms.

Late fusion is the procedure of first incorporating multi-omics information into artificial intelligence models, then fusing for future assignments. Directly evaluating these approaches is difficult because of the mismatch in source omics data and activities downstream. To ensure comparability across different methodologies, this study first eliminated the information fusion element from the basic architecture and then performed comparisons of performance with unifying samples and goals. Two particular factors guided the selection of these multi-omics analysis techniques: (a) The initial prototypes for the indicated approaches use freely available software; (b) the first models used a multi-omics arrangement, as well as the data fusion element of the original structure may be recovered individually, allowing the assessment of data fusion when combined into datasets and goals.

To undertake a thorough evaluation of the programmes' effectiveness, this study comprised three unique kinds of multi-omics evidence collections: simulations details, single-cell development facts, and cancer-related material. This discovery shows the separation of evaluation models into two categories: supervised models and unsupervised algorithms. As a result, each dataset had two unique objectives: classification of models under supervision and aggregation of unorganised structures. Furthermore, this work performed a thorough evaluation of the approaches' usefulness in capturing the link among multi-omics dimensionality reduction results, their survival, and medical labelling in illness multi-omics data sets. Table 7.3 compares several deep learning architectures and applications in data fusion.

Table 7.3 Comparative analysis of various deep learning architectures and applications in data fusion.

DL architecture	Description	Example applications
Convolutional Neural Networks	Designed for processing grid-like data, such as images. It uses convolutional layers to extract features and pooling layers to reduce spatial dimensions.	Image classification, object detection, and medical image analysis.
Recurrent Neural Networks	Suited for sequential data processing, with feedback loops that allow information to persist. Used for tasks requiring memory of past inputs, such as natural language processing.	Language translation, speech recognition, time series prediction.
Long Short-Term Memory (LSTM)	A type of recurrent neural network that addresses the vanishing gradient problem, allowing it to learn long-term dependencies.	Sentiment analysis, speech recognition, financial forecasting.
Autoencoders	Neural networks are trained to copy input data to output, typically with a smaller number of hidden units in the middle layer, forcing the network to learn efficient representations.	Dimensionality reduction, anomaly detection, feature learning.
Generative Adversarial Networks	Comprising two networks, a generator, and a discriminator, that are trained together in a competitive setting. Used to generate new data instances similar to the training data.	Image generation, data augmentation, generative modeling.
Deep Belief Networks	Composed of multiple layers of stochastic, latent variables. Pre-trained in an unsupervised manner before fine-tuning in a supervised setting.	Feature learning, collaborative filtering, anomaly detection.

7.5 Case Studies and Applications

Multimodal clinical information fusion has become a revolutionary method in intelligent healthcare, allowing a thorough comprehension of patient well-being and tailored treatment strategies. Table 7.4 presents a comparative analysis of various case studies of multimodal data fusion (Yang, 2022). The critical areas in the field of multimodal data fusion with bioinformatics are as follows.

Table 7.4 A comparative analysis of various case studies of multimodal data fusion.

Case study/ application	Description	Data sources/ modalities	Methods/ techniques	Key findings/ results
Healthcare Monitoring	Integrating data from wearable sensors, electronic health records, and genomic data for patient monitoring.	Wearable sensors, EHRs, genomic data	Machine learning algorithms for real-time monitoring and predictive analytics.	Improved patient monitoring, early detection of health issues, and personalized treatment plans.
Autonomous Vehicles	Fusion of data from cameras, LiDAR, radar, and GPS for autonomous navigation.	Cameras, LiDAR, radar, GPS	Sensor fusion algorithms (e.g., Kalman filters, neural networks) for environment perception and decision-making.	Enhanced situational awareness, improved navigation accuracy, and increased safety on the roads.
Environmental Monitoring	Integration of data from satellite imagery, weather stations, and ground sensors for environmental analysis.	Satellite imagery, weather stations, ground sensors	Remote sensing techniques, spatial analysis, and statistical modeling for environmental monitoring and forecasting.	Enhanced understanding of environmental changes, better prediction of natural disasters, and improved resource management.
Finance and Stock Market	Fusion of financial data, news articles, and social media data for stock market prediction.	Financial data, news articles, social media data	Sentiment analysis, natural language processing, machine learning for stock price prediction, and trend analysis.	Improved stock market predictions, better investment strategies, enhanced risk management.

(*Continued*)

Table 7.4 A comparative analysis of various case studies of multimodal data fusion. (*Continued*)

Case study/ application	Description	Data sources/ modalities	Methods/ techniques	Key findings/ results
Smart Cities	Integrating data from IoT devices, traffic cameras, and social media for urban planning.	IoT devices, traffic cameras, social media	Big data analytics, machine learning, and simulation modeling for traffic management, energy optimization, and public safety.	Efficient resource allocation, reduced traffic congestion, improved public services, and enhanced quality of life.
Industrial IoT	Fusion of data from sensors, machines, and production systems for predictive maintenance.	Sensors, machines, production systems	Predictive analytics, machine learning algorithms for anomaly detection, and maintenance scheduling.	Reduced downtime, improved equipment efficiency, and cost savings from proactive maintenance.
Weather Forecasting	Integration of meteorological data, satellite imagery, and climate models for weather prediction.	Meteorological data, satellite imagery, climate models	Data assimilation techniques, ensemble modeling, and machine learning for weather forecasting.	Improved accuracy of weather forecasts and better preparedness for extreme weather events.
Precision Agriculture	Fusion of data from drones, sensors, and satellite imagery for crop monitoring and management.	Drones, sensors, satellite imagery	Remote sensing, machine learning algorithms for crop health assessment, irrigation optimization, and yield prediction.	Increased crop yield, reduced water and pesticide usage, improved farm management practices.
Energy Management	Integrating data from smart meters, weather forecasts, and energy demand models for energy optimization.	Smart meters, weather forecasts, energy demand models	Data analytics, optimization algorithms, and demand response strategies for efficient energy consumption and grid management.	Reduced energy costs, improved grid stability, and increased use of renewable energy sources.

7.5.1 Neuro-Imaging and Genetic Data Fusion

Neuroimaging data is characterized by its extensive size and intricate nature since it incorporates several parameters pertaining to anatomy, function, and disease. Neuroimaging research has increasingly prioritized the application of machine learning techniques to analyze intricate brain imaging data. The effectiveness of machine learning methods relies heavily on the presence of extensive research that is supplemented with comprehensive and in-depth phenotyping. In recent years, there has been a growing trend in the collection of imaging data using enormous sample sizes, leading to the emergence of mega-analysis techniques that include the pooling of thousands of samples. The scientific field of brain imaging genomics has gained prominence because of the progress made in high-throughput genome sequencing and multimodal neuroimaging methodologies. The primary objective of this study is to investigate the correlation between genetic markers, namely polymorphisms in one nucleotide, and statistical characteristics derived from multimodal neurological imaging data. The possibility for enhancing our mechanistic knowledge of normal or abnormal brain functioning lies in the integration of imaging and genetic components, as well as the exploration of their interconnections. Over the last ten years, the utilization of statistical and machine learning techniques has been prevalent in this field of study. This has significantly enhanced the identification of associations through the application of univariate in multilocus analysis, bi-multivariate neuroimaging and genomic association analysis, and route and network saturation analysis.

7.5.2 Multi-Omics Data Fusion for Cancer Classification

The multi-omics predictors created by [21, 34] possess the ability to categorize both individual kinds of data and fused data with better accuracy levels. SCCA-CC exhibited its advantage over iCluster by its ability to discover subgroups characterized by stronger coherence, clinical significance, and time efficiency. The collection of multi-omics data is becoming more prevalent in the study of intricate disorders, such as cancer. Nevertheless, the problems of integrated analysis are significant because of the high complexity, short sample size, and variability of many omics types. Omics pertains to the quantification of several molecular entities, such as transcriptomics, the field of proteomics epigenomics research, and others, which are associated with distinct molecular pathways, including genetics and epigenetics, inside a singular organism and tissue the specimen (Yuan, H. and Xu, H., 2023).

The utilization of high-performance "omics" technology is becoming more prevalent in unraveling the fundamental molecular pathways and devising innovative treatment approaches for intricate illnesses like cancer. Cancer may be understood as a macroevolutionary phenomenon that is influenced by the specific tissue environment present in individuals. The advantages of employing a customized therapeutic strategy in the management of cancer are becoming more evident and have consequently been embraced by a growing number of healthcare professionals. The Cancer Genome Atlas (TCGA) and similar initiatives have collected significant quantities of multi-omics information gathered from several human participants. The pursuit of efficient biological technology has resulted in a significant surge of multi-omics data with large dimensions, necessitating innovative approaches for data processing. The presence of high complexity and diversity significantly challenges the integration and assessment of multi-omics.

7.5.3 Clinical and Wearable Sensor Data Fusion

Distinctive integration into commonplace items, both within the house and on the individual, is now possible because of advances in technology in networking and sensing. The collection of data through the observation of physiological, behavioral in nature, and social aspects of individuals' lives has the potential to provide beneficial outcomes in terms of enhancing quality of life, promoting health, and fostering overall well-being. Wearable sensors are on the verge of achieving widespread adoption, with the potential to be integrated into our clothing and accessories in a manner that renders them omnipresent and imperceptible. In order to analyze the intricate and multifaceted data obtained from various sensors, data fusion methods are utilised to generate a coherent and significant depiction of the sensor output by Hemker *et al.* (2023).

7.6 Future Directions

It is anticipated that the domain of multimodal health information integration for intelligent healthcare will progress in accordance with the four Ps of medical care, namely Preventive, Predictive, Participatory, and Personalized. The primary objective of predicting healthcare information fusion is to integrate data from several sources in order to forecast health occurrences and consequences. Conversely, preventative data fusion is centered on the identification of risk factors and the promotion of healthy behaviours (Alwazzan *et al.*, 2023). Personalized fusion is a method that addresses the unique data of individuals to provide tailored treatment, while participative fusion is the active involvement of consumers and other partners in the process of data fusion, hence promoting transparency and fostering confidence. The advancement towards these objectives becomes the central focus of our subsequent study. Table 7.5 presents a comparison of future directions of multimodal data fusion (Ryan *et al.*, 2023).

Table 7.5 Future directions of multimodal data fusion.

Future directions	Description	Challenges	Potential solutions/ approaches
Integration of AI and IoT	Leveraging AI techniques such as machine learning and deep learning to enhance data fusion in IoT applications.	Interoperability between AI and IoT devices, data privacy and security.	Standardization of communication protocols development of secure AI models for edge devices.
Explainable AI	Developing transparent and interpretable AI models for data fusion to enhance trust and understanding of automated decisions.	Complexity of AI models, balancing between model complexity and interpretability.	Use of explainable AI techniques (e.g., LIME, SHAP), model simplification approaches.
Federated Learning	Utilizing federated learning to train models across distributed data sources without centralized data aggregation, enhancing privacy and scalability.	Communication and synchronization overhead, model heterogeneity.	Optimization of federated learning algorithms, privacy-preserving techniques (e.g., differential privacy).
Quantum Computing	Exploring the potential of quantum computing for data fusion to handle complex computations and large-scale datasets more efficiently.	Quantum hardware limitations, error rates and qubit coherence.	Development of quantum error correction codes, improvements in quantum hardware.

(*Continued*)

Table 7.5 Future directions of multimodal data fusion. (*Continued*)

Future directions	Description	Challenges	Potential solutions/ approaches
Blockchain Technology	Using blockchain technology to secure and validate data transactions in distributed data fusion systems, ensuring data integrity and trustworthiness.	Scalability and performance issues, energy consumption.	Implementation of scalable blockchain solutions (e.g., sharding), energy-efficient consensus mechanisms.
Edge Computing	Moving data processing and analysis closer to the data source (e.g., IoT devices) to reduce latency and bandwidth usage, improving real-time data fusion capabilities.	Limited computational resources, security and privacy concerns.	Optimization of edge computing algorithms, use of secure communication protocols (e.g., TLS).
Hybrid Data Fusion	Integrating multiple data fusion techniques (e.g., model-based and data-driven) to leverage the strengths of each approach for enhanced fusion performance.	Complexity of hybrid models, integration of heterogeneous data sources.	Development of hybrid fusion frameworks, model ensembles for combining different fusion techniques.
Cross-Domain Fusion	Extending data fusion beyond single domains (e.g., healthcare, finance) to enable insights and discoveries across diverse fields, promoting interdisciplinary research.	Domain-specific challenges and terminology, data integration from disparate sources.	Interdisciplinary collaboration, development of cross-domain fusion frameworks and ontologies.
Autonomous Data Fusion	Advancing autonomous data fusion capabilities to enable systems to adapt, learn, and evolve in dynamic environments without human intervention.	Trust and reliability of autonomous systems, interpretability and explainability.	Incorporation of human oversight and feedback, development of transparent autonomous fusion algorithms.

7.7 Conclusion

The integration of many modalities, such as electronic health records (EHRs), medical imaging, wearable devices, genetic data, sensor data, environmental data, and behavioral data, known as multimodal medical data fusion, can transform innovative healthcare. Practitioners may enhance their understanding and expertise in healthcare by utilizing several methodologies, including feature selection, rule-based systems, machine learning (ML), deep learning, and natural language processing (NL). These techniques enable the extraction of essential insights from a wide range of varied sources.

Nonetheless, it is imperative to acknowledge and tackle the obstacles pertaining to data quality, interoperability, privacy, security, data processing, clinical integration, and ethical issues. Future research should prioritize the investigation of Predictive, Preventive, Personalised, and Participatory approaches. The integration or amalgamation of these approaches has the potential to enhance the ability to anticipate health events, identify risk factors, administer customized interventions, and empower patients in their healthcare endeavors. Seizing these opportunities will revolutionize healthcare by enhancing patient welfare, treatment results, and the general operation of the healthcare sector.

References

1. Vincenzo, M.D., *Review on multi-modal AI models to integrate imaging and omics data*, 2024, (Master's thesis).
2. Jiao, C.N., Gao, Y.L., Ge, D.H., Shang, J., Liu, J.X., Multi-modal imaging genetics data fusion by deep auto-encoder and self-representation network for Alzheimer's disease diagnosis and biomarkers extraction. *Eng. Appl. Artif. Intell.*, *130*, 107782, 2024.
3. Burugadda, V.R., Pawar, P.S., Kumar, A., Bhati, N., Predicting Hospital Readmission Risk for Heart Failure Patients Using Machine Learning Techniques: A Comparative Study of Classification Algorithms, in: *2023 Second International Conference on Trends in Electrical, Electronics, and Computer Engineering (TEECCON)*, Bangalore, India, pp. 223–228, 2023, doi: 10.1109/TEECCON59234.2023.10335817.
4. Duan, J., Xiong, J., Li, Y., Ding, W., Deep learning based multimodal biomedical data fusion: An overview and comparative review. *Inf. Fusion*, 102536, 2024.

5. Burugadda, V.R., Jadhav, N., Vyas, N., Duggar, R., Exploring the Potential of Deep Reinforcement Learning for Autonomous Navigation in Complex Environments, in: *2023 7th International Conference on Computing, Communication, Control and Automation (ICCUBEA)*, Pune, India, pp. 1–6, 2023, doi: 10.1109/ICCUBEA58933.2023.10392109.
6. Nikolaou, N., Salazar, D., RaviPrakash, H., Goncalves, M., Mulla, R., Burlutskiy, N., Markuzon, N., Jacob, E., Quantifying the advantage of multimodal data fusion for survival prediction in cancer patients. *bioRxiv*, 2024-01, 2024.
7. Kumar, A., Kumar, S.A., Dutt, V., Dubey, A.K., Narang, S., A Hybrid Secure Cloud Platform Maintenance Based on Improved Attribute-Based Encryption Strategies. *Int. J. Interact. Multimed. Artif. Intell.*, 8, 2, 150, 2023. doi: 10.9781/ijimai.2021.11.004.
8. Punugoti, R., Dutt, V., Anand, A., Bhati, N., Exploring the Impact of Edge Intelligence and IoT on Healthcare: A Comprehensive Survey, in: *2023 International Conference on Sustainable Computing and Smart Systems (ICSCSS)*, Coimbatore, India, pp. 1108–1114, 2023, doi: 10.1109/ICSCSS57650.2023.10169733.
9. Bhati, N., Duggar, R., Alzahrani, A., Exploring few-shot learning approaches for bioinformatics advancements, in: *Applying Machine Learning Techniques to Bioinformatics*, pp. 303–316, IGI Global, 2024.
10. Dalal, S., Lilhore, U.K., Manoharan, P., Rani, U., Dahan, F., Hajjej, F., Keshta, I., Sharma, A., Simaiya, S., Raahemifar, K., An Efficient Brain Tumor Segmentation Method Based on Adaptive Moving Self-Organizing Map and Fuzzy K-Mean Clustering. *Sensors*, *23*, 18, 7816, 2023.
11. Kumar, S.A., Kumar, H., Dutt, V., Soni, H., Self-Health Analysis with Two Step Histogram based Procedure using Machine Learning, in: *2021 Third International Conference on Intelligent Communication Technologies and Virtual Mobile Networks (ICICV)*, Tirunelveli, India, pp. 794–799, 2021, doi: 10.1109/ICICV50876.2021.9388427.
12. Tang, X., Zhang, J., He, Y., Zhang, X., Lin, Z., Partarrieu, S., Hanna, E.B., Ren, Z., Shen, H., Yang, Y., Wang, X., Explainable multi-task learning for multi-modality biological data analysis. *Nat. Commun.*, *14*, 1, 2546, 2023.
13. Xie, W., Fang, Y., Yang, G., Yu, K., Li, W., Transformer-Based Multi-Modal Data Fusion Method for COPD Classification and Physiological and Biochemical Indicators Identification. *Biomolecules*, *13*, 9, 1391, 2023.
14. Srinivas, I.V., Alzubaidi, L.H., Singh, R., Sundaram, N.K., Nirmala, D., Disease Prediction Models Using Machine Learning Algorithms, in: *2023 3rd International Conference on Technological Advancements in Computational Sciences (ICTACS)*, IEEE, pp. 802–810, 2023, November.
15. Kumar, A., Sharma, N.K., Reshmi, B., Saini, R., Thanganadar, H., Singhal, A., Rao, P.V., A Novel Deep Learning Approach for Retinopathy Prediction Using Multimodal Data Fusion. *Int. J. Intell. Syst. Appl. Eng.*, *12*, 11s, 70–77, 2024.

16. Burugadda, V.R., Mane, P.M., Kumar, A., Bhati, N., A Machine Learning-Based Algorithm for Early Detection of Sepsis in Hospitalized Patients: Development and Evaluation, in: *2023 1st International Conference on Circuits, Power and Intelligent Systems (CCPIS)*, Bhubaneswar, India, pp. 1–6, 2023, doi: 10.1109/CCPIS59145.2023.10291447.
17. Sasubilli, S.M., Kumar, A., Dutt, V., Improving Health Care by Help of Internet of Things and Bigdata Analytics and Cloud Computing, in: *2020 International Conference on Advances in Computing and Communication Engineering (ICACCE)*, Las Vegas, NV, USA, pp. 1–4, 2020, doi: 10.1109/ICACCE49060.2020.9155042.
18. Li, J., Han, X., Qin, Y., Tan, F., Chen, Y., Wang, Z., Song, H., Zhou, X., Zhang, Y., Hu, L., Hu, P., Artificial intelligence accelerates multi-modal biomedical process: A survey. *Neurocomputing*, *558*, 126720, 2023.
19. D'Souza, N.S., Wang, H., Giovannini, A., Foncubierta-Rodriguez, A., Beck, K.L., Boyko, O., Syeda-Mahmood, T.F., Fusing modalities by multiplexed graph neural networks for outcome prediction from medical data and beyond. *Med. Image Anal.*, *93*, 103064, 2024.
20. Stahlschmidt, S.R., Ulfenborg, B., Synnergren, J., Multimodal deep learning for biomedical data fusion: a review. *Briefings Bioinf.*, *23*, 2, bbab569, 2022.
21. Swarna, S.R., Kumar, A., Dixit, P., Sairam, T.V.M., Parkinson's Disease Prediction using Adaptive Quantum Computing, in: *2021 Third International Conference on Intelligent Communication Technologies and Virtual Mobile Networks (ICICV)*, Tirunelveli, India, pp. 1396–1401, 2021, doi: 10.1109/ICICV50876.2021.9388628.
22. Holzinger, A., Malle, B., Saranti, A., Pfeifer, B., Towards multi-modal causability with graph neural networks enabling information fusion for explainable AI. *Inf. Fusion*, *71*, 28–37, 2021.
23. Rahaman, M.A., Chen, J., Fu, Z., Lewis, N., Iraji, A., Calhoun, V.D., Multimodal deep learning of functional and structural neuroimaging and genomic data to predict mental illness, in: *2021 43rd Annual International Conference of the IEEE Engineering in Medicine & Biology Society (EMBC)*, IEEE, pp. 3267–3272, 2021, November.
24. M'Sabah, C.E.L., Bouziane, A., Ferdi, Y., A survey on deep learning methods for cancer diagnosis using multimodal data fusion, in: *2021 International Conference on E-health and Bioengineering (EHB)*, IEEE, pp. 1–4, 2021, November.
25. Wen, H., Ding, J., Jin, W., Wang, Y., Xie, Y., Tang, J., Graph neural networks for multimodal single-cell data integration, in: *Proceedings of the 28th ACM SIGKDD Conference on Knowledge Discovery and Data Mining*, pp. 4153–4163, 2022, August.
26. D'Souza, N.S., Wang, H., Giovannini, A., Foncubierta-Rodriguez, A., Beck, K.L., Boyko, O., Syeda-Mahmood, T., MaxCorrMGNN: A Multi-graph Neural Network Framework for Generalized Multimodal Fusion of Medical Data for Outcome Prediction, in: *Workshop on Machine Learning*

for Multimodal Healthcare Data, Springer Nature Switzerland, Cham, pp. 141–154, 2023, July.

27. Zhang, Y., Zhang, H., Xiao, L., Bai, Y., Calhoun, V.D., Wang, Y.P., Multimodal imaging genetics data fusion via a hypergraph-based manifold regularization: Application to schizophrenia study. *IEEE Trans. Med. Imaging*, *41*, 9, 2263–2272, 2022.
28. Vahabi, N. and Michailidis, G., Unsupervised multi-omics data integration methods: a comprehensive review. *Front. Genet.*, *13*, 854752, 2022.
29. Punugoti, R., Dutt, V., Kumar, A., Bhati, N., Boosting the Accuracy of Cardiovascular Disease Prediction Through SMOTE, in: *2023 International Conference on IoT, Communication and Automation Technology (ICICAT)*, Gorakhpur, India, pp. 1–6, 2023, doi: 10.1109/ICICAT57735.2023.10263703.
30. Yang, K., *Machine Learning Approaches to Multi-Modal Data Integration and Translation in Single-Cell Biology*, Massachusetts Institute of Technology, 2022, Doctoral dissertation.
31. Yuan, H. and Xu, H., Deep multi-modal fusion network with gated unit for breast cancer survival prediction, in: *Computer Methods in Biomechanics and Biomedical Engineering*, pp. 1–14, 2023.
32. Hemker, K., Simidjievski, N., Jamnik, M., Hybrid Early Fusion for Multi-Modal Biomedical Representations, in: *UniReps: the First Workshop on Unifying Representations in Neural Models*, 2023, December.
33. Mylavarapu, R.T., Pokhriyal, A., Dhargalkar, R.R., Bhati, N., Empowering Healthcare with AI: Addressing Challenges and Envisioning the Future, in: *2023 4th International Conference on Electronics and Sustainable Communication Systems (ICESC)*, Coimbatore, India, pp. 1393–1398, 2023, doi: 10.1109/ICESC57686.2023.10193228.
34. Ryan, B., Marioni, R.E., Simpson, T.I., Multi-Omic Graph Diagnosis (MOGDx): A data integration tool to perform classification tasks for heterogeneous diseases. *medRxiv*, 2023. doi: https://doi.org/10.1101/2023.07.09.23 292410.

8

Machine Learning Approaches for Integrating Imaging and Molecular Data in Bioinformatics

Mandeep Kaur[1], Dankan Gowda V.[2*], Priya. S.[3], K.D.V. Prasad[4] and Venkatesan Hariram[5]

[1]*Department of Electronics and Communication Engineering, Punjabi University, Patiala, Punjab, India*
[2]*Department of Electronics and Communication Engineering, BMS Institute of Technology and Management, Bangalore, Karnataka, India*
[3]*Department of Computer Science and Engineering, Coimbatore Institute of Technology, Coimbatore, Tamil Nadu, India*
[4]*Symbiosis Institute of Business Management, Hyderabad and Symbiosis International (Deemed University), Pune, India*
[5]*Department of Practice of Medicine, Vinayaka Mission's Homoeopathic Medical College and Hospital, A Constituent College of Vinayaka Mission's Research Foundation Deemed to be University, Salem, Tamil Nadu, India*

Abstract
The bioinformatics field is getting more and more complex because there are lots of biological data types being integrated. This means that not only do we have a problem in integrating the data but we are also given an opportunity to understand and solve problems concerning biological systems. Of note is the ability of ML to assist undertaking imaging and molecular analyses. This fusion might mean a whole new domain in disease diagnosis, prognosis, and study of pathological processes. This chapter explores the different machine-learning methods which support a proper identification of associations between imaging and molecular data to inspire and advance the bioinformatics field including the development, problems and solutions involved. We introduce base-level ML concepts, fused methods, and sophisticated AI methods, including deep learning, to create the bridge

**Corresponding author*: dankan.v@bmsit.in

Umesh Kumar Lilhore, Abhishek Kumar, Narayan Vyas, Sarita Simaiya and Vishal Dutt (eds.) Multimodal Data Fusion for Bioinformatics Artificial Intelligence, (147–178) © 2025 Scrivener Publishing LLC

between mechanical and symbolic syntaxes. The chapter goes on to deal with the practical implementations that include diagnostics, prognostics, drug discoveries and demonstration of how integrated data analysis helps transform many things. We also discuss present difficulties and envisage future orientations of research in this field of the connection of imaging, machine learning, and molecular biology. The analysis of strategies and case studies in this chapter aims at providing practitioners and researchers with the most updated information on the avenue of this field and possibly ignite further improvement.

Keywords: Bioinformatics, machine learning, data integration, imaging data, molecular data, deep learning, multimodal fusion, disease diagnosis

8.1 Introduction

Imaging combined with molecular sequencing stands at the forefront of bioinformatics. It draws the synergy between different data types to explore more effective approaches to a better understanding of biological issues. The picture data compose and a wide range of modalities—magnetic resonance imaging (MRI), computed tomography (CT) scans, and microscopy pictures—provide rather spatial and architectural information of trabecula and organs. Molecular datas, such as genomic, transcriptomic, and proteomic, describe the occurrence in a cell or some other cellular organelles at a molecular level [1], exposing biological processes at the atomic or molecular level. A diverse range of omics data types coming together and being analysed through highly refined methods offer possibilities for better understanding of disease processes, higher accuracy in diagnosis, and more customized therapy per individual patient. These links are vital especially nowadays when the aim is to create personalized medicine by having each one personalized, whereby all the medical decisions will be taken personally to the individual patient based on their detailed reports.

Importance of Integrating Imaging and Molecular Data in Bioinformatics

The encompassing of images' and molecular data into a single data set constitutes a feature that is seen as a vital opportunity in bioinformatics for many different reasons. First of all, it permits a complete insight into diseases by connecting the visible phenotypic extremities shown on the image with the molecular or genetics disturbances that lay down the root of a disease. Take, for example advanced cancer research, where integration of various data types [2, 3], may identify the molecular marker that can predict the progression and expected treatment response of a certain tumour.

Besides, this integration provides an endowing context for the generation of more accurate models of diagnostics and prognostics that integrate the obtained data on a spatial scale by combining the molecular information with the detail of the imaging data. The introduction of these devices is an accurate way of diagnosis earlier and has shown more reliable prognosis, which could guide in timely and appropriate treatments. Also, the integration of the two types of data described above can advance the field of systems biology by simulations of the systems of endogenous complex biology [4], revealing the disease pathways and mechanisms with greater scale and depth than before.

Brief Overview of Machine Learning (ML) in Bioinformatics

The application of machine learning, an area of artificial intelligence, makes bioinformatics complete by being used to visualize, analyse, and make deductions and predictions from complex biological information which is received. Using the algorithms of ML, we can discover the patterns and connections storing in a big-data dataset that otherwise is beyond reach of the independent human mind [5, 6]. Bioinformatics algorithms work in the framework of supervised learning for model identifying, such as gene-based or other features for diseases prediction. Also, they are involved in building predicting systems which give the clinical data information on patient outcome. But the second category refers to the unsupervised learning, that is the eternal pursuit to detect the latent structures embedded into data, such as clustering genes with a similar expression pattern [7]. Quite recently, DL, a more sophisticated corner of ML, has proven quite efficient in reading high-throughput genetic sequences, predicting the structure of proteins and analysing medical images thanks to its competency of learning sequential data representations.

Figure 8.1 is an infographic that depicts different machine learning paradigms types. In a very central and visible position the red rectangle, "Types of Machine Learning" appears, signalling that the diagram's focus is on classifying different learning strategies within the field [8, 9]. Central to this model will be the arrow cutting through five elliptical or oval shapes which represent the five different machine learning learning methodologies. At the top, two ovals, one yellow and another green, portray the supervised and the unsupervised, respectively [10, 11]. These are two key learning algorithm methods of machine learning: supervised learning learns from the data that is labelled and unsupervised learning finds hidden patterns or intrinsic structures in unlabelled data. On the right, the green oval is connected to reinforcement learning, also in green, that means the kind of learning where the agent makes decisions based on rewards or punishment

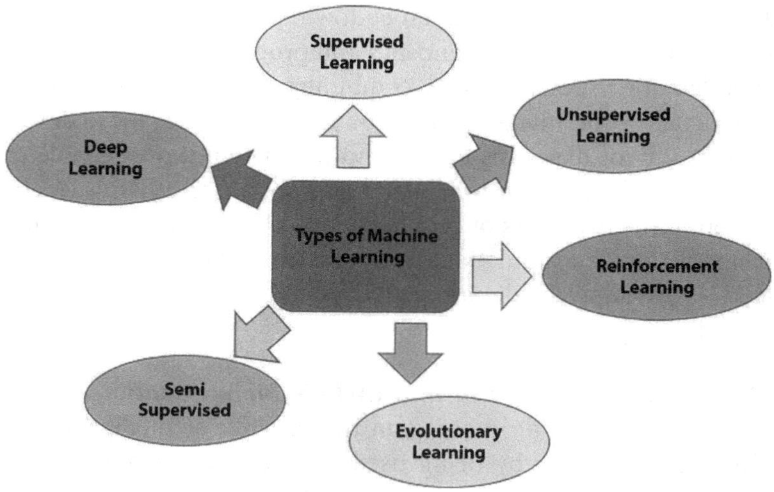

Figure 8.1 Overview of learning methodologies.

for its actions. In the bottom left corner is a brown oval representing deep learning, which is a method of machine learning featuring neural networks with many layers and the ability to learn from large and complex sets of data. Right next to it, a light blue arrow directs toward semi-supervised learning, which is shown in grey. It combines both supervised and unsupervised methods, using a small amount of labelled data as well as a large amount of unlabelled data. The grey arrow at the lower part of the diagram moves downwards to an oval that represents evolutionary learning in a lighter shade of grey. Here, natural selection is mimicked by algorithms known as genetic algorithms where a population of solutions evolves to adapt better to a specific problem over several generations.

Figure 8.2 provides the basic structure of the brain in the highlighted labels' arrangement. It shows those main parts of the brain and the functions they associate with. The frontal lobe lies in the upper part of the diagram and is best known for its role in executive functions, decision-making, and working voluntary movements. The lobe temporal labelled here in the side brain is responsible for processing auditory information and is crucial to memory and emotions, as well as its importance. Approximately one inch below, the cerebellum is seen, a structure that aids in the regulation of voluntary movements, such as balance, coordination, and speech. Visual cortex, in the occipital lobe of the brain, behind its visual aspects lies the main area of interpretation of the visual information [12, 13]. This image additionally refers to the auditory cortex responsible for the processing

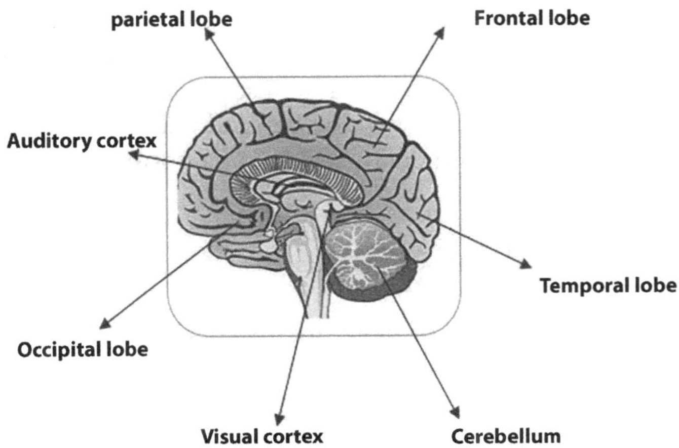

Figure 8.2 Main anatomical features of the human brain.

sounds information. Tom top and the parietal lobe is denoted, which is described processor sensory information arising from different forms of the body, space orientation and language and mathematics management. The parts of the brain are easily understandable and are clearly labelled in each slideshow, and the arrows always point to the actual locations on the sagittal section of the brain explaining the functions of the human brain.

Challenges and Opportunities in Integrating Heterogeneous Data Types

Along with opportunity of integration of imaging and molecular data, the associated bioinformatics generates not a few difficulties. The first feature of the data is that it has natural heterogeneity. The imaging data collection will be three-dimensional, and the molecular data will also be two-dimensional. This is because it is time [14, 15]. This implies the creation of new ML (machine learning) techniques scalable enough to address such multimedia type of data. However, magnitude of the data is also an issue since medical and molecular images are full of data and have complex structure and therefore, they require different approaches to processing. The issues of data privacy and sharing surely constitute another significant barrier while dealing with these data that are from different sources.

Regardless of the obstacles, the harmonization of molecular and image data has already shown a critical contribution to the field. It possibly may announce the emergence of more accurate and custom-made diagnostic and prognostic models helping physicians to develop patients' therapy on the basis of specificity of their diseases and biological peculiarities considering. Since this metabolization process allows for scavenging of novel biomarkers and targets hence [16], biomedical approach towards precision medicine and drug development is nourished. In addition, the combination of these types of data forge an interdisciplinary interaction among computer scientists, biologists and doctors, and help in generating ideas that bring more knowledge about the field of bioinformatics.

8.2 Background and Motivation

The development trajectory of bioinformatics has been highly dynamic ever since it began, thanks to technological growth and unprecedented growth of biological data. First, bioinformatics was narrowed down to DNA management and analysis and then gained a broader meaning that includes different datasets, such as complex molecular and imaging data [17]. This evolution highlights a progression from sequence analysis of primitive form to the coalescence of biological complexity through integrating different kinds of information on the molecular level.

Historically, bioinformatics attempts were sequestered and many researchers were engaged in the same domains. The data integration at the early stage was mostly human-powered, and it was done through the tedious review of literature, which connected the genotypic information with phenotypic observations. Meanwhile, the creation of searchable databases and algorithmic ways to analyse data were of paramount importance in the process of obtaining information. Nowadays, integrated databases, NCBI's Entrez and EMBL-EBI's Ensemble, are the critical tools for the cross-linking of genetic [18, 19], proteomic, and phenotypic data. Correspondingly, computational algorithms have evolved for analysing and interpreting intertwined datasets; therefore, a full understanding of biological processes seems to be possible.

Imaging data, which offers an added dimension of visual information with regard to biological structures and processes, is of vital importance for this integrated vision. Ranging from microscopic images of cells to whole-body examinations as in the case of MRI and CT scans, imaging data visualizes macroscopic aspects of biological phenomena, thus giving information about the structure and function of living bodies. Its outstanding contribution in the disease diagnosing, treatment monitoring and structural biology investigations is unequalled.

Figure 8.3 visualizes image processing as a sequence of actions making up a flowchart—the most typical case of digital image processing. Firstly, exiting stage is Image Acquisition, where the image is taken and then digitized. Then, the image gives the Image Enhancement process which is for

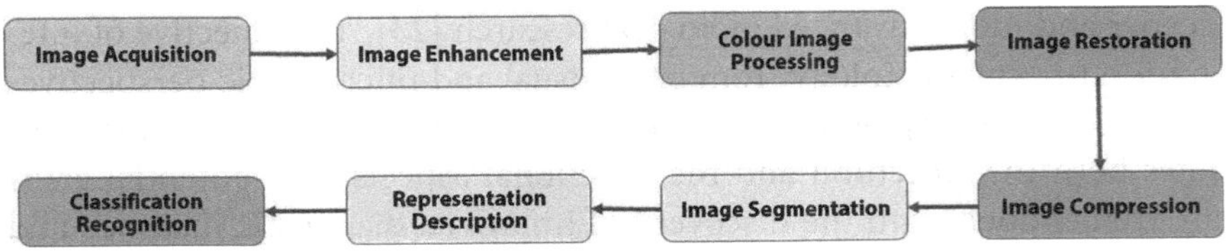

Figure 8.3 Sequential steps in image processing.

improving the visual appearance of the image or converting the image to a form well suited for further analysis [20]. After highlighting the enhancement, Colour Image Processing is indicated, pointing to the particular set of techniques used to deal with the complications that arise with colour images, such as self-calibration and colour space conversion. Image Restoration is discussed after the colour processing, and the removal of degradation from images, noise removal or deblurring, to restore the original impression on the images is the main theme. This is the branching point where our flow chart forks into two separate yet parallel processes. Feature extraction is the process that the upper path employs, Representation/Description, to capture the content and shapes of the image. Sometimes it is used as a precursor for the final stage, Classification/Recognition, in this branch, where the image or features in the image are identified and classified in predefined classes. On the other path, Image Segmentation is illustrated; this step is an important one where the image is divided up into a number of segments or regions oftentimes based on features, e.g., colour and texture [21, 22]. Usually the process implies extracting or selecting specific components from the image like things or the boundaries. Image Compression is the last stage, which encodes the image to make the file size saleable for storing or transmitting it so as to ensure the balance between the data amount required to represent the image and the quality.

At the same time, molecular data genomic, proteomic, transcriptomic, and metabolic by means of an independent microscopic perspective of biological world. Genomic data contributes to the knowledge of the genetic constitution of cells, making it possible to deal with genetic differences and diseases that individuals may be predisposed to, in addition to having an effect on evolutionary biology. Extending this analysis to the protein level through proteomics and the RNA level through transcriptomics allows the unravelling of the functional consequences of genetic information, as well as challenges the dynamic features of biological regulation.

The blending of imaging and molecular data is the current bioinformatics trend which not only leads to precision medicine but also promises deeper and more advanced biological research [23]. The objective of integration to explain biology from both visual and microscopic perspectives is to bridge the gap as well as providing an overall picture that incorporates both the structural and the functional aspects. The potential gains are tremendous, with the discovery of improved diagnostic methods and the possibility of developing personalized therapeutic approaches that are tailored to the patient's specific needs, to name a few. Furthermore, this breakthrough research may lead to groundbreaking developments of complex biological systems and disease mechanisms' understanding.

Moreover, the way to any successful integration will never be a smooth road, meeting obstacles such as the variety of data formats, the high computational requirements of data processing, and the need for advanced algorithms for data with modalities [24]. These impediments notwithstanding, there is a huge discovering avenue for the advancement of knowledge and the improvement of human health. Given that bioinformatics is a fast-growing field and is continuously changing, I am convinced that in the days to come, the connection of imaging and molecular data will have utmost significance for the advancement of the biological sciences and medicine.

8.3 Machine Learning Basics

In bioinformatics, machine learning (ML) now occupies a central position, having redesigned how biological data is handled and recognised. The ML (machine learning) approach, at the very core, mobilizes algorithms to draw experiences with data and make choices from it according to the desired outcomes. This process is typically categorized into three main types of learning: without supervision, with supervision, and reward learning.

Supervised machine learning which is also known as the most spread type of machine learning is the most applicable form of machine learning, especially in bioinformatics applications. It is a training tool of producing algorithms that has two parts [25]. One part is a labelled dataset with the correct output known and the other part is to produce the algorithm. It is aimed at finding a function responding to given mapping requests, such as determining output values for unknown data. Among the popular supervised learning algorithms you will find logistic regression, linear regression, support vector machines (SVM), and deep networks. Bioinformatic is a field that makes it possible to solve different tasks using supervised learning [26]. For example, this can be a disease classification based on genetic information, prediction of protein structures, and finding drug targets.

Unsupervised learning is another learning mode, which is not devoted to data that is not labelled. The aim in is to observe unidentified trends like built-in structures from the data. The two primary approaches in unsupervised learning, which are also known as clustering and dimensionality reduction, are K-means clustering and principal component analysis (PCA). These models are very popular. The reason why unsupervised learning is essential in bioinformatics for the purposes of studying processes of gene expression, detecting gene clusters by having the same expression patterns, and analysis of patient data that helps to identify the subtypes of diseases without pre-established categories is that it frees researchers to take advantage of the great possibilities available in data comparison and clustering techniques.

Reinforcement learning is the second kind of learning. It allows an agent to communicate the actions via the setting of some goals and this is quite difficult to collect. Through this learning mechanism, the agent develops competence by capitalizing on the lessons got from the outcomes of the actions, using the cues of the rewards or the punishments [27]. Reinforcement learning is much less commonly used compared to the other two types of machine learning in bioinformatics; however, it has certain areas it can apply in, which is optimising parameters for biological experiments for example, or in silico modelling of biological processes.

Challenges in Bioinformatics Data: The use of ML by biologists also has numerous issues though. Data used in the area of bioinformatics are often high-dimensional, as they contain many features as compared to the number of samples. Knowing how data from different regions will differ, the model can be created as the model learns noise in the training data rather than the actual signal, so that it cannot be generalized to other data [28]. Techniques like feature selection, regularization, and dimensionality reduction are the options generally employed to fight against the curse of dimensionality.

The other major difficulty is the diversity of bioinformatics data that can be presented in different formats and levels, such as genomics and proteins as structures and images on a cellular scale. One of the major research challenges is that the integration of various data types, be they from sensor networks, social media or visual observations, into a comprehensive analysis framework generally requires complicated pre-processing and normalization procedures, as well as algorithms that are capable of processing multisensory information in a joint manner.

Common ML Algorithms in Bioinformatics: From vast algorithms to confined ones, only some of these algorithms enjoy wide use and prove very effective in bioinformatics. Decision Trees and Random Forests are commonly chosen for their abilities to automatically justify themselves, which is very important for non-technical audience (low skill level) and robustness for classification and regression tasks, such as predicting disease susceptibility based on genetic variants. SVMs are quite effective for classification problems, particularly when the dimension is high, and consequently they are suited to analyze gene expression or protein classification. Neural Networks as a type of the data processing where Deep Learning models, such as Convolutional Neural Networks (CNNs) and Recurrent Neural Networks (RNNs) have become the main force in biomedical research field, engaging into sequence analysis and structure modeling as well as biomedical image analysis.

Finally, we conclude that machine learning in bioinformatics gives the most resolute devices to decode enigmas in complicated biological data. Concurrently, there are persistent impediments, but the improvements of machine learning algorithms and the computational techniques are the door openers to what can be achieved in bioinformatics by giving scientists the necessary tools to obtain more conclusive and accurate results which equip them in discovering life at a molecular level and improving their prediction abilities.

8.4 Approaches for Data Integration

The heterogenous data type integration, imaging and molecular data in bioinformatics of today is one of the hardest problems requiring the invention of advanced strategies and techniques. The purpose of data fusion is to exploit the augmentative information available from the myriad sources of data in order to get a more holistic grasp of the intricate biologic processes. Data integration can be essentially categorized into first, middle and terminal integration methods; this brings out the effective approaches and methods of implementation. The first step is Brokadnanie (Blend of Data) and repurposes particular data types coupled at the data level, without any analytics. Considering the approach where information integration is perceiving as golden fusion operation, features from different datastores are concatenated to make a single and combined dataset. The suggested benefit of pre-integration is that it possibly allows the direct implementation of classical machine learning algorithms to the melted dataset, thus, a chance of acquiring feature relationships from different sources. Nonetheless, the data must be available beforehand for all of them to be submitted into the same data type which is very bottlenecking in cases of data types that are essentially different or if there are missing or incomplete data sources.

This (Feature-Level Integration) represents Intermediate-Level Integration in that it involves features extraction and integration. The method extract features separately from each data form with the help of appropriate techniques then combines the set of extracted features to train the model. Each data type would be followed by a slightly different extraction method which would be more specialized to the data type. Those approaches are likely to produce better features which may enhance the way the machine learning models work. Intermediate-level correlation is particularly helpful when it comes to processing data formats that require feature extraction or pre-processing techniques such as imaging and sequences.

Figure 8.4 shows a detailed structure of pre-processing strategies that are conventionally employed during brain MRI scans before subsequent

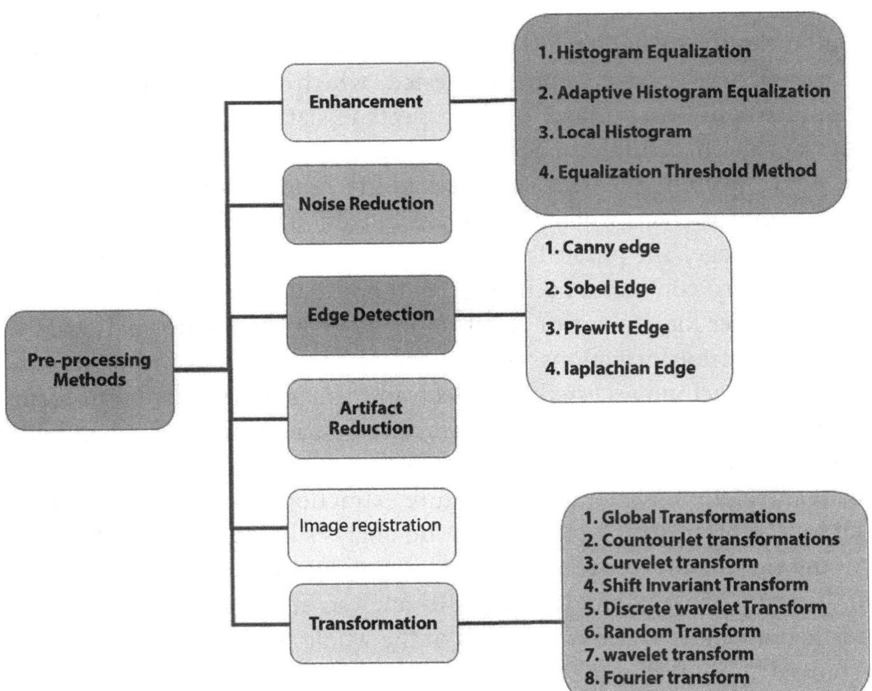

Figure 8.4 Pre-processing strategies for brain MRI scans.

study or diagnosis. The diagram shows the pre-processing of data and it is categorized into clear and relevant methods with more details on the specific techniques for each method. It commences with Pre-processing Methods, which is marked as a burnt orange rectangle on the flowchart that connects and paves the way for the following activities. From there, the work flow diverges into five main pre-processing methods, each inscribed as a rectangle and linked by a vertical line in the central area to symbolize a sequence or interdependence. The Enhancement, captured in yellow, includes scene elements that can be applied to provide better image quality and contrast. Consequently, these tools employ such techniques as Histogram Equalization, Adaptive Histogram Equalization, Local Histogram, and Equalization Threshold Method, all aimed at improving the scans' clarity and visibility. Also, Noise Reduction, written inside a light green rectangle, is included; it is the function which eliminates the noise or random fluctuations from the pictures. This is a vital step and is a necessity for ensuring that the accuracy of the subsequent analyses would be at a high level. Strategy number 3 is portrayed in a blue rectangular box, Edge Detection, which is very important and is needed for differentiating anatomical structures through MRI image by identifying the edges and contours of the image. Techniques such as Canny edge, Sobel edge, Prewitt edge, and Laplacian edge are suggested, which covers all the common approaches to bringing out useful aspects in data. After RGB space and edge detection, Artifact Reduction is displayed in a shade of tan, the red rectangle meaning the next step is a set of techniques for getting rid of or minimizing artefacts which may be attributed to the process of generating the MRI image. The phase Transformation, as the last stage and placed in the beige box, contains a number of methods that can change an image to make it easier for analysis or registration. The Global transformations, the Contourlet Transformations, and the Discrete wavelet transformations are a few of the techniques listed: curvelet transform, shift invariant transform, random transform, wavelet transform, and Fourier transform. Their wide usage is specifically for the image pre-processing to prepare the data, e.g., for segmentation, registration or feature extraction tasks, which are essential for the brain structure and function analysis based on the MRI scans. All the varying pre-processing procedures along with techniques involved in the setup phase of an extensive MRI analysis are important to the diagnostic outcome and the correctness of the whole process. So, the diagram arranged these techniques in an associated structure, which is a helpful guide for building up information out of a complicated MRI data in a thorough and thoughtful way.

Towards the end sprint (Decision-Level Integration), separate models are trained to make predictions on every data type, whose results are combined to produce the final decision. This might be a simple approach by using voting, averaging, or more complex approaches like meta-learning, etc. Late integration gives us a chance to explore different possibilities. We could choose each model optimized without constraints, for corresponding data type. Nevertheless, the methods of this type cannot make interactions between different data sets as well as recent or mid-stage integration can.

Acquisition of Multimodal Information is a critical strand for the integration of imaging and molecular data. These methods are intended to unify the differences among data categories, and appropriately select and use different data sources. A rapid development of technologies, including intelligent deep learning-oriented fusion models, has demonstrated outstanding results in the wide-scale data integration allowing for flexible and powerful multimodal data analysis and exploitation.

Feature-Level vs. Instructional-Level Integration is the most decisive point in having the data integration process. Feature-level integration, a technique with the ability to use combined extracted features from different data types as inputs for machine learning methods, might thus exploit interactions between attributes, but also can be burdened with the curse of dimensionality, and practical solutions should be used for feature engineering. The integration at the decision level, on the other hand, allows simple and flexible use of separate models, which were originally developed as independent models for different data fields and may, thus, miss hidden interactions of data fields.

Figure 8.5 illustrates the actualization of several MLT in disease diagnostics. In the upper part of the figure, an enclosed yellow shape named MLT made Diagnoses shows the ultimate category of medical diagnoses that are performed through machine learning algorithms. Through this node central area, five arms emerge toward various oval-shaped clusters, where every one of them signifies a particular disease identified with machine learning technology. The ecologically green oval to the extreme left is Hepatitis. Other techniques following in the retro coated are offered in the orange rectangle under it. The methods that are being used are the Naive Bayes, Naive Bayes Updateable, FT, Kstar, J48, LMT, NN, C4.5, ID3, and CART. This are algorithms and classifiers of decision trees applied to identify patterns in hepatitis patient data that are adaptive. The olive oval label of the next node, Dengue, is connected to the darker orange rectangle node listing: MFNN, DT, ANN, and RSVM as the algorithms used for its diagnosis. These abbreviations stand for the neural network models

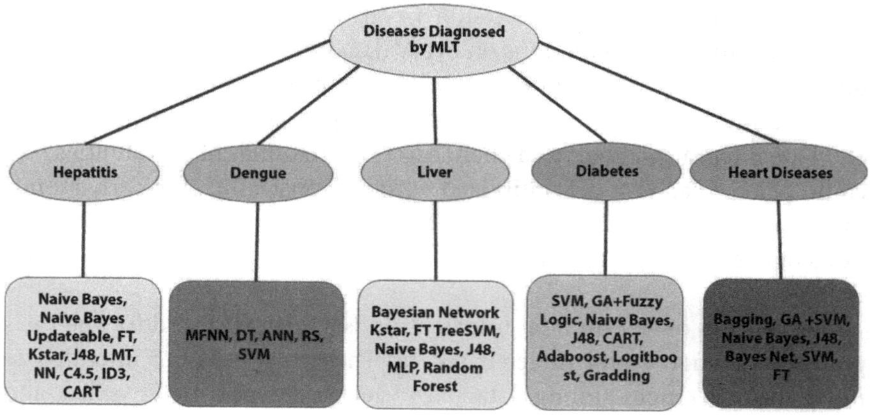

Figure 8.5 Health issues diagnosed with the help of ML techniques.

such as perceptron and the non-linear classification technique known as support vector machine. They are used to model the complex relationships in the data that define the development of the dengue disease. The main entity, Liver disease, is represented by the central orange oval with a brown rectangle attached to it having details about Manifold Learning (ML) techniques like J48, Bayesian Network, F Tw Frame Vector, Naive Bayes, K star and Multilayer Perceptron (MLP). The techniques involve probabilistic modalities, as well as tree-based and ensemble methods for the detection of liver-related diseases. The light blue signlet denotes Diabesity, while the dark blue block beneath it is the technique used for diagnosing diabetes with techniques like SVM, GA+Fuzzy Logic, Naive Bayes, J48, CART, Adaboost, Logitboost, and stGraddia listed in it. The approaches involve evolutionary discipline, fuzzy systems, boosting techniques, and some others whose suitability for the analyses of the numerical and categorical data representative of diabetes symptoms and indicators have been demonstrated. Lastly, Heart Diseases are to the far right, and are visualized by a purple oval with Specific Area, Genetic Autoencoder, Naive Bayes, J48, Bayes Net, SVM and FE as the applied ML algorithms. Such an extensively used group is defined by classification methods such as ensembles, genetic algorithms, and Bayesian networks, that are based on different ways of making diagnosis of cardiovascular problems. Every trade assemblage of techniques is given a disease name with which the diagnostic process relates, and this corresponds to how machine learning is specifically applied to unclear and multi-layered regulatory issues. This diagram uses color codes in depicting the associations between ML techniques and clinical diagnostics helping us visualize the significant role of ML in modern medical diagnosis.

Case Studies: A bioinformatics-data-integration review cannot be considered to be complete without selected examples of implementation with evaluation demonstrating their results. Examples of the cases that appeal are the compilation of genomic and transcriptomic data in order to identify new cancer subtypes, the integration of radiomic and genomic data to improve the prognostic assessment through molecular profiling, or using the multiple mode data integration to assemble the target molecules for the successful application of the drug. These cases can be used, in part, to show to data unification/ maintenance difficulties and the potential of such an approach of working towards development in bioinformatics and custom medical treatment.

Figure 8.6, on a technical note, graphically portrays a comparative assessment of bioinformatics dataset across the leading machine learning algorithms, captured in a closely packed, well-structured bar chart. This visualization methodically segments classifier performance across four pivotal metrics: accuracy, precision, recall, and F1-scores. Each one

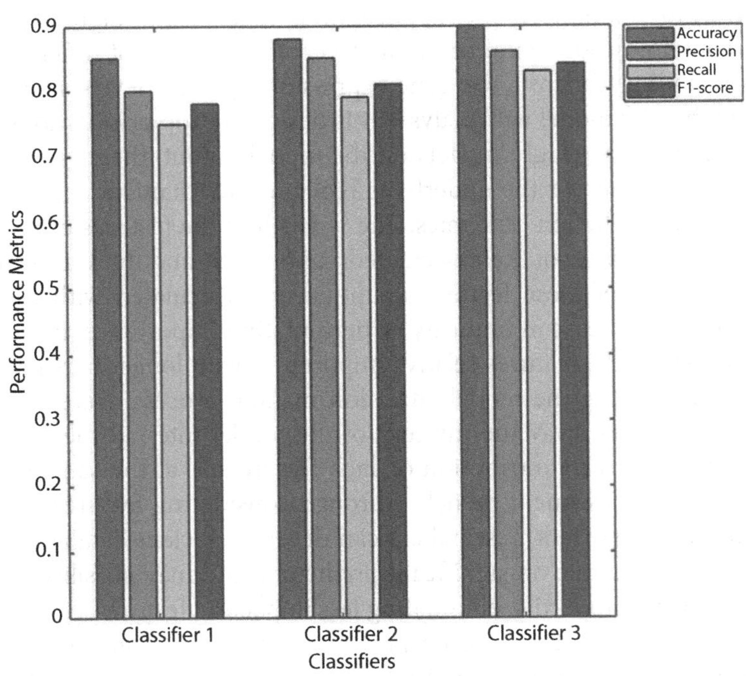

Figure 8.6 Classifier performance on a bioinformatics dataset.

of the metrics provides different view of accuracy of classifiers like SVM, Random Forests, and Neural Networks of effectiveness against biological data. This collective approach helps us to have a broader understanding of prediction capabilities in the context of work of biology. Accuracy, being the main indicator of how well a model performs, determines close to the actual dataset whether it is a positive or a negative outcome; it is calculated by dividing the number of correct predictions to the total number of all data. The proficiency primarily highlights the ratio of TP to TN prediction as a measure of the exactness of the classifier which can be interpreted as failure of the model to identify positive instances in certain cases. On the other hand, the recall takes a look at the skills of the classifier too to identifying positives from the dataset, all of which mitigates false negatives from occurring frequently. The F1-score is the form of the precision-recall trade-off where both ratios will be considered to balance the metric. The figure nicely employs color-coding for bars as well as emphasizes axis labels with bold fonts thereby improving legibility but most importantly, the graph demonstrates the aptness of different models for tribes against definite configurable parameters for computational estimations in biological science research.

A model output for a feature importance derived from a machine learning model for a bioinformatics application is visualized in Figure 8.7. The figure contains a horizontal bar chart to explain the role of different elements including, for instance, gene expressions, protein levels, and other markers that the model will analyse. This design is a top priority to decide which features have high impacts on the model output, thereby allowing researchers to uncover the underlying biological mechanism and its contributions to prediction outcomes. The y-axis lists the features examined, arranged in the order of their calculated importance, and the x-axis shows the importance of these features quantitatively, calculated with metrics such as mean decrease in impurity or permutation importance. Each bar's length indicates the feature's relative importance with longer bars proposing traits impacting the model's decision-making process. Herewith, the visualization takes away the mystery of the model internal mechanisms as it emphasizes the contribution of each feature and at the same time it helps improve subsequent models. Through considering features that are very and less important, researchers can develop efficient data collection processes, concentrate on significant predictors, and may possibly reduce computational complexity, eliminating less impacting features.

Figure 8.8 is a gene expression heatmap, which is a main tool in bioinformatics for displaying complicated datasets, most importantly those with the characteristic of a large-scale gene expression study. This table

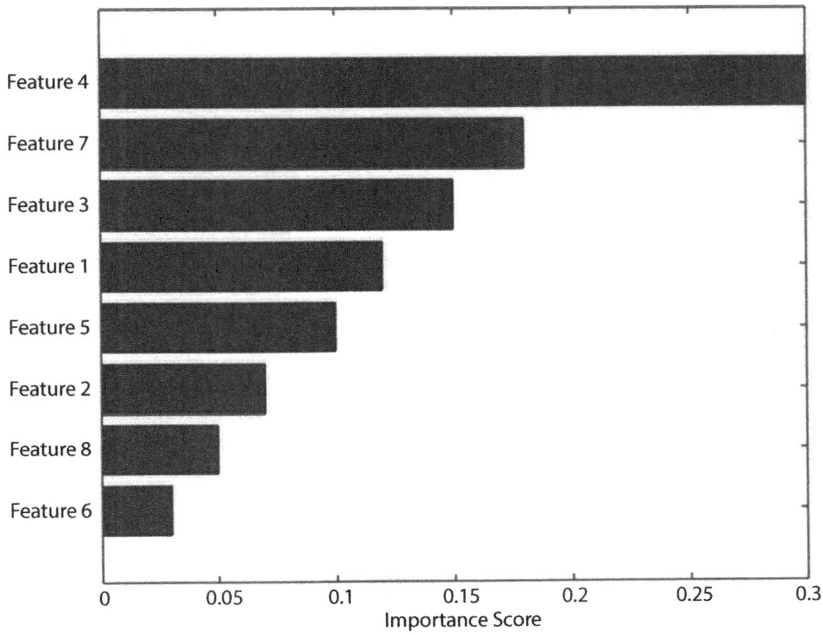

Figure 8.7 Feature importance from a machine learning model.

illustrates the expression levels of many genes across different samples or conditions with a gradient of blue for low expression intensity to dark red for maximum expression levels. The vertical axis shows individual genes. At the same time, the horizontal axis displays different experimental conditions or sample types so to obtain a global view of gene expression across the whole dataset. Colour hue in every cell of the heatmap is proportional to the extent of gene expression; the given colour scale ranging from blue (lower levels of expression) to yellow (medium levels) to red (higher levels) gives an immediate sense of clusters of gene expression or the sense of trends. Such clustering patterns might reveal genes that are co-expressed in the same conditions indicating a chance of co-regulation or, otherwise, the involvement in the same biological processes. In addition, the secondary heatmap of Figure 8.8 includes hierarchical clustering dendrograms. These dendrograms were obtained as a result of the cluster analysis, which associates genes with similar expression profiles each other, thus reflecting the structure of data and assisting in finding biologically relevant groupings. The addition of these data trees introduces an element of explanatory or guiding value for the researchers as they muse about gene functioning, regulatory activities, or the effect of specific conditions on gene activity.

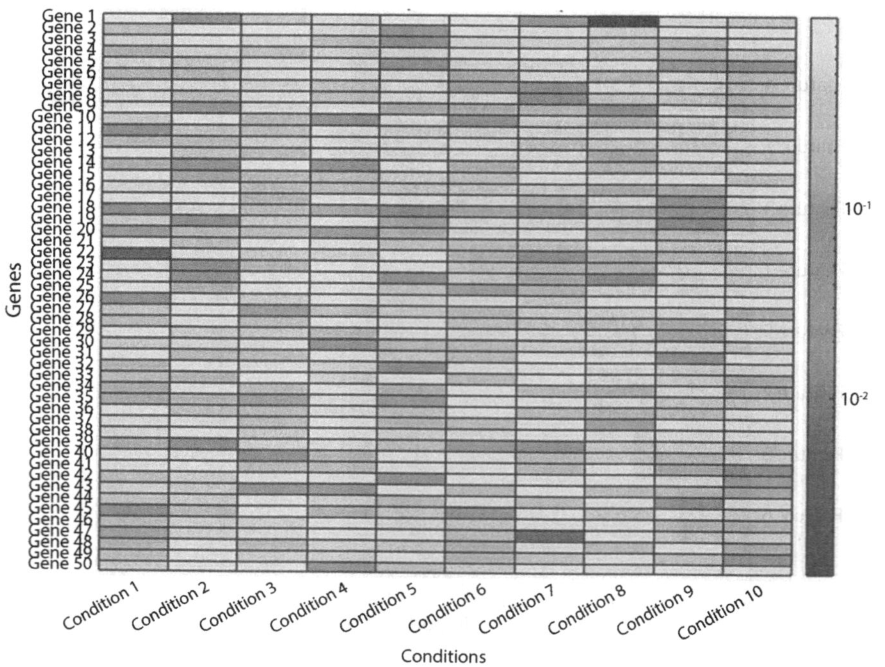

Figure 8.8 Gene expression heatmap.

Finally, the figure usually contains a legend next to it which describes what the color scale includes; as a result, the viewer can measure the degree of different colors according to the gene expression levels. Another possible thing that may occur is annotations or extra markers which provide the information about the interesting genes, genetic paths, etc. This helps to give a closer look into the essential parts of the data.

Figure 8.9 impeccably features a PCA (Principal Component Analysis) biplot, an analytical technique that reduces the dimensionality and reveals the contributions of some multivariate data types commonly dominating bioinformatic applications. The figure here comes handy to present high-dimensional data on a two-dimensional plane while keeping all sorts of variance intact. Therefore, it is easier to interpret and obtain a clear view of the structure of the dataset. The PCA biplot achieves this by facilitating the visualization of the first two principal components that are the eigenvectors with the highest associated eigenvalues among all the eigenvectors. Each point on the biplot equals a sample with scores for these principal components arranged so that the principle of similarities and differences among them becomes evident. The position of points fairly close to each

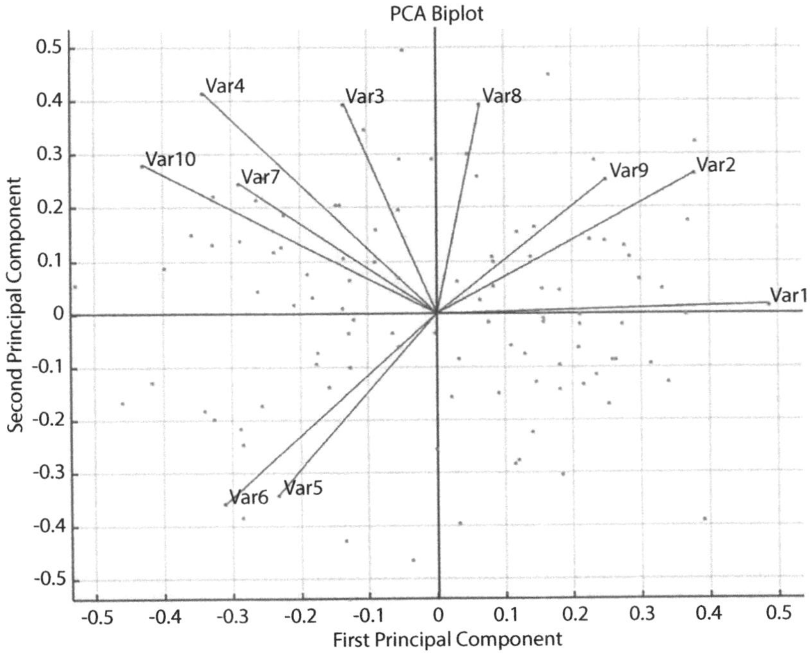

Figure 8.9 PCA biplot for dimensionality reduction.

other and to every axis is advantageous for observation of the intrinsic structure of the dataset in terms of clustering and expression profile similarity, which, in its turn, may point to outliers and clusters of samples with shared patterns of expression. Again, the start of the feature vector is represented by arrows emanating from the origin of the biplot. These arrows depict the original features (such as genes among many others) which influence the dataset, with their direction and angles showing how each feature affects the principal components. The magnitude of these vectors indicates the value of feature importance, and the angle between vectors allows measuring consonance. In this lattice, it is possible to identify the influential variables which drive the deviation captured by the main elements of variation and to close the gap between data reduction and interpretability.

Figure 8.10 depicts Kaplan-Meier curves as a main statistical tool in the survival analysis, very much applicable in the field of bioinformatics and medical science because these types of curves estimate and visualize survival probabilities over time. This figure is a generalized plot of the survival probability (percent) of a cohort(s), so during the duration of a study, the time (increments) is shown on the x-axis and the percentage of

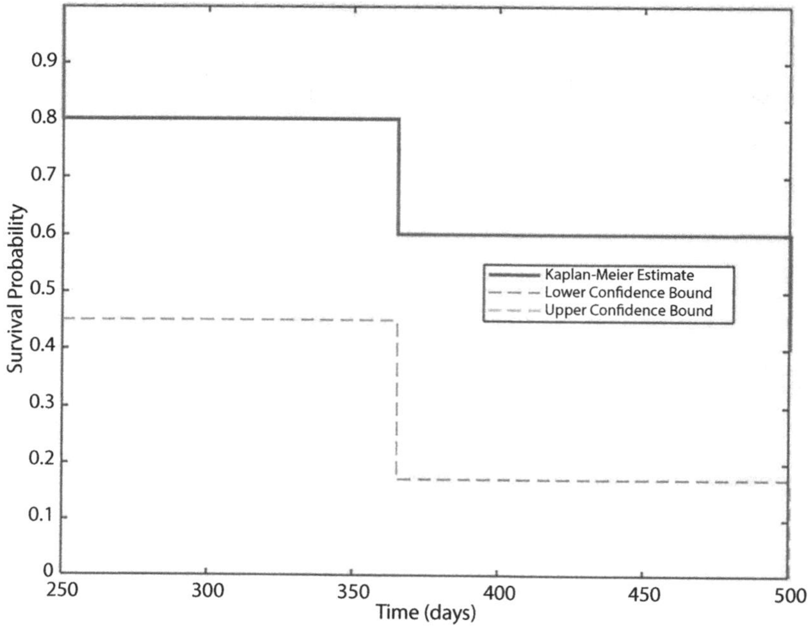

Figure 8.10 Survival analysis using Kaplan-Meier curves.

the population surviving is shown on the y-axis, yielding a visual representation of this particular survival function. Projected to bioandicity, the setting where analysis often expands to explore the effect of genetic alterations, biomarkers, and treatment on an individual or population survival, the Kaplan-Meier curve becomes a vital tool. It makes comparison of overall survival time of different groups possible—for example, patients with various treatment backgrounds or different genetic phenotypes. Overall survival times of such groups widely differ and these differences are statistically significant. The Kaplan-Meier curve is typically (or conventionally) a stepwise decline with each downward step representing a happening, mostly death or failure, followed by computation of the survival probability of the patients, hence being progressively lowered. Censored data consisting of people whose end-point information is missing due to the follow-up or study termination ending before the event happened, is also taken care of in the analysis of survival analysis. The process of censoring is manifested by means of small vertical inclined ticks parallel to the curve at the time points at which censoring takes place without affecting the probability of survival; therefore, the survival statistics remain valid.

8.5 Machine Learning Techniques for Imaging and Molecular Data

Deep Learning Models for Image Analysis in Bioinformatics

The development of Convolutional Neural Networks (CNN) brought about a significant change in image analysis in bioinformatics which nowadays can be used as a tool capable of not only extracting but also characterizing the image patterns. Without CNNs there would be no microscopic cellular imaging and whole-slide images in histopathology, which speed up and give a better insight into high-throughput and high-accuracy analysis. They naturally learn, respectively, the aspects that are behaving as the evidence or prediction of the particular physical condition or the results what are surpassing the conventional photo analysing methodologies.

It is GANs that give another unique chance by applying the technology in image generation as well as augmentation. The bioinformatics have adopted GANs in producing fake images for the machine learning model that is used later to enhance a model's effectiveness in cases where data is a constraint. Moreover, GANs have recently been utilized to decrease noise in microscopic images and optimize the image clarity and analysis, which are subsequently very dependable.

Machine Learning Models for Molecular Data Analysis

Support Vector Machines (SVMs) and Random Forests represent classifiers extensively used in omics data analysis where SVMs are widely used to classify disease states based on genetic or proteomic profiles. These models might help to uncover the main markers of biomarkers and genetic features as disease indicators.

Deep Learning in Molecular Data: Because of the aid which they have had from deep learning techniques, particularly with the help of Deep Belief Networks (DBNs) and Recurrent Neural Networks (RNNs), they are no longer only involved in the processing and understanding of the complex relationship in the molecular data. The tools developed stand out in their ability to analyse sequence data, for example, DNA, RNA, and protein sequences, and thus help to predict the sequence function and identify the genetic changes contributing to the diseases.

Techniques for Bridging Imaging and Molecular Data

Imaging and molecular data coming into a multimodal neural network and analysing them is the main goal of the department, and it serves to process multiple modalities data simultaneously. Such would allow for the integration of the composite data either to a particular data type or to a single view of the event under study.

Another useful method is Transfer Learning, which takes place when training a model on data from one domain and then transferring the knowledge gained to another domain. Through the transferring of knowledge that comes through training with one data modality (e.g., imaging) to enhance the research via another data modality (e.g., molecular data), scientists can customize their models and reach more precise predictions.

Evaluation Metrics and Validation Strategies for Integrated Models

Evaluation Metrics: The kind of evaluation metrics that are chosen depends on the jobs at hand. Classification tasks have Accuracy, Precision, Recall, and the F1 score as the metrics that are commonly used, while for the regression task, the mean squared errors (MSE) and coefficient of determination (R^2) prototypes are the most commonly used indicators. For models that combine the assessments of imaging and molecular data, we need to select metrics that can comprehensively display the model's accuracy for both data types.

Validation Strategies: The validation should be accredited to the success of the system and it is also a proof that the model consists all the components that will achieve the goal. Cross-validation, a technique loved by machine learning individuals, is the most frequently used like k-fold cross-validation that makes sure that the model runs well across different subsets of the data. Overall, apart from the external validation based on data that is not seen during the training, measuring the real-world performance of the model is also quite essential.

8.6 Applications

Recent progress in the combination of machine learning (ML) with image-based and molecular data not only revolutionized the field of bioinformatics but also positively affected diagnostic, prognostic, and drug discovery operations. This is not just an academic development; it is one that is entirely changing the face of clinical practices and advancing the precision of medical interventions, all the while accelerating the path towards personalized medicine.

Diagnostic Model

The union of radiomics (quantitative features that are extracted from medical images) with genomics in the field of diagnostics has revealed positive outcomes especially in the diagnosis of cancer diseases. Radiomics analyses characteristic patterns of tumours from standard medical imaging which are imperceptible to the human eye. While integrated with the genomic data, which is a source of information on genetic mutations and the pathways involved in cancer development, machine learning models can make a more precise and comprehensive diagnosis. Taking for an example a deep learning model based on radiomic and genomic data could predict the existence of several cancer subtypes or discriminate tumours with a higher probability to respond to particular therapies. This approach leverages the strengths of both data types: the spatial and temporal resolution of the imaging data, along with the molecular specificity of the genomic data. Trough training the models on the datasets that are integrated, researchers have developed diagnostic tools that surpass those based on either of the datasets, which has huge influence on early diagnosis and personalized treatment plans.

Prognostic Models

As a consequence, prognostic models are able to incorporate such modalities as imaging and molecular biomarkers, which makes it possible to predict disease progression and outcomes with exceptional precision. Using these models, clinicians can predict the risk of disease recurrence, metastasis, and patient survival rates, which will help them in making an informed treatment decision.

For instance, a machine learning model could be trained using MRI or CT images of tumours to determine their size, shape and texture while also analysing molecular biomarkers that are related to tumour aggressiveness and patient genetic predisposition. This multifaceted approach enables a thorough comprehension of the disease, taking into account both the demonstrable tumour appearance and its underlying molecular features. Models based on this complete data set with prognostic characteristics will drastically increase the accuracy of the predictions and as such allow the targeting of the treatment plans enabling them to be more effective and, to sum up, lead to better patient outcomes.

Drug Discovery and Development

Integration of imaging data and molecular information is bringing about a revolution in drug development cycle as well. By analysing integrated datasets, researchers can pinpoint new drug targets, uncover the mechanisms of drug actions, and model the therapeutic activities more accurately. First, this method is based on processing a large amount of data so as to find out possible targets, which then requires validation and optimization to produce effective and harmless drugs.

The frameworks which integrate multiple datasets with the deep learning models have been used to detect the molecular targets associated with specific disease phenotypes through imaging. In addition, these models may assist in predicting how particular genetic mutations may impact drug effectiveness that promotes the design of targeted drugs that are more likely to be successful in the clinical trial. Moreover, the use of imaging data as early as drug development provides a non-invasive monitoring of treatment effects in preclinical models, resulting in acceleration of the drug optimization and validation.

By integrating molecular information, which is very detailed, with a functional point of view (which is made possible through imaging data), researchers can get a complete picture of disease and drug action. Beyond that, this holistic approach contributes to faster drug discovery and development, as well as increasing the precision and effectiveness of treatments, thus providing a chance of more proper therapies in the struggle to overcome complicated diseases.

8.7 Challenges and Future Directions

A synergy between ML and imagery and molecular data of bioinformatics is making possible fantastic progress in biomedical informatics. This is making it possible to better understand and new ways to treat complex diseases. The road ahead on this journey is indeed highly demanding, presenting equally diversified obstacles and a field of opportunity that will forever make bioinformatics and personalized medicine the next threshold in health care for many.

Data Privacy and Ethical Considerations

With big data becoming the norm in this day and age, the protection of patient information regarding individual privacy and security is now top of the urgency list. Feeding in the most various dataset types, for instance, medical imaging and genetic data, introduces great ethical dilemmas. The risk of misuse of data, if they are breached or exploited deliberately, require the share of watertight data governance framework. In addition to that, ethical concerns are not only limited to the application of these discoveries; rather, they also identify that innovations should get equitably accessed by a wider range of populations. The innovations should not make the health disparity worse.

While the next phase must aim for the extensive growing of privacy-preserving technologies such as federated learning, which enables ML models to be learnt across many decentralized apps and servers while holding local data samples without transmitting each other, we cannot avoid the fact that there will also be the possibility of overtaking the current privacy shield. Ethical rules and regulatory frameworks have to get updated and also never lag behind the technology. This will ensure that bioinformatics investigate does not misbehave, it will be fair and focus on health well-being for individuals and societies.

Managing Data Heterogeneity and Ensuring Model Interpretability

The presence of heterogeneous imaging and molecular data is a tricky challenge which has to be resolved using delicate analytical methods to handle various and intricate data sets. The major problem of complex ML models, including deep neural networks is the opaque "black box" nature of these models. Such complexity makes it very difficult to determine the reasons for the ML model's decisions and might raise privacy issues related to patient-provider interaction.

To tackle these issues we need combined undertaking of the creation of more transparency ML models and methodologies for incorporating heterogenous data that address informational features of the dataset. XAI (Explainable AI) is the main technique now to be a high priority of researchers and developers. And it is able to apply human understanding to the AI models. Multimodal learning architectures have been another line of attack to this heterogeneous data.

The Need for Standardized Datasets and Benchmarks

The lack of the sanctioned datasets and the benchmarks for ML procedures and the integration techniques have a patent implication on the advancement of bioinformatics because it is hard to compare the relative performance of the models and techniques. The varying ways in which data is collected, modelled, and labelled between studies can be much attributed to the difficulties, as the studies are rendered unable to give robust and predictable results. Efforts for the future goal should primarily be in creating interconnected, unified datasets and metadata techniques, making it possible for better interpretation and communication between different research groups in the research field. Framework like digitizing the available resources and consortia meant for the data-sharing and standardization will be the avenues where bioinformatics research will be possible.

Future Trends in Machine Learning and Bioinformatics Integration
In the near future, ML integration with imaging and molecular data in bioinformatics is likely to encourage building of knowledge, given that the modern computational techniques as well as data analytics and organization is in the vanguard. Predicted future trends could include more ML transformer models usage, for example, for complex biological data analysis and decrease of individualized medicine limits, for example, through the integration bioinformatics into current approaches.

Additionally, the confronting of bioinformatics with other revolutionary technologies, including quantum computation, and synthetic biology results in the unlocking of new dimensions in disease modeling, leads in medicine discovery, and therapy realization. Within the expanding horizons of the bioinformatics field, scientists should have the readiness to use new tactics for implementing technological advancements but also meet the ethical, privacy and methodological challenges which accompany technological improvements.

8.8 Case Studies

In a rapidly developing area of oncology, the process of searching for individual diagnostic and therapeutic methods involves the use of ML and the integration of different types of data for predictive purposes. A very exciting path is the concept of hybridizing the radiomics (which means extracting quantitative features from medical images) and genomics (which are concerned about the genetic background of diseases). This case study on lung cancer is about an innovative project that seeks to customize the radiomic signatures obtained from Computed Tomography (CT) scans and associate them with the patients' genomic data.

The project has a strong data collection system, which consists of CT scans with high resolution from a cohort of lung cancer sufferers. These scans were painstakingly processed to acquire more than 100 radiomic features that describe the tumor's phenotypic characteristics in detail, such as pattern, shape, gradients, and wavelet-transformed attributes. At the same time, genomic data was obtained through whole sequence efforts, concentrating on detecting mutations, levels of gene expression, and some molecular features important for lung cancer development and response to treatment.

The crux was the creation of an ML model that was capable of combining and processing these two sets of data, from the radiomic and genomics ones. The research group applied a multimodal deep learning strategy putting together the spatial pattern recognition power of convolutional neural networks (CNN) and genomic data sequence modeling techniques, which are adept at analyzing genomic data. This dual-stream model thus went under a regimen of training, validation and the process of calibration and optimization, the strategies of which were cross-validation and regularization, in order to provide a better predictive accuracy and a wider applicability.

The integrated ML model that was first evaluated had a better predictive performance on the response of patients to lung cancer treatment from drugs as compared to the models based on either radiomic or genetic data alone. Our proposed model achieved impressive accuracy, greatly surpassing both the earlier diagnosis and prediction procedures. This breakthrough showed the strong synergy in combining such radiomic and genomic data in order to provide a deeper understanding of the biological processes behind tumor progression as well as its interaction with drug agents.

Such diagnostic potentials of these findings are wide-ranging. The illustrated integrated approach to treatment will assist in accurately predicting treatment outcomes, hence guiding oncologists in selecting the best available treatments for individual patients, thus improving survival rates and minimizing exposure to ineffective treatments as well as their related side effects. Additionally, the research demonstrated that ML algorithms might be a powerful tool for the detection of the intricate interactions between the genotypic and phenotypic components of the oncology progression process and resistance to treatment.

The road was not without hurdles. Yet there existed data-related challenges like the one of data heterogeneity which necessitated the use of advanced preprocessing techniques to standardize and consolidate. The "black box" nature of deep learning models was problematic in terms of understanding the specific reasons behind radiomic and genomic features looked at in models predicting disease. The need for deeper research in explainable AI methods in clinical application was thus highlighted.

With positive outcomes of this study, there is possible application of the integrated radiomic and genomic analysis for other types of cancer. The future approach would involve an expansion of the dataset to include more subtypes and stages of cancer as well as consideration of other molecular data types and models' refinement to increase the interpretability and applicability in practice. Through this case study we can not only illustrate the applicability and value of merging radiomics and genomics through ML but also start a new generation of personalized cancer therapy when the treatment plans are based on all dimensional and comprehensive aspects of the disease.

8.9 Conclusion

The use of ML with imaging and molecular data in bioinformatics is a giant step in the evolution of the field and a gift of unimaginable opportunities to study complex biological systems and enable the treatment of patients. This chapter has shown the multi-pronged approaches to integrating this complex data, starting with the foundations of machine learning and then moving on to the specific algorithms and models that are best suited for bioinformatics applications, and lastly the new techniques for melding imaging and molecular data. ML has been shown, as exemplified through the extensive investigation of diagnostic, prognostic, and drug discovery models, to be able to use the best of all the data types, for more accurate diagnostics, predicting disease progression, and for finding new therapeutic targets.

The discussion of the existing challenges and further directions for the future has shown the present problems that still exist like the privacy of data, the non-unified datasets and model interpretability that are persisting topics. The challenges notwithstanding, the machine learning capability to proffer personalized medicine and expeditious improvements in the life sciences are immense. The use cases mentioned above demonstrate practical applications and the gains from integrating the machine learning and imaging and molecular data to address biomedical challenges and complex bioinformatics problems.

As we examine the effects of integrating imaging and molecular data with ML, we come to a conclusion that combining these technologies not just improves our capability to study diseases but also advances us towards the goal of personalized medicine. This approach creates an opportunity to better understand the impact of disease on an individual patient concerning their specific biological data and a personalized treatment. As bioinformatics fueled by continuous integration of ML, imaging, and molecular data will only lead to the invention of more powerful and sophisticated techniques and methodologies. It goes without saying that this will be a defining period for the field of medicine marked by the revolution that takes place, with respect to how diseases are diagnosed, treated, and understood.

In the light of this new era, multidisciplinary cooperation should not be undervalued. Successful integration of these domains demands in-depth knowledge and a good command of both biological and medical concepts. Through stimulating the collaboration among computer scientists, biologists, and clinicians, we can ensure that the benefits of the technological applications are manifested, eventually resulting in improved patient experience globally. Upon us is a complex quest where each step is fraught with bumps and hurdles, but the sky is as wide as the community's creative dreaming and active dedication.

References

1. Prasad, K., Dekka, S., c. Tanguturi, R., Poornima, G., An Intelligent System for Remote Monitoring of Patients Health and the Early Detection of Coronary Artery Disease, in: *2022 International Conference on Smart Generation Computing, Communication and Networking (SMART GENCON)*, Bangalore, India, pp. 1–6, 2022.
2. Kishore Kumar, R., Pandidurai, M., Senthil Kamalesh, M.S.C., Design of IoT based Rural Health Helper using Natural Language Processing, in: *2023 4th International Conference on Electronics and Sustainable Communication Systems (ICESC)*, Coimbatore, India, pp. 328–333, 2023.
3. Kumar, A., Kumar, S.A., Dutt, V., Dubey, A.K., Narang, S., A Hybrid Secure Cloud Platform Maintenance Based on Improved Attribute-Based Encryption Strategies. *Int. J. Interact. Multimed. Artif. Intell.*, 8, 2, 150, 2023. Universidad Internacional de La Rioja, doi: 10.9781/ijimai.2021.11.004.
4. Burugadda, V.R., Mane, P.M., Kumar, A., Bhati, N., A Machine Learning-Based Algorithm for Early Detection of Sepsis in Hospitalized Patients: Development and Evaluation, in: *2023 1st International Conference on Circuits, Power and Intelligent Systems (CCPIS)*, Bhubaneswar, India, pp. 1–6, 2023, doi: 10.1109/CCPIS59145.2023.10291447.
5. Tanguturi, R.C., L., S.V.S.L., S. R. C., K., V., C.H., Implementation of Machine Learning Approach for Detecting Cardiovascular Diseases, in: *2023 3rd International Conference on Intelligent Technologies (CONIT)*, Hubli, India, pp. 1–6, 2023.
6. Bhati, N., Duggar, R., Alzahrani, A., Exploring few-shot learning approaches for bioinformatics advancements, in: *Applying Machine Learning Techniques to Bioinformatics*, pp. 303–316, IGI Global, 2024.
7. Burugadda, V.R., Jadhav, N., Vyas, N., Duggar, R., Exploring the Potential of Deep Reinforcement Learning for Autonomous Navigation in Complex Environments, in: *2023 7th International Conference on Computing, Communication, Control And Automation (ICCUBEA)*, Pune, India, pp. 1–6, 2023, doi: 10.1109/ICCUBEA58933.2023.10392109.

8. Ramesh Naidu, P. and Guruprasad, N., Design and implementation of crypt-cloud system for securing files in cloud. *Adv. Math. Sci. J.*, 9, 7, 4485–4493, 2020.
9. Mylavarapu, R.T., Pokhriyal, A., Dhargalkar, R.R., Bhati, N., Empowering Healthcare with AI: Addressing Challenges and Envisioning the Future, in: *2023 4th International Conference on Electronics and Sustainable Communication Systems (ICESC)*, Coimbatore, India, pp. 1393–1398, 2023, doi: 10.1109/ICESC57686.2023.10193228.
10. Chakrasali, S.V., Kumar, C., Chaturvedi, A., Azhagu Jaisudhan Pazhani, A., Computer vision based healthcare system for identification of diabetes & its types using AI. *Meas.: Sens.*, 27, 10075, 2023.
11. Hombalimath, Palanikkumar, D., Patwari, N., Symmetrized Feature Selection with Stacked Generalization based Machine Learning Algorithm for the Early Diagnosis of Chronic Diseases, in: *2023 5th International Conference on Smart Systems and Inventive Technology (ICSSIT)*, Tirunelveli, India, pp. 838–844, 2023.
12. Burugadda, V.R., Pawar, P.S., Kumar, A., Bhati, N., Predicting Hospital Readmission Risk for Heart Failure Patients Using Machine Learning Techniques: A Comparative Study of Classification Algorithms, in: *2023 Second International Conference on Trends in Electrical, Electronics, and Computer Engineering (TEECCON)*, Bangalore, India, pp. 223–228, 2023, doi: 10.1109/TEECCON59234.2023.10335817.
13. Ramesh Naidu, P. and Guruprasad, N., A High-Availability and Integrity Layer for Cloud Storage, Cloud Computing Security: From Single to Multi-Clouds. *J. Phys. Conf. Ser.*, 1921, 1, 012072, 2021.
14. Punugoti, R., Dutt, V., Kumar, A., Bhati, N., Boosting the Accuracy of Cardiovascular Disease Prediction Through SMOTE, in: *2023 International Conference on IoT, Communication and Automation Technology (ICICAT)*, Gorakhpur, India, pp. 1–6, 2023, doi: 10.1109/ICICAT57735.2023.10263703.
15. Jeevan, K. and Sathisha, B.M., Implementation of IoT Based Wireless Electronic Stethoscope, in: *2020 Third International Conference on Multimedia Processing, Communication & Information Technology (MPCIT)*, pp. 103–106, 2020.
16. Upendra, K.N., and Rajashekara, V.M., Arduino based COVID-19 Suspect Detection Device, in: *2022 6th International Conference on Electronics, Communication and Aerospace Technology*, Coimbatore, India, pp. 158–163, 2022.
17. Madasamy Raja, G. and Anandaram, H., Extraction of Fetal ECG Using ANFIS and the Undecimated-Wavelet Transform, in: *2022 IEEE 3rd Global Conference for Advancement in Technology (GCAT)*, pp. 1–5, 2022.
18. Punugoti, R., Dutt, V., Anand, A., Bhati, N., Exploring the Impact of Edge Intelligence and IoT on Healthcare: A Comprehensive Survey, in: *2023 International Conference on Sustainable Computing and Smart*

Systems (ICSCSS), Coimbatore, India, pp. 1108–1114, 2023, doi: 10.1109/ICSCSS57650.2023.10169733.

19. Anandaram, H., Nithya, B.A., Gupta, N., Verma, B.K., IoT Wearable Breast Temperature Assessment System, in: *2023 7th International Conference on Computing Methodologies and Communication (ICCMC)*, Erode, India, pp. 1236–1241, 2023.
20. Prasad, K., Anil Kumar, N., Reddy, N.S., Ashreetha, B., Technologies for Comprehensive Information Security in the IoT, in: *2023 International Conference for Advancement in Technology (ICONAT)*, Goa, India, pp. 1–5, 2023.
21. Palanikkumar, D., Mary, P.A., Begum, A.Y., A Novel IoT Framework and Device Architecture for Efficient Smart city Implementation, in: *2023 7th International Conference on Trends in Electronics and Informatics (ICOEI)*, Tirunelveli, India, pp. 420–426, 2023.
22. Swarna, S.R., Kumar, A., Dixit, P., Sairam, T.V.M., Parkinson's Disease Prediction using Adaptive Quantum Computing, in: *2021 Third International Conference on Intelligent Communication Technologies and Virtual Mobile Networks (ICICV)*, Tirunelveli, India, pp. 1396–1401, 2021, doi: 10.1109/ICICV50876.2021.9388628.
23. Kavitha, R., Kumar, A., Kalpana, V., Hariram, V., Artificial Intelligence based Health Monitoring System on IoTH platform, in: *2023 Second International Conference on Augmented Intelligence and Sustainable Systems (ICAISS)*, Trichy, India, pp. 1458–1463, 2023.
24. Kumar, S.A., Kumar, H., Dutt, V., Soni, H., Self-Health Analysis with Two Step Histogram based Procedure using Machine Learning, in: *2021 Third International Conference on Intelligent Communication Technologies and Virtual Mobile Networks (ICICV)*, Tirunelveli, India, pp. 794–799, 2021, doi: 10.1109/ICICV50876.2021.9388427.
25. Santosh Reddy, P. and Patwal, P.S., Data Analytics and Cloud-Based Platform for Internet of Things Applications in Smart Cities, in: *2022 International Conference on Industry 4.0 Technology (I4Tech)*, pp. 1–6, 2022.
26. Kawale, S.R. and Diwan, S.P., Intelligent Breast Abnormality Framework for Detection and Evaluation of Breast Abnormal Parameters, in: *2022 International Conference on Edge Computing and Applications (ICECAA)*, pp. 1503–1508, 2022.
27. Kameswara Rao, B., Chaturvedi, A., Hussain, N., Industrial quality healthcare services using Internet of Things and fog computing approach. *Meas.: Sens.*, 24, 100517, 2022.
28. Sasubilli, S.M., Kumar, A., Dutt, V., Improving Health Care by Help of Internet of Things and Bigdata Analytics and Cloud Computing, in: *2020 International Conference on Advances in Computing and Communication Engineering (ICACCE)*, Las Vegas, NV, USA, pp. 1–4, 2020, doi: 10.1109/ICACCE49060.2020.9155042.

9

Time Series Analysis in Functional Genomics

Yash Mahajan[1*], Inderjeet Singh[1], Muskan Sharma[1] and Shweta Sharma[2]

[1]*Department of Computer Science and Engineering, Chandigarh University, Mohali, India*
[2]*Department of Computer Science, R.K. Patni Girls' College, Kishangarh, Rajasthan, India*

Abstract

Time series analysis has emerged as a vital analytical framework in the field of functional genomics, offering insights into the temporal dynamics of gene expression, protein synthesis, and other molecular interactions. By focusing on the temporal dimension, time series analysis enables researchers to observe changes in biological systems over time, capturing the complex interplay between genes, their products, and external stimuli. This method is especially useful for understanding dynamic regulatory functions, such as patterns in gene expression and protein activity, providing a high-resolution perspective on biological processes. With the integration of multimodal data, such as transcriptomics, proteomics, and metabolomics, time series analysis can further deepen our understanding of cellular mechanisms, offering a holistic view of genetic functions in various physiological and pathological contexts. This chapter aims to explore the foundational concepts, methodologies, and applications of time series analysis in functional genomics, emphasizing the potential of this approach to uncover temporal trends and interactions that are crucial for advancing genomic research. Additionally, the chapter highlights the challenges associated with analyzing dynamic biological data and the benefits of combining different data sources to improve the accuracy and depth of genomic insights.

***Keywords*:** Time series analysis, functional genomics, gene expression, protein synthesis, temporal dynamics, multimodal data integration, transcriptomics

**Corresponding author*: gyash724@gmail.com

Umesh Kumar Lilhore, Abhishek Kumar, Narayan Vyas, Sarita Simaiya and Vishal Dutt (eds.) Multimodal Data Fusion for Bioinformatics Artificial Intelligence, (179–204) © 2025 Scrivener Publishing LLC

9.1 Introduction

Time series analysis has expanded rapidly out of genomics (which itself bridges data science, biology and technology). The convergence field that it primarily deals in is called functional genomics. But functional genomics wants to uncover the interactive relationships between genes, their products and nonstatic mechanisms for coordinating biological operations. A commitment to unravel the genetic code is its base. The biological activities and the underlying molecular mechanisms interact. This broader perspective requires scientists to use new methods and analytic frameworks.

In the field of functional genomics, time series data integration is now a powerful tool to catch temporal aspects within biological systems. Time series analysis provides a dynamic perspective which is essential to viewing the flow of biological activity. Life itself is built from the complex web of several internal and external factors affecting biological phenomena, these being relatively dynamic but developing over time.

Accompanying these efforts is functional genomics, which tries to systematically predict gene functions and the products of those genes using a variety of high-throughput technologies. Transformational tools: These three techniques—transcriptomics, proteomics and metabolistics—all provide a whole-picture town of biological activity (Shi *et al.*, 2019). Transcriptomics takes a look at the powerful world of RNA and also tells us how genes are expressed. Proteomics is the study of a powerful type of protein that regulates many bodily functions—the proteome. Meanwhile, metabolomics provides that last piece in the trio of molecular omics studying those tiny molecules responsible for these enormously complex functions (Rathour *et al.*, 2023).

A key starting point for getting a handle on these kinds of dynamic phenomena is to create high-level logical techniques that can deal with such temporal issues as are found in biological systems. Indeed, static and fixed-structure annotations cannot fully capture the richness that comes with incorporating time.

Pathology to poetry: From patterns of protein production or destruction at specific times, right through gene expression artwork chugging along rhythmically after being turned on—all the measuring subjects are oddly alive. The science of functional genomics revolves around time series analysis (Yang *et al.*, 2023), which offers people access to a qualitative perspective on when things occur. After this data is passed through analysis, a few things can be determined. Temporal trends may occur in regulatory function across time and even how different genes and their products respond at timespace ranges vary under various stimuli triggers. While the former may all yield useful information about cellular mechanisms, only time series analysis permits researchers to see how small differences are unfolded in a system and thus understand its deepest secrets.

The importance of this temporal window cannot be overemphasized, nor is it simply a technical anomaly, but an essential necessity for the study of biological mechanisms. But the biological world is in constant flux, responding to physiological disorders (You *et al.*, 2023), growth stages and environmental conditions. Time series analysis, by allowing researchers to interpret these temporal subtleties in turn allows for meaningful insight into the functional significance of genetic data.

The primary objective of this chapter is to initiate a comprehensive discussion about time series analysis in the general area of practical genomics. We aim to investigate the techniques, applications and problems involved in temporal data analysis (Wu *et al.*, 2023). We hope that this will help readers gain a more mature understanding of the significance and opportunities for time-based research toward unraveling biological systems.

Time series analysis has numerous possible applications in functional genomics, but to what limits and degrees? Everything from the basics of time series analysis, key techniques and applications in gene expression profiling to basic functional annotation will be thoroughly discussed. In addition, we plan to study the combination of multimodal data with time series data in order to clarify why combining different biological information sources may be advantageous or difficult (Manna and Sarkar, 2021). As we pass through these dimensions, we will keep an eye on the rapid changes of our technological environment and the problems that are encountered by studying phenomena in science which change with time.

We hope we can give a clear and objective review of the state of time series analysis in functional genomics keeping all these limitations in mind (Madeddu *et al.*, 2022). Through in-depth exploration of methods and applications we hope to make our own contribution towards advancing the knowledge which provides thrust for research, while also helping people understand better that genetic data are not stable but alive.

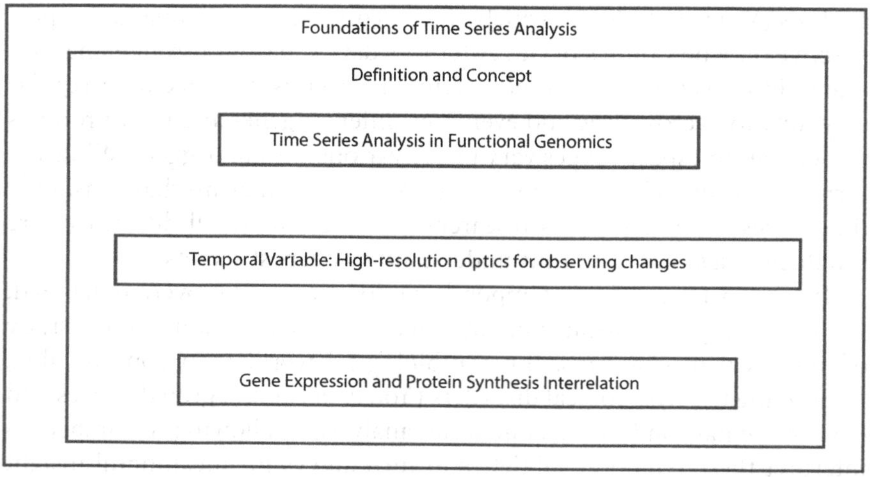

Figure 9.1 Outline of foundations of time series analysis.

9.2 Foundations of Time Series Analysis in Functional Genomics

9.2.1 Definition and Concept

Time series analysis is a state-of-the art framework developed to gain valuable insights from the ever-changing web of biological data in an emerging field called functional genomics. As mentioned in Figure 9.1 the outline of the subsection (Fugazzola *et al.*, 2020), This kind of analyze- away is the simplest possible method which looks at each data point as a temporal instance reflecting one moment in time within our dynamic biological systems. Driven by time, the temporal variable adds a dynamic element to the picture, providing high-resolution optics for observing fine gradual changes occurring inside cells and organisms. One of the most important parts of functional genomics is time series analysis, since it lets us see how gene expression and protein synthesis interrelate across differences in flow (Khan, Manoj and Pramod, 2016).

9.2.1.1 Time Series Data in Genomics

Genomics represents a new canvas on which the history of biological activity, in time series form, is recorded. Each data dot becomes a footnote and witness to the dance of cellular activity precisely documenting each molecular moment. Take for example the way a temporarily changing gene expression pattern can be conceived of as a form of molecular symphony responding rhythmically to internal and external stimuli (Cabanos and Hata, 2021). In these molecular time spans, one takes a journey to explore the regulatory processes controlling cellular function. Therefore, time series data is more than mere observation. It can also open up a dynamic window onto the molecular interactions that exist in real time within live organisms and overcome some of those former notions of superficiality among other types of life.

9.2.1.2 *Key Terminology*

Time series analysis lingo: All of these terms call for a degree of mastery and they are also useful to researchers themselves in understanding the temporal coloring of the data. Autocorrelation quantifies the similarity of any given point to following points in a chain. That kind of data (Zhou *et al.*, 2021), which is constantly changing as it's measured and sampled repeatedly across time, contains information on the patterns that get repeated. In time series analysis, stationarity refers to the issue of whether statistical properties are varying with time in a uniform way. It helps researchers differentiate between long-term trends and short-term cycles that might occur within them. Periodicity is supposed to help the visualization of light by demonstrating whether or not there are periodic cycles in time-related data. This reflects the beating heart of genome activity, but also provides

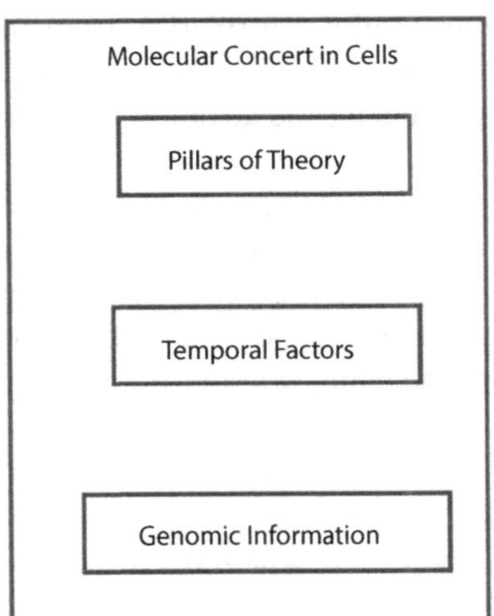

Figure 9.2 Molecular concert in cells.

information about how biological synchrony controls cellular functioning (Mansoori *et al.*, 2017).

The definitions and concepts that comprise this framework are not merely explanations of what is. Instead, as we enter into the realm of time series analysis they also become mechanisms by which one may gain access to understanding a kind of molecular concert taking place within these cells (Mahgoub, Bolad and Mergani, 2014). Figure 9.2 shows the molecular concert in Cells with Temporal Factors. Concepts of this nature make up the pillars of theory, which help to illuminate many temporal factors that accompany genomic information. Now they can never look back—to not only notice but witness how time is the player in a changing genetic script.

9.2.2 Challenges in Analyzing Functional Genomic Time Series Data

The potential for the application of time series analysis in functional genomics is high, but attendant problems are even greater—these reflect the richness and subtlety of temporal data as well as biological complexity.

9.2.2.1 Noise and Variability

One of the greatest headaches brought by processing functionally significant genomic time series is noise and uncertainty. But since biological systems are living, numerous variables can influence any type of test (varying conditions, etc.), so data could vary in a large range. But it then devolves into distinguishing meaningful information from the surrounding wave of meaningless oscillations, which calls for knowledgeable application methodology, signal processing and advanced statistical techniques (Omer Mahgoub *et al.*, 2023).

But it is not enough to acknowledge noise and variability; you also have to understand their source and nature, as well as how much they affect the data. But biological systems are extremely complex, and respond to any number of internal or external stimuli with temporal fluctuations. Any changes could be small, so telling whether something was a real biological signal or just random oscillations would require some discrimination (Guo *et al.*, 2023). To deal with this problem, scholars study things ranging from machine learning techniques for time series data to Bayesian methods and wavelet analysis. The objective is unambiguous: How can one tease out the most useful biological information from this temporal hullabaloo while at the same time making sure that what is being observed really exists and isn't just another kind of corruption.

9.2.2.2 Data Preprocessing Considerations

Analyzing time series in functional genomics is closely connected to the most important step of processing data, which forms a necessary condition for doing meaningful analysis. Learning to be professional: This step is not just a technical process; it's also an effort to enhance the quality and readability of the data, so as to prepare better for analytical research.

Since all kinds of outliers affect a thorough analysis, data cleaning is the most important task. Artifacts from experiments, equipment that has broken down and true biological anomalies are all possible culprits. Giving everything a good once-over is like applying the polish to an important work of art, making sure that nothing draws your attention away from its message.

Synchronization turns into a conductor, coordinating data under different experimental conditions. If comparisons are to be made, data should be normalized because mismatching measurement units or experimental environments could introduce unnecessary variables. Normalization methods (Huang *et al.*, 2023), from z-score normalisation to the various more sophisticated methods, all seek dispersion of these disparate data points so that they can give researchers a clear picture.

But missing data points are a frequent problem in longitudinal studies, and imputation eases this predicament as smoothly as an artisan's brush. Gaps in the timeline may arise from biological systems "intrinsic unpredictability, experimental limitations or measurement error" (Agathokleous *et al.*, 2023). To preserve the continuity of such a temporal narrative, various techniques including imputation procedures (which may involve mean imputation or other forms) seek to "smoothly" patch over these holes.

The analysis of the effects of such procedures is as critical for success in this data preparation work, if not more so. It's a tricky balancing act, because you want to ensure that the quality of all data collected in preparation remains intact and isn't spoiled by anything picked up during the trip.

Time series analysis is the very foundation of functional genomics, and only after gaining a good understanding of its flaws will one be able to hope negotiate such hornets 'nests. However, these difficulties are in reality not impediments but doors leading to scientists bravely and correctly crossing through the tricky woodland of biological ups and downs (Burugadda *et al.*, 2023). Such applications and methods reveal open space because we are brought above the foundation of obstacles, which allows us to glimpse one door always ajar—the long-range significance for that still-evolving branch of our knowledge about genetic data.

9.3 Methodologies for Time Series Analysis

Mastering time series: In the larger field of functional genomics, selecting appropriate generative methodology is essential when confronted with statistical and temporal theories. The book begins with a detailed description of what is available today, from familiar old ways to exploiting the new possibilities offered by computers. As illustrated in Figure 9.3, there are various methods for time series analysis.

9.3.1 Overview of Existing Approaches

9.3.1.1 Classical Methods

Classical time series analysis draws on studies from past decades to give researchers a set of methodologies that have lasted through the ages. Backed up statistical analyses, these methods offer an elementary understanding of the intentional and accidental temporal structures underlying genomic data.

A. Statistical Descriptives

What is their foundation? For the most part, they are statistical descriptives that enable researchers to identify and reduce time series. He notes that although the numbers may seem to be very basic, indicators such as mean, median value and variance show what is at least a beginning—the

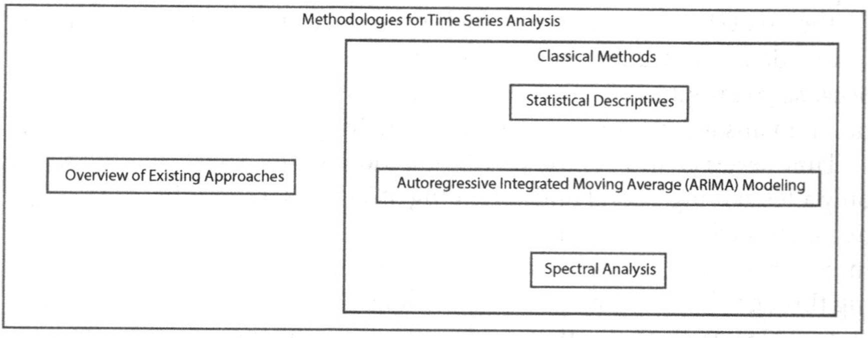

Figure 9.3 Methodologies for time series analysis.

first brush strokes of core trends with their veinings drawn out in diversity (Fakhar *et al.*, 2023). But these statistical bedrocks allow researchers to get an early feel for the textural nature of genetic time, and are a prerequisite before tackling more challenging research.

B. Autoregressive Integrated Moving Average (ARIMA) Modeling
In the classical tool set, only ARIMA modeling can be relied on as a mainstay when processing temporal data with patterns and seasonality. The advantage of this method is that it can be employed in very different ways so as to first transform a non-stationary time series into one which meets the moving average and autoregressive conditions (Liu, Hou and Chen, 2023). For this reason, the adaptability of ARIMA makes it useful in bringing out spatial and temporal characteristics embodied within gene expression dynamic events.

C. Spectral Analysis
Based on the old Fourier transformations, this is also a method in the standard repertory. This method, by revealing the frequency domain of time series data is able to lay bare many subtle aspects that are hidden within temporal signals. If such signals can be decomposed into their individual frequencies, scientists could discover a lot about oscillatory behavior and periodic phenomena (Lou, Deng and Gao, 2023). Spectral analysis is extremely useful when investigating cyclic genomic mechanisms or analyzing rhythms in gene expression patterns.

9.3.1.2 Advanced Computational Techniques

The burgeoning area of functional genomics is calling increasingly upon advanced computer tools. Because these methods are designed to cope with the challenges of high-dimensional and dynamic genomic data, they demonstrate the leading edge in methodological advances (Altmann *et al.*, 2020).

A. Machine Learning Approaches
Time series research Sense and sensitivity: In addition to supplying the field of functional genomics with tools for its transformational work, machine learning also enters another arena in this way (Sasubilli *et al.*, 2020). Examples include support vector machines, random forests and neural networks. These are all nonlinear methods that exceed traditional boundaries; as shown in Figure 9.4, various machine learning models excel at discovering important patterns in temporal data. As these models were

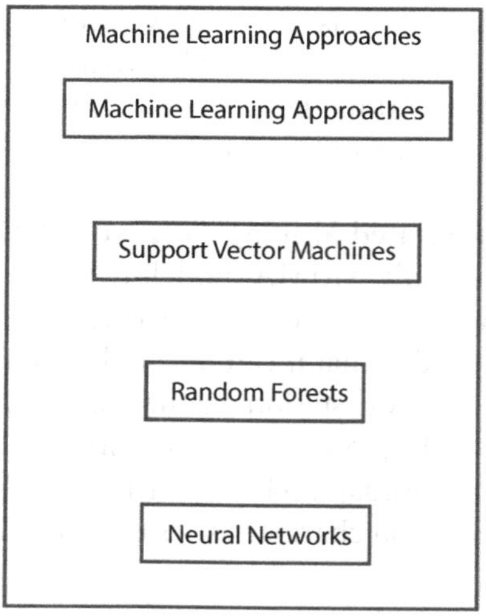

Figure 9.4 Machine learning approaches.

trained on vast amounts of genomic data, they track the ever-changing symphony of gene expression, protein interactions and metabolite changes.

B. Dynamic Bayesian Networks (DBNs)

All these probabilistic graphical modelling frameworks, known as DBNs, represent a paradigm shift. The reason these networks are particularly suited to elucidating gene regulatory networks and signaling pathways is precisely that they excel at representing relationships between variables over time. As illustrated in Figure 9.5, by seamlessly traversing temporal relationships (Burugadda *et al.*, 2023), DBNs enhance our ability to recognize causal connections amidst the tangle of genetic interactions.

C. Functional Data Analysis (FDA)

FDA adds to and joins with the development of traditional statistical methods by interpreting functional data (time series) as time-series samples. This state-of-the art technique treats every time series as a smooth function, thereby opening the door to more in-depth exploration of temporal patterns (Han *et al.*, 2023). Further, researchers can use techniques such as functional regression and functional principal component analysis to search for hidden trends and relationships of unknown meaning in the high-dimensional time series data of gene expression.

It is necessary when exploring the zillions of different ways that computer methods can be applied to time series analysis under functional

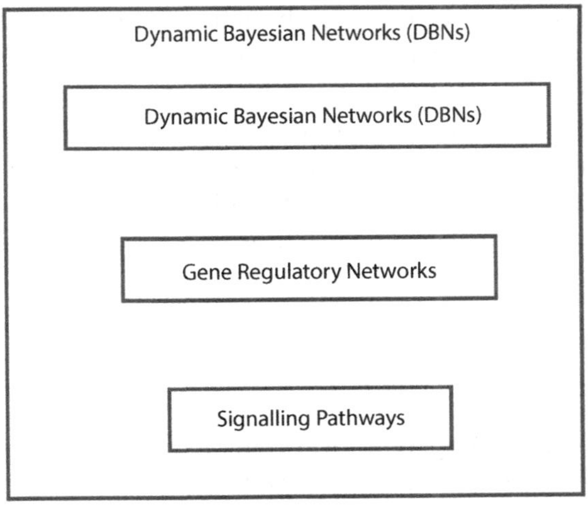

Figure 9.5 Dynamic bayesian networks (DBNs).

genomics, which involves both high-end and low tech. These traditional methods offer a solid foundation that gives researchers interpretable and statistically sound results. Figure 9.6 shows the functional data analysis of the methodology during the process. Meanwhile, advanced computer techniques allow researchers to quickly and accurately navigate the dense terrain of high-dimension genetic data.

A methodological cloth woven from the fabric of many different approaches not only makes it possible for researchers to understand, but also analyze in detail the temporal variations among functional genomes.

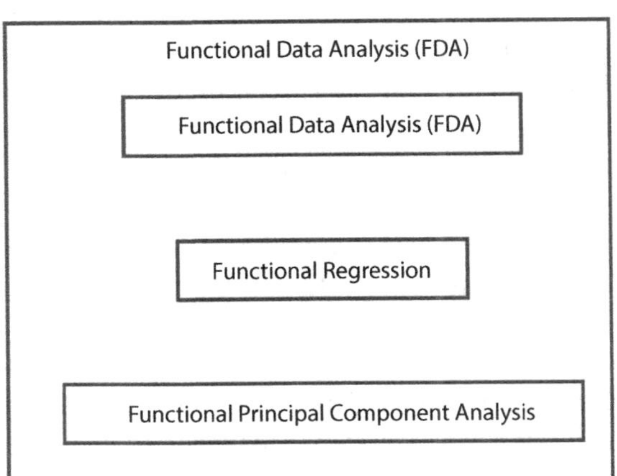

Figure 9.6 Functional data analysis.

When we go into the specifics of each methodology, we find that they are all driven by a same goal: This unchanging universe of genetic data is the common pursuit in history through time (McWhite *et al.*, 2020). But even methodological differences cannot destroy this common goal. This organized, now deepened approach will serve as a strong foundation for the ensuing practical application of these techniques in the chapters that follow and is part of our formal goal to give time series analysis its due treatment.

9.3.2 Case Studies

9.3.2.1 Successful Applications

Case Study 1: Unraveling Temporal Gene Expression Dynamics
In a major publication, researchers used the powerful modelling approach of autoregressive integrated moving average (ARIMA) to study temporal variations in gene expression triggered by environmental stresses (Feng *et al.*, 2023). The project was aimed at investigating the fine-tuned reaction of all kinds of genes to imposed external stresses, in order to gain an understanding into the exquisite coordination within cells.

Statistical methodology forms the basis of this investigation, and its starting point was the ARIMA modeling system. More than just a tool, it was like having a guide help you through the forest of temporal gene expression patterns (Sekhar *et al.*, 2023). The power of the research lay in its ability to identify tiny patterns within gene temporal expression, as a person can interpret the delicate movements expressed by molecules responding to stimulae from an environment. That was, statistical descriptives were the narrators of trends and fluctuation in gene expression over time (Kocakulak *et al.*, 2023). Far more than simple measures at the heart of a research program. Besides offering a concrete understanding of the temporal subtleties essential for interpretation by cellular machines, mean, median, variance and skewness were also used as paint brushes to produce an image allowing us to see how stress makes cells respond (Lihore *et al.*, 2024).

In this particular case study, we looked at the difficulties of applying ARIMA modeling and how important it is for learning about temporal relationships governing gene expression. The concept was not simply a mathematical puzzle to be solved, but also an interesting story about the temporal relationship between genes and their environmental stimuli. From each and every ARIMA cycle we managed to excavate data not only from the temporal patterns (Almusaylim and Zaman, 2019), but that gave us a more comprehensive understanding than would normally be possible.

The significance of this case study goes beyond its direct implications. It highlighted the importance of time series analysis in gene expression research, particularly ARIMA modeling. What was really significant, however, is the ability to translate these patterns into a narrative description of how cells respond individually and collectively.

In sum, this case study demonstrated that applications of these techniques for time series analysis ideas (such as in the context of computer games) are by no means limited to information technology. They offer a better understanding of the organized responses embodied in this dynamic scenery underlying gene expression. These are highly penetrating explorations of the temporal resonances generated by biological phenomena. But this kind of investigation sets the stage for further efforts during which time series analysis can serve as a transformational lens to help us fathom temporal relationships in functional genomics.

Case Study 2: Machine Learning Deciphers Disease Progression

In addition to these, probably the greatest triumph of functional genomics was made in machine learning. Here they present a seminal case of applying machine learning techniques to using long-term accumulations of genomic information as the model, which not only explains how illness comes into being but also why. N. Vyas, V. Dutt *et al.* (2023) start with an explanation of support vector machines (SVMs), which are a type of machine learning algorithm that is particularly useful for tasks involving classification. SVMs can look for patterns of illness indicators that are weaved together over time and hidden within the huge amount of longitudinal genomic data. These revelations were only possible with computer assistance.

This model was developed with long-term genetic information, making the age of adventure data driven. It was not only math, but the study of how gene expression and disease change with time. As SVMs swept across the broad canvas that is genomic data, they uncovered not only patterns but also miniscule details picked up from time series data which would help predict the course of an illness.

The reason for this success, however, was as much the case study's accuracy in making predictions than it finding previously unknown links between gene expression and clinical characteristics. From this model was developed a virtual detective that could introduce relationships and patterns invisible to standard modes of analysis. Not only did this constitute a purely academic discovery, it also fired new ideas about individualized treatment methods.

This case study illustrates how the illness was accurately foreseen and, at the same time, showed new levels of understanding. This demonstrated that genetic interactions are time-dependent; it was not a black box effect, but human. With this long-term data providing perspective, the SVMs were finally able to read a genetic language that clearly expressed much about how diseases mutate.

From this case study, we can see that machine learning applied to time series analysis breaks through a number of barriers. In doing so, it serves as a beacon we can use to guide ourselves along the path towards an illness—one that provides not just prognosis but also meaning. Rethinking it, this case shows how machine learning can help us to humanize the interpretation of temporal and intratemporal changes in functional genetics, helping lay a track towards an era when tailored interventions can be guided by dynamic patterns formed by single genes over time.

Case Study 3: Dynamic Bayesian Networks Unveil Regulatory Networks
The use of dynamic Bayesian networks (DBN) marks another page in the wonderland that is functional genomics. This landmark case study reveals how much DBNs have clarified gene regulation networks during early embryonic development.

The story begins with realization that embryonic development is a dynamic process of gene dancing in an extremely choreographed way. In addition, there were static ones which apparently grew as you looked at them. All that it needed was dynamic interactions between people themselves; a technology that could simulate this process had to be developed first. Then came DBNs, a precise probability-theoretic model that eventually became the basis for breaking through to understanding gene regulation in embryogenesis. DBNs are especially advantageous, because they innately meet the requirements of temporal dependency, which is important for modeling developmental processes. They are no longer cold mathematical objects to be manipulated. Instead, this model takes into account the probabilities of genes interacting in line with embryonic types and has thereby given rise to a dynamic developmental process.

DBNs were therefore not only able to provide a temporary glimpse of gene interactions. But in fact, there was even more looking into temporal relations that brought out the flow of regulatory networks. DBNs provided a window to such knowledge, giving people the ability to explain not just the central regulatory nodes themselves but also their interactions over time and how they regulate development. What is unique about this case study, however, is that the degree of description allows a greater understanding than most methodologies do into how development looks. So

DNBs are no longer mere tools. They start to understand the language of genes and a narrative gradually takes shape. This application of DBNs gives us a whole new perspective on the subtle rhythms that govern gene expression during embryonic development.

From looking at this case study, it is not hard to realize that by focusing on temporal interdependence DBNs bring our investigation of functional genomics to a whole new level. They shed light on the interrelationships that govern biological activities and also suggest a direction for research into gene control networks. Such a case study brings us one step closer to the day where using DBNs will be as natural and routine in functional genomics research as working with spatial information is today. They do this by bringing together sophistication with revelation.

Case Study 4: Functional Data Analysis Explores Temporal Metabolite Profiles

Thus FDA is a golden new opportunity for research into the much talked-about subject of metabolomics. From this example, we see the value of knowing metabolite profiles through temporal data. One source of information on this is the FDA. The second is to explore the impact of environmental factors and physiological conditions on metabolite levels. However, the subtle variations in time are usually too slight for conventional techniques to pick up. The FDA, on the other hand, viewed metabolite time series as smooth functional objects. In this way, researchers can focus on these temporal metabolite profiles' subtle patterns and deviations.

Take this case study. Moving beyond mere computer analysis, the FDA application delves into a real-world field of research—metabolomics (Kumar *et al.*, 2021). But there's another way of dealing with this problem if you treat metabolite time series as smooth functions. In addition to being able to measure the metabolites, it is also essential to know how they vary over time and in response with biological surroundings. Yet, functional regression techniques are also part of the FDA's armory and can make it easier to link metabolite changes with specific physiological states. By providing researchers with this jump across that huge gap of traversing a costume-like world, they can not only identify these metabolites but also observe changes in them over time relative to physiological events.

Victory in this type of case study is not only due to the ability to detect the minute fluctuations that exist over time in metabolites, but also because it captures patterns and associations among them with their relationship to a person's physiological state, like researchers who use linguistics as a prism to interpret the metabolite, which in turn varies with time resembles grammar. FDA is called upon to tell stories each one of which has its own beginning and ending over more or less time frames.

9.4 Applications of Time Series Analysis in Functional Genomics

The possibilities for its application to functional genomics have already unfolded broad vistas by helping people gain insight into the subtle changes visible in biological data. In this section we discuss three types of application: fundamental annotation, comparative analysis and gene expression profiling.

9.4.1 Gene Expression Profiling

9.4.1.1 Identification of Temporal Patterns

The temporal shift in expression profiles is something that can't be overlooked, and time series analysis has become an indispensable tool complementing gene profiling. In addition, through the observation of successive points and minute temporal differences they intend to identify small-scale provisions in gene organization made according to internal or external conditions. This goes beyond still photographs to capture the passing of time through a kaleidoscope and reveal patterns underlying gene expression.

Many factors influence the ever-changing gene expression process. Time series analysis can be employed by researchers to identify patterns of gene activation or repression over time. Temporal pattern detection: With improved statistical methods and computer programs, the search for temporal patterns becomes a journey through time into how genes regulate each other. Identifying the functions of genes and their complex relationships thus involves sophisticated understanding of temporal dynamics.

9.4.1.2 Regulatory Network Inference

Time series analysis expertise allows the inference of regulatory networks that control gene interactions. Scientists believe time-series data can help them understand the relationship between genes, leading to the construction of regulatory networks. This provides a detailed explanation of the various links and relationships which coordinate this complicated machinery.

Thus, they are dynamic systems that vary in response to changes of gene-gene interrelationships and how genes regulate each other. Thanks to time series analysis, researchers can now investigate not only the patterns of expression for individual genes but also relationships and regulation between them. A complete view of the whole thing helps make it easier to construct a regulatory network, since we already have an idea about all the complex interactions between different things that constitute biological processes. This is an advanced study of the temporal vocabulary for gene control.

9.4.2 Functional Annotation

9.4.2.1 Enrichment Analysis

Time series analysis is a crucial complement to functional annotation, the most basic element of all genomes research and particularly helpful with enrichment analysis. Through time series measurements of gene sets, researchers can potentially uncover increased biological activities or pathways. This allows us to sort out the functional meaning of changes in gene expression over time.

Traditionally, enrichment analysis seeks the biological words most frequently found in a gene set. By extending this technique to time series analysis, researchers can not only discover phrases in context but also explore the way they change over time. This temporal perspective thus provides a more refined understanding of functional annotation by providing insights into when certain biological processes are active or suppressed.

9.4.2.2 Pathway Analysis

Pathway analysis, the key to assessing the functional significance of genetic data is given temporal context by time series analysis. How genes in a pathway change at different points over time can be researched to help better inspect how biological networks are dynamically regulated and the temporal sequence for activating or inhibiting them. This technique of time series analysis is able to reveal the patterns of increases or decreases in gene activity within pathways over periods of time. The advantage of this temporal perspective is that it helps in the analysis of routes, providing a more complete picture of how biological processes progress over some period.

9.4.3 Comparative Analysis

9.4.3.1 Contrasting Time Series Data Across Genomic Entities

Comparative analysis is a basic approach to genomics research, but time series data gives the technique an added dimension. By comparing temporal patterns among different genetic units, scientists can identify static and dynamic differences between organisms, enabling them to better understand the exquisite nuances in time that define living things.

The purpose of comparative analysis traditionally has been to identify either similarities or dissimilarity among genetic entities. Time series analysis takes this a step further by allowing researchers to compare dynamic temporal patterns as well as static properties. This temporal perspective gives an even richer account of dynamic shifts, be they in the control patterns between gene expression and different cell types or in pathway dynamics across experimental conditions (comparative genomics).

From the various applications of time series analysis within functional genomics, it is abundantly apparent how important a role time plays in understanding biological phenomena. We can study the evolutionary nature of language in new ways through time series analysis, such as by identifying dynamic regulatory networks or temporal gene expression patterns. This comprehensive approach will allow more of the riddles in functional genomics to be understood, as it becomes clear that temporal variation is a factor highly relevant even for solving puzzles within dynamic life processes-genes and pathways.

9.5 Integration with Multimodal Data

Synthesis of multidimensional information: Nevertheless, what is extremely challenging and is at the cutting edge in this fast-moving field involves threads or how to integrate all kinds of views on biological coordination. The first section provides an in-depth analysis of multimodal integration, providing a broad perspective on the pros and cons associated with integrating time-series data. It also explores how successful programs succeed by transcending this obstacle to cooperation between different modes.

9.5.1 Overview of Multimodal Data Fusion

Multimodal Data Fusion: A Synergistic Approach

Meanwhile, the field of functional genomics has already moved from single-mode to multimodal fusion. The idea behind this system paradigm is to create a more detailed structure that can be composed of many different types of data, like proteomics or metabolites being brought together with genomes. This symphony shows that time series data, which documents the changes in a phenomenon through specific intervals of time, can indeed be one of the most powerful tools for researchers. Incorporating information from multiple molecular levels, multimodal fusion can help researchers to delve still deeper into the world of biologicalEs. Genomics, transcriptomics and proteomes all await piecing together into a picture of cellular activity. Second, time series can locate the temporal relationships between many different molecular entities and achieve a dynamic integration. Perhaps with this kind of synergistic research style, researchers might be able grasp the relationships over time among biological phenomena in a much more integrated manner.

9.5.2 Challenges and Opportunities in Integrating Time Series Data

9.5.2.1 Challenges in Integrating Time Series Data

Fusion of time series data with multimodal information has great potential. It just needs a few hurdles to be overcome first. Time adds to the difficulties, as do many other questions which require careful consideration. Other difficulties arise from the fact that biological systems are not static, missing data points must be organized and managed in some way, temporal scales sometimes do not offset. Statistical analysis and computer systems that bring together temporal data from different modalities can reduce these problems. Temporal information, being dynamic in nature, can create problems when time series data spans several modalities. But, particularly when using data gathered in different experimental environments or with different technologies, it is crucial to unify time scales if meaningful comparisons are ever to be possible. To ensure the coherence of integrated datasets, however, specialized imputation methods need to be applied for missing data points (common in time series), etc. In addition, the dynamic nature of biological systems also renders it harder to illustrate changes over time in relationships among modalities. These obstacles can only be overcome through innovative computer methods and statistical strategies that cater to the demands of integrated time series data.

9.5.2.2 *Opportunities in Integrating Time Series Data*

The challenges may also be opportunities for revolutionary breakthroughs. Both of these combine multimodal data, with the former increasing interpretability of it and the latter giving one insight into hard-to-understand biological processes. For example, these might include new associations discovered during certain periods of time or a deeper understanding about how dynamic biomarkers and marker networks work. Therefore, the practical result of exploiting integrated time series data to its maximum is that one can more easily seek dynamic variables, which serve as a means for defining natural phenomena.

When time series data is added to the multimodal results, even more inferences can be made. The fourth is the addition of temporal information, so that researchers can see how certain molecular layers change over time. This enables us to discover dynamic biomarkers not readily revealed by static analysis. This large amount of integrated time series data enables one to discover the temporal regulatory networks by which genes, proteins and metabolites are coordinated. In addition, the inter-variable linkages that arise at various times are best for discovering new trends and associations. Thus, adding time series data gives us a glimpse of these quieter temporal qualities that say so much about biological systems.

9.5.3 Case Studies on Successful Integration

9.5.3.1 *Unveiling Temporal Interactions Across Multiple Modalities*

Afterwards they used time series data from genomes, transcriptomics and metabolomics to decipher temporal relationships in a new case study of cellular responses to one particular stressor. They then integrated this data into dynamic regulatory networks that revealed how genes respond to changes in their environment, interacting with other transcripts and metabolites over time. This is such a good case study for the use of time series in combining data to give an explanation for dynamic cross talk between different molecular levels.

This case study had relied on the seamless fusion of time series data acquired from different modalities in order to achieve accurate temporal relationships. Analyzing how genes and metabolites change under the influence of a stressor, researchers have discovered some dynamic regulatory networks. This integrated method takes you well beyond the molecular level, making it possible to understand how thousands of different components are coordinating their reactions over set periods of time as part and parcel of the cell's machine.

9.5.3.2 Temporal Biomarkers in Disease Progression

In addition, it demonstrates another valuable case study—the integration of time series data about the spread of illness. Combining clinical time-series data with proteomic and genetic information enabled scientists to identify temporal biomarkers of illness. It was discovered that besides the temporal change in illness over its course, this kind of integrated approach can offer clues about which biomarker at what time will be best for diagnosis.

It is an excellent example of how time series data can be used to look for biomarkers related to the course of disease. The gradual integration of clinical, proteomic and genomic data helped scientists to grasp the timing behind biomarker expression. In this way, by employing an integrated approach some biomarkers that appear at specific times have been discovered and a time frame has been mapped out for understanding the pathological process of illness development. This case illustrates how time series analysis can utilize integrated data to discern the subtle temporal patterns underlying molecular changes in illness.

From examining the topography of integrating time series data with multimodal information, this combination has opened up new areas where biological complexity can be understood. The difficulties inherent in integration are solved through innovative means, and the chance is taken.

9.6 Conclusion

The comprehensive study of time series analysis within functional genomics has been more than just a journey through data and methods; it's also reflected the longing to better examine dynamical aggregates which guide biological process. In closing this chapter, we need to do more than just reach a condensation of the most salient points; we should also illuminate for our readers the wide implications for bioinformatics artificial intelligence and suggest future lines of research.

A comprehensive introduction established the importance of time series analysis in functional genomics. Then we examined the utility of time series data for properly representing temporal relationships in describing various interactions within biological systems, moving into a new interdisciplinary realm called functional genomics. The chapter's goals and its desire to conduct a comprehensive study of time series analytic methods were described, with applications well beyond time-series acoustic records. We reviewed the basics of time series analysis, from definitions and concepts to understanding time series in genomics and mastering terminology. The problems inherent in the process of analysing functional genomic time series data were discussed, and helped to clarify such technical concepts as noise, variability and preprocessing. In addition, we explored time series analytic methods where the approaches and computer tools are integrated into one single approach. From careful case studies, the applicability of such methods was stressed. There is a practical understanding to how well they work at unraveling temporal processes.

Our research is applicable everywhere. In the corridors of Bioinformatics AI, everything has entered a revolutionary era—someone needs computers to save their body? Blending classic human wit with the latest tools of information technology yields a toolbox that lets scientists tame dynamic, high-dimensional data. These include the still-emerging fields of machine learning, dynamic Bayesian networks and functional data analysis—your everyday tools for plotting gene expression; protein synthesis and metabolite variation over time. When time series data is combined with multimodal information, there are innumerable possibilities for bioinformatics AI. Such a collaborative approach lets researchers understand cellular activity on many different levels, providing clear sight across the limitations of various types of data. Besides making the data more interpretable, this integration will make it possible to identify dynamic biomarkers or clarify temporal regulatory networks involving them—and gain an even deeper understanding of the subtle nuances that underlie biological cycles.

In the future, time series analysis of functional genomics seems to have many different directions in which study can be pursued. Another major objective focuses on developing new computational methods capable of dealing with the non-stationary nature of multimodal time series. We hope that researchers will still be able to address issues such as dealing with missing data points, bringing temporal scales into synchrony and encompassing the dynamic nature of biological systems in integrated information.

The unexplored world of temporal biomarkers, dynamic regulatory networks and the complex interactions between different molecular levels hold out great prospects for future discoveries. Through that and the pursuit of better methodology, functional genomics will progress towards an even deeper understanding of temporal relations. To sum up, our story of working with time series analysis in the field of functional genomics is a microcosm for understanding bioinformatics artificial intelligence.

The road ahead beckons with more questions and new answers, at the interface of data, computers and biology. The reason for this pursuit is the desire to grasp at a model of life that unfolds in time.

References

Agathokleous, E., *et al.*, One hundred important questions facing plant science derived using a large language model, in: *Trends in Plant Science*, 2023, [Preprint], Available at: https://doi.org/10.1016/j.tplants.2023.06.008.

Dutt, V., Sasubilli, S.M., Yerrapati, A.E., Dynamic Information Retrieval with Chatbots: A Review of Artificial Intelligence Methodology, in: *2020 4th International Conference on Electronics, Communication and Aerospace Technology (ICECA)*, Coimbatore, India, pp. 1299–1303, 2020, doi: 10.1109/ICECA49313.2020.9297533.

Burugadda, V.R., Pawar, P.S., Kumar, A., Bhati, N., Predicting Hospital Readmission Risk for Heart Failure Patients Using Machine Learning Techniques: A Comparative Study of Classification Algorithms, in: *2023 Second International Conference on Trends in Electrical, Electronics, and Computer Engineering (TEECCON)*, Bangalore, India, pp. 223–228, 2023, doi: 10.1109/TEECCON59234.2023.10335817.

Altmann, M., *et al.*, Extensive signal integration by the phytohormone protein network. *Nature*, 583, 7815, 271–276, 2020. Available at: https://doi.org/10.1038/S41586-020-2460-0.

Cabanos, H.F. and Hata, A.N., Emerging insights into targeted therapy-tolerant persister cells in cancer. *Cancers*, 13, 11, 2021. Available at: https://doi.org/10.3390/CANCERS13112666.

Fakhar, A.Z., *et al.*, The ORFans' tale: new insights in plant biology. *Trends Plant Sci.*, 28, 12, 1379–1390, 2023. Available at: https://doi.org/10.1016/j.tplants.2023.06.011.

Burugadda, V.R., Jadhav, N., Vyas, N., Duggar, R., Exploring the Potential of Deep Reinforcement Learning for Autonomous Navigation in Complex Environments, in: *2023 7th International Conference on Computing, Communication, Control and Automation (ICCUBEA)*, Pune, India, pp. 1–6, 2023, doi: 10.1109/ICCUBEA58933.2023.10392109.

Feng, J.W., *et al.*, MaizeNetome: A multi-omics network database for functional genomics in maize. *Mol. Plant*, 16, 8, 1229–1231, 2023. Available at: https://doi.org/10.1016/J.MOLP.2023.08.002.

Fugazzola, L., *et al.*, Intratumoral genetic heterogeneity in papillary thyroid cancer: Occurrence and clinical significance. *Cancers*, 12, 2, 2020. Available at: https://doi.org/10.3390/CANCERS12020383.

Kumar, A., Kumar, S.A., Dutt, V., Dubey, A.K., Narang, S., A Hybrid Secure Cloud Platform Maintenance Based on Improved Attribute-Based Encryption

Strategies. *Int. J. Interact. Multimed. Artif. Intell.*, 8, 2, 150, 2023. Universidad Internacional de La Rioja, doi: 10.9781/ijimai.2021.11.004.

Guo, J., *et al.*, A tripartite rheostat controls self-regulated host plant resistance to insects. *Nature*, 618, 7966, 799–807, 2023. Available at: https://doi.org/10.1038/S41586-023-06197-Z.

Chandrasekaran, S., Dutt, V., Vyas, N., Kumar, R., Student Sentiment Analysis Using Various Machine Learning Techniques, in: *2023 International Conference on Artificial Intelligence and Smart Communication (AISC)*, Greater Noida, India, pp. 104–107, 2023, doi: 10.1109/AISC56616.2023.10085018.

Huang, J., *et al.*, Discovery of deaminase functions by structure-based protein clustering. *Cell*, 186, 15, 3182–3195.e14, 2023. Available at: https://doi.org/10.1016/J.CELL.2023.05.041.

Khan, M.H., Manoj, K., Pramod, S., Reproductive disorders in dairy cattle under semi-intensive system of rearing in North-Eastern India. *Vet. World*, 9, 5, 512–518, 2016. Available at: https://doi.org/10.14202/VETWORLD.2016.512-518.

Punugoti, R., Dutt, V., Anand, A., Bhati, N., Exploring the Impact of Edge Intelligence and IoT on Healthcare: A Comprehensive Survey, in: *2023 International Conference on Sustainable Computing and Smart Systems (ICSCSS)*, Coimbatore, India, pp. 1108–1114, 2023, doi: 10.1109/ICSCSS57650.2023.10169733.

Kocakulak, T., *et al.*, Determination of optimum operating parameters of MWCNT-doped ethanol fueled HCCI engine for emission reduction. *Sci. Total Environ.*, 895, 2023. Available at: https://doi.org/10.1016/j.scitotenv.2023.165196.

Liu, Y., Hou, S., Chen, S., Kinase fusion proteins: intracellular R-proteins in plant immunity, in: *Trends in Plant Science*, 2023, [Preprint], Available at: https://doi.org/10.1016/j.tplants.2023.11.002.

Kumar, S.A., Kumar, H., Dutt, V., Soni, H., Self-Health Analysis with Two Step Histogram based Procedure using Machine Learning, in: *2021 Third International Conference on Intelligent Communication Technologies and Virtual Mobile Networks (ICICV)*, Tirunelveli, India, pp. 794–799, 2021, doi: 10.1109/ICICV50876.2021.9388427.

Lou, Y., Deng, Z., Gao, J., Genomics refined: AI-powered perspectives on structural analysis, in: *Trends in Plant Science*, 2023, [Preprint], Available at: https://doi.org/10.1016/J.TPLANTS.2023.10.005.

Madeddu, C., *et al.*, EGFR-Mutated Non-Small Cell Lung Cancer and Resistance to Immunotherapy: Role of the Tumor Microenvironment. *Int. J. Mol. Sci.*, 23, 12, 2022. Available at: https://doi.org/10.3390/IJMS23126489.

Sekhar, U.S., Vyas, N., Dutt, V., Kumar, A., Multimodal Neuroimaging Data in Early Detection of Alzheimer's Disease: Exploring the Role of Ensemble Models and GAN Algorithm, in: *2023 International Conference on Circuit Power and Computing Technologies (ICCPCT)*, Kollam, India, pp. 1664–1669, 2023, doi: 10.1109/ICCPCT58313.2023.10245177.

Manna, D. and Sarkar, D., Multifunctional role of astrocyte elevated gene-1 (Aeg-1) in cancer: Focus on drug resistance. *Cancers*, 13, 8, 2021. Available at: https://doi.org/10.3390/CANCERS13081792.

Sasubilli, S.M., Kumar, A., Dutt, V., Improving Health Care by Help of Internet of Things and Bigdata Analytics and Cloud Computing, in: *2020 International Conference on Advances in Computing and Communication Engineering (ICACCE)*, Las Vegas, NV, USA, pp. 1–4, 2020, doi: 10.1109/ICACCE49060.2020.9155042.

Swarna, S.R., Boyapati, S., Dutt, V., Bajaj, K., Deep Learning in Dynamic Modeling of Medical Imaging: A Review Study, in: *2020 3rd International Conference on Intelligent Sustainable Systems (ICISS)*, Thoothukudi, India, pp. 745–749, 2020, 10.1109/ICISS49785.2020.9315990.

McWhite, C.D., *et al.*, A Pan-plant Protein Complex Map Reveals Deep Conservation and Novel Assemblies. *Cell*, 181, 2, 460–474.e14, 2020. Available at: https://doi.org/10.1016/j.cell.2020.02.049.

Omer Mahgoub, E., *et al.*, Role of functional genomics in identifying cancer drug resistance and overcoming cancer therapy relapse. *Heliyon*, e22095, 2023. Available at: https://doi.org/10.1016/J.HELIYON.2023.E22095.

Rathour, R., *et al.*, Metagenomic analysis of a bioreactor biofilm treating raw textile effluent and biochemical characterization of a novel azoreductase gene. *Biocatal. Agric. Biotechnol.*, 53, 2023. Available at: https://doi.org/10.1016/j.bcab.2023.102876.

Shi, Y., *et al.*, *In vitro* and *in vivo* evaluation of Lactobacillus strains and comparative genomic analysis of Lactobacillus plantarum CGMCC12436 reveal candidates of colonise-related genes. *Food Res. Int.*, 119, 813–821, 2019. Available at: https://doi.org/10.1016/j.foodres.2018.10.064.

Swarna, S.R., Kumar, A., Dixit, P., Sairam, T.V.M., Parkinson's Disease Prediction using Adaptive Quantum Computing, in: *2021 Third International Conference on Intelligent Communication Technologies and Virtual Mobile Networks (ICICV)*, Tirunelveli, India, pp. 1396–1401, 2021, doi: 10.1109/ICICV50876.2021.9388628.

Wu, T., *et al.*, Comparison of volatile metabolic profiles in fermented milk of Streptococcus thermophilus during the postripening period at different incubation temperatures. *J. Dairy Sci.*, 106, 4, 2303–2313, 2023. Available at: https://doi.org/10.3168/jds.2022-22331.

Yang, Y., *et al.*, Optimization of lactic acid bacterial starter culture to improve the quality and flavor characteristics of traditional Hurood. *J. Dairy Sci.*, 2023. [Preprint], Available at: https://doi.org/10.3168/jds.2023-23754.

Boyapati, S., Swarna, S.R., Dutt, V., Vyas, N., Big Data Approach for Medical Data Classification: A Review Study, in: *2020 3rd International Conference on Intelligent Sustainable Systems (ICISS)*, Thoothukudi, India, pp. 762–766, 2020, doi: 10.1109/ICISS49785.2020.9315870.

Zhou, H.-T., *et al.*, *Broadband acoustic carpet cloak with dynamic or static metasurface*, p. 62, 2021, Available at: https://doi.org/10.1117/12.2583943.

10

Review of Multimodal Data Fusion in Machine Learning: Methods, Challenges, Opportunities

Leena Arya[1], Yogesh Kumar Sharma[1]*, Smitha[2] and Sreelakshmi Doma[3]

[1]*Koneru Lakshmaiah Education Foundation, Vaddeswaram, Guntur, AP, India*
[2]*Muscat college, Affiliated to University of Stirling, Bousher, Muscat, Oman*
[3]*Institute of Aeronautical Engineering, Dundigal, Hyderabad, India*

Abstract
In many fields, data on the same phenomenon can be derived from a variety of sources, including different detectors, different conditions, different experiments, and different subjects. In this article, we refer to every one of the acquisitions mentioned above frames as a "modality." It is quite uncommon for one method to provide a thorough comprehension of the issue under research, considering the diversity of natural events. There are concerns beyond employing each modality individually when a growing number of techniques can provide information on an identical framework. It is generating further levels of flexibility. Many of these issues and "challenges," as we describe them, are cross-disciplinary. The two main topics that this article addresses are "The reason why data combination is required" and "In what ways can one accomplish this?" Inspired by different instances in the areas of science and technology, the primary issue is followed by a structure based on mathematics exhibiting some of the benefits of data fusion. We address the second concern by defining "diversity" and applying many methods based on data that make use of tensor as well as matrix subdivisions. These approaches demonstrate their ability to account for variability across databases. This article aims to provide readers with an overview of the scope, possibilities, and promise of the topic, regardless of their prior knowledge.

***Keywords*:** Multimodal, data fusion, fusion methods, machine learning, data integrations, multimodal learning

**Corresponding author*: dr.sharmayogeshkumar@gmail.com

Umesh Kumar Lilhore, Abhishek Kumar, Narayan Vyas, Sarita Simaiya and Vishal Dutt (eds.) Multimodal Data Fusion for Bioinformatics Artificial Intelligence, (205–226) © 2025 Scrivener Publishing LLC

10.1 Introduction

One of the critical challenges in robotic data processing is the successful construction of shared and multimodal representations. A new paradigm for data fusion based on multimodal learning is able to make intelligent use of the vast amounts of raw data that are at our fingertips. Several methods for creating multimodal representations have been developed, but none of them have been tested in a real-world production environment [1].

Educational organizations need to be competent in handling technologies that produce huge volumes of different data, particularly due to the emergence of the Internet of Things (IoT), which is followed by ubiquitous monitoring and additional forms of hyper-digitalization. The ability to model and anticipate organizational learning is dependent on the quality of multimodal representations, which is why this process is a primary focus of multimodal data study [2].

Text, pictures, music, numbers, and behavioral data are all examples of modalities that may be used in multimodal learning. The 1980s saw the beginning of multimodal learning's meteoric rise to prominence. Early work on the topic showed that a speech recognition sensor system could effectively integrate visual and audio data [3]. They beat the audio data model by combining the two modalities.

Additional research has shown that different modalities may really work together and that with proper data fusion, model performance can be significantly enhanced [4]. It is impossible to resolve the examined machine learning (ML) issue without taking into account all modalities because modalities may exist in tandem by definition. Lastly, a suitable fusion method is needed to adapt the ML issue to the high-quality modalities that have been supplied by recent advancements in multisensory systems [5]. Choosing or even developing the right data fusion solution can decide whether the data fusion tactics employed by data analysis groups in businesses are successful or unsuccessful. A key aspect of multimodal learning additionally involves the integration of information [6].

The concept in question possesses the capacity to serve as a "universal approach," adaptable to a broad range of artificial intelligence paradigms, i.e., machine and deep learning models. There is not presently a one-size-fits-all approach, as mentioned in [7]. Based on their findings, the authors conclude that there are two significant problems with all state-of-the-art data fusion models available today. They are not adaptable or interpretable, or they are very complex or task-specific [8].

Multimodal, such as multisensory perspectives, are essential to individual cognitive growth from childhood onward [9]. As an example, throughout operational cognitive development, the meaning of the word "joy" is never wholly formed apart from visual and auditory inputs; this is in addition to the semantic and syntactic accompaniments that humans use to understand word meaning.

Reading a book, for example, is an example of a situation when modalities are absent, yet the learned structures from multisensory experiences are used similarly. It is common in the field of machine learning to acquire knowledge using unimodal nature input when the subsequent assignment also happens to be unimodal. It is common practice to choose and thoroughly investigate the modality that is most prevalent in a given study subject. One may alternatively use multimodal data to train a model that can handle unimodal situations; this approach is more in line with how humans' brains evolve. In the context of our research, we use the acronym MCl to describe this phenomenon [10].

The distinction between MCl and unimodal learning may be better articulated and understood by comparing two sentiment analysis models: one using unimodal textual information and the other employing multimodal data to perform training. Which of the following will hold up better under test using unimodal textual facts? Although the task might appear simple if the assessment turned out to be multimodal, the outcome is not widely recognized due to the unimodal nature of the subsequent tasks. In this research, we compare and contrast MCl with unimodal learning from a theoretical and empirical vantage point [12]. Here is a brief overview of what we have accomplished:

- We begin by conducting an empirical evaluation of MCl and comparing its performance to that of situations when unimodal data is used for learning. Our primary emphasis is on the auditory modality, and we choose language-related downstream tasks.
- We present mathematical evidence that suggests particular modalities are able to acquire information from different modalities and outperform them on single-modal activities with the use of parameters associated with the model. We prove that MCl has upper-bound entropy limits from unimodal learning and remove performance limitations for it. Moreover, we investigate MCl's lower bounds and suggest a regularization strategy that might promote MCl.

The structure of the entire article is as follows: The second section describes deep learning techniques, including multimodal analysis, while covering relevant work in Multimodal Fusion. The third section provides a thorough explanation of multimodal and information merging; the fourth section discusses applications, possibilities, and obstacles; the fifth section concludes the study and suggests future developments.

10.2 Related Work

In this part, we will go over the many kinds of modalities that might arise in a machine-learning task. We classify modalities into three broad categories in accordance with [13]:

- Tabular data: rows represent observations and columns their attributes;
- Graphical data: In a graph, each statement is a node, and the relationships between them are the edges;
- Signal-based data: the data included in files with the correct extension constitute observations.

In sequences, characteristics are represented by certain types of letters or phrases in texts. Each of the recognized categories is represented in our research using the following modalities: Examples of tabular data include labels; examples of textual data (sequences) include reviews, titles, and descriptions; examples of visual data include product pictures and movie posters; and graphs depict relations between movies [14].

Furthermore, the authors of [15] focused on the job of picture segmentation in order to develop the best joint representation from rich and complementary scene information using images obtained from several sensors. There seemed to be no limitations on the modalities that may be investigated in tandem to address a particular issue in any of these investigations. The multimodal model outperformed the unimodal ones, proving that combining modalities improves performance [1].

10.2.1 Machine and Deep Learning Methods with Multimodal

There is much activity in the field of multimodal machine learning. Using a variety of sensory inputs, this field attempts to replicate real-world situations [16]. One subfield of natural language processing that is more pertinent to the experiments presented here is the study of human multimodal language. The use of data from visual, auditory, and linguistic modalities has the potential to boost NLP model performance, according to research [17]. Using a multimodal paradigm, sentiment analysis has been the subject of substantial research [18]. In recent years, other research has also shown success in using multimodal language data for tasks including emotion detection [19] and personality characteristics recognition [20]. Research has focused on various natural language processing (NLP) problems that make use of multimodal language data and innovative ML methods, such as the Recurrent Dynamic Fusion Network (RDF) [21], Memory Fusion Network (MFN) [22], and the Low-rank Multimodal Fusion Fusion model [5] for tasks involving many modalities.

There has been much activity in the field of machine learning pertaining to transfer learning, which involves moving data from one job to another [23]. One example is the transmission of information from one modality or domain to another, as shown in [24]. Another area of transfer learning that is currently active is learning distributed representations of inputs [25]. The practice of never seeing class labels during training in areas like zero-shot learning [26] is another example of information transfer. As far as we are aware, this is the first publication to thoroughly examine the Multimodal Co-learning (MCl) paradigm from both a theoretical and empirical perspective.

10.2.2 Evaluation of Multimodal

There is currently no uniform metric that can be used to assess the aspect of collected inter- and cross-modalities, making it difficult to evaluate the multimodal data fusion method [27]. We can, however, test the hypothesis that learning from many kinds of data at once improves task performance. Comparing the multimodal fusion model's performance scores (precision, AUC, etc.) against those of models that only examine one modality is the most common method for ensuring the model's quality [28]. This method allows us to determine whether and to what degree mixing modalities yields novel insights. We also strive to maintain consistency between observations by making sure that related comments have similar multimodal representations. As a result, NN algorithms have been compared to multimodal models in a number of studies [29], providing a solid foundation.

In conclusion, it is recommended to evaluate multimodal models before making adjustments to additional modalities. Adding more modalities improves performance somewhat but drastically increases training duration in certain circumstances [30]. Consequently, even while the model performs very well, it may not be practical to use in production settings. Therefore, we need to think about the model's simplicity and adaptability in addition to its ratings. Our study evaluates and contrasts three methods: sketch, late Fusion, and early Fusion for creating multimodal representations in sensor systems. In this part, we have covered the essential points of each of them. The following section provides an overview of the datasets used for the analysis [31]. Table 10.1 presents a comparative analysis of existing multimodal research.

Table 10.1 A comparative analysis of existing research in multimodal research.

References	Research objective	Modalities	Data fusion methods	Key findings
[10]	Enhance surveillance by combining speech and video data	Speech, Video	Fusion of Hidden Markov Models (HMM) for speech and Convolutional Neural Networks (CNN) for video	Improved accuracy in identifying and tracking individuals in crowded environments.
[11]	Improve retrieval of art images using textual queries	Text, Image	Cross-Modal Embeddings, Siamese Networks	Achieved significant gains in retrieval accuracy, mainly when dealing with diverse art collections.
[12]	Monitor health parameters using data from wearables	Accelerometer, Heart Rate, Temperature	Sensor Fusion, Ensemble Learning	Enhanced accuracy in predicting health conditions, especially during dynamic activities.
[13]	Improve underwater object detection and mapping	Radar, Sonar	Fusion of Convolutional Neural Networks (CNN) and Echo State Networks	Achieved better object detection and mapping accuracy in underwater environments.
[14]	Enhance perception capabilities for autonomous vehicles	LiDAR, Radar, Camera	Sensor Fusion, Deep Neural Networks (DNN)	Improved object recognition and trajectory prediction, leading to safer autonomous driving.

(*Continued*)

Table 10.1 A comparative analysis of existing research in multimodal research. (*Continued*)

References	Research objective	Modalities	Data fusion methods	Key findings
[15]	Analyze sentiment in social media using text and images	Text, Image	Natural Language Processing (NLP), Image Classification	Achieved better sentiment analysis accuracy by considering both textual and visual cues.
[1]	Investigate brain connectivity using EEG and fMRI	EEG, fMRI	Joint Independent Component Analysis (jICA)	Identified novel patterns of brain connectivity, leading to a deeper understanding of neural networks.
[16]	Recognize daily activities using smartphone sensors	Accelerometer, Gyroscope, GPS	Ensemble Methods, Decision Trees	High accuracy in identifying various activities, contributing to personalized health monitoring.
[17]	Improve image retrieval by incorporating audio information	Image, Audio	Fusion of Convolutional Neural Networks (CNN) and Audio Processing	Demonstrated the effectiveness of audio cues in refining image retrieval results.
[18]	Monitor environmental conditions using sensor networks	Temperature, Humidity, Air Quality	Sensor Fusion, Clustering	Enabled real-time monitoring and early detection of environmental changes, aiding in timely interventions.

10.3 Multimodal and Data Fusion

Gathering data from different formats and combining it into a single format is the aim behind multimodal data fusion methods. A multimodal data fusion paradigm is shown in Figure 10.1.

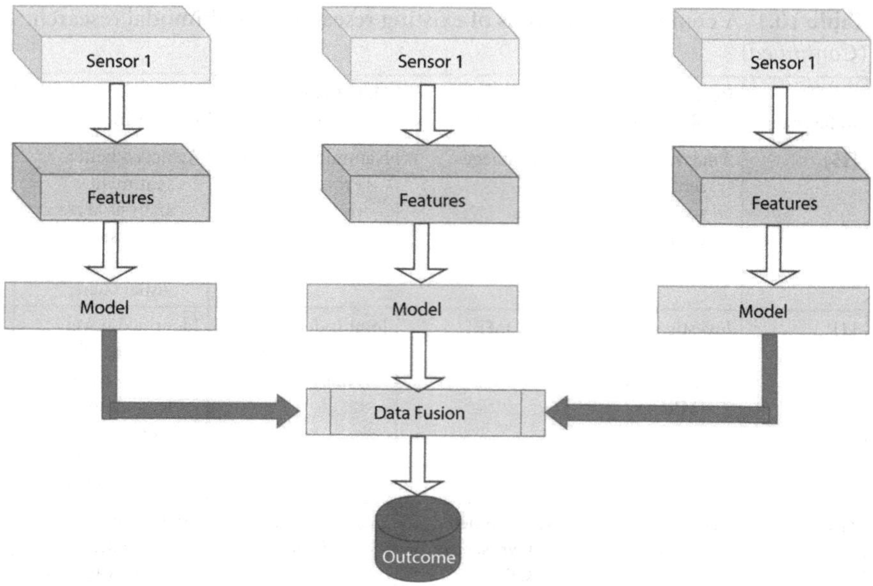

Figure 10.1 Data fusion model.

When combining several modalities, there are a few things to keep in mind [32]: Better and more robust model predictions are achieved by the merging of different modalities, a process known as intermodality [33].

- Cross-modality: Assuming inseparable interactions across modalities, this characteristic is known as cross-modality. Data cannot be used to derive fair conclusions until all of its modalities are combined [34].
- Data gaps: Not all cases may be able to take advantage of certain modalities. A perfect multimodal data integration method ought to be able to tolerate missing modalities and exploit additional modalities in order to compensate for the heavy losses of data in recommendation systems.
- Early Fusion: This focuses on features, and late Fusion, which takes decisions into account, are the two traditional branches of multimodal representation approaches [35].

The early feature method integrates all available modalities. One standard way to do this is to first combine their vector representations before training a single model [36]. Late Fusion connects the outputs of many separately trained models for each modality. The link may be established at will. To get a final result, one may either average the outcomes and choose the most common one (for classification tasks) or combine them into a model [37]. Both of these data fusion methods have shown promise in different contexts, but none can be called the best [38]. Table 10.2 presents a comparison of various fusion models used in Multimodal.

Table 10.2 Comparison of various fusion models used in multimodal.

Aspect	Sensor fusion	Feature fusion	Decision fusion
Definition	Integrates raw data from different sensors to create a unified representation.	Combines extracted features from each modality into a joint feature space.	Merges decisions or outputs from individual modalities to make a final decision.
Data Integration Level	Low-level data integration, combining raw signals from sensors.	Intermediate-level integration, combining feature vectors.	High-level integration, merging decisions or predictions.
Example Applications	Autonomous vehicles, robotics, sensor networks.	Image and speech recognition, sentiment analysis.	Medical diagnosis, security systems, human-computer interaction.
Challenges	Alignment of sensor data, dealing with different modalities and data formats.	Feature selection, dealing with heterogeneity in feature spaces.	Handling uncertainty and addressing conflicts in decision outputs.
Benefits	Improved accuracy through complementary information from multiple sensors.	Enhanced feature representation capturing diverse aspects of data.	Robust decision-making increased reliability.

(*Continued*)

Table 10.2 Comparison of various fusion models used in multimodal. (*Continued*)

Aspect	Sensor fusion	Feature fusion	Decision fusion
Computational Complexity	Can be computationally intensive, especially with a large number of sensors.	Moderate complexity, depending on the dimensionality of feature spaces.	Generally lower computational demands compared to sensor and feature fusion.
Flexibility	Less flexible in handling variations in feature spaces across sensors.	Offers flexibility in accommodating diverse feature types and dimensions.	Provides flexibility in choosing fusion strategies based on the problem at hand.
Scalability	May face scalability challenges as the number of sensors increases.	Scalable for a moderate number of features, it may face challenges with high dimensionality.	Generally more scalable, especially when dealing with large-scale decision networks.
Data Privacy Concerns	This may raise privacy concerns due to the direct integration of raw sensor data.	Reduces privacy concerns as it works with pre-processed features.	Decision-level Fusion minimizes privacy issues, as the final decision is often less sensitive than raw data.

There is no universally accepted metric for what constitutes a high-quality representation, and learning to represent is inherently unsupervised. The critical requirements for obtaining a numerical model of any modality, however, have been outlined in a number of publications. For example, textual data has BERT [39], and picture data has ResNet [40]; these and other modality-dedicated models have previously addressed the issue of Unimodal representation. Nevertheless, there is still no proven, all-encompassing approach to multimodal data that machine learning tasks may use [41]. Figure 10.2 presents the relationship of Multimodal with machine learning in various sectors.

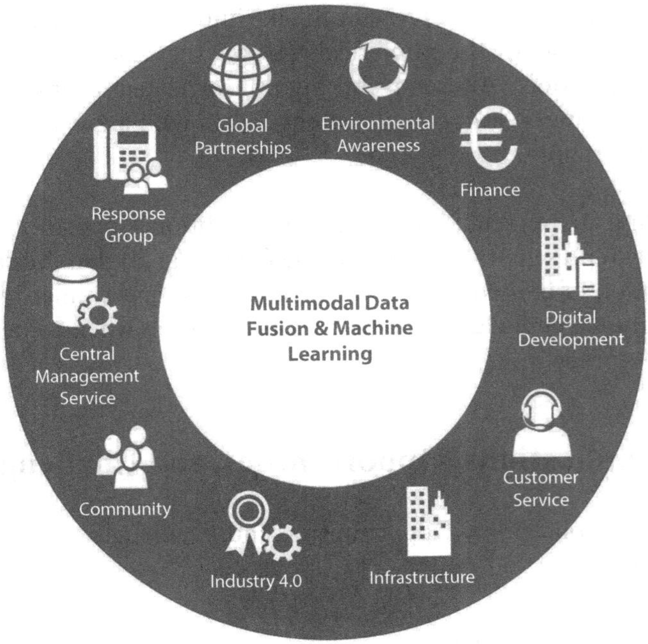

Figure 10.2 The relationship of multimodal with machine learning in various sectors.

According to [42], a suitable vector representation should have a number of characteristics, such as:

- Smoothness: The smoothness of a transformation is defined mathematically as the degree to which it maintains the objects' similarities. As an example, it is anticipated that the terms "read" and "book" would have comparable embeddings.
- Manifolds: For example, employing manifolds, one can predict that the terms "USA," "France," and "Poland" are going to possess embedded data in one region, whereas the terms "ride," "jump," and "run" can possess incorporation in a separate area. All of these zones likely have lower dimensionality than the space that started.
- Natural clustering: Putting a numerical value on observations that are contained within the same manifold facilitates natural categorization; for example, a region that contains the terms "Poland," "USA," and "France" could be classified as nations.

- Sparsity: Sparsity forces one to take into account just a small percentage of the numerical features that characterize an observation. Alternatively, highly correlated characteristics may result in complex embeddings with a great deal of uncertainty.

According to reference [43], there are additional considerations for multimodal representation, including the following: (a) that the combined representation of individual modalities maintains their similarity, and (b) that multimodal embedding can be constructed even when some modalities are not present.

10.4 Applications, Opportunities, and Challenges

The critical Applications, Opportunities, and Challenges of Multimodal are as follows.

10.4.1 Audio-Visual Multimodality

Because it makes use of our two main perceptual instruments, multimodality is likely the most natural. When people talk to one another, they usually do so while looking at the speaker [44]. The use of human voice and vision is integral to many audio-visual applications. It is typical for the audio channel to communicate the relevant information in these types of applications. The complementary nature of audio and video in conveying information is well-known. Unlike television, audio does not need a direct line of sight. Contrarily, visual processing is unaffected by acoustic disturbances such as reverberations and ambient noise, which may make it challenging to comprehend speech and audio [45].

10.4.2 Human-Machine Interaction (HML)

Here at HMI, we draw much inspiration from the multimodality seen in nature. The goal of human-machine interface (HMI) design should be to create an interface that is as easy to use, efficient, and natural as possible [46]. A number of multimodal functionalities, including vision, touch, smell, motion (such as gesture detection and user tracking), and the interpretation of human language instructions, are proposed for integration into future interaction modes. Among the numerous multimodal applications we have mentioned, HMI stands out due to the fact that its modalities are often interactive. Data fusion not only aims to interpret each system's output but also actively conveys information between these two systems; unlike other multimodal applications we mention, this one involves not one but two very different types of systems, human and machine, with each variety of sensors "observing" the other. Adding insult to injury, this work is often meant to be completed in real time. Multimodal HMI is unique in its complexity since it usually involves the human user in both the selection of modalities (from a set that is accessible) and their actual implementation. Therefore, it is not enough to know which data streams would be most useful when combined; the design of the multimodal setup and data fusion process also has to take the user's subjective cognitive preferences into account [47].

10.4.3 Understanding Brain Functionality

Investigating the roles played by distinct brain regions in processing visual and cognitive information is the focus of functional brain research. Relevant neuroscience studies largely use non-invasive methods of imaging to produce high-resolution images and spatiotemporal visualization of the activity of neurons in the brain. Dipoles are a common way to represent the ionic currents produced by neuronal activity in the brain. These dipoles are able to capture the magnetic and electrical fields that they create using two different forms of magnetic resonance imaging (MEG) and electroencephalogram (EEG). The hemodynamic response, which occurs as a result of neural activity, also alters the magnetization of blood based on its oxygen content. Functional magnetic resonance imaging (fMRI) may detect this phenomenon, which is also known as blood-oxygen-level dependent (BOLD) alterations. Thus, functional magnetic resonance imaging (fMRI) acts as a surrogate for actual brain activity [48].

10.4.4 Medical Diagnosis

A single kind of evaluation is unable to identify particular health issues, including possibly cancerous tumors, due to an assortment of variables, such as minimal positive forecasting values, specificity (high false-positive), and unsuitable sensitivity. Additionally, there are a small amount of spatial samples available (like in the biopsy). It is essential to do several medical evaluations using a variety of medical diagnostic methods to enhance the accuracy of the diagnosis, the assessment of risk, and the selection of treatment alternatives [49]. Combining genetic, environmental, and personal risk factors with traditional diagnostic tools like a physical exam, blood tests, biopsies, and MRI (both static and functional) is one example. With so many options accessible at once, it is hard to say how to do an analysis. At present, human medical specialists are primarily responsible for this work.

10.4.5 Smart Patient Monitoring

These days, medical facilities are more interested in health monitoring systems that use a variety of sensors. We want to provide a suite of affordable sensors that are both non-invasive and obtrusive so the patient may go about their daily life as usual while receiving accurate real-time alerts. Here, we concentrate on keeping an eye on epileptic patients, making predictions about when they could have severe seizures, and alerting them when they do [50]. The most effective method for tracking epileptic seizures is a combination of electroencephalogram (EEG) and video, which needs a hospital stay of several days for professional manual analysis of the EEG. The patient will experience financial strain, inconvenience, and wasted time due to this operation. Obviously, it will not work for regular life. A large percentage of potentially fatal seizures are almost undetectable by EEG, and while much work has gone into trying to predict epileptic seizures using EEG, there have been no definitive findings so far.

10.4.6 Remote Sensing and Earth Observations

There are a variety of sensor technologies that can provide information on various parts of Earth's objects. Technologies that use passive optical hyperspectral (or multispectral) imaging may determine the surface's material composition by piecing together its spectral properties from a variety of neighboring visible and non-visible spectral bands. Panchromatic imaging is the third kind of optical sensor; it creates a monochrome picture with a somewhat wider band. Hyperspectral pictures often have a spatial resolution of tens of meters, multispectral images of a few meters, and panchromatic images of less than one meter [51].

10.4.7 Meteorological Monitoring

The study and forecasting of meteorological events, including precipitation, water vapor, dew, fog, and snow, as well as their precise measurement, are essential for many uses in hydrology, agriculture, and aviation. In addition to using already commercial microwave connections, data may be obtained from a variety of sources, including rain gauges, radars, and remote sensing devices carried by satellites (see Example II-C.1) [52]. For instance, rain gauges are nothing more than cups that gather the rainwater. Their limited sample size suggests highly localized representation and, hence, low spatial resolution, even if it is the most direct and dependable method (e.g., [53]). A rain gauge may be programmed to read the precipitation level every few seconds automatically. In order to report on a variety of atmospheric phenomena, including water vapor concentration and temperature, satellites survey Earth at many frequencies, comprising visible, microwave infrared, and wavelength infrared. Factors such as terrain, beam effects, and distance from the radar may all impede the precision of radar rainfall estimates.

While satellite and radar systems cover much land, they do not always provide the most precise readings when it comes to ground-level precipitation (e.g., [54]). Cellular service providers use microwave networks for base station-to-base station backhaul communication. There are a number of meteorological events that impact the signals that the base stations send, the most common of which is attenuation caused by rainfall [55, 56]. The cellular provider's records will include these variations in signal strength at predetermined periods. This information is really "reverse-engineered" into the precipitation data. Average precipitation throughout the whole link and near ground level is provided by the data taken by the microwave links [57]. Taken collectively, these technologies complement one another in a number of ways, including their capacity to identify and differentiate between various meteorological events, as well as their coverage area, temporal resolution, measurement error, and other attributes. To improve accuracy, coverage, and resolution, meteorological data is routinely integrated; for example, see [58, 59] and the references therein.

10.5 Conclusion and Future Directions

10.5.1 Conclusion

We are entering an age when there are so many different kinds of data that it is almost impossible to avoid seeing many datasets that may be connected. An ensemble of linked datasets is probably "more than the sum of its parts" as it includes valuable information that would be lost without these linkages. However, the relevant data stored in these databases is not always easy to get to. In contrast to other forms of aggregated datasets, multimodal and multiset data have unique characteristics, which must be understood and identified before any further value can be derived from them. Additionally, multi-dataset analysis "stands on the shoulders of" a single-set study. As a result, state-of-the-art data fusion relies on building procedures and strategies for single-set analysis. In this research, we demonstrated that approaches that correctly consider the relationships between datasets may obtain advantages and gains above what is achievable when processing each dataset alone. This paper argues that these gains could have far-reaching consequences, touching on a wide range of topics such as the medical, environmental, psychological, social, and technological spheres, among many others. It goes on to say that these gains could even solve theoretical problems that defy solutions by using single-set scenarios. Using a data-driven approach, we have shown that the problems are widespread; hence, there is a need to address these issues and potential solutions at a level that includes all relevant populations.

10.5.2 Future Directions

There are now additional options for high-quality modalities because of advancements in sensor systems. As a result, some new possibilities and problems need fixing in order to produce a multimodal data fusion method that works for everyone. We identified three main topics of study: designing a multimodal benchmark, expanding multimodal applications, and boosting multimodal interpretability. To set the bar for multimodal representation research, it is essential to create a multimodal benchmark for natural language processing (NLP) applications comparable to GLUE [28]. Everything that has been found in prior and forthcoming research on this topic would be validated by this. One possible contender for this kind of benchmark is Multibench [29]. Included in this bundle are fifteen datasets that cover seven distinct uses. The next logical step may be to build state-of-the-art models and integrate them with Multibench while also adding a dynamic scoreboard and supporting additional applications.

In order to develop a data fusion approach that works for every situation, it is crucial to find new multimodal applications. For example, current multimodal fusion techniques have had their merits and weaknesses highlighted by recent research on biological applications [30, 31]. Therefore, investigating other uses would bring attention to the ongoing research and development in the area of multimodal representation. The capacity to comprehend multimodal deep neural networks is known as multimodal interpretability. Deep neural networks perform very well, yet they are not widely used or accepted because of their complexity, opaqueness, and black-box nature. Therefore, for every multimodal application, it is vital to understand the influence of separate modalities and particularly how they interact.

References

1. Gandhi, A., Adhvaryu, K., Poria, S., Cambria, E., Hussain, A., Multimodal sentiment analysis: A systematic review of history, datasets, multimodal fusion methods, applications, challenges, and future directions. *Inf. Fusion*, *91*, 424–444, 2023.
2. Barua, A., Ahmed, M.U., Begum, S., A Systematic Literature Review on Multimodal Machine Learning: Applications, Challenges, Gaps and Future Directions. *IEEE Access*, 2023.
3. Pawłowski, M., Wróblewska, A., Sysko-Romańczuk, S., Effective Techniques for Multimodal Data Fusion: A Comparative Analysis. *Sensors*, 23, 5, 2381, 2023.
4. Dai, Y., Yan, Z., Cheng, J., Duan, X., Wang, G., Analysis of multimodal data fusion from an information theory perspective. *Inf. Sci.*, 623, 164–183, 2023.
5. Swarna, S.R., Kumar, A., Dixit, P., Sairam, T.V.M., Parkinson's Disease Prediction using Adaptive Quantum Computing, in: *2021 Third International Conference on Intelligent Communication Technologies and Virtual Mobile Networks (ICICV)*, Tirunelveli, India, pp. 1396–1401, 2021, doi: 10.1109/ICICV50876.2021.9388628.
6. Aguilar-Lazcano, C.A., Espinosa-Curiel, I.E., Ríos-Martínez, J.A., Madera-Ramírez, F.A., Pérez-Espinosa, H., Machine Learning-Based Sensor Data Fusion for Animal Monitoring: Scoping Review. *Sensors*, 23, 12, 5732, 2023.
7. Lipkova, J., Chen, R.J., Chen, B., Lu, M.Y., Barbieri, M., Shao, D., Vaidya, A.J., Chen, C., Zhuang, L., Williamson, D.F., Shaban, M., Artificial intelligence for multimodal data integration in oncology. *Cancer Cell*, 40, 10, 1095–1110, 2022.
8. Lance, C., Luecken, M.D., Burkhardt, D.B., Cannoodt, R., Rautenstrauch, P., Laddach, A., Ubingazhibov, A., Cao, Z.J., Deng, K., Khan, S., Liu, Q., Multimodal single cell data integration challenge: results and lessons learned. *BioRxiv*, 2022–04, 2022.
9. Gao, J., Li, P., Chen, Z., Zhang, J., A survey on deep learning for multimodal data fusion. *Neural Comput.*, 32, 5, 829–864, 2020.
10. Sasubilli, S.M., Kumar, A., Dutt, V., Improving Health Care by Help of Internet of Things and Bigdata Analytics and Cloud Computing, in: *2020 International Conference on Advances in Computing and Communication Engineering (ICACCE)*, Las Vegas, NV, USA, pp. 1–4, 2020, doi: 10.1109/ICACCE49060.2020.9155042.

11. Dahiya, N., Sharma, Y.K., Rani, U., Hussain, S., Nabilal, K.V., Mohan, A., Nuristani, N., Hyper-parameter tuned deep learning approach for effective human monkeypox disease detection. *Sci. Rep.*, 13, 1, 15930, 2023.
12. Qi, W., Fan, H., Karimi, H.R., Su, H., An adaptive reinforcement learning-based multimodal data fusion framework for human–robot confrontation gaming. *Neural Netw.*, 164, 489–496, 2023.
13. Kunduru, A.R., Machine Learning in Drug Discovery: A Comprehensive Analysis of Applications, Challenges, and Future Directions. *Int. J. Orange Technol.*, 5, 8, 29–37, 2023.
14. Li, J., Hong, D., Gao, L., Yao, J., Zheng, K., Zhang, B., Chanussot, J., Deep learning in multimodal remote sensing data fusion: A comprehensive review. *Int. J. Appl. Earth Obs. Geoinf.*, 112, 102926, 2022.
15. Mu, S., Cui, M., Huang, X., Multimodal data fusion in learning analytics: A systematic review. *Sensors*, 20, 23, 6856, 2020.
16. Pradeep, S., Sharma, Y.K., Lilhore, U.K., Simaiya, S., Kumar, A., Ahuja, S., Chakrabarti, T., Developing an SDN security model (EnsureS) based on lightweight service path validation with batch hashing and tag verification. *Sci. Rep.*, 13, 1, 17381, 2023.
17. Punugoti, R., Dutt, V., Kumar, A., Bhati, N., Boosting the Accuracy of Cardiovascular Disease Prediction Through SMOTE, in: *2023 International Conference on IoT, Communication and Automation Technology (ICICAT)*, Gorakhpur, India, pp. 1–6, 2023, doi: 10.1109/ICICAT57735.2023.10263703.
18. Gaw, N., Yousefi, S., Gahrooei, M.R., Multimodal data fusion for systems improvement: A review. *IISE Trans.*, 54, 11, 1098–1116, 2022.
19. Wang, Z., Ma, Y., Zhang, Y., Review of pixel-level remote sensing image fusion based on deep learning. *Inf. Fusion*, 90, 2023.
20. Punugoti, R., Dutt, V., Anand, A., Bhati, N., Exploring the Impact of Edge Intelligence and IoT on Healthcare: A Comprehensive Survey, in: *2023 International Conference on Sustainable Computing and Smart Systems (ICSCSS)*, Coimbatore, India, pp. 1108–1114, 2023, doi: 10.1109/ICSCSS57650.2023.10169733.
21. Comito, C., Caroprese, L., Zumpano, E., Multimodal fake news detection on social media: a survey of deep learning techniques. *Soc. Netw. Anal. Min.*, 13, 1, 101, 2023.
22. Mylavarapu, R.T., Pokhriyal, A., Dhargalkar, R.R., Bhati, N., Empowering Healthcare with AI: Addressing Challenges and Envisioning the Future, in: *2023 4th International Conference on Electronics and Sustainable Communication Systems (ICESC)*, Coimbatore, India, pp. 1393–1398, 2023, doi: 10.1109/ICESC57686.2023.10193228.
23. Swarna, S.R., Boyapati, S., Dutt, V., Bajaj, K., Deep Learning in Dynamic Modeling of Medical Imaging: A Review Study, in: *2020 3rd International Conference on Intelligent Sustainable Systems (ICISS)*, Thoothukudi, India, pp. 745–749, 2020, doi: 10.1109/ICISS49785.2020.9315990.

24. Nayak, S. and Sharma, Y.K., A modified Bayesian boosting algorithm with weight-guided optimal feature selection for sentiment analysis. *Decis. Anal. J.*, 8, 100289, 2023.
25. Rangineni, S., Marupaka, D., Bhardwaj, A.K., An examination of machine learning in the process of data integration. *Int. J. Comput. Trends Technol.*, 71, 6, 79–85, 2023.
26. Qiu, S., Zhao, H., Jiang, N., Wang, Z., Liu, L., An, Y., Zhao, H., Miao, X., Liu, R., Fortino, G., Multi-sensor information fusion based on machine learning for real applications in human activity recognition: State-of-the-art and research challenges. *Inf. Fusion*, 80, 241–265, 2022.
27. Zhu, L., Zhu, Z., Zhang, C., Xu, Y., Kong, X., Multimodal sentiment analysis based on fusion methods: A survey. *Inf. Fusion*, 95, 306–325, 2023.
28. Burugadda, V.R., Mane, P.M., Kumar, A., Bhati, N., A Machine Learning-Based Algorithm for Early Detection of Sepsis in Hospitalized Patients: Development and Evaluation, in: *2023 1st International Conference on Circuits, Power and Intelligent Systems (CCPIS)*, Bhubaneswar, India, pp. 1–6, 2023, doi: 10.1109/CCPIS59145.2023.10291447.
29. Kumar, N., Verma, H., Sharma, Y.K., Adversarial Attacks on Graph Neural Network: Techniques and Countermeasures, in: *Concepts and Techniques of Graph Neural Networks*, pp. 58–73, IGI Global, 2023.
30. Amal, S., Safarnejad, L., Omiye, J.A., Ghanzouri, I., Cabot, J.H., Ross, E.G., Use of multi-modal data and machine learning to improve cardiovascular disease care. *Front. Cardiovasc. Med.*, 9, 840262, 2022.
31. Albahri, A.S., Duhaim, A.M., Fadhel, M.A., Alnoor, A., Baqer, N.S., Alzubaidi, L., Albahri, O.S., Alamoodi, A.H., Bai, J., Salhi, A., Santamaría, J., A systematic review of trustworthy and explainable artificial intelligence in healthcare: Assessment of quality, bias risk, and data fusion. *Inf. Fusion*, 2023.
32. Kumar, N., Verma, H., Sharma, Y.K., Graph Convolutional Neural Networks for Link Prediction in Social Networks, in: *Concepts and Techniques of Graph Neural Networks*, pp. 86–107, IGI Global, 2023.
33. Mohd Ali, M., Hashim, N., Abd Aziz, S., Lasekan, O., Utilisation of Deep Learning with Multimodal Data Fusion for Determination of Pineapple Quality Using Thermal Imaging. *Agronomy*, 13, 2, 401, 2023.
34. Babadian, R.P., Faez, K., Amiri, M., Falotico, E., Fusion of tactile and visual information in deep learning models for object recognition. *Inf. Fusion*, 92, 313–325, 2023.
35. Heiliger, L., Sekuboyina, A., Menze, B., Egger, J., Kleesiek, J., *Beyond medical imaging - A review of multimodal deep learning in radiology*, Authorea Preprints, 2023.
36. Kumar, A., Kumar, S.A., Dutt, V., Dubey, A.K., Narang, S., A Hybrid Secure Cloud Platform Maintenance Based on Improved Attribute-Based Encryption Strategies. *Int. J. Interact. Multimed. Artif. Intell.*, 8, 2, 150, 2023. Universidad Internacional de La Rioja, doi: 10.9781/ijimai.2021.11.004.

37. Richards, C.J., Valliani, N., Johnson, B.A., Wong, N.K.K., Pennati, A., Saeed, A.K., Rodriguez, B.M., Multimodal data fusion using signal/image processing methods for multi-class machine learning, in: *Signal Processing, Sensor/Information Fusion, and Target Recognition XXXII*, vol. 12547, pp. 194–210, SPIE, 2023, June.
38. Sharma, Y.K., Athithan, S., Sachi, S., Singh, A.K., Jain, A., Devi, S., Copy and Move Forged Image Detection by Deep Learning, in: *2023 World Conference on Communication & Computing (WCONF)*, IEEE, pp. 1–6, 2023, July.
39. Bhati, N., Duggar, R., Alzahrani, A., Exploring few-shot learning approaches for bioinformatics advancements, in: *Applying Machine Learning Techniques to Bioinformatics*, pp. 303–316, IGI Global, 2024.
40. Qiu, S., Cui, X., Ping, Z., Shan, N., Li, Z., Bao, X., Xu, X., Deep Learning Techniques in Intelligent Fault Diagnosis and Prognosis for Industrial Systems: A Review. *Sensors*, 23, 3, 1305, 2023.
41. Sachi, S., Singh, A.K., Jain, A., Devi, S., Sharma, Y.K., Athithan, S., Hate Speech Detection Using the GPT-2 and Natural Language Processing, in: *2023 Intelligent Methods, Systems, and Applications (IMSA)*, pp. 276–280, IEEE, 2023, July.
42. Jony, R.I., *Multimodal data fusion of remote sensing and social media using machine learning for natural disaster detection and assessment*, Queensland University of Technology, 2023, Doctoral dissertation.
43. Sharma, Y.K. and Khatal Sunil, S., Health Care Patient Monitoring using IoT and Machine Learning, in: *IOSR Journal of Engineering (IOSR JEN) National Conference on "Recent Innovations in Engineering and Technology" MOMENTUM-19*, 2019.
44. Wu, P., Wang, Z., Zheng, B., Li, H., Alsaadi, F.E., Zeng, N., AGGN: Attention-based glioma grading network with multi-scale feature extraction and multi-modal information fusion. *Comput. Biol. Med.*, 152, 106457, 2023.
45. Burugadda, V.R., Jadhav, N., Vyas, N., Duggar, R., Exploring the Potential of Deep Reinforcement Learning for Autonomous Navigation in Complex Environments, in: *2023 7th International Conference on Computing, Communication, Control And Automation (ICCUBEA)*, Pune, India, pp. 1–6, 2023, doi: 10.1109/ICCUBEA58933.2023.10392109.
46. Boyapati, S., Swarna, S.R., Dutt, V., Vyas, N., Big Data Approach for Medical Data Classification: A Review Study, in: *2020 3rd International Conference on Intelligent Sustainable Systems (ICISS)*, Thoothukudi, India, pp. 762–766, 2020, doi: 10.1109/ICISS49785.2020.9315870.
47. Sharma, Y.K. and Rokade, M.D., Deep and machine learning approaches for anomaly-based intrusion detection of imbalanced network traffic. *IOSR J. Eng.*, 63–67, 2019.

48. Salcedo-Sanz, S., Ghamisi, P., Piles, M., Werner, M., Cuadra, L., Moreno-Martínez, A., Izquierdo-Verdiguier, E., Muñoz-Marí, J., Mosavi, A., Camps-Valls, G., Machine learning information fusion in Earth observation: A comprehensive review of methods, applications and data sources. *Inf. Fusion*, 63, 256–272, 2020.
49. Sekhar, U.S., Vyas, N., Dutt, V., Kumar, A., Multimodal Neuroimaging Data in Early Detection of Alzheimer's Disease: Exploring the Role of Ensemble Models and GAN Algorithm, in: *2023 International Conference on Circuit Power and Computing Technologies (ICCPCT)*, Kollam, India, pp. 1664–1669, 2023, doi: 10.1109/ICCPCT58313.2023.10245177.
50. Balyan, A.K., Ahuja, S., Sharma, S.K., Lilhore, U.K., Machine learning-based intrusion detection system for healthcare data, in: *2022 IEEE VLSI Device Circuit and System (VLSI DCS)*, pp. 290–294, IEEE, 2022, February.
51. Swapna, M., Sharma, Y.K., Prasad, B.M.G., A survey on face recognition using convolutional neural network, in: *Data Engineering and Communication Technology: Proceedings of 3rd ICDECT-2K19*, Springer Singapore, Singapore, pp. 649–661, 2020.
52. Boehm, K.M., Aherne, E.A., Ellenson, L., Nikolovski, I., Alghamdi, M., Vázquez-García, I., Zamarin, D., Long Roche, K., Liu, Y., Patel, D., Aukerman, A., Multimodal data integration using machine learning improves risk stratification of high-grade serous ovarian cancer. *Nat. Cancer*, 3, 6, 723–733, 2022.
53. Burugadda, V.R., Pawar, P.S., Kumar, A., Bhati, N., Predicting Hospital Readmission Risk for Heart Failure Patients Using Machine Learning Techniques: A Comparative Study of Classification Algorithms, in: *2023 Second International Conference on Trends in Electrical, Electronics, and Computer Engineering (TEECCON)*, Bangalore, India, pp. 223–228, 2023, doi: 10.1109/TEECCON59234.2023.10335817.
54. Jadhav, D., Sharma, Y.K., Arora, D.P., Profound Learning Approach for Shot Boundary Location, in: *2nd International Conference on Communication & Information Processing (ICCIP)*, 2020, April.
55. Jadhav, M., Kumar Sharma, Y., Bhandari, G.M., Currency identification and forged banknote detection using deep learning, in: *2019 International Conference on Innovative Trends and Advances in Engineering and Technology (ICITAET)*, IEEE, pp. 178–183, 2019, December.
56. Zhang, H., Xu, H., Tian, X., Jiang, J., Ma, J., Image fusion meets deep learning: A survey and perspective. *Inf. Fusion*, 76, 323–336, 2021.
57. Chandrasekaran, S., Dutt, V., Vyas, N., Kumar, R., Student Sentiment Analysis Using Various Machine Learning Techniques, in: *2023 International Conference on Artificial Intelligence and Smart Communication (AISC)*, Greater Noida, India, pp. 104–107, 2023, doi: 10.1109/AISC56616.2023.10085018.

58. Shaheed, K., Mao, A., Qureshi, I., Kumar, M., Hussain, S., Zhang, X., Recent advancements in finger vein recognition technology: methodology, challenges and opportunities. *Inf. Fusion*, 79, 84–109, 2022.
59. Dutt, V., Sasubilli, S.M., Yerrapati, A.E., Dynamic Information Retrieval With Chatbots: A Review of Artificial Intelligence Methodology, in: *2020 4th International Conference on Electronics, Communication and Aerospace Technology (ICECA)*, Coimbatore, India, pp. 1299–1303, 2020, doi: 10.1109/ICECA49313.2020.9297533.

11

Recent Advancement in Bioinformatics: An In-Depth Analysis of AI Techniques

Yogesh Kumar Sharma[1]*, Leena Arya[1], Smitha[2] and Shaik Saddam Hussain[3]

[1]*Koneru Lakshmaiah Education Foundation, Vaddeswaram, Guntur, AP, India*
[2]*Muscat College, University of Stirling, Bousher, Muscat, Oman*
[3]*VNR Vignana Jyothi Institute of Engineering and Technology, Hyderabad, India*

Abstract

Computational systems biology is one of the scientific and technical domains where artificial intelligence (AI) has shown its worth and even triumphed. Typically, computational biologists use mathematical modelling and statistical analysis to solve issues involving biological systems at all levels, including those involving specific species, internal biological subsystems, cells, membranes, DNAs, and pertinent external environments. Genomics and bioinformatics are two subfields of computational systems biology that have a lot in common and where AI can shine. When it comes to tackling problems in the fields, artificial intelligence provides a more sophisticated toolbox than traditional computer techniques. Machine learning approaches, such as developing deeper learning models and neural networks, are now in vogue in bioinformatics and genomics as a means of artificial intelligence. However, they are not the only applications of AI. Molecular structure analysis and biological data classification are two practical applications of artificial intelligence. This paper examines and analyses the advancements in two types of deep learning algorithms applied to the bioinformatics domain: AutoMLDL and DeepMLDL. The present research strives for publications that demonstrate and deal with the most recent advancements in AI techniques with the goal of addressing the challenges within bioinformatics.

Keywords: Machine learning, AutoMLDL, bioinformatics, deep learning, artificial intelligence

**Corresponding author*: dr.sharmayogeshkumar@gmail.com

Umesh Kumar Lilhore, Abhishek Kumar, Narayan Vyas, Sarita Simaiya and Vishal Dutt (eds.) Multimodal Data Fusion for Bioinformatics Artificial Intelligence, (227–246) © 2025 Scrivener Publishing LLC

11.1 Introduction

An average 50-layer ResNet-50 model [1–5] structure has about 25 million variables. The first stage contains 64 filters; the subsequent phase contains 128 filters; the third stage contains 256 filters; the next stage contains 512 filters; and the fifth level contains 1,024 filters. Each residual block within the framework has three (3 × 3) layers of convolution as well as an alternative connection. At least one shortcut link and two (3 × 3) convolutional layers may be found in each model residual block. The development of high-performing mathematical models, for the most seasoned experts, requires a significant investment of both money and time because, before the introduction of ResNet, the model had to be developed independently using experimentation and failure [6–9].

The exorbitant expenses of model creation have given rise to a revolutionary idea: automating the whole machine-learning workflow. One tactic to reduce the burden of costs associated with development involves automatic artificial intelligence [7]. Utilizing the AutoMLDL techniques that can automatically integrate many approaches, one can now easily build an end-to-end machine learning pipeline functionality architecture. The goal we have is to construct the most technologically sophisticated AI system we can, which includes creating a multitude of customized AutoMLDL techniques. The phases in the AutoMLDL techniques procedure include model building, integrating features, preparing information, and the assessment of the model. Subdivisions of model generation include search space exploration as well as optimization approaches.

The search space distinguishes between two primary types of machine learning techniques: neural networks and standard models for machine learning (ML). The core ideas for the design of such models are defined by exploring space. The two different types of optimization strategies are hyperparameter optimization (HPO) [11] and structural optimization (AO) [10].

AO enhances the internal workings of the model, while the HPO concentrates on training metrics such as comprehension rate as well as batch size. Architectural optimization (AO) may optimize KNN model neighbours or neural architecture layers. Neural architecture search automates neural network topology construction and optimization [12]. This technology automates design space exploration to increase neural network performance and simplify human designers' responsibilities. Neural architecture search (NAS) uses gradient-based techniques, evolutionary algorithms, and reinforcement learning to find the best structures for high accuracy with little processing resources. Any neural architecture search seeks a robust and performant model. We concentrate on a defined search zone and integrate fundamental processes [13].

Recent developments in AutoMLDL approaches have the potential to revolutionize robotics. Machine learning algorithms used in robotic systems may now be effectively constructed without the requirement for specialized expertise and a substantial amount of human labour. The method of machine learning can potentially be automated by utilizing AutoML, also known as AML techniques in robotics, for data preparatory work, design of features, selection models, hyperparameter adjustment, and implementation. In the part that follows, we have gone into depth on this. There are a lot of great reviews out there on AutoMLDL methods, but ours distinguishes us as it delves into more AutoMLDL methods and AutoDL methods approaches than just NAS strategies [14].

Dedicated researchers engaged with computational intelligence, including its associated fields, such as neural networks, deep learning, learning through reinforcement, and machine learning models, find great attraction in this subject since it remains in its early stages. Data preparation, algorithm selection, and hyperparameter tweaking are three of the most tedious and time-consuming parts of building machine learning models.

Automating these processes is now the main focus of AutoMLDL research. By streamlining and improving the machine learning process, AutoMLDL hopes to free up academics and practitioners to concentrate on more strategic endeavours, including creating problems and understanding their results. Also, by making machine learning accessible to those without extensive training in the field, AutoMLDL hopes to democratize machine learning. This might spur innovation and advancement in many different areas. However, the primary goal of this review article is to establish specific standards to tackle the outstanding difficulties and limits [15]. In order to meet the issues in bioinformatics, this research is looking for works that reflect and address the newest breakthroughs in AI approaches. When it comes to AutoMLDL performance, there are four key needs:

- AutoMLDL systems should aim for high accuracy in forecasts or models. The aim is to ensure automated operations provide accurate outcomes with minimal errors.
- AutoMLDL requires efficiency in time and computational power. Automation should maximize resource usage and reduce training and prediction time.

- An advanced AutoMLDL solution may handle massive data sets and challenging machine-learning tasks. Despite sacrificing effectiveness or speed, they must manage increasing data volumes and computing demands.
- Versatility: AutoMLDL must be flexible to deal with multiple machine-learning approaches, frameworks, and models. It should be possible for users to try various methods until they discover an automated method that fits them. These four criteria are essential for assessing AutoMLDL systems' machine learning cycle automation efforts. These four performance and accuracy elements will conclude our open problem discussion.

The entire chapter is divided into multiple subsections, with the second section focusing on AutoMLDL methods, the third section discussing the practical use of AutoMLDL within bioinformatics, the fourth section discussing more advanced methods in AutoMLDL with bioinformatics, and the final section concluding and outlining the work's future course.

11.2 AutoMLDL Methods

AutoMLDL technologies boost efficiency by improving machine learning model development and selection. These developments may spur AI-related discoveries. The optimum neural network design and hyperparameters for deep learning tasks are automatically chosen using "evolutionary algorithms" (EAs) and cutting-edge collaborative computing architectures for "Earth Observation Fusion".

To facilitate the testing and improvement of automatic machine learning algorithms, the open-source AutoMLDL benchmark, also known as AutoML -Zero, aspires to provide a straightforward and comprehensive setting. This study compares four AutoMLDL systems on 39 datasets to find out how effective automated machine-learning approaches are [17]. Figure 11.1 illustrates the primary techniques used in both deep learning and machine learning models.

Table 11.1 provides a comparison of previous studies utilizing AutoMLDL techniques in the field of bioinformatics.

Employing "automatic machine learning and deep learning" (AutoMLDL) strategies on more than 300 datasets collected through OpenML [22], one may get an improved awareness of the effectiveness and efficiency of these programmes in a variety of machine learning use cases.

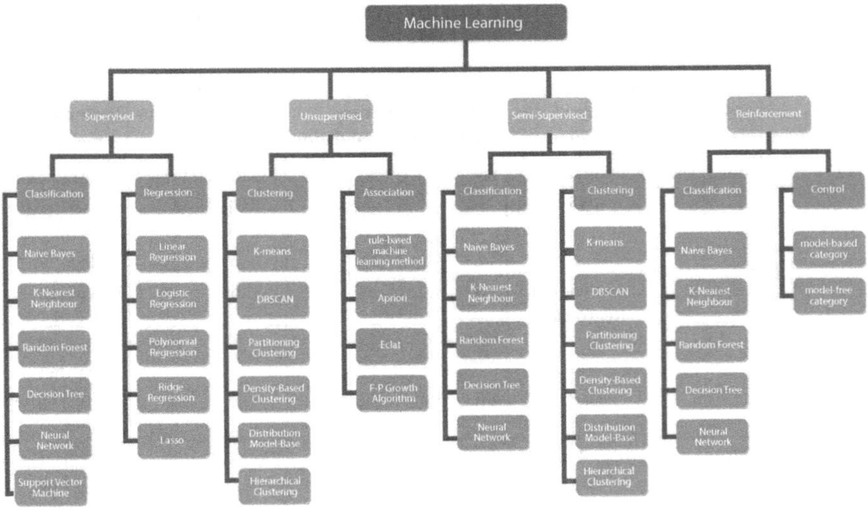

Figure 11.1 Comprehensive analysis of important models of machine learning and deep learning methods.

The Decathlon competition benchmark for the analysis of medical images uses 11 databases collected for the MedMNIST categorization test to assess the effectiveness of multiple states' AutoMLDL techniques in categorizing different kinds of healthcare images [23]. By improving search space decomposition, VolcanoML, an AutoMLDL framework, speeds up the whole AutoML process. As a result, the area for designing deep learning models may be efficiently explored [24]. Possible benefits, as discussed in a new level-based taxonomy for AutoML systems, include making AI more accessible and democratizing machine learning [25].

Multi-label classification using AutoMLDL approaches is a challenging machine-learning problem. The data, as mentioned earlier, offer useful information for a quantitative assessment of these strategies using the grammar-based method (BFS) best-first search [26]. To evaluate and contrast different AutoMLDL frameworks, three scenarios—General machine learning (ML), the XGBoost and advanced machine learning methods deployment and tuning—are utilized for standards [27]. Unsupervised anomaly detection using AutoMLDL methods highlights the most pressing issues with hyperparameter tuning and data cleaning while also suggesting avenues for further study [28]. Meta-learning techniques that identify dataset attributes by combining MetaBu meta-features alongside the OpenML condition of completeness-18 standard are advantageous for contemporary AutoMLDL implementations [29]. Regarding further

Table 11.1 Comparative analysis of existing research of AutoMLDL methods in Bioinformatics research.

References	AutoMLDL method	Algorithm types included	Feature selection	Cross-validation	Integration with bioinformatics tools	Performance metrics
[12]	AutoSklearn	Classification, Regression	Yes	Yes	Bioconductor, Biopython, BioPerl	Accuracy, F1, AUC-ROC, Sensitivity, Specificity
[13]	TPOT	Classification, Regression	Yes	Yes	Python,	Precision, Recall, AUC-PR, Matthews Correlation Coef.
[14]	H2O.ai	GLM, Random Forest, etc.	Yes	Yes	Bioconductor, Python, R	AUC-ROC, Log Loss, Accuracy, Sensitivity
[15]	AutoML by Data-Robot	Linear Models, RF, XGBoost, etc.	Yes	Yes	Python,	R-squared, MAE, RMSE, Precision, Recall
[16]	MLBox	Regression, Classification	Yes	Yes	Bioconductor, Python, R	Accuracy, F1, AUC-ROC, Sensitivity, Specificity
[17]	AutoSklearn	Classification, Regression	Yes	Yes	Bioconductor, Biopython, BioPerl	Accuracy, Precision, Recall, AUC-ROC
[18]	TPOT	Regression	Yes	Yes	Python,	RMSE, MAE, R-squared
[19]	H2O.ai	GLM, Random Forest, etc.	Yes	Yes	Bioconductor, Python, R	AUC-ROC, Log Loss, Accuracy, Precision, Recall
[20]	AutoML by Data-Robot	RF, Gradient Boosting, Neural Networks	Yes	Yes	Python,	AUC-ROC, Log Loss, Accuracy, Sensitivity
[21]	MLBox	Classification	Yes	Yes	Bioconductor, Python, R	Accuracy, F1, AUC-ROC, Precision, Recall

machine learning uses, FLAML serves as an inexpensive, basic AutoMLDL module that optimizes choosing models and the hyperparameters for speedy training of models and placement [30].

The cognitive system's AutoMLDL transferred learning has the potential to save time when dealing with large volumes of data that are labelled by utilizing RL-based structural search to speed up the training of models [31]. With the support of the Oracle AutoMLDL automatic processing method, highly precise machine-learning algorithms may be quickly and effectively constructed, especially when compared with cutting-edge open-source AutoMLDL solutions such as auto-sklearn with water droplets [32]. With the use of neural networks and evolutionary algorithms, a groundbreaking new study called AutoMLDL -Zero builds and optimizes mathematical models for machine learning naturally, all the way through, without our intervention. Automated modelling utilizing AutoMLDL for the compression of models may be investigated for portable device applications to save computational expenses. In order to maintain exceptional precision and significant compression, AMC uses VGG-16 algorithms for ImageNet [33].

11.3 Application of AutoMLDL in Bioinformatics

AutoMLDL methods are widely used in bioinformatics. This section covers the key applications of AutoMLDL methods in bioinformatics.

11.3.1 Bioinformatics and the Categorization of Cardiovascular Diseases

For an extended period, the consensus has been that coronary artery disease is the primary cause of death globally. Over 17 million individuals worldwide suffered from heart disease in 2018, according to estimates by the World Health Organization WHO [34]. Data mining approaches have consequently been researched in recent decades to enhance medical processes for predicting the occurrence of heart issues [35]. The method of finding and removing useful details from huge datasets by using a variety of techniques such as data preparation, forecasting, categorization and clusters can be referred to as data mining. It constitutes a crucial phase in the cycle of (KDD) knowledge discovery in databases procedure, which entails a number of other processes such as preparation, alteration, and decision-making regarding data.

Quantitative research found an astounding 97.8% accuracy rate for classifying cardiac illnesses using the ensemble model and brute force as a feature selection approach. In terms of classifying cardiac diseases, the proposed stacking model is more effective than current methods [36].

11.3.2 Diagnostics of Coronavirus Disease and Bioinformatics

As it spreads over the world, the COVID-19 pandemic has cast a pall over public discourse and endangered many lives. As the COVID-19 case count continued to rise, it became clear that resource allocation for viral detection was a major concern for all nations. Due to the rapid spread of the virus, the limited resources for detecting this highly contagious illness are under great pressure. To successfully fight the spread of COVID-19, an easily accessible, cost-effective, and automatable COVID-19 detection device is essential [37].

Detection methods based on radiography have arisen as a potential solution to the scarcity of viral testing kits, thanks to the ubiquitous radiology imaging equipment in healthcare institutions. Thanks to advancements in machine learning and other forms of deep learning, artificial intelligence has grown into a core discipline. Therefore, incorporating these technologies into radiography-based testing procedures may provide a productive and accurate way to identify COVID-19 [29]. The use of deep learning algorithms to automatically identify and classify COVID-19 is a topic of intense research [30]. So, deep learning is becoming an essential part of AI-powered medical decisions [31]. An investigation of the COVID-19 diagnostic process that made use of chest computed tomography (CT) and x-ray pictures yielded multi-classifiers as opposed to a single classifier trained via ensemble stacking. When tested on X-ray and CT scan datasets, the proposed ensemble stacking method performed quantitatively well, with percentages close to 99% [38].

11.3.3 Genomic and Bioinformatic Correlation with Clinical Data and Progress of Disease

A PCR-based investigation that used polymorphisms like INSR exon seventeen, LEPR Gln223Arg, as well as the UCP2 G 866 to connect obesity to these disorders also demonstrated that gender affects some of the variations in risk [39]. Furthermore, a study that analyzed the whole genomes of nine Egyptian women using an Illumina short-read sequencer discovered that the majority of the subjects had 12 obesity-related SNPs in common, which matched their medical diagnosis according to 30 times genome coverage.

11.3.4 Bioinformatics in the Study of Drug Resistance

Globally, bloodstream and urinary tract infections are most often caused by Escherichia coli. Worldwide, healthcare facilities are feeling the effects of the increasing antibiotic resistance in Escherichia coli, which is making patients sick and making treatment more challenging [40]. Germs that cause food poisoning may infect humans and increase their pathogenicity by acquiring drug-resistant genetic patterns in mobile elements such as plasmids, transposons, and integrons [36].

The development of next-generation sequencing (NGS) has opened up new possibilities for the effective characterization of bacterial infections, leading to the identification of virulence-associated factors and antibiotic-resistant genes [41]. Keep in mind that next-generation sequencing (NGS) is a widely used method for studying the connections between Escherichia coli strains that have developed resistance to many drugs. This allows for the analysis of genetic differences in distinct E. coli plasmids collected from different locations to predict resistance features from genomic sequences [42].

Using the bioinformatics workflow and sequencing the latest generation of sequencing technology for chromosomal shot-gun DNA sequencing, "carbapenem-resistant Escherichia coli" (CRE) isolated organisms were evaluated for resistance to quinolones and aminoglycosides. Only one of the two isolates that had virulence factors linked to the Imogene cluster was found. The findings raise the possibility of resistance gene and plasmid transfer across species and are not limited to nosocomial infections in healthcare facilities [43]. Table 11.2 presents a comparative analysis of applications of AutoMLDL methods in bioinformatics in various sectors. Figure 11.2 presents an application of AutoMLDL in bioinformatics and coverage.

Table 11.2 Comparative analysis of applications of AutoMLDL methods in bioinformatics in various sectors.

References	AutoMLDL method	Methods used	Applications	Key benefits	Challenges
[21]	AutoKeras, TPOT	Neural Networks, Decision Trees, TPOT	Genomic Sequencing, Disease Prediction	Improved Prediction Accuracy, Automated Feature Selection	Interpretability of Complex Models, Large Dataset Handling
[22]	H2O.ai, DeepAutoML	Deep Learning, Random Forest, H2O.ai	Protein Structure Prediction, Drug Discovery	Enhanced Model Generalization, Reduced Model Bias	Computationally Intensive, Hyperparameter Tuning
[23]	AutoML, TensorFlow	Support Vector Machines, Neural Networks	Gene Expression Analysis, Biomarker Identification	Time Efficiency, Scalability	Limited Explainability, Data Privacy Concerns
[24]	AutoGluon, Keras-Tuner	AutoML, Neural Networks	Functional Genomics, Pathway Analysis	Increased Research Productivity, Automated Hyper-parameter Tuning	Model Overfitting, Limited Benchmarking Tools
[25]	Google AutoML	Gradient Boosting Machines, Google AutoML	Drug Response Prediction, Biomolecular Interaction	Increased Accessibility to ML, Reduced Human Bias	Model Interpretability, Limited Customization Capabilities

(Continued)

Table 11.2 Comparative analysis of applications of AutoMLDL methods in bioinformatics in various sectors. (*Continued*)

References	AutoMLDL method	Methods used	Applications	Key benefits	Challenges
[26]	AutoML, DeepChem	Random Forest, Graph Convolutional Networks	Integrative Omics Analysis, Multi-Omics Integration	Improved Robustness, Reduced Bias and Variance	Model Complexity, Limited Biological Interpretability
[27]	AutoBias	Logistic Regression, Neural Networks	Disease Risk Prediction, Population Health Studies	Enhanced Fairness, Addressing Bias in Data	Ethical Concerns, Algorithmic Fairness Considerations
[28]	scikit-learn, AutoEncoder	AutoML, AutoEncoder	Single-cell RNA Sequencing, Cell Type Classification	Improved Clustering Accuracy, Dimensionality Reduction	High Dimensionality, Batch Effects in Single-Cell Data
[29]	PathAI, AutoML	Decision Trees, Random Forest	Pathway Analysis, Biological Function Prediction	Increased Reproducibility, Reduced Manual Annotation	Limited Training Data for Rare Pathways
[30]	AlphaFold, AutoDock	DeepMind AlphaFold, Molecular Docking Methods	Protein Folding Prediction, Drug Design	Unprecedented Accuracy in Structure Prediction	Computational Intensity, Limited Training Data

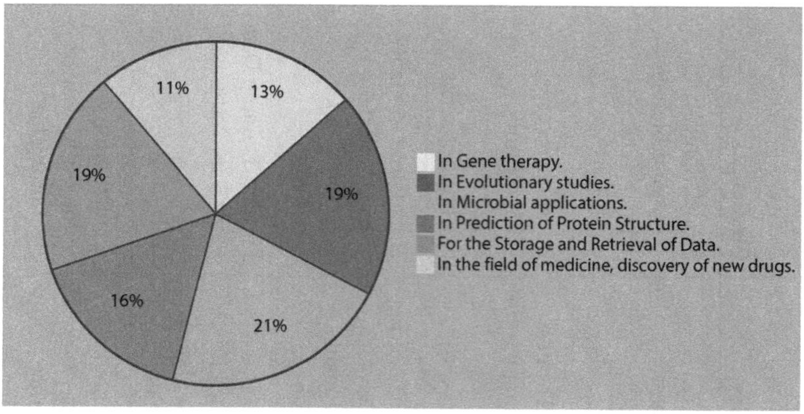

Figure 11.2 The application of AutoMLDL in bioinformatics and coverage.

11.4 Advanced Algorithm in AutoMLDL for Bioinformatics

11.4.1 Optimization with Hybrid Harris Hawks along with Cuckoo Search Applying Chemo Bioinformatics

One of the main problems in cheminformatics is dealing with large datasets that contain an excessive amount of duplicate data. To prevent premature convergence, CHHO-CS, an integrated metaheuristic technique, is capable of balancing the exploration and extraction phases. It solves the redundant calculation issue in similarity measures associated with drug design and discovery by combining the Harris-Hawks optimizer (HHO) along with two operators such as Cuckoo Search (CS) as well as Chaotic Maps (CMs). Findings from the statistical and experimental investigations demonstrate that CHHO-CS outperforms its rival algorithms. The recommended methodology ought to improve the effectiveness and precision of similarity measurements when implemented in drug study and construction procedures [44].

11.4.2 The Integration of Chemoinformatics and Bioinformatics with AI

One of the main reasons why clinical studies are terminated is because the treatment is not effective enough. This is due to problems with the drug's availability in the body and adverse responses. There is an enormous variety of variables that may cause a chemical to fail or have negative consequences. Furthermore, substantial time and financial commitment may be required to evaluate a compound's properties using *in vitro* and *in vivo* methodologies. The development of computer models capable of predicting ADME-Tox properties absorption, distribution, metabolism, excretion, and toxicity has therefore been an area of intense focus [45]. The need to enhance and simplify the medication development process is motivating these efforts, particularly in identifying possible hazards linked to novel chemicals.

Artificial intelligence algorithms have greatly improved the accuracy of early medication safety and effectiveness forecasts by using the extensive data offered by diverse ADME-Tox datasets. More and more projects in both the public and commercial sectors are being launched to develop and evaluate potential models that might assist in decision-making and come up with new ways to anticipate ADME-Tox characteristics. So, there are continuous endeavours to make ML/DL models available for public use and comparison in an attempt to increase trust and embrace these forecasts. Among them, one may find the treatments Data Commons (TDC), an open Python framework that provides a platform for the systematic access and assessment of ML models across all treatments [46].

Several models have been created within the field of machine learning (ML) to either define *in vivo* qualities using data from *in vitro* assays or to construct hypothetical features from limited experimental data. The precision of such models, however, may have certain restrictions. Regarding this matter, Rodríguez-Pérez *et al.* showed that MT-GNN, a multitask learning method based on graph neural networks, outperformed previous ML methods that depend just on data from *in vitro* brain penetration experiments [47].

Integrating ML and DL with known bioinformatics approaches is possible in four domains of computational biology: disease genomics, systems biology, molecular evolution, and protein structure analysis. Moreover, machine learning techniques such as k-nearest neighbours (KNNs), support vector machines (SVMs), convolutional neural networks (CNNs), recurrent neural networks (RNNs), principal component analysis (PCA), t-distributed stochastic neighbour embedding (t-SNE), and non-negative matrix factorization (NMF) are frequently used in bioinformatics studies [48].

11.5 Security and Privacy Issues in AutoMLDL

11.5.1 Security and Privacy

The need to guarantee ethical practices is growing in importance and urgency because of the fast development of AutoMLDL and neural networks. Regulating the development and deployment of AutoML technologies requires the enforcement of guidelines and regulations. In recent years, there has been much speculation about the potential influence of machine learning technology on people's privacy. Because of the delicate nature of the subject, careful consideration is required throughout the development of related apps and services. Several people are worried about the possibility that Intelligent Personal Assistants (IPAs) like Siri and Alexa are constantly picking up data [49].

The data subjects or sources have little rights over the exploitation of their data, even though these technologies need vast amounts of data. Anyone who creates data that can be stored has their past tracked for a long time. Digital history may be located using algorithms that have pattern recognition capabilities. As a result, the presumption of being undetectable is broken. Facial recognition software and data from social media tendencies can identify anybody. Our political leanings and other personal information may be gleaned from our online behaviour and patterns of interaction. It is possible to infer a person's personality type and even their life events from their social media behaviour [50].

A person's emotional state and truthfulness may be inferred from their word choice or the pressure of their handwriting on a digital stylus. Technologies like AutoMLDL and Neural Networks have limitless potential. Additionally, there are an infinite number of potential outcomes and abuses of them. So, the issue of responsibility for these technologies' usage and abuse arises. Regarding artificial intelligence, a resolution passed by the European Parliament in 2017 stipulates that whosoever owns, develops, or operates an AI shall be legally liable for its actions or inactions. Human and civil rights must be prioritized throughout the design process of these systems. The scientific community holds the view that the only way to gain confidence in these technologies is via laws, clarity, answerability, and doing what is right [51].

11.5.2 Open Issues

These four points, with an emphasis on precision and performance, will form the basis of our final open problem discussion segment. Our analysis of the tabled comparisons has also shown the shortcomings of the currently available neural architecture search methods in fulfilling the criteria. Future research and improvements are needed to address these problems [52]. It is a continuous struggle to improve the sampling efficiency of NAS algorithms. It now takes many attempts with NAS approaches to identify the best designs. Improving methods to efficiently find high-performing designs with fewer samples is a key topic for development. The need for scalable NAS approaches capable of handling large-scale datasets and complicated models is driven by the ever-increasing processing demands and datasets. For real-world use, it is essential to provide NAS algorithms that can search for designs efficiently and scalable [53].

The goal of NAS approaches should be to design structures that can effectively apply to new types of data. One of the main challenges in NAS is making sure that the designs that are found perform well on the training set and also show strong generalization on new data. There is a lack of clear integration of domain knowledge in current NAS approaches, which mainly depend on automated search algorithms. More effective and interpretable designs may be achieved by incorporating domain-specific constraints or previous knowledge into the NAS process [54].

The inability of NAS algorithms to be applied to new jobs or domains is a common issue. Research on NAS methods that can generalize designs and knowledge acquired from one dataset or job to another is crucial for cutting down on computing costs and search space. It may be quite a challenge to read and comprehend the complex designs generated by NAS approaches. If we can figure out how to make the found architectures more interpretable, we can learn more about the logic and principles that drive automated design. Better model creation and optimization may be achieved by resolving these outstanding challenges in AutoMLDL that are dependent on NAS performance. This will lead to more advanced and practical automated machine-learning systems [55].

11.6 Conclusion and Future Works

Many considerations arise for practitioners as they work to construct an efficient AutoMLDL system such as this. Expertise in data selection, optimization of models, hyperparameter modification, etc., has evolved into a must-have skill for machine learning practitioners. All of the potential approaches for utilizing AutoMLDL have been covered in this overview, along with descriptions of their respective elements. The recently attracted AutoMLDL future system may be developed using this explanation by immediately building on top of it. The goal of NAS is to find efficient neural network designs automatically with the use of algorithms and computer resources.

The brilliant concept of Neural Architecture Search discovers task-specific neural network topologies by using automation and computing resources. Research in this area is still going strong, and it has helped deep learning make great strides forward. Thanks to the review's thorough citations and condensed experimental results, readers will have a much better grasp of NAS and AutoMLDL. In the years to come, AutoMLDL will undoubtedly shape AI's advanced domain and the AI age as a whole.

References

1. Bhatt, M. and Shende, P., Advancement in machine learning: a strategic look-out from cancer identification to treatment. *Arch. Comput. Methods Eng.*, *30*, 4, 2777–2792, 2023.
2. Liu, Y., Chen, Y., Han, L., Bioinformatics: advancing biomedical discovery and innovation in the era of big data and artificial intelligence. *Innov. Med.*, *1*, 1, 100012–1, 2023.
3. Pur, D.R., Krance, S., Pucchio, A., Bassi, A., Miranda, R.N., Felfeli, T., Emerging applications of bioinformatics and artificial intelligence in the analysis of biofluid markers involved in retinal occlusive diseases: a systematic review. *Graefe's Arch. Clin. Exp. Ophthalmol.*, *261*, 2, 317–336, 2023.
4. Tufail, S., Riggs, H., Tariq, M., Sarwat, A.I., Advancements and Challenges in Machine Learning: A Comprehensive Review of Models, Libraries, Applications, and Algorithms. *Electronics*, *12*, 8, 1789, 2023.
5. Mufassirin, M.M., Newton, M.H., Sattar, A., Artificial intelligence for template-free protein structure prediction: a comprehensive review. *Artif. Intell. Rev.*, *56*, 8, 7665–7732, 2023.
6. Priyamvada, P., Debroy, R., Anbarasu, A., Ramaiah, S., A comprehensive review on genomics, systems biology and structural biology approaches for combating antimicrobial resistance in ESKAPE pathogens: computational tools and recent advancements. *World J. Microbiol. Biotechnol.*, *38*, 9, 153, 2022.
7. Xu, X., Li, J., Zhu, Z., Zhao, L., Wang, H., Song, C., Chen, Y., Zhao, Q., Yang, J., Pei, Y.A., Comprehensive Review on Synergy of Multi-Modal Data and AI Technologies in Medical Diagnosis. *Bioengineering*, 11, 3, 219, 2024.
8. Dahiya, N., Sharma, Y.K., Rani, U., Hussain, S., Nabilal, K.V., Mohan, A., Nuristani, N., Hyper-parameter tuned deep learning approach for effective human monkeypox disease detection. *Sci. Rep.*, 13, 1, 15930, 2023.
9. Swarna, S.R., Kumar, A., Dixit, P., Sairam, T.V.M., Parkinson's Disease Prediction using Adaptive Quantum Computing, in: *2021 Third International*

Conference on Intelligent Communication Technologies and Virtual Mobile Networks (ICICV), Tirunelveli, India, pp. 1396–1401, 2021, doi: 10.1109/ICICV50876.2021.9388628.
10. Lee, M., Recent Advances in Deep Learning for Protein-Protein Interaction Analysis: A Comprehensive Review. *Molecules*, *28*, 13, 5169, 2023.
11. Parvez, M. and Khan, T., Applications in the Field of Bioinformatics, in: *A Guide to Applied Machine Learning for Biologists*, pp. 175–188, Springer International Publishing, Cham, 2023.
12. Stahlschmidt, S.R., Ulfenborg, B., Synnergren, J., Multimodal deep learning for biomedical data fusion: a review. *Brief. Bioinform.*, 2, bbab569, 2022.
13. Pradeep, S., Sharma, Y.K., Lilhore, U.K., Simaiya, S., Kumar, A., Ahuja, S., Chakrabarti, T., Developing an SDN security model (EnsureS) based on lightweight service path validation with batch hashing and tag verification. *Sci. Rep.*, 13, 1, 17381, 2023.
14. Iqbal, N. and Kumar, P., From Data Science to Bioscience: Emerging era of bioinformatics applications, tools and challenges. *Procedia Comput. Sci.*, *218*, 1516–1528, 2023.
15. Sasubilli, S.M., Kumar, A., Dutt, V., Improving Health Care by Help of Internet of Things and Bigdata Analytics and Cloud Computing, in: *2020 International Conference on Advances in Computing and Communication Engineering (ICACCE)*, Las Vegas, NV, USA, pp. 1–4, 2020, doi: 10.1109/ICACCE49060.2020.9155042.
16. Patra, P., Disha, B.R., Kundu, P., Das, M., Ghosh, A., Recent advances in machine learning applications in metabolic engineering. *Biotechnol. Adv.*, *62*, 108069, 2023.
17. Kumar, N., Verma, H., Sharma, Y.K., Adversarial Attacks on Graph Neural Network: Techniques and Countermeasures, in: *Concepts and Techniques of Graph Neural Networks*, pp. 58–73, IGI Global, 2023.
18. Choi, S.R. and Lee, M., Transformer architecture and attention mechanisms in genome data analysis: a comprehensive review. *Biology*, *12*, 7, 1033, 2023.
19. Singh, A.V., Varma, M., Laux, P., Choudhary, S., Datusalia, A.K., Gupta, N., Luch, A., Gandhi, A., Kulkarni, P., Nath, B., Artificial intelligence and machine learning disciplines with the potential to improve the nanotoxicology and nanomedicine fields: a comprehensive review. *Arch. Toxicol.*, *97*, 4, 963–979, 2023.
20. Bhardwaj, K.K., Banyal, S., Sharma, D.K., Artificial intelligence based diagnostics, therapeutics and applications in biomedical engineering and bioinformatics, in: *Internet of Things in Biomedical Engineering*, pp. 161–187, Academic Press, 2019.
21. Nagarajan, N., Yapp, E.K., Le, N.Q.K., Kamaraj, B., Al-Subaie, A.M., Yeh, H.Y., Application of computational biology and artificial intelligence technologies in cancer precision drug discovery. *Biomed Res. Int.*, *2019*, 2019.
22. Punugoti, R., Dutt, V., Anand, A., Bhati, N., Exploring the Impact of Edge Intelligence and IoT on Healthcare: A Comprehensive Survey,

in: *2023 International Conference on Sustainable Computing and Smart Systems (ICSCSS)*, Coimbatore, India, pp. 1108–1114, 2023, doi: 10.1109/ICSCSS57650.2023.10169733.
23. Abiodun, O.I., Jantan, A., Omolara, A.E., Dada, K.V., Umar, A.M., Linus, O.U., Arshad, H., Kazaure, A.A., Gana, U., Kiru, M.U., Comprehensive review of artificial neural network applications to pattern recognition. *IEEE Access, 7*, 158820–158846, 2019.
24. Boyapati, S., Swarna, S.R., Dutt, V., Vyas, N., Big Data Approach for Medical Data Classification: A Review Study, in: *2020 3rd International Conference on Intelligent Sustainable Systems (ICISS)*, Thoothukudi India, pp. 762–766, 2020, doi: 10.1109/ICISS49785.2020.9315870.
25. Singh, K., Kumar, A., Sharma, Y.K., Rai, A.K., AIoT-based e-commerce. *AIoT Technol. Appl. Smart Environ.*, 215, 2023.
26. Kumar, A., Kumar, S.A., Dutt, V., Dubey, A.K., Narang, S., A Hybrid Secure Cloud Platform Maintenance Based on Improved Attribute-Based Encryption Strategies. *Int. J. Interact. Multimed. Artif. Intell.*, 8, 2, 150, 2023. Universidad Internacional de La Rioja, doi: 10.9781/ijimai.2021.11.004.
27. Sharma, Y.K., Athithan, S., Sachi, S., Singh, A.K., Jain, A., Devi, S., Copy and Move Forged Image Detection by Deep Learning, in: *2023 World Conference on Communication & Computing (WCONF)*, pp. 1–6, IEEE, 2023, July.
28. Lee, M., Deep Learning Techniques with Genomic Data in Cancer Prognosis: A Comprehensive Review of the 2021–2023 Literature. *Biology, 12*, 7, 893, 2023.
29. Sachi, S., Singh, A.K., Jain, A., Devi, S., Sharma, Y.K., Athithan, S., Hate Speech Detection Using the GPT-2 and Natural Language Processing, in: *2023 Intelligent Methods, Systems, and Applications (IMSA)*, pp. 276–280, IEEE, 2023, July.
30. Ghods, K., Azizi, A., Jafari, A., Ghods, K., Application of Artificial Intelligence in Clinical Dentistry, a Comprehensive Review of literature. *J. Dent.*, 2023.
31. Sekhar, U.S., Vyas, N., Dutt, V., Kumar, A., Multimodal Neuroimaging Data in Early Detection of Alzheimer's Disease: Exploring the Role of Ensemble Models and GAN Algorithm, in: *2023 International Conference on Circuit Power and Computing Technologies (ICCPCT)*, Kollam, India, pp. 1664–1669, 2023, doi: 10.1109/ICCPCT58313.2023.10245177.
32. Burugadda, V.R., Jadhav, N., Vyas, N., Duggar, R., Exploring the Potential of Deep Reinforcement Learning for Autonomous Navigation in Complex Environments, in: *2023 7th International Conference on Computing, Communication, Control and Automation (ICCUBEA)*, Pune, India, pp. 1–6, 2023, doi: 10.1109/ICCUBEA58933.2023.10392109.
33. Pradeep, S. and Sharma, Y.K., A pragmatic evaluation of stress and performance testing technologies for web-based applications, in: *2019 Amity International Conference on Artificial Intelligence (AICAI)*, pp. 399–403, IEEE, 2019, February.

34. Vobugari, N., Raja, V., Sethi, U., Gandhi, K., Raja, K., Surani, S.R., Advancements in oncology with artificial intelligence—A review article. *Cancers*, *14*, 5, 1349, 2022.
35. Li, H., Tian, S., Li, Y., Fang, Q., Tan, R., Pan, Y., Huang, C., Xu, Y., Gao, X., Modern deep learning in bioinformatics. *J. Mol. Cell Biol.*, *12*, 11, 823–827, 2020.
36. Mazlan, A.U., Sahabudin, N.A., Remli, M.A., Ismail, N.S.N., Mohamad, M.S., Nies, H.W., Abd Warif, N.B., A review on recent progress in machine learning and deep learning methods for cancer classification on gene expression data. *Processes*, *9*, 8, 1466, 2021.
37. Sharma, Y.K. and Rokade, M.D., Deep and machine learning approaches for anomaly-based intrusion detection of imbalanced network traffic. *IOSR J. Eng.*, 63–67, 2019.
38. Dhakal, A., McKay, C., Tanner, J.J., Cheng, J., Artificial intelligence in the prediction of protein–ligand interactions: recent advances and future directions. *Briefings Bioinf.*, *23*, 1, bbab476, 2022.
39. Sharma, A. and Rani, R., A systematic review of applications of machine learning in cancer prediction and diagnosis. *Arch. Comput. Methods Eng.*, *28*, 7, 4875–4896, 2021.
40. Burugadda, V.R., Pawar, P.S., Kumar, A., Bhati, N., Predicting Hospital Readmission Risk for Heart Failure Patients Using Machine Learning Techniques: A Comparative Study of Classification Algorithms, in: *2023 Second International Conference on Trends in Electrical, Electronics, and Computer Engineering (TEECCON)*, Bangalore, India, pp. 223–228, 2023, doi: 10.1109/TEECCON59234.2023.10335817.
41. Painuli, D. and Bhardwaj, S., Recent advancement in cancer diagnosis using machine learning and deep learning techniques: A comprehensive review. *Comput. Biol. Med.*, *146*, 105580, 2022.
42. Chandrasekaran, S., Dutt, V., Vyas, N., Kumar, R., Student Sentiment Analysis Using Various Machine Learning Techniques, in: *2023 International Conference on Artificial Intelligence and Smart Communication (AISC)*, Greater Noida, India, pp. 104–107, 2023, doi: 10.1109/AISC56616.2023.10085018.
43. Cao, Y., Geddes, T.A., Yang, J.Y.H., Yang, P., Ensemble deep learning in bioinformatics. *Nat. Mach. Intell.*, *2*, 9, 500–508, 2020.
44. Dutt, V., Sasubilli, S.M., Yerrapati, A.E., Dynamic Information Retrieval With Chatbots: A Review of Artificial Intelligence Methodology, in: *2020 4th International Conference on Electronics, Communication and Aerospace Technology (ICECA)*, Coimbatore, India, pp. 1299–1303, 2020, doi: 10.1109/ICECA49313.2020.9297533.
45. Athanasopoulou, K., Daneva, G.N., Adamopoulos, P.G., Scorilas, A., Artificial intelligence: the milestone in modern biomedical research. *BioMedInformatics*, *2*, 4, 727–744, 2022.

46. Beg, A. and Parveen, R., Review of Bioinformatics Tools and Techniques to Accelerate Ovarian Cancer Research. *Int. J. Bioinf. Intell. Comput.*, *1*, 1, 1–10, 2022.
47. Swapna, M., Sharma, Y.K., Prasad, B.M.G., A survey on face recognition using convolutional neural network, in: *Data Engineering and Communication Technology: Proceedings of 3rd ICDECT-2K19*, Springer Singapore, Singapore, pp. 649–661, 2020.
48. Pandiyan, S. and Wang, L., A comprehensive review on recent approaches for cancer drug discovery associated with artificial intelligence. *Comput. Biol. Med.*, 106140, 2022.
49. Rokade, M.D. and Sharma, Y.K., MLIDS: A machine learning approach for intrusion detection for real-time network datasets, in: *2021 International Conference on Emerging Smart Computing and Informatics (ESCI)*, pp. 533–536, IEEE, 2021, March.
50. Mishra, S., Abbas, M., Jindal, K., Narayan, J., Dwivedy, S.K., Artificial intelligence-based technological advancements in clinical healthcare applications: A systematic review, in: *Revolutions in Product Design for Healthcare: Advances in Product Design and Design Methods for Healthcare*, pp. 207–227, 2022.
51. Jadhav, D., Sharma, Y.K., Arora, D.P., Profound Learning Approach for Shot Boundary Location, in: *2nd International Conference on Communication & Information Processing (ICCIP)*, 2020, April.
52. Waqas, A., Tripathi, A., Ramachandran, R.P., Stewart, P.A., Rasool, G., Multimodal data integration for oncology in the era of deep neural networks: a review. *Front. Artif. Intell.*, 7, 1408843, 2024.
53. Jadhav, M., Kumar Sharma, Y., Bhandari, G.M., Currency identification and forged banknote detection using deep learning, in: *2019 International Conference on Innovative Trends and Advances in Engineering and Technology (ICITAET)*, IEEE, pp. 178–183, 2019, December.
54. Swarna, S.R., Boyapati, S., Dutt, V., Bajaj, K., Deep Learning in Dynamic Modeling of Medical Imaging: A Review Study, in: *2020 3rd International Conference on Intelligent Sustainable Systems (ICISS)*, Thoothukudi, India, pp. 745–749, 2020, doi: 10.1109/ICISS49785.2020.9315990.
55. Cui, C., Yang, H., Wang, Y., Zhao, S., Asad, Z., Coburn, L.A., Wilson, K.T., Landman, B.A., Huo, Y., Deep multimodal fusion of image and non-image data in disease diagnosis and prognosis: a review. *Prog. Biomed. Eng.*, 52, 022001, 2023.

12

Future Directions and Emerging Trends in Multimodal Data Fusion for Bioinformatics

Dankan Gowda V.[1*], D. Palanikkumar[2], K.D.V. Prasad[3], Mandeep Kaur[4] and Shivoham Singh[5]

[1]*Department of Electronics and Communication Engineering, BMS Institute of Technology and Management, Bangalore, Karnataka, India*
[2]*Department of Computer Science and Engineering, Dr. NGP Institute of Technology, Coimbatore, Tamil Nadu, India*
[3]*Symbiosis Institute of Business Management, Hyderabad and Symbiosis International (Deemed University), Pune, India*
[4]*Department of Electronics and Communication Engineering, Punjabi University, Patiala, Punjab, India*
[5]*Symbiosis Institute of Business Management, Hyderabad, Symbiosis International (Deemed University), Pune, India*

Abstract
Bioinformatics has just been the nexus of the dynamic field that amalgamation of multiple data types now represents the cutting-edge technology for research in biology and medicine. The present chapter addresses present status, nascent trends, and next steps in multimodal data integration for bioinformatics, which provides cues about underlying tactics, messes, and challenges of this fast-growing field. As the technology of high-throughput and the increasing richness of the diversified biological data are entrenched, data fusion, which should not be ignored, has played a vital role in the exploration of complex biological mechanisms, precision medicine, and new drug development. This chapter gives a complete review covering the successive incorporation of genomics, proteomics, metabolomics, imaging and among maybe others this transformation will be highlighted. It goes into depth about the cutting-edge computational strategies that are based on machine

**Corresponding author*: dankan.v@bmsit.in

Umesh Kumar Lilhore, Abhishek Kumar, Narayan Vyas, Sarita Simaiya and Vishal Dutt (eds.) Multimodal Data Fusion for Bioinformatics Artificial Intelligence, (247–282) © 2025 Scrivener Publishing LLC

learning and deep learning models, which are constantly increasing the limits of biological data analysis and interpretation. Secondly, it gives a solution to not only the tech issues but ethical dilemmas linked with the data fusion; thus, it is a passageway for researchers and bioinformatics practitioners. In this chapter, we have put together all the fragmentized knowledge into a whole conclusion and also presented future openings; thus this chapter is meant to propel further improvement in this field and unfold the complexities of life.

***Keywords*:** Multimodal data fusion, bioinformatics, machine learning in bioinformatics, precision medicine, systems biology, deep learning, computational biology, genomic data integration, proteomics, metabolomics, data privacy in bioinformatics

12.1 Introduction

Bioinformatics is undeniably an important branch of life sciences at the crossroads of IT as it is concerned with the collection, processing and analysis of huge biological data, particularly genetic and genomic data. Fast development of sequencing-based technologies brought about the rise in biological data volume, meaning that science has to cope with both numerous new opportunities and challenges of data processing and study. Data integration, the process of combining various data sources or types so that they are more consistent, accurate, and advantageous, empowers the bioinformatics discipline [1]. It helps researchers to consolidate the various heterogeneous cut datasets, for example, genomic, proteomic, and metabolonic, to attain a more in-depth knowledge of how biological entities function [2]. The aim of data fusion is to improve the ability of data analysis accuracy of forecasts, as well as facilitation of discovery that cannot be obtained from single-source data.

Figure 12.1 shows the canonical architecture of a biometric system, which is broken down into four phases making up the identity validation stream. The Enrollment Module is the beginning step. It appears when a user's finger or an eye is captured by a sensor. It may be any type of biometric sign such as, fingerprint, iris pattern, or facial shapes [3]. The records of the raw data move on to the feature extraction stage, a crucial step where character features are identified and digitally transformed into a template. Now, the biometric "template" is moved into the system database which takes the role of storage for enrolled users' biometric templates. Yet, Animal Handling Module runs in conjunction with the Identification Module which reflects the first part of the Enrollment Module while an individual is posing for login hence, during an access request. The user

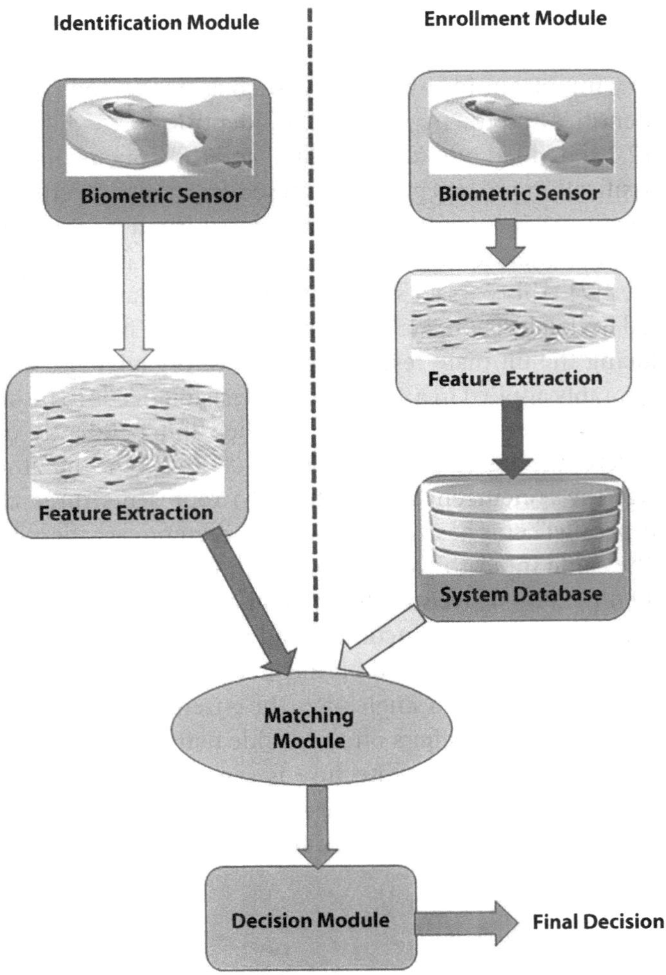

Figure 12.1 Standard biometric system configuration.

then provides the system with the rest of their biometric specs through the sensor and the system will retrieve information from the same area it has previously stored [4]. The expression features obtained are further fed to the Matching Module which is instrumental because it compares them with the pre-existing templates in the system database to evaluate the possible match. What results from the two different approaches is the signal sent on to the Decision Module for the definite final decision [5, 6]. If it is indeed a match, entry is granted, and it is confirmed that it is a positive identification; in case of a failure to spot a match, access to the alley is restricted, and thus, it is a negative identification. This is a way to show that the system has capacity to allow secure and effective identity verification, which is very important for occupations such as access control, authentication of identities and the management of identities.

Figure 12.2 is divided into (a) Sequential and (b) Concurrent flow schemas for classification process purposes. In sequential architecture (consecutive architectures), it is evident that classifiers form a row of a hierarchy classifier (b). For these classifiers, this output serves as the input of the next classifier [7]. This passage's both linear structure and classifiers "may refine or add to the decision-making process" with the final classifier at the end "producing the ultimate result". This way of organizing could be, for example, favorably applied in a case where a decision needs to be iteratively optimized. Besides, every classifier would then independently deal with assessing different levels of detail within the data [8]. On the other hand, the wording "the concurrent architecture (b) represents three classifiers working in parallel" emphasizes this point. Different classifiers undoubtedly have the same input to work with, which they each process on their own and then pass their decision to a fusion center. The algorithm of the fusion center is to collect the outcomes of all classifiers and return the final choice [9, 10]. This model is based on the idea that many predictions provide more information than a single one. The ensemble learning paradigm assumes that disparate classifiers often provide better results than any one classifier alone. Convergent architecture is especially suitable for classes that are diverse, each of them giving essential probes to the data and the whole set being treated as a bundle results in a more accurate and reliable final decision.

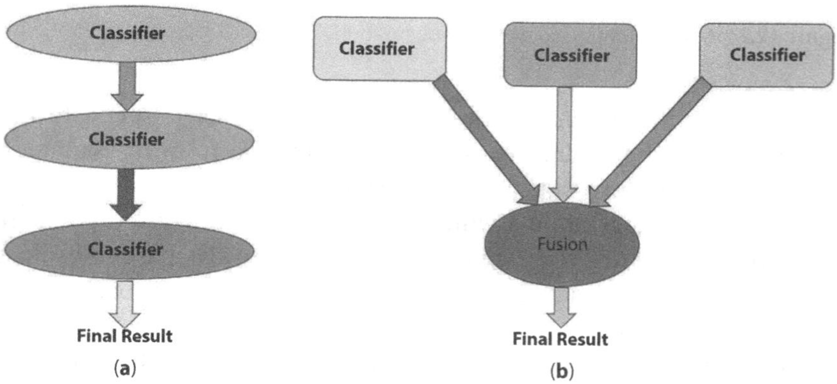

Figure 12.2 (a) Sequential and (b) Concurrent system architectures.

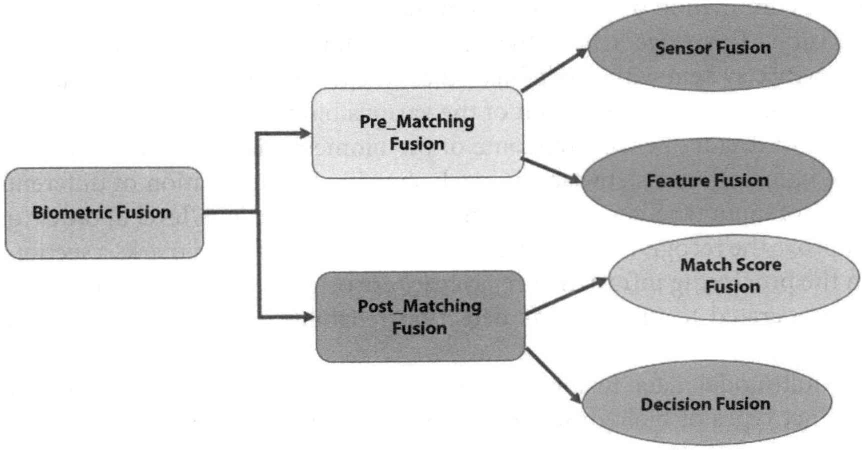

Figure 12.3 Classification of biometric fusion levels.

Figure 12.3 provides the classification of biometric fusion levels, which is a biometric system framework part responsible for data reliability and accuracy through identification. Biometric fusion can be categorized mainly into two levels: The origin of the technology is the fundamentals of the Biometric Fusion. However, there are modifications called the Pre-Matching Fusion and Post-Matching Fusion.

In Pre-Matching Fusion, two approaches are highlighted: Sensor Fusion and Feature Fusion. Fusion happens when some biosensors inputs are merged before the process of matching is done [11]. It might even involve all of these, using different sensors to capture the same biometric marker (taken by level or combined from different modalities). The source for feature fusion is usually integration of those features extracted from different types of biometric models, which are then presented as an input for the matching algorithm. This level classes the data to come up with features that are distinct, informative and reliable [12], while at the same time combining them to create an in-depth feature set.

After Post-matching Fusion like Match Score Fusion and Decision Fusion, a fusion is performed. The satellite match system merges the outputs after the individual pattern matchers have calibrated the inputs. Multi-match scores are the result of the matching algorithms which combine to one unique score that indicates the confidence level in the match. The symbiosis between the components of this algorithm allows the system to seize individual merits and gain the most accurate performance out of the matching process [13]. To conclude, the Decision Fusion tool is the culmination of all the different matchmaker decisions to give a final decision. This stage acts as the decision-making authority for the entire biometric system with predefined rules (the frequently-used being majority voting) by taking the input of the various biometric systems and using them to decide the final outcome of the biometric identification process. The figure offers a stepwise approach showing the integration of different types of input whether sensors, feature, score, or decisions/level in order to improve the recognition accuracy [14]. Each level of fusion marks a section in the processing infrastructure layer where originally gained information is cooperated to improve the detection reliability and the identification accuracy.

Multimodal data fusion in bioinformatics represents connecting of distinct types of biological data to arrive at the conclusions that not one single type of data would bring. By integrating computational methods capable to tackle data from different modalities like DNA sequencing, RNA sequencing, protein expression ratios, and image data, this technique brings together a variety of data for a comprehensive look at tissue organization and identity. Beyond simple data fusion that includes aggregation multimodal data fusion also includes the design and use of concepts and approaches that are able to deal with the data multifurcates [15], diversity and huge amount of data. Such techniques represent a method of discovering regularities, determination of the connections among different data sources as well as building predictions that may be made possible by their combined characteristics. Hence, the main purpose of multimodal data fusion is to create an overall image of a phenomenon, resulting in breakthroughs in such areas as disease diagnosis and drug development as well as understanding of interactions between genetics and environment.

Data fusion as far as bioinformatics is concerned is not a new idea but rather a trend that has evolved at high speed for the last two decades. Before, biological studies were filled with restrictions due to the modes and procedures of gathering data and analysing it. Most of such procedures were oriented to single-modal data formats [16]. In the 2000s the Human Genome Project, which provided the first-ever sequence of the human genome, marked the beginning of the genomic research that is geared towards better understanding of biological processes and is the basis for generation of huge amounts of data. It was this influx of data coupled with new computing capabilities and the growth of machine learning technology that brought forth the emergence of specialist data fusion techniques.

The first attempts in data fusion were centered on the amalgamation of genomic and transcriptomic information with the goal of fully comprehending the process by which genes are expressed and regulated [17].

Technologies evolved, which resulted in widening the scope of potential techniques which included proteomic, metabolomic, and epigenomic data. Besides this, techniques such as the CRISPR and screening techniques are extensively used. Over the last few years, a newer generation of hybrid models has become evident, whose main focus is the use of AI and machine-learning technologies, especially of deep learning, to deal with data inputs that are rich in formats.

Data fusion in bioinformatics is a significant part of the wider systems biology orientation where the focus is on understanding biological systems as whole clusters instead of attached segments. It follows a pattern of merging multimodal data to catch the complexity of those groups, consequently enabling researchers to investigate problems from human health and illness standpoints.

12.2 Foundational Concepts

The world of bioinformatics incorporates various types of biological data which are all a part of the complex life machinery, adding to the different dimensions of our knowledge about the core parts of the entire biological architecture. The right interpretation of these classifications of data types is without a doubt paramount for getting ahold of the fine details of multimodal data fusion and, hopefully, unraveling some of the biological secrets.

Types of Biological Data

Genomic Data: The initial basis of biological data types is genomic data, which are the carriers of information inheritance of organisms. This genetic type, specifically obtained from DNA sequencing, gives insights into the structures, the variations, and the evolutionary process of genes. The genomic data analysis has been the basis of discovering genes connected to diseases, determining genetic variations, and revealing evolutionary routs.

Proteomic Data: The proteomics discipline is committed to the whole field of proteome study that is the set of proteins formed by a given organism. Proteomics encompasses information concerning the expression of protein species, modifications [18], associations as well as functions. This information is the fundamental of cellular functions exploration, like revealing disease mechanisms, target proteins for drug development, and unveiling cell's protein networks.

Metabolomic Data: The metabolomics of living systems assess comprehensively the metabolites that constitute a living system, in essence, providing a metabolic fingerprint of a given cell, tissue or living being. The metabolomics data are clearly of good importance for understanding metabolic pathways [19], developing disease biomarkers and also for assessing the intervention responses of therapeutic and environmental changes.

Imaging Data: We call biological imaging a whole collection of techniques which involves microscopy, that is X-ray microscopy and digital microscopy, and advanced imaging modalities such as MRI and NPS. This specific data form is a source of visual visualization of structure, function and dynamic of cells, tissues and organs allowing to determine development and diagnose diseases, study developmental biology and research neurobiology.

Figure 12.4 shows cutting-edge sensor-level fusion software to be used with biometric system. However, it is not just a two-step verification process; rather it involves biometric parameters to do the trait confirmation [20]. At the first module, each Identity or Trait detail move to the pre-processing part. Such modules do the first stage of data scrubbing and preparing, including hypothetical noise reduction, normalization or other methods that are supposed to improve the quality of the data. Secondly, when the data has been prepared, it can be subsequently processed. Feeding the readings of both characteristics into Fusion Module becomes the next step of the pre-processing. This feature module merges the datasets, which were initially pre-processed from the two biometric source types and which when combined, contain additional information from both sources [21]. The system tends to harmonize the whole sensory integration by merging all data which makes the system unravel the power that each biometric feature has and improves accuracy and reliability. To clarify, after the integration of these two modules, the Feature Extraction Model comes again. This module integrates the knowledge of face recognition in depth to enable the system to capture unique features that differentiate one person from the next [22]. The feature extraction function is vital since it begins by reducing the size of the data, while preserving and excluding unimportant characteristic information. Subsequently, the specific features are input into the Matching Schema to extract those features which match the templates stored in the database. These templates work as ready-to-use components that allow the system to find or verify the identity of the user. If those templates, generated from biometric data, are fully coincident to the existing one, then match is declared to decide [23]. The Last Decision Module provides the ultimate decision, thereby concluding the suspect's personality. The kind of decision will be based on whether we have biometric data supporting the identity since Matching Module is completely based on the output. This procedure is the compilation of the

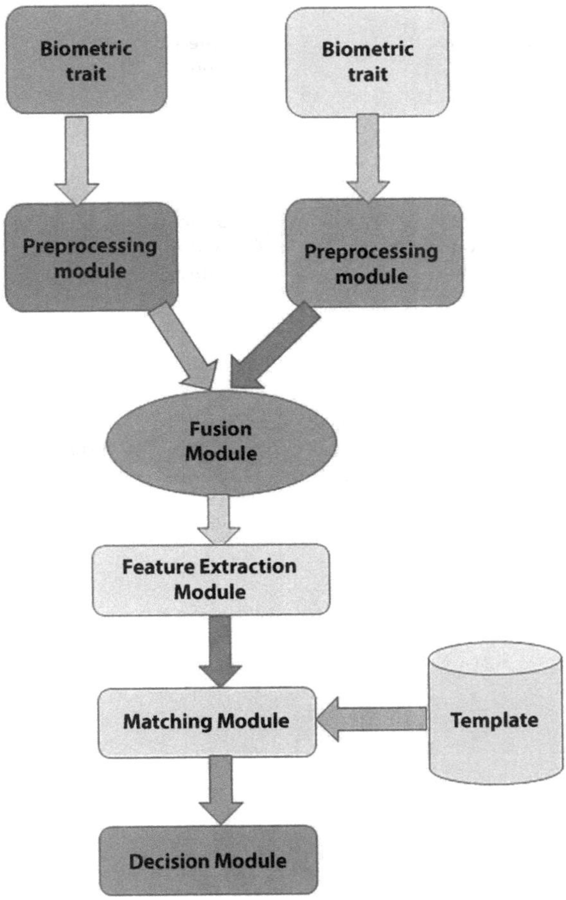

Figure 12.4 Sensor-level fusion technique.

system describing a multimodal biometric system, which combines sensor-level fusion and thus enhances accuracy [24]. The system at first stages uses several features together; if one feature or several of them are weak or have errors, then the identification method will not be effective or reliable and have less certainty, and so unification of features will make it safer and more reliable.

Figure 12.5 demonstrates the schematic the feature-level data mix is practiced in the biometric systems. It starts with the individual parts through which the different biometric features are being processed separately. Fear, stress, and mental health problems are often consequences of modern-day life. In particular, each of the traits possesses its specific

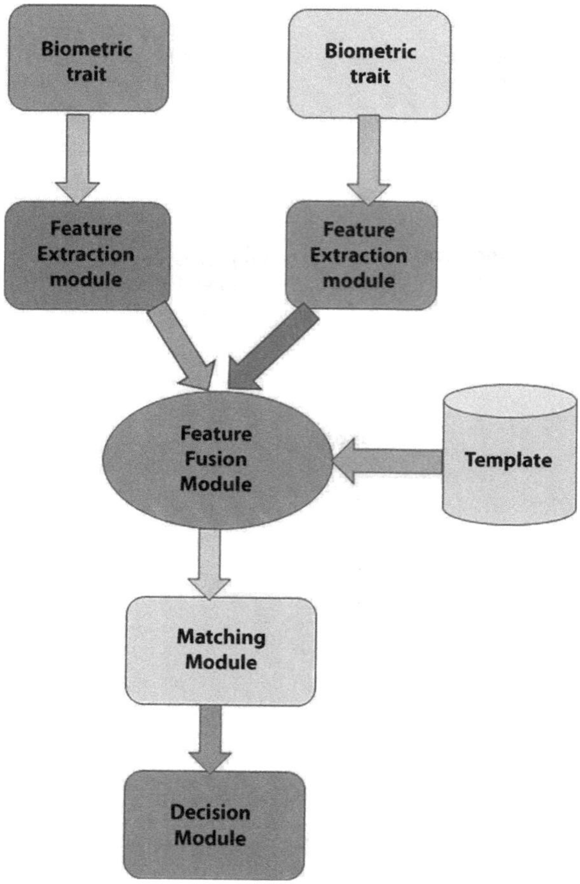

Figure 12.5 Feature-level data combination techniques.

Feature Extraction Module that is responsible for extraction of the distinctive features which are the most informative aspects of the biometric data that can be used for individual identification. From there this module takes the biometric trait features and transits them to the Feature Fusion Module. This module serves the main function of the system which is to concatenate the output features from the both biometric sensors into a single set of features [25]. Such interconnection at this level increases the ability of the system to exploit this collaborative information that is generated from each biometric property and thereby make an improvement in reliability, particularly in terms of accuracy and resistance to interference. The next step is feature fusion; what follows is that matching module that takes the combined feature set output. In fusion, the new created curve is called with data templates which had been previously stored in a database [26]. The templates in question are actually patterns or prototypes of features where previously demonstrated enrolments were used. Matching Module's job is to decode how accurate are they comparable with the saved ones.

After the appropriate matching process completion, the system will advance to the Decision Module. This next process, which is based on the information previously provided by the Matching Module, finally takes the decision of making a verification of the biometric data corresponding to known individuals or to identify the specific identity among the database of users (identification). With this example, fusion of feature-level application is provided to refine biometric process and verify the authenticity of the information [27]. Instead of the separate, the system works before the procedure that would combine features in order to improve the discrimination power of the biometric identifiers which would result in a more precise and effective decision-making process.

Challenges in Multimodal Data Integration

The combination of these various types of data implies numerous challenges of a different nature (spatial, multi-scale and formats representation).

Heterogeneity: The primary barrier stands for the disparity of data that includes, for example, numerical differences together with the differences of scales (e.g., molecular/molecular level) whether at the cellular (such as interactions at molecular levels), or dimensional level (for example, radio images vs. 3D structures).

Volume and Velocity: The intensity of data generated from large-scale machines in addition to the speed at which it accumulates calls for complex computational strategies to store, handle and analyse all the captured data effectively.

Interoperability: Astronomies interoperability becomes an obstruction due to variation of formats and standards of databases and systems that have multimodal datasets.

Complexity: We shall encounter a variety of data types, ranging from genomic [28], transcriptomic, proteomic, and metabolomic data, to name but a few; and all these data types require very complex models that can correctly interpret the interplay between the various biological entities and processes.

Data Ties and Overflow Techniques: the Overview

Several data fusion methods have been developed, exact within methods and applications.

Early Integration: Data-level integration, or a type of integration realized at the initial stage of datasets, refers to their amalgamation at the stage of raw data before the analysis begins. This method allow us to go deeper in and more complex data, but it is necessary to make sure the data is compatible in terms of format and measure.
Late Integration: Finally, higher-level integration (late-integration), similar to combining the results of separate analyses done on different data types. This method is good when the detailed analysis cannot be incorporated at the initial raw level. It is helpful, for instance, in integrating data on a different level to combine the conclusions drawn from different analytics.
Model-Based Integration: The model-based approach combines statistical or computational models in order to connect data from different sources. The latter one has the ability to address the heterogeneity and complex nature through the designing of models which explicitly contain the relationships between different kinds of data. Model base implementation is an outstanding tool that stands of various sections such as the hypothesis testing and making predictions based on the merged datasets.

12.3 Current State of Multimodal Data Fusion in Bioinformatics

In bioinformatics, multimodal data fusion methods have changed the landscape as it prevailed once broadcasted. Hence, those advancements allow for gaining biomedical perspectives that are impossible to achieve otherwise, but at the same time, opportunities are followed by new difficulties. Here, a discussion on the existing multimodal data fusion methodologies, the spectrum of recent real-world applications, and the main shortcomings in the field of bioinformatics is presented.

Review of Current Methods and Technologies in Data Fusion
Modern bioinformatics involves the adaptation and implementation of multifaceted data fusion methods which aim to combat the complexity and disparity of the biological data. The algorithms of machine learning, like supervised and unsupervised learning, have created a permanent tool for connecting all omics data, such as genomics, proteomics, etc. It has made the algorithm that can help us to find out the patterns and correlations inside all of the data. Deep learning architectures, amongst which convolutional neural networks (CNNs) and recurrent neural networks (RNNs) stand out for their powerful ability to handle complex multivariable data

such as sequence and imaging data, shine at the issue of complex structures within the biological portfolio. They reveal subtleties found in those areas of cellular processes, mechanisms of disease and therapeutic responses and others as well.

A network-based method of integration constructed on a graph model to represent the interaction of biological molecules is used by data passed through different biological levels provided to picture the complex networks at the basis of biological functions and diseases. Statisticians use Bayesian models and multivariate analysis (e.g., in order to account for uncertainty and variability) as sources of combining various types of biological data, thus taking advantage from their joint usefulness. Thus, statistically meaningful relationships between different biological data types as well as their contribution to understanding the underlying mechanisms can be determined.

Key Applications and Success Stories in Bioinformatics

It is the line of multimodal data that did rapid development and enhances various areas of bioinformatics. Splicing data in precision medicine has led to development of complex models that explain the full spectrum of various diseases partially by stratifying genetic, environmental and clinical data for personalized treatments. In molecular biology, the genomic, transcriptomic, and epigenomic data are merged under the banner of cancer genomics. It ultimately leads to the discovery of new oncogenes and tumour suppressors, as well as biomarkers that help in cancer diagnosis and prognosis.

Neuroinformatic is the most promising of them, successfully combining structural and functional neuroimaging data with genetics and clinical information, which has resulted in advancement of researchers' knowledge on the topic of neurological disorders like Alzheimer's, autism spectrum disorders, and schizophrenia. Model systems biology based on the combination of omics data have been tremendously popular in laying a foundation of metabolic and signalling pathways which in turn has proven to be illuminative of overarching properties of biological systems.

Limitations and Challenges of Current Approaches

A few of what the field of data fusion in bioinformatics has succeeded are not without these obstacles. The heterogeneity of data is still a big challenge as the data types could be heterogenous, i.e., ranging from sequences and structures to images and clinical records which are all quite different in nature. Thus, the integration of this heterogeneous nature of data demands very diverse automatic processes and complex biocomputing technologies that can accommodate their difference. Scalability is an issue as well as the steep rate of growth of biological data is reaching a point where there is no sufficient tools to process and study the big datasets.

One of the biggest challenges provided by the data fusion models, especially the deep learning approaches, is interpretability, because models like this have a "black box" nature, which means it is often hard to establish a connection between very complex results and biological significance. Data privacy and ethical matters also emerge as the crucial issues, especially in the medical applications when the combination of genetic, clinical and lifestyle information of human beings asks for the stricter measures and makes sure that no one's privacy might be violated and data usage to be ethical.

Summing it up together, presently we have the emerging multimodal data integration in bioinformatics which shows us some exiting option for advancement of our biological system and the diseases understanding, yet we need still the future research and development for solving the broader issues. The critical progress of computational methods, working in collaboration with multiple disciplines, will hold back the utilization of the full data fusion capacity in the search for the next new discoveries in the field of bioinformatics.

12.4 Emerging Trends in Data Fusion

The bioinformatics scene is currently experiencing profoundly moving shifts through the emergence of intelligent algorithms which are driven by the latest machine learning and artificial intelligence technologies. This progress, however, is not only giving us the tool to get to the unification of different bioscience but also fundamentally igniting a new dimension of our comprehension of the complex systems in the bioscience. This part investigates the state-of-the-art trend in data integration by underlining the decisive role of ML and AI, how deep learning influences multimodal dataset analysis, development of highly efficient algorithms, and modeling approaches that try to work on the speed and quality of integration processes.

Advances in Machine Learning and AI for Data Integration

The trend nowadays is for utilization of machine learning and artificial intelligence techniques for the purpose of resolving the problems in bioinformatic integration. These technologies bring about a futuristic way of researching and analysing the biological data's size, depth, and the rate of it.

The method of predicting with using many different machine learning model predictions is known as "ensemble learning". It has given positive results to make integrated data robust and convenient. In contrast to AI, the transferring learning principles allows the training of models that are used for one type of data or task to be used across other domains facilitating the cross-modal integration of biological data.

In the case of federated learning, a special technique in multi-institutional studies come into play, whereby we merely require the collaboration of our models on different datasets without the need to them share the data directly. Such an approach helps address the privacy concerns stemming from data sharing, therefore making it a suitable method for sharing data such as the one from genomic and clinical analyses. Reinforcement learning as an emerging technology is being considered to be an efficient tool for decision-making process in data integration. Models could then make learning and adaptations based on the feedback they receive during the integration process.

The Role of Deep Learning in Handling Complex, Multimodal Datasets

It was deep learning that was recently hailed as the star in the context of managing multimodal data complexity. It has enabled one to create the most functional tools, including feature extraction, dimensionality reduction and pattern recognition. Convolutional neural networks (CNNs) have been found to be good for analysing spatial data. They consequently are the most appropriate ones for including imaging data into other data types. RNNs and their sequels network, LSTM, were developed to process sequential information as the genomes. This is realized through capturing any of the dependencies that are beyond the short-term sequence of events.

Graph neural networks (GNNs) are a huge step towards effectively utilizing data in different forms of graphs, e.g. protein-protein interaction graphs or the gene regulatory graphs. GNNs greatly collecting the complicated relationships and the interactions within such data, thus providing a profound analysis of the hidden mechanisms of organisms Auto coilers during unsupervised learning tasks in the data integration have been used, which facilitates the dimension reduction of the large data sets in order to discover latent representations that can summarize the underlying and inherent patterns from the different data modalities.

Novel Algorithms and Models for Efficient and Effective Data Fusion

The brains behind bioinformatics data fusion lie in algorithms and models that are constantly being innovated to make them more precise and effective. Multiple view learning models are meant to have data from numerous perspectives or sources; they incorporate the different information to generate a clustered output that depicts the amalgamated knowledge of all involved data types. These models prove a great aid in such cases where each data type is itself gives different viewpoints about the system under study.

Currently, hybrid methods are taking shape that can apply ML and DL together with traditional statistics-based solutions for fusing the data. Such methods are very attractive for the data fusion problems. Utilizing hybrid models as a joint approach opens the door for comprehensively dealing with diverse types of biological data, tackle many scales, and produce decipherable results that shorten biological discovery pathways.

Zero-shot and few-shot learning models are particularly becoming popular in various NLP tasks, mainly because they have a knack to generalize to a new dataset or class that was not seen during the training process. This simulation capacity becomes a strength in bioinformatics where there are uncommon diseases or a presence of biomolecules at a low diffuse might not be sufficient in training datasets for machine learning models.

Data fusion in the bioinformatics field is increasingly becoming an area that is being rapidly expanded by the technological leaps forward in machine learning and artificial intelligence taking place now. These technologies are not only exclusively offering solutions to the current problems of data integration but also are presenting prospects for newer explorations and discoveries in the domain of biological research. Weaved deep learning algorithm is becoming irreplaceable in the context of analysing modal complex and multistructure datasets. New capable algorithms assist in ensuring integration of data fusion that was impossible until today. With these developing trends a horizon of surprises is promised, which would in turn enable even deeper insights into the abyss of living things and thus help to put rank among the bioinformatics and computational biology courses.

Figure 12.6 shows a comparative study on data fusion methods used in biometrics system. The bar graph represents three distinct fusion methodologies: New data-based machine learning techniques with the plot in the graph show categories of early integration, late integration and model-based Integration, and on the y-axis the corresponding rate of accuracy. The vertical bars show up as indication that each methodology is relevant within the establishing of the truth of biometric data matches. The chart gives a clean, visual comparison, illustrating in this synthetic example the possibility that the model-based integration is always the best option. Such a figure is a display of the correlation between different integration strategies and fusion techniques, and therefore it emphasizes the significance

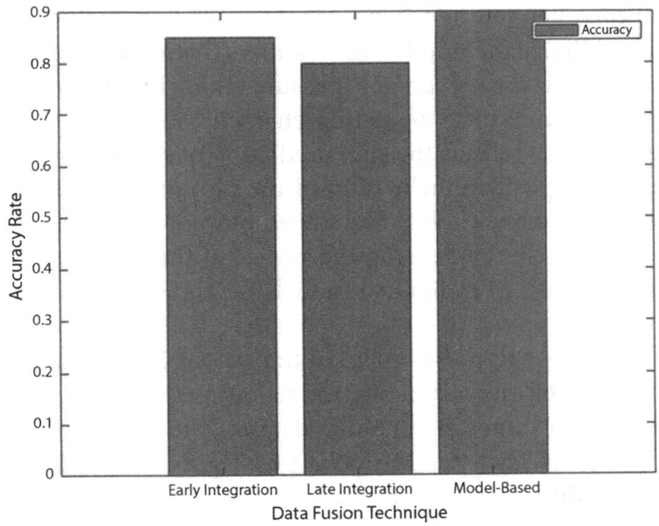

Figure 12.6 Accuracy comparison of data fusion techniques.

of choosing the most appropriate integrative method applicable to specific kinds of biometric applications.

Figure 12.7 draws a graph which describes the quantitative (precision/performance parameter) development as a consequence of the (number

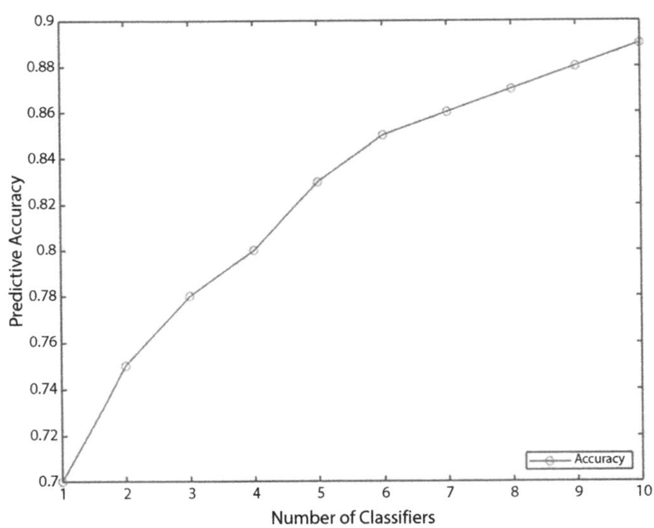

Figure 12.7 Performance improvement through ensemble learning.

of discrete) classifier adding when learning ensembles' method is applied. The horizontal line is the number of classifiers that make up the ensemble and the vertical axis is the accuracy measure taking implied average under the area under the receiver operating characteristic curve (ROC). Each dot on the line chart reflects the sum prediction of the appending number of classifiers. The positive inclination of the plot indicates the trend: the more classifiers aforementioned that are employed, the more accurate the ensemble that is built, evidencing the power of the ensemble in collecting the strong points of individual models for the sake of more accurate predictions.

Figure 12.8 allows to present data in the way of 2D scatter picture that shows the output of dimensionality reduction methods which have been applied to the high-dimensional omics dataset. The Principal Component Analysis (PCA) or t-Distributed Stochastic Neighbor Embedding (t-SNE) algorithms are utilized to assign different points with specific colors, and therefore, show the distinct groups or conditions in the data. The axes represent the feature space capturing the possible transformations of the original data where separation of data clusters is depicted. This visualization, therefore, is of utmost importance for clustering out the natural groupings and revealing hidden structures that are potentially associated with clinical or od biologic factors.

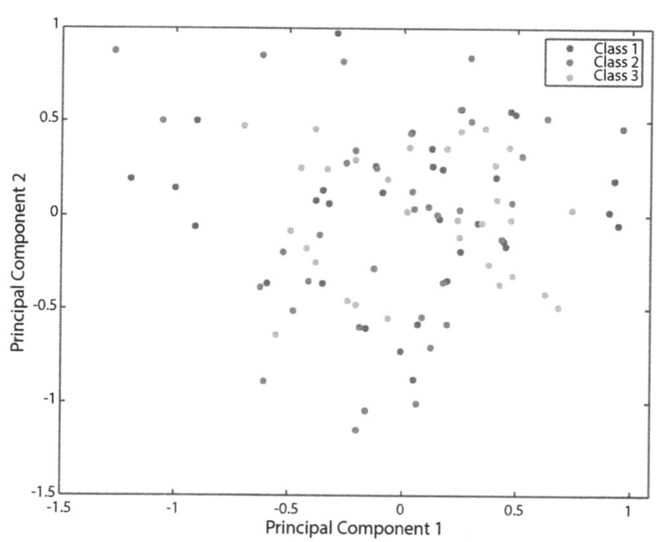

Figure 12.8 Dimensionality reduction visualization.

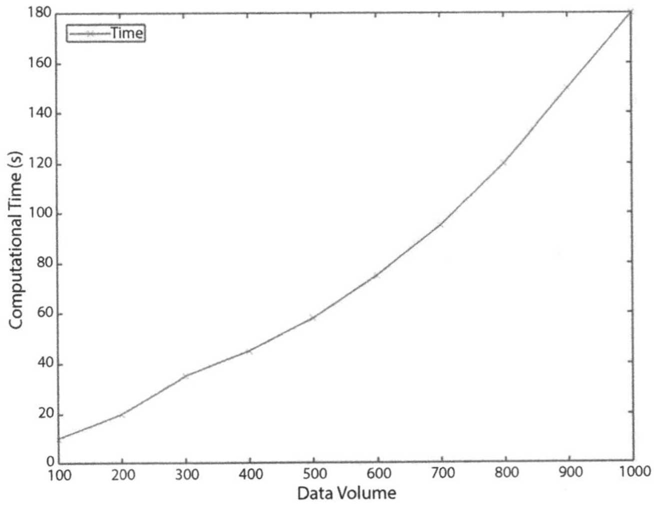

Figure 12.9 Computational time vs. data volume.

In Figure 12.9, however, the graphical element shows that the computation time function is seen in respect to data size, giving a measure of scaling of these different data fusion techniques. The x-axis is related to data volumes that grow in complexity and reach higher figures as they are shown on them while the y-axis represents the computational time that is necessary for data processing. The sustained upward action of the graph suggests that upon increase of the volume of data computational demands rise, displaying the trend of algorithm efficiencies. A figure of this kind is considered an effective way to spotlight the speed of data fusion schemes, which becomes more and more significant in a large number of bioinformatics applications in light of the data volumes being huge.

Figure 12.10 displays a set of pie charts expressing the respective bioinformatics problem solving figures of merit derived when data fusion techniques are employed. The segment of each pie chart represents the portion of successful reactions with each scenario case studies, visualizing the practical use of multimodality data clustering and as an example, medical diagnosis or medication command prediction. The pictures in combination clarify the practical benefits of data fusion in bioinformatics respectively, which substantiate the construct in success metrics with empirical success metrics.

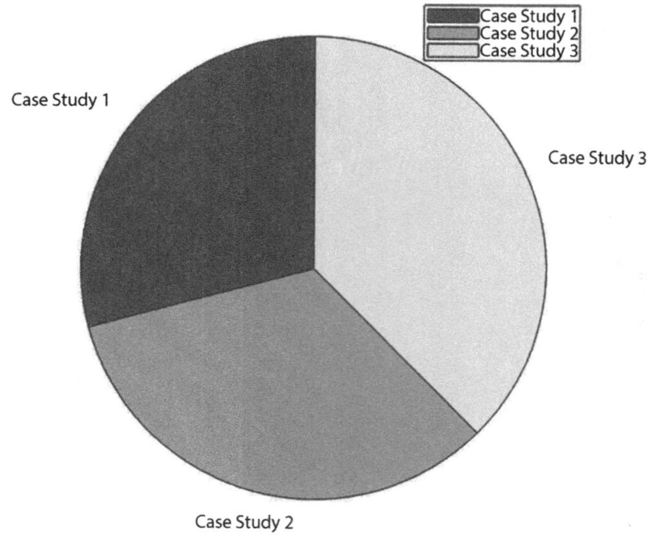

Figure 12.10 Real-world application success rate.

12.5 Algorithms

12.5.1 Deep Learning Architectures for Data Fusion

Convolutional Neural Networks (CNNs): Moreover, CNNs are one of the pillars of deep learning, especially well known for their ability to process principally the three types of data in the images. This architecture, which mimics the data interconnection within the animal visual cortex, exceptionally excels at detecting the intricate complexities within the huge datasets which makes it eminently fit for applications that deal with imaging data or the genomic sequence pattern. Computerized neural networks with their capabilities in terms of disease diagnosis and prognosis also are remarkable. In another sense, imaging data which are obtained from the scanners such as MRI or CT and genomics are fused in the convolutional networks which, then, increases the level of accuracy of cancer diagnosis and prediction of treatment outcomes. It is this fusion of imaging with genomic data that provides this contextual element, thereby offering an encompassing view that is fundamental to the precision oncology. This not only provides ways to identify disease biomarkers, but also unveils the contacts between molecular mechanisms of disease and its progression, which gives an idea on the development of targeted therapies.

Recurrent Neural Networks (RNNs) and Long Short-Term Memory (LSTM) Networks: RNN and LSTM which support sequence capturing the temporal dependencies and their relation are the special design that are capable to process the sequential data. This is really what saves them the best job of studying the DNA sequences, such as the patient health records or longitudinal study data, etc. In bioinformatics, where understanding the sequence and evolution of various biological phenomena is essential, RNNs and LSTMs make it possible for information to be compiled for static genetic elements and to integrate them with dynamic, temporal biological processes. The process of observing the evolution of gene expressions over time in response to a specific treatment as well as connecting those expressions with the static genomic information will reveal key information about the gene regulation mechanism and the impact of genetic variants in the treatment effect. This stepwise curation of the genomic and disease progression data helps in precision medicine, in which treatments are exclusively formulated for an individual patient.
Graph Neural Networks (GNNs): GNNs are tailored to deal with data organized as graphs, which holds as extremely valuable for many bioinformatics cases, where the problem of interest involves interaction networks, for instance, protein-protein interactions or gene regulatory networks. To learn about the relationships and interactions among entities in a graph, GNNs can discover the underlying biological processes that are used to maintain health or diseased state. Indeed, the fusion of molecular data with protein-protein interaction networks through GNNs could reveal crucial targets for drugs by visualizing proteins that play central linkages in the networks related to disease. Correspondingly, GNNs can be used to enrich by integrating genomic data with gene regulatory network data, leading to understanding of gene expression regulation and gene basis of disease. This capability to combine intentions and activity networks together with other data sources provides further possibilities to explain the molecular mechanisms of diseases and the development of precise treatment options.

12.5.2 Ensemble Methods for Heterogeneous Data Integration

Random Forests: Interestingly, one of Random Forests' key characteristics is the ability to build numerous decision trees at training time and output the class that is predominantly voted for in the resulting class table (classification) or the mean prediction (regression) of these individual trees. This approach, for instance, involves platforms that are specifically designed for bioinformatics domains where data comes at different forms and scales, such as genetic, proteomic and clinical data. The outstanding feature of Random Forests is their ability to process data of a high dimension while providing information on feature importance that makes it possible for researchers to have an idea of which variables are playing a critical part in their research.

In the view of multimodal information fusion, Random Forests can combine data from several sources, enhancing the prediction ability of disease diagnosis, patient outcomes prediction or potential biomarkers exploration. As an instance, in which way one can combine clinics genomics with genomic data, the art of Random Forests could be able to detect and provide predictive features in disease progression or treatment response, which will result in personalized medicines. The Figurative character of Random Forests in terms of feature importance also plays a key role in learning about these multiple biological and clinical factors which interact with each other.

Boosting Algorithms (e.g., XGBoost, AdaBoost): Ensemble classifiers that employ different boosting algorithms, such as XGBoost and AdaBoost, are also very powerful techniques focused on successively eliminating errors of the susceptible classifiers and building a more durable classifier. The multimodal integration algorithms have been specially developed for the cases where such a kind of integration is indispensable for a marked increase in the predictive character of the models and robustness to the input data.

Boosting algorithms in bioinformatics is unequivocally essential for data integration from multimodal sources like genomic, transcriptomic, and metabolomic data. It results in improved disease diagnosis, better prognosis, and detection of therapeutic targets with accuracy beyond single datasets. As an example, XGBoost has been shown to enable classifying cancer making use of variety of datasets, where each dataset is built on an individual data type and their results combined are superior to any one data type considered, which is achieved by the XGBoost merging the data to provide the best result. Additionally, AdaBoost can aid in combining information form gene mutations, mRNA amounts and clinical features to analyze the extent of reaction to the treatment of the patient, delivering a kind, which is principally multidimensional, that conveys the complexity of the disease. Studies of integrating biological data from various sources and developing boost algorithms can facilitate exceedingly accurate predictions as well as supply deeper insights into the molecular nature of the diseases. The sequential model correction mechanism that comes with boosting gives rise to increasing accuracy over time as the training dataset queries each prediction which reinforces its adaptability to the complex bioinformatics data fusions tasks.

12.5.3 Dimensionality Reduction and Feature Extraction

Principal Component Analysis (PCA) and t-Distributed Stochastic Neighbor Embedding (t-SNE): Principal Component Analysis (PCA) and t-Distributed Stochastic Neighbor Embedding (t-SNE) are two out of many possible techniques for dimensionality reduction in bioinformatic, with each one used in a unique way in the analysis of high-throughput molecular analysis results. PCA, a linear dimensionality reduction technique, takes in a large number of variables and ends up with a smaller set of variables that carry almost all the information that was in the large set. PCA reduces the complexity of omics data in the manner that it extracts the main components that capture the largest amount of variance in data leaving less variables for analysis and subsequent visualisation. It allows to not only discover the latent structures in the data but it is also one of the major steps in making integrated datasets by aligning them to principal axes.

Among the t-SNE which is non-linear and specially designed for the visualization of data of a very high dimension. Transforming data point resemblances to joint probabilities and compensating for Kullback-Leibler divergence between the low-dimensional odds and the high-dimensional whatsoever data is a way in which t-SNE enables us to show very complex omics data on a level of two or three dimensions. This approach is especially good at depicting the underlying structure of the data, stressing gains of clustering and patterns that can't be demonstrated in higher dimensions. If t-SNE is used in multimodal data fusion, it can be one of the most effective tools in exposing dataset's relationships. It helps to visualize clusters and patterns that span multiple input data types so that this type of information fusion is possible.

Autoencoders, Particularly Variational Autoencoders (VAEs): Autoencoder and VAEs are the neural networks, which most specifically are for unsupervised learning tasks, including dimensionality reduction and feature extraction. Through an unfolding process of input data encoding into latent space that is compressed and then decoding it back to its original input, autoencoders are capable of grasping the crucial peculiarities of data in a way that captures them in the lower-dimensional space. In essence, this process helps both in reducing dimensionality as well as converge on the most characteristic components, ultimately facilitating the integration and analysis of multimodal data sets.

VAEs go beyond the scope of the typical autoencoders by introducing a probabilistic aspect encoding inputs into a distribution of space over space rather than a single point. One reason for this approach is the ability to create new data points in the latent space. It offers a more flexible and powerful means of modeling complex distributions of data, something that cannot be achieved through the use of simple manifolds alone. With respect to bioinformatics, VAEs can particularly offer such a possibility to interact with the latent space, which might possibly share some common properties with different data modalities, e.g., VAEs provide a platform for connecting genomic and transcriptomic data via identifying hidden variables that direct gene expression, bringing into focus the mechanism behind different biological states.

12.5.4 Multi-View Learning Algorithms

Co-training: Co-training is a semi-supervised learning method aimed at improving efficiency by using two or more different views of the same data for training. The scenario of bioinformatics is different where the data can come from a diverse source like genomic sequences and proteomic profiles. Alternatively training helps the model to learn more comprehensive representation by alternately training on each view and using the predictions form one view to enhance the training set of the other. This iterative procedure exploits the different and complementary information stored within each data type, elevating the appropriateness of the models to make the correct predictions or uncover hidden designs.

In the example we mentioned of cancer, a complex disease, to integrate genetic alterations and gene expression data through co-training is to identify potential biomarkers or therapeutic targets. Through analyzing genomic and transcriptomic views at the same time, the algorithm would be able to detect relationships and limit the number of possible connections that might not be evident when studying these data types separately. This, in turn, leads to a more comprehensive understanding of disease mechanisms.

Multi-view Canonical Correlation Analysis (CCA): The multi-view CCA algorithm is a statistical method that seeks to find linked variables among two or more sets of data. In bioinformatics, where studies often apply multi-omics techniques (such as genomics, proteomics or metabolomics), CCA can be of benefit, for instance by highlighting how alterations in one layer (e.g., genomic mutations) are related to changes in another one (e.g., protein expression levels).

CCA achieves this through the process of optimizing the correlation between given linear combination of variables from the different aspects, while identifying the commonalities between them. This is particularly worthy for integration of multimodal datasets, since the biologic connections behind different types of data are highlighted. For instance, CCA applied to genomic and proteomic data set from a cohort of cancer patients can identify gene-protein pairs that are correlated with clinical outcomes and select them as a target for designing personalized treatment plans and targeted therapies.

Integration into Bioinformatics: Co-training as well as CCA in bioinformatics demonstrate the capacity of multi-view learning algorithms to merge and process data observed from different biological layers, yielding insights unattainable from single-modal data sources. These algorithms allow the researchers to maximize the utilization of all biological data available and create a clearer picture of the way intricate molecular mechanisms interact contributing to the development of health issues or diseases.

12.5.5 Federated Learning for Privacy-Preserving Data Fusion

Federated Learning Frameworks: One of the novel approaches to machine learning is referred to as Federated Learning (FL) which allows organizations and institutions with local data samples to collaboratively train models across decentralized nodes such as hospitals and research institutions without having to share or centralize the data. This approach is vital to bioinformatics because of the unique combination of different and delicate datasets that enables research advancement and enhancing patient care, at the same time, managing the ethical issues related to privacy and consent.

A global model is sent to every party where it is trained on local data. Sending only the updates, not the entire data, and combining the outcome at the central server to improve the global model are on the contrary. This process is repeated in which the training is performed on the redistributed global model at each node. This decentralized approach on the one hand mitigates privacy concerns by keeping data on-premise but on the other hand offers a scalable solution for integrating data from various independent sources.

Application in Bioinformatics: The application of FL bioinformatics makes possible the combination of many data sets from different institutions all over the globe without jeopardizing patient confidentiality. Considering precision medicine, federated learning serves as a means for collaborative development of predictive models with which diagnostics and treatment outcomes can be illuminated using the genetic, clinical and lifestyle data from various population groups, improving the models' generalizability and accuracy.

On top of this, FL can thereby greatly influence the research of uncommon diseases. Thanks to a decentralized environment where data come from patients worldwide, the challenge of limited data access is successfully overcome and it allows various universities to find answers to questions of rare genetic disorders that otherwise would never be possible.

Challenges and Opportunities: While federated learning looks like a promising solution for privacy-preserving data conciliation, it also brings new features. Enhancing the robustness of the global model under various data distributions across nodes and preventing the possible security flaws originated during the model update aggregation are the vital areas where we need to invest our research and innovation efforts. Moreover, the excess computational needs and bandwidth of FL are of prime importance for the development of algorithms and communication protocols. The application of federated learning in bioinformatics could be the prelude to a new era of collective and collaborative research, in which the knowledge gathered from integrated, multiple data sets can accelerate the discoveries and understanding of how biological systems and diseases work. This technology will develop, and enable more inclusive as well as ethically sound research practices, with respect for privacy-by-design in the handling of sensitive biological data.

12.6 Future Directions

Data fusion can be considered as one of the fields in bioinformatics that is realizing modern times. These are the most important benefits of data fusion that are still to be exploited and they include huge predictive modeling achievements, tailored medicine and the inclusion of a wider variety of data sets. These innovations are aimed at transforming medical care paradigms by revolutionizing the notion of biological systems, raising the bar for therapeutic precision, and paving the way for a comprehensive health management approach.

Predictive Modeling and Simulation of Biological Systems

The direction of bioinformatics is very much inclusive of the rise of predictive modeling and simulating a complex system; the latter stands as a renaissance of the biological system. The recently developed computational models are progressively growing its ability to capture the complicated dynamics of cellular activities and organ functions, including the behaviors of the whole organism. The composing of multimodal data with these models leads to the generation of comprehensive simulations which are independent of the type of output environment that can predict results in divergent cases such as drug responses or disease progression.

The growth in technology, especially the computational powers and algorithms, is opening a new horizon of simulating big biological systems which can never be achieved. These models possess data from genomics, proteomics, metabolomics and other omics layers, as well as clinical and phenotypic data together, thus the developed predictions are based on the real biological available cell material. It is quite safe to say that quantum computing will be applied to advanced predictive models ever so soon, due to the fact that it will enable more complicated systems to be simulated with greater exactness and better speed.

Personalized Medicine and Patient-Specific Data Fusion

The integration of medical information on an individual basis continues to be the main characteristic of the rapidly developing area of multimodal data synergy. Combining genetics, environmental, lifestyle and clinical data would lead to personalized treatment of patients by doctors. This personalized treatment focuses on the maximization of treatment efficiency while minimizing negative effects and promoting the improvement of outcomes in the healthcare sphere.

The essence of what is needed in applying personalized medicine is the assembling of multimodal observations to get detailed patient charts. Through the use of machine learning and AI techniques, there has come about development that enables models to properly handle the complexities and widen heterogeneity of this data, hence providing insights that are more accurate and individualized. Moving forward, there are going to be advanced, adaptive models that will use real-time patient data on the spot, which includes progress clinical data, lifestyle changes and environmental exposures, all to refine treatment courses of action continually.

Integration of Broader Data Types (Environmental, Lifestyle, Socioeconomic Data)

The purview of bioinformatics has expanded not only to include clinical and biological information, but also the environment, lifestyle behaviours, and socioeconomic conditions. This multifactorial way of thinking sees healthcare comprising all the internal and external factors that affect human health, singling them all out as the major contributors. This wider variety of data integration adds a layer of complexity which provides a more complete picture of the cause of the disease, its development, and its response to treatment.

Progress of technological developments in data collection for individual lifestyles, like wearable devices and sensors of IoT that are sending continuous, real-time data, are being helpful now. The main task is the successful integration of side-huge, multisided data with related biological and medical datasets for positive derived outcomes. It can be foreseen that future developments in data fusion techniques will involve major advances in scaling, privacy and interoperability issues to effectively take advantage of the broadened data types in both bioinformatics research and healthcare applications.

Multimodal data fusion of the future in bioinformatics is expected to demonstrate positive outcomes of predictive modeling, personalization medicine, and an integration of all the possible types of data to be processed. The directions point out the evolving aspect of bioinformatics and hereby to the interdisciplinary collaboration needed to manoeuvre the future advancements in bioinformatics. As we develop more computationally sophisticated methods and data becomes more complex and intertwined, bioinformatics opens pathways to discovering a new depth in the complexity of life and health enabling us to make advancement which could push healthcare to new heights and improve our lives.

12.7 Case Studies and Applications

The multimodal data fusion in bioinformatics has proven to be a real game-changer that is delivering amazing data insights across biology and healthcare. From the standpoint of precision oncology, neuroinformatic, and systems biology, we can appreciate how the integration of various data sets enhances our knowledge about and leads to treatments of complex diseases.

Precision Oncology: Integrating Genomic, Transcriptomic, and Imaging Data for Cancer Diagnosis and Treatment

Oncology precision is a comprehensive form of multimodal data fusion, and genomic, transcriptomic, and imaging data all are utilized to personalize the cancer therapy. These multiple data sources blended provides a profound overview of the molecular profile of a particular tumor, disclosing unique genetic mutations and specific expression patterns that can be targeted by precisely directed therapies. Receiving imaging data is an extremely valuable extra level of spatial and morphological context that the clinician can use to determine the location of the tumor, the size of the tumor and the response to treatment.

In difference with this didactic case study, multimodal data fusion is applied for glioblastoma, an aggressive brain tumor. They have seamlessly integrated genomic sequencing data with improved MRI imaging to define molecular subtypes of glioblastoma, which have distinct genetic alterations and clinical outcomes. This fusion has made it possible for scientists to develop more definite and powerful cancer therapies, whose purpose is to treat the genetic abnormalities of the tumors, thus improving patients' prognoses. Moreover, the feedback loop of tumor response by means of imaging systems permits changes in treatment in real time, which leads to the precision and efficacy of cancer treatment.

Neuroinformatics: Fusion of Neuroimaging and Genetic Data for Understanding Neurological Disorders

Neuroinformatics is, perhaps, one of those frontiers where this multimodal data fusion is making a great leap in understanding and treatment of neurological diseases. Thus, the integration applications for neuroimaging information with genetic information offer an opportunity to know the relationships between genetic factors in the context of changes in brain structure and function associated with disorders like Alzheimer's disease, autism spectrum disorders, and schizophrenia, among others.

An important example for this purpose may be an ongoing investigation of Alzheimer's illness, where a combination of MR and PET with genetic data revealed the fact that there are some markers of DNA responsible for brain atrophy and amyloid deposits. This integrated approach has not only contributed to the increased understanding of the disease's pathology but also allowed developing biomarkers for early detection and the building of targeted pharmacological interventions. In addition, the possibility to connect to genetics conveying risk factors with neuroimaging signatures of disease development may be a highly effective tool for predicting disease onset and course, which, in consequence, may lead to preventive strategies and personalized treatment types.

Systems Biology: Modeling Complex Biological Systems through Integrated Datasets

System biology is a fine example of the holistic approach that has been made possible by multimodal data fusion whereby a systematically effort is employed to model and understand complex biological systems using various data sets. "This field comprises data from genomics, proteomics, metabolomics, and other omics layers as well as it includes phenotypic and environmental data to build multilevel models representative of biological processes and systems."

A convincing example of systems biology practically would be the investigation of the human microbiome and how it is connected to health and disease. Researchers have joined genomic data obtained from host organisms with metagenomic data and metabolomic data obtained from microbial communities to look at the complex interactions between humans and the microbes in their microbiomes. Integrative assessment of the critical role of the microbiome in metabolic diseases, immune responses and even in emotional disorders has illuminated the possibility of using the microbiome as a new therapeutic target for prevention or treatment of diseases. The integrated perspective supplied by systems biology, which ultimately arrives with the data fusion techniques, provides the foundation for a new philosophy of the multilevel interactions between health and disease which leads to the discovery of new drugs and interventions.

12.8 Challenges and Opportunities

The assimilation of multimodal information in bioinformatics on the one hand promises unprecedented possibilities for advanced research and health applications but on the other hand remains at the same time with challenging issues matching the simultaneous solutions. The issues that arise are the data privacy and the ethical pros and cons, the system requirements of scalability and computation power, and the impossibility standards and fusion methods between data topics. To realize the full power of the multimodal data fusion we should handle the following two questions efficiently by being responsible.

Data Privacy and Ethical Considerations in Handling Personal Biological Data

This sort of merger of biological data, especially when it goes far beyond public and personal boundaries, causes really critical problems of privacy and ethical issues. Now as bioinformatics is widely used to combine genetic data with the data acquired from the channel, lifestyle and environment, the threat to individuals' privacy also goes up. The risk of re-identification, even when the datasets are anonymized, remains a one-of-a-kind ethical problem that needs to be concerned with the balance of scientific progress and people's personal privacy protection.

Moreover, biological data collection and use covers concerns that involve individual privacy, property rights and fair accord of advances. The question regarding the application of personal data for the sake of research, in which there is no express approval nor the explicit identification of the benefits for the collective from which the personal data were taken, demands a very careful consideration of ethical principles along with the appropriate regulatory framework. Promulgation of thorough guidelines enabling participants to sign permissive consent forms, cautioning the public on data uses and fair distribution of study outcomes is of the essence as it is the only way of sustaining public support and scientific credibility in bioinformatics.

Scalability and Computational Challenges in Processing Large-Scale, Multimodal Datasets

The phenomenon of exponential growth in the size of the data, type of data, and speed of data generation is a frontier area for both large-scale data handling and computation. Processing, handling as well as analysing data that is massive, multimodal, requires a lot of the computations along with the very well-designed algorithms that can be used for addressing the complexity and uniqueness of these data sets. The scale of genomics, proteomics, and imaging data integrated with continuous health monitoring data imposes rigorous excess computational infrastructure and data storage systems.

These obstacles, however, can be overcome only through technological development, where at the forefront will be more effective algorithms, while cloud computing and distributed computing will serve as a platform. At the end of the day, the possible implementation of quantum computing can help with data processing. Moreover, utilizing machine learning and artificial intelligence as analytical tools able to scale up to cover multimodal data integration can offer flexible solutions that are able to meet the ever-growing needs of futuristic data fusion. The technological improvement must be accompanied by literacy in computational by scientists and bioinformaticians. Therefore, no part the scientific community will lose the chance to fully exploit such tools.

The Need for Standardization and Interoperability among Data Formats and Fusion Methodologies

The major roadblock on the way of harmony among multimodal data fusion is that there is no unification and harmony among data formats and fusion process. Disparity in data storage and analysis platforms results in diversity of formats, metadata and other specification. The integration of data becomes a real pain which impedes the free flow and analysis of data between different services and studies. Moreover, the wide spread of data fusion methods, however without common standards or steps, will result in the difficulty of validation and comparison in research concerning bio-computing, downgrading the re-creation and credibility of this science.

With this, a focused effort and adoption of data standards that allow integration and data sharing are required to accomplish this goal. Consequently, the creation of the consent platforms, which facilitate the design and the use of common data fusion tactics, facilitates the reasonable and accurate reproduction of biocomputational studies. There is also a need to build cross-disciplinary cooperation among biologists, computer scientists and statisticians for bridging the divides between different data modalities and algorithms, supporting the growth of strong frameworks for proper data integration.

The issues and prospects of multimodal data combination further emphasizes fusion character of different biological dataset with bioinformatics data integration. Nevertheless, the decision-making has to be directed toward the solutions of the ethical and privacy challenges, solving the scalability and computational issues and favouring the standardization and interoperability, which are the keys to achieve the complete potential of multimodal data collecting. This community can use their potential to solve the problems by helping the bioinformatics community to integrate datasets to get the new scientific findings in healthcare which help to unravel some of the complex biological systems that will in turn improve the health and well-being of human beings.

12.9 Conclusion

The review of potential futures and the trends of multimodal data integration in bioinformatics has explicated a bird's-eye view of a sphere which is in the forefront of fresh discoveries and innovations. And on this journey, from the basics of concepts to the frontline of modern methodologies and the space beyond, we definitely understand that biological systems are quite complicated and so is the data they generate, and the only way that sophisticated computational approaches can solve this is using cutting-edge strategies. The integration of various biological data types, from genomic and proteomic to imaging data sets, has shown paths to novel achievements in such disciplines as precision medicine and systems biology, supposedly ushering in the new era of the biomedical sciences that is ever more data-driven. While so much effort is poured in by the researchers in these challenges a broad field of obstacles and opportunities likes the conflicting issue of data privacy and shaping the ethical considerations to overcoming the escalation problem to the scalability and computational barriers to the basic need for standardization and interoperability issues that seem to crop up among diverse data formats and fusion methodologies.

Data fusion in bioinformatics, however, puts a great stress on the role of interdisciplinary collaboration amongst the participating scientists. The bringing together of knowhow from biology, computer science, statistics, and ethics is an imperative for more creative and everlasting solutions that cover the edges of only one field. This cooperative spirit is the technical wire that leads to designing the new computational models, ethical frameworks and implementation of large data sets to get actionable clinical information. While peering into the not-so-distant future, we now witness the sky of possibilities contemplating the multi-event data fusion in bioinformatics. Picture a meme where you can see multiple layers of biological data coming together in one place and providing you with a complete, organized knowledge base. Combining those ways of investigation promises not only to change our perception of the design of illnesses and enhance diagnostics and treatment strategies, but also to open the secret of nature code itself.

These are the types of future that are ethically and privacy awareness design and we should take care of it. The accomplishment of the bioinformatics research was done in an ethical and privacy manner to make sure that everything was done fairly. There is no denial that there will be a lot of risks along the way but the principle of interdisciplinary cooperation as well as the rapid improvements in computational devices and the ever-growing library of biological data give bioinformatics an edge over other fields, meaning that it is the discipline that will bring forth the next scientific revolution. The prophecy of multimodal data fusion in bioinformatics to enhance the knowledge from biology as well as medicine is, without a shadow of a doubt, incomparable. Developing the identify of bioinformatics to catch up with the ever-increasing complex biological data, creating multi-disciplinary partnerships and the challenge of putting an innovative way of overcoming the ethical and computational issues will ensure that the bioinformatics community becomes ever innovating in scientific and health care. By means of this concluding reflection, I not only bring together the universal observations and the discovered things from the entire chapter but also clearly reveal the inspiring future of the multidisciplinary data in bioinformatics—the future of the data which is not dark with the shadow of the defect but lit with the glowing of discovery, understanding, and the possibility of changing human health and well-being.

References

1. Reddy P, S. and Patwal, P.S., Data Analytics and Cloud-Based Platform for Internet of Things Applications in Smart Cities. *2022 International Conference on Industry 4.0 Technology (I4Tech)*, pp. 1–6, 2022.
2. Kawale, S.R. and Diwan, S.P., Intelligent Breast Abnormality Framework for Detection and Evaluation of Breast Abnormal Parameters. *2022 International Conference on Edge Computing and Applications (ICECAA)*, pp. 1503–1508, 2022.
3. Kameswara Rao, B., Chaturvedi, A., Hussain, N., Industrial quality healthcare services using Internet of Things and fog computing approach. *Meas.: Sens.*, 24, 100517, 2022.
4. Swathi Pai, M., Shruthi, M., Naveen K, B., Internet of Things: A Survey on Devices, Ecosystem, Components and Communication Protocols. *2020 4th International Conference on Electronics, Communication and Aerospace Technology (ICECA)*, pp. 611–616, 2020.
5. Burugadda, V.R., Pawar, P.S., Kumar, A., Bhati, N., Predicting Hospital Readmission Risk for Heart Failure Patients Using Machine Learning Techniques: A Comparative Study of Classification Algorithms. *2023 Second International Conference on Trends in Electrical, Electronics, and Computer Engineering (TEECCON)*, Bangalore, India, pp. 223–228, 2023, doi: 10.1109/TEECCON59234.2023.10335817.
6. Sasubilli, S.M., Kumar, A., Dutt, V., Improving Health Care by Help of Internet of Things and Bigdata Analytics and Cloud Computing. *2020 International Conference on Advances in Computing and Communication Engineering (ICACCE)*, Las Vegas, NV, USA, pp. 1–4, 2020, doi: 10.1109/ICACCE49060.2020.9155042.
7. Prasad, K., Dekka, S., Tanguturi, R.C., Poornima, G., An Intelligent System for Remote Monitoring of Patients Health and the Early Detection of Coronary Artery Disease. *2022 International Conference on Smart Generation Computing, Communication and Networking (SMART GENCON)*, Bangalore, India, pp. 1–6, 2022.
8. Burugadda, V.R., Jadhav, N., Vyas, N., Duggar, R., Exploring the Potential of Deep Reinforcement Learning for Autonomous Navigation in Complex Environments. *2023 7th International Conference On Computing, Communication, Control And Automation (ICCUBEA)*, Pune, India, pp. 1–6, 2023, doi: 10.1109/ICCUBEA58933.2023.10392109.

9. Ram Vishal, B., Shankar, M.U., M, K.A., Cardiovascular Disease Prediction Using LSTM Algorithm based on Cytokines. *2023 4th International Conference for Emerging Technology (INCET)*, Belgaum, India, pp. 1–5, 2023.
10. Kranthi, M. and Tanguturi, R.C., Design of Intelligent Medical Integrity Authentication and Secure Information for Public Cloud in Hospital Administration. *2023 2nd International Conference on Edge Computing and Applications (ICECAA)*, Namakkal, India, pp. 256–261, 2023.
11. Swarna, S.R., Kumar, A., Dixit, P., Sairam, T.V.M., Parkinson's Disease Prediction using Adaptive Quantum Computing. *2021 Third International Conference on Intelligent Communication Technologies and Virtual Mobile Networks (ICICV)*, Tirunelveli, India, pp. 1396–1401, 2021, doi: 10.1109/ICICV50876.2021.9388628.
12. Mailapur, R.V. and K, M., Implementation of GUI based Vital Track Ambulance for Patient Health Monitoring. *2023 8th International Conference on Communication and Electronics Systems (ICCES)*, Coimbatore, India, pp. 1417–1424, 2023.
13. Kumar, A., Kumar, S.A., Dutt, V., Dubey, A.K., Narang, S., A Hybrid Secure Cloud Platform Maintenance Based on Improved Attribute-Based Encryption Strategies. *Int. J. Interact. Multimed. Artif. Intell.*, 8, 2, Universidad Internacional de La Rioja, 150, 2023, doi: 10.9781/ijimai.2021.11.004.
14. Chakrasali, S.V., Kumar, C., Chaturvedi, A., Azhagu Jaisudhan Pazhani, A., Computer vision based healthcare system for identification of diabetes & its types using AI. *Meas.: Sens.*, 27, 10075, 2023.
15. Hombalimath, Palanikkumar, D., Patwari, N., Symmetrized Feature Selection with Stacked Generalization based Machine Learning Algorithm for the Early Diagnosis of Chronic Diseases. *2023 5th International Conference on Smart Systems and Inventive Technology (ICSSIT)*, Tirunelveli, India, pp. 838–844, 2023.
16. Namitha, A.R., Manu, Y.M., Rashmi, G.R., Chinamuttevi, V.S., IOT Based Smart Health Care System to Monitor Covid-19 Patients. *IJEER*, 10, 1, 36–40, 2022.
17. Ramesh Naidu, P. and Guruprasad, N., A High-Availability and Integrity Layer for Cloud Storage, Cloud Computing Security: From Single to Multi-Clouds. *J. Phys. Conf. Ser.*, 1921, 1, 012072, 2021.
18. A, G., Naik, A.B., HG, N., Covid-19 Prevention Kit Based on an Infrared Touchless Thermometer and Distance Detector. *2021 5th International Conference on Electronics, Communication and Aerospace Technology (ICECA)*, pp. 358–362, 2021.
19. Jeevan, K. and Sathisha, B.M., Implementation of IoT Based Wireless Electronic Stethoscope. *2020 Third International Conference on Multimedia Processing, Communication & Information Technology (MPCIT)*, pp. 103–106, 2020.

20. K N, U. and V M, R., Arduino based COVID-19 Suspect Detection Device. *2022 6th International Conference on Electronics, Communication and Aerospace Technology*, Coimbatore, India, pp. 158–163, 2022.
21. Punugoti, R., Dutt, V., Anand, A., Bhati, N., Exploring the Impact of Edge Intelligence and IoT on Healthcare: A Comprehensive Survey. *2023 International Conference on Sustainable Computing and Smart Systems (ICSCSS)*, Coimbatore, India, pp. 1108–1114, 2023, doi: 10.1109/ICSCSS57650.2023.10169733.
22. C R, R., Kameswara Rao, B., Sarma, P., Enhanced Diagnostic Methods for Identifying Anomalies in Imaging of Skin Lesions. *IJEER*, 10, 4, 1077–1085, 2022.
23. Anandaram, H., B A, N., Gupta, N., Verma, B.K., IoT Wearable Breast Temperature Assessment System. *2023 7th International Conference on Computing Methodologies and Communication (ICCMC)*, Erode, India, pp. 1236–1241, 2023.
24. Prasad, K., Anil Kumar, N., Reddy, N.S., Ashreetha, B., Technologies for Comprehensive Information Security in the IoT. *2023 International Conference for Advancement in Technology (ICONAT)*, Goa, India, pp. 1–5, 2023.
25. Palanikkumar, D., Mary, P.A., Begum, A.Y., A Novel IoT Framework and Device Architecture for Efficient Smart city Implementation. *2023 7th International Conference on Trends in Electronics and Informatics (ICOEI)*, Tirunelveli, India, pp. 420–426, 2023.
26. Nareshkumar, and Gururaj, B., An Integrated IoT Technology for Health and Traffic Monitoring System with Smart Ambulance. *2022 IEEE North Karnataka Subsection Flagship International Conference (NKCon)*, Vijaypur, India, pp. 1–6, 2022.
27. Kumar, S.A., Kumar, H., Dutt, V., Soni, H., Self-Health Analysis with Two Step Histogram based Procedure using Machine Learning. *2021 Third International Conference on Intelligent Communication Technologies and Virtual Mobile Networks (ICICV)*, Tirunelveli, India, pp. 794–799, 2021, doi: 10.1109/ICICV50876.2021.9388427.
28. Archana Shreee, S., Maheshwari, B., Jeevitha Sai, G., A Novel Method of Identification of Delirium in Patients from Electronic Health Records Using Machine Learning. *2023 World Conference on Communication & Computing (WCONF)*, Raipur, India, pp. 1–6, 2023.

13

Future Trends in Bioinformatics AI Integration

Srinivas Kumar Palvadi[1]* and G. Kadiravan[2]

[1]Department of Computer Science and Engineering, SRK Institute of Technology, Vijayawada, Andhra Pradesh, India
[2]Department of Computer Science and Engineering, Koneru Lakshmaiah Education Foundation, Vaddeswaram, Guntur, Andhra Pradesh, India

Abstract
The convergence of Artificial Intelligence (AI) and bioinformatics is reshaping the future of biological research and data analytics. This paper delves into emerging trends within this dynamic field, emphasizing the transformative capabilities of AI in handling and interpreting extensive biological datasets. With the ever-increasing volume of biological information, traditional bioinformatics approaches often struggle with issues of speed and the ability to derive meaningful insights. AI introduces innovative methods, such as machine learning, deep learning, and natural language processing, which significantly enhance data analysis, optimize workflows, and unlock new avenues for discovery.

A key trend is the utilization of machine learning algorithms for predictive analytics in genomics and proteomics. These algorithms are adept at recognizing patterns within large datasets, contributing to advancements in personalized medicine and targeted treatment options. For example, AI can assess genetic data to predict individual disease risks and treatment responses, thereby facilitating more tailored healthcare solutions. Additionally, deep learning techniques are becoming increasingly valuable in the realm of image analysis for bioinformatics, particularly in histopathology and medical imaging. By automating the interpretation of complex visual data, AI tools can support pathologists in delivering more accurate diagnoses while enhancing efficiency. This not only improves diagnostic precision but also minimizes the potential for human error, ensuring timely patient care.

**Corresponding author*: srinivaskumarpalvadi@gmail.com

Umesh Kumar Lilhore, Abhishek Kumar, Narayan Vyas, Sarita Simaiya and Vishal Dutt (eds.) Multimodal Data Fusion for Bioinformatics Artificial Intelligence, (283–304) © 2025 Scrivener Publishing LLC

Natural language processing (NLP) is another critical component in bioinformatics, allowing for the extraction of pertinent information from extensive scientific literature and unstructured datasets. AI-enabled NLP applications can assist researchers in sifting through vast amounts of information, identifying relevant studies, and summarizing key findings, thus accelerating the research process.However, several challenges persist, including concerns regarding data privacy, the necessity for high-quality datasets, and the interpretability of AI models. Addressing these issues is vital for the effective integration of AI within bioinformatics.

In overall, the future of bioinformatics is intricately linked to the integration of AI technologies, which hold great promise for deepening our understanding of complex biological systems and enhancing health outcomes. As the field progresses, collaboration between scientists and technologists will be crucial to ensure ethical standards and data integrity are upheld. This paper aims to provide a thorough overview of contemporary trends and future directions in the integration of AI within bioinformatics, highlighting its potential to drive significant advancements in the discipline.

Keywords: AI, bioinformatics, machine learning, predictive analytics, deep learning, natural language processing, personalized medicine, data integration

Introduction

This chapter investigates the developing scene of bioinformatics research, imagining a future where man-made reasoning procedures and multimodal information combination strategies merge to open further experiences into organic frameworks. Conventional bioinformatics approaches have frequently worked inside disengaged information storehouses, yet the development of incorporated structures promises to upset the field via flawlessly mixing different information modalities like genomics, proteomics, metabolomics, and imaging information. This coordination holds tremendous commitment for accuracy medication and customized medical care, empowering the improvement of custom-made mediations in light of thorough examinations of individual patient profiles. Nonetheless, close by these valuable open doors come difficulties, including moral contemplations, information security concerns, and the requirement for powerful information normalization and quality affirmation conventions. By tending to these difficulties and utilizing the collaborations among simulated intelligence and multimodal information combination, the future of bioinformatics promises to introduce another period of extraordinary experiences and developments in biomedical exploration and medical care conveyance [1].

What Is Multimodal Data Fusion?

Multimodal information combination, as investigated in this chapter, alludes to the most common way of coordinating data from different information modalities inside the field of bioinformatics. This approach includes joining information from different sources [2], like genomics, proteomics, metabolomics, imaging, and clinical records to get a more thorough comprehension of natural frameworks. Multimodal information combination use man-made reasoning (computer-based intelligence) methods to consolidate, examine, and separate significant bits of knowledge from these heterogeneous datasets, empowering specialists to uncover stowed away affiliations and relationships that may not be clear while dissecting individual information modalities in isolation. By coordinating different layers of organic data, multimodal information combination works with a comprehensive perspective on complex natural peculiarities, driving progress in accuracy medication, customized medical care, and biomedical examination. Moreover, this approach engages scientists in fostering custom-fitted intercessions and treatment systems in light of a more profound comprehension of the fundamental sub-atomic components and patient-explicit qualities. Generally speaking, multimodal information combination addresses a strong worldview inside bioinformatics, offering extraordinary opportunities to disentangle the intricacies of organic frameworks and increase the speed of revelation in the existence sciences.

Multimodal information combination in the setting of this chapter includes the mind-boggling blend of heterogeneous information types and sources. It envelops a refined course of incorporating data from genomics, proteomics, metabolomics, imaging, clinical information, and more. This combination rises above conventional disciplinary limits [3], drawing from different fields like software engineering, insights, and science. By tackling the force of man-made reasoning (simulated intelligence), multimodal information combination empowers scientists to consolidate these unique information modalities as well as to separate synergistic experiences that go past what every methodology could give independently [4].

This approach uses progressed AI calculations, including profound learning structures, group strategies, and Bayesian induction procedures, to really blend, examine, and decipher complex datasets. Through multimodal information combination, specialists can reveal multifaceted connections, recognize biomarkers, explain organic pathways, and at last gain a more profound comprehension of natural frameworks' way of behaving and capability.

Besides, multimodal information combination holds colossal commitment for tending to pressing difficulties in biomedicine, including sickness analysis, anticipation, and therapy [5]. By incorporating multimodal patient information, including sub-atomic profiles, clinical records, and imaging information, computer-based intelligence driven bioinformatics approaches can work with accuracy medication drives. This empowers the advancement of customized treatment methodologies custom-made to individual patients' distinctive organic attributes, prompting more viable mediations and worked on quiet results.

However, the excursion towards understanding the maximum capacity of multimodal information combination in bioinformatics simulated intelligence mix isn't without its difficulties. Moral contemplations, information security concerns, interoperability issues, and the interpretability of simulated intelligence models stay basic areas of concentration [6]. Tending to these difficulties will require interdisciplinary coordinated effort, strong information administration systems, and the improvement of norms and best practices for information joining and investigation.

Types of Multimodal Data in Bioinformatics

In this chapter, different sorts of multimodal information in bioinformatics are investigated, each offering exceptional bits of knowledge into natural frameworks. Genomics information addresses one urgent methodology, including data about a living being's DNA grouping, quality articulation levels, and hereditary varieties. This incorporates information from strategies, for example, next-generation sequencing (NGS) [7], microarrays [8], and polymerase chain response (PCR) [9], giving insight into hereditary inclinations, changes, and quality administrative organizations.

Proteomics information comprises one more fundamental methodology, zeroing in on the investigation of proteins and their communications inside natural frameworks. Methods, for example, mass spectrometry and protein microarrays create huge measures of information connecting with protein articulation levels, post-translational adjustments, and protein cooperation. This information offers significant understanding of cell flagging pathways, protein capabilities, and sickness systems.

Metabolomics information provides one more aspect in the mix of multimodal data in the field of bioinformatics, zeroing in on the thorough examination of little particles, metabolites, and metabolic pathways inside natural examples. Strategies like nuclear magnetic resonance (NMR) [10] spectroscopy and liquid chromatography-mass spectrometry (LC-MS) consider the recognizable proof of dynamic changes in metabolic profiles related with physiological cycles, natural upgrades, and illness conditions.

Imaging information assumes a critical role in explaining natural designs, tissues, and cell constituents. Modalities, for example, microscopy, attractive reverberation imaging (X-ray) [11], and positron emission tomography (PET) produce a range of imaging yields, including underlying, utilitarian, and sub-atomic data. This information gives comprehension of spatial connections, morphological changes, and illness movement at different levels, from subcellular designs to entire living beings.

Clinical information, including electronic health records (EHRs) [12], patient socioeconomics, and clinical imaging translations, address one more fundamental part in the combination of multimodal information. This information gives essential setting and clinical importance to sub-atomic revelations, associating sub-atomic experiences with patient results, infection determinations, and reactions to treatment.

With the help of automatic procedures that have different data techniques, which can give lot of data for various data models? These frameworks give various solutions for a complex process which gives single information procedure. The scope in dealing with the multimodal data which has lot of dedication for doing biomedical operations, accuracy as well as medical service communication [13].

Taking the general information which was time to time defined by the complex task in field of bioinformatics offers the way of defining techniques which consists of passing data, geographical data, micro elements as well as various natural situations. Coordinating ecological information with atomic and clinical datasets empowers investigation of the complicated interchange between hereditary inclinations [14], natural openings, and defencelessness to infection.

Furthermore, transient data adds one more layer of intricacy to multimodal information mix, catching remarkable vacillations in natural cycles over the long run. This incorporates longitudinal examinations, time-series information from investigations, and fleeting examples separated from clinical records. Dissecting transient information close by different modalities gives bits of knowledge into infection movement [15], treatment reactions, and the elements of natural frameworks.

Furthermore, spatial information gives important data about the spatial association of natural designs and cycles inside tissues and organic entities. Methods, for example, spatial transcriptomics, spatial proteomics, and spatial metabolomics empower specialists to plan sub-atomic profiles inside spatial settings, uncovering spatially settled examples of quality articulation, protein restriction, and metabolite circulations.

Finally, multi-omics information coordination addresses a high-level type of multimodal information combination, joining data from different omics modalities like genomics, transcriptomics, proteomics, and metabolomics.

Challenges in Multimodal Data Fusion

A few difficulties in multimodal information combination are distinguished, featuring the intricacies innate in coordinating different information modalities inside bioinformatics. One basic test lies in information heterogeneity, originating from contrasts in information configurations, scales, and quality across different modalities. Organizing the treatment of heterogeneous information involves strong pre-processing, normalization, and harmonization techniques to guarantee consistency and similarity. Moreover, the test procedure is defined with unknown datasets from large volumes of data. For dealing with the designing of large amount of data some of the calculations as well as computer resources were basic sources for completion of the task.

Giving guarantee for the data transfer from one device to another is a greater task; a few operations have to improve for storage space purposes or defining the type of the data. For this purpose we need converters, ontologies as well as data trading configuring for working constantly across all the modules [16].

Communication results with the AI-driven mechanisms, because of changes in procedures. Moreover, developing communication techniques helps in gaining security as well as establishing trust in bioinformatics.

Privacy as well as security were of primary importance while taking patient data. Data safety, guarantee of privacy for patient information, giving security for patient information are the basic things we need to follow while taking public data and we should not break the people's trust.

Multimodal Data Integration Approaches

Performing the analysis of large volumes of data collection techniques helps to merge various types of data over bioinformatics. One of the best techniques is giving connection to various techniques that means to define communication among various strategies using numerical values to authenticate relation investigation [17].

People defined techniques have various difficult mechanisms which use mathematical procedures like Support Vector Machine (SVM) technique, which groups the various processes for extracting difficult patterns as well as collaborating over datasets.

Developing various critical datasets helps in data identification as well as many techniques in bioinformatics. One of the models is defining the categories of various heterogeneous data for defining the quality of the data. For doing this we need to perform the pre-processing, making data in the normalised form for the purpose of data consistency as well as defining uniqueness of data.

Other tests which have lot of scope as well as datasets from long waiting time has lot of creativity. Adopting the new techniques for development for general data needs a lot of time as well as computational power for performing the tests as well as performing various operations.

Giving a secure connection for various users is the greatest improvement of performing mathematical calculations for various data types. Developing general conventions, ontology, as well as data trade helps in designing with various privacy features as well as consistency in co-operation.

Giving the security by merging various types of results especially for AI techniques. As AI techniques have more difficult for processing as well as testing the data. Developing the privacy features is a good metric for trust as well as repetition in bioinformatics.

Summary of the data as well as privacy were both important while taking patient data. Data protecting, information guarantee, and privacy as well as developing the rules were the basic things for maintaining trust among people.

Feature Representation and Selection

The future development of the various types of heterogenous data includes changing crude data at the time of making safe data. Techniques such as decrease in dimension, improving the designing as well as data extracting by the help of dimension data intricacy while making hold of unwanted information among the various mechanisms.

Various procedures were defined like examining the data, reducing high-level data to low-level data, making secure from inconsistency information which helps in defining the difficult datasets by giving various permissions to verify connections as well as samples in all of the data.

Various types of designs including developing new prototypes, datasets from lot of data from various techniques may bring change over the basic operations in database like create, retrieve, and update as well as delete. There exists the numerical terms in the data factors which includes developing as well as analysis for differentiating data from various datasets. The data extraction techniques bring the direct data from other techniques such as Convolution Neural Networks (CNN) as well as Recurrent Neural Networks (RNN) which help in multimodal information datasets.

Highlighting the data is the one of the type of data in multimodal data combining technique. Distinguishing the data is one of the most important things for data defining in data co-ordination as well as data examination. Include determination strategies plan to lessen overt repetitiveness, commotion, and over fitting by choosing a subset of elements that contribute fundamentally to the prescient or discriminative force of the incorporated dataset. Strategies like channel techniques, covering strategies, or installed strategies survey include significance in view of measurable tests, model execution, or regularization procedures.

In summary, highlight portrayal and determination are basic in multimodal information combination, permitting analysts to change crude information into enlightening portrayals and select important elements for examination. Through dimensionality decrease, highlight designing, highlight extraction, and component choice strategies, specialists can actually catch and influence important data from heterogeneous information modalities, empowering more hearty and interpretable examinations in bioinformatics.

Integration of Omics Data

Future depiction and decision are urgent parts of multimodal information combination, assuming a vital part in successfully catching significant data from heterogeneous information modalities. Include portrayal includes changing crude information into a more enlightening and conservative portrayal that extracts significant qualities for ensuing examination. These techniques have a lot of strategies for decreasing the dimensions, improving in terms of designing, extraction of important data for diminishing data from various different sources.

Multiple techniques give more tasks for giving multiple calculations as well as defining of undefined datasets which gives more examples in more mechanisms. Making new techniques over the domain of data strategies. This technique results in various factors like increasing or reducing data, defining mathematical elements.

Improving as well as defining the basic terms of data gives the data analytics by performing certain examinations like dimensionality, examination as well as importing data with the help of data extraction in the field of bioinformatics. Identifying the type of the data and removing unwanted information by the help of create, read, update, and delete (CRUD) operations for upgrading or deleting the data which includes the data extracting technique for taking information. The data have lot of versatile techniques for complex as well as adaptability techniques for the improved datasets. Highlight determination is one more basic move toward multimodal information combination, zeroing in on distinguishing the most useful and significant elements from every methodology to remember for the coordinated examination. This cycle includes distinguishing the most instructive and pertinent components from each way to deal with remember for the planned assessment. Highlight choice techniques intend to lessen overt repetitiveness, clamor, and over fitting by choosing a subset of elements that contribute most fundamentally to the prescient or discriminative force of the coordinated dataset. This interaction might include procedures like channel strategies, covering techniques, or implanted techniques, which assess highlight significance in view of measurable tests, model execution, or regularization methods.

In general, highlight portrayal and determination assume an essential part in multimodal information combination, empowering scientists to change crude information into enlightening portrayals and select important elements for examination. By utilizing dimensionality decrease, highlight designing, include extraction, and element choice strategies, analysts can successfully catch and use significant data from heterogeneous information modalities, working with additional vigorous and interpretable examinations in bioinformatics.

Clinical Applications

Clinical applications address a key region where multimodal information combination holds gigantic commitment, offering creative answers for medical services difficulties and improving patient results. By incorporating different information modalities, including sub-atomic profiles, imaging information, clinical records, and ecological elements, scientists and clinicians can acquire an extensive comprehension of individual patients' health status, illness dangers, and treatment reactions.

One clinical utilization of multimodal information combination is in the field of accuracy medication, which plans to fit clinical medicines and mediations to individual patients' novel attributes and sub-atomic profiles. By incorporating genomic, proteomic, and metabolomic information with clinical records and imaging information, clinicians can separate patients in view of their atomic subtypes, recognize prescient biomarkers, and customize treatment regimens to enhance restorative results.

Besides, multimodal information combination works with infection determination and forecast by coordinating different wellsprings of analytic data, including sub-atomic marks, imaging discoveries, and clinical biomarkers. By consolidating integral information modalities, clinicians can upgrade analytic precision, distinguish infections at beginning phases, and anticipate sickness movement with more prominent certainty, prompting all the more opportune mediations and worked on tolerant results.

Besides, multimodal information combination empowers prescient demonstrating and risk evaluation by incorporating longitudinal patient information with ecological elements and way of life factors. By utilizing AI calculations and factual models, clinicians can foster prescient models for sickness risk separation, patient anticipation, and therapy reaction expectation, empowering early mediations and customized preventive systems to alleviate infection chances. Also, multimodal information combination works with clinical choice emotionally supportive networks, which help clinicians in pursuing proof-based choices by coordinating different information sources, clinical rules, and patient-explicit data. These frameworks influence computer-based intelligence–driven calculations to break down complex datasets, create significant bits of knowledge, and give proposals to determination, therapy arranging, and patient administration, in this manner working on clinical results and diminishing clinical mistakes.

By and large, clinical uses of multimodal information combination address a ground-breaking worldview in medical services, offering customized, information-driven ways to deal with illness the executives and patient consideration. By coordinating different information modalities and utilizing progressed simulated intelligence–driven examination, clinicians can open new bits of knowledge into sickness systems, streamline therapy techniques, and work on persistent results, introducing another time of accuracy medication and customized medical care.

Imaging Data Fusion

Imaging information combination arises as an extraordinary methodology for incorporating data from different imaging modalities to improve how we might interpret natural designs, capabilities, and infections. Imaging information combination includes the mix of information from different imaging methods, for example, attractive reverberation imaging (X-ray), computed tomography (CT), positron emission tomography (PET), single-photon *emission computed* tomography (SPECT), ultrasound, and optical imaging, among others.

One critical goal of imaging information combination is to use the corresponding qualities of various imaging modalities to defeat their singular constraints and give more complete and exact data about natural frameworks. For instance, X-ray offers amazing delicate tissue difference and physical detail, while PET gives practical data about metabolic action, and CT offers high-goal primary imaging. By melding information from these modalities, specialists can acquire multi-parametric imaging datasets that catch both primary and utilitarian parts of natural tissues and organs.

A few methodologies have been produced for imaging information combination, going from enlistment and co-enrollment strategies to cutting-edge computational techniques in view of AI and man-made brainpower. Enrollment methods adjust pictures from various modalities into a typical direction space, empowering direct examination and combination of information. Co-enlistment methods expect to adjust pictures procured from a similar methodology yet at various time focuses or imaging boundaries, working with longitudinal examinations and quantitative investigation.

AI and computerized reasoning methodologies offer incredible assets for imaging information combination, empowering mechanized investigation, highlight extraction, and combination of multi-parametric imaging datasets. Profound learning structures, for example, convolutional neural networks (CNNs), recurrent neural networks (RNNs), and generative adversarial networks (GANs), have shown guarantee in coordinating data from different imaging modalities and extricating significant highlights for errands like picture division, characterization, and illness analysis.

Besides, imaging information combination has various clinical applications across different fields, including oncology, nervous system science, cardiology, and radiology. In oncology, for instance, multi-parametric imaging information combination can further develop growth location, portrayal, and treatment arranging by consolidating underlying, utilitarian, and atomic imaging data. In nervous system science, imaging information combination empowers the examination of mind availability, utilitarian organizations, and sickness biomarkers in neurological issues like Alzheimer's disease, Parkinson's disease, and multiple sclerosis.

In general, imaging information combination addresses a strong methodology for coordinating data from different imaging modalities to upgrade how we might interpret natural frameworks and further develop clinical navigation. By utilizing progressed computational strategies and man-made reasoning, imaging information combination can possibly upset diagnostics, customized medication, and remedial mediations, prompting worked on persistent results and medical services conveyance.

Biological Network Integration

Organic organization reconciliation arises as a strong methodology for incorporating different natural information modalities into network-based portrayals. Organic organizations, for example, protein connection organizations, quality administrative organizations, metabolic organizations, and flagging organizations, give an all-encompassing system to demonstrating and breaking down complex communications and connections between natural substances.

One vital target of organic organization incorporation is to coordinate heterogeneous information modalities, like genomics, transcriptomics, proteomics, metabolomics, and phenomics, into a brought together organization structure. By addressing natural elements (e.g., qualities, proteins, metabolites) as hubs and their communications as edges, organic organizations empower scientists to catch the complicated interchange between various sub-atomic parts and pathways inside an organic framework.

A few methodologies have been created for natural organization mix, going from measurable strategies to AI calculations and organization arrangement procedures. Measurable techniques, for example, connection-based approaches and co-articulation network examination, empower scientists to distinguish affiliations and co-administrative connections between qualities or proteins in light of examples of articulation across various datasets.

AI calculations, including chart-based strategies, profound learning structures, and organization implanting procedures, offer elective ways to deal with natural organization incorporation. Diagram-based strategies influence the topological design of organic organizations to focus on naturally applicable communications and foresee novel cooperation in view of organization properties. Profound learning designs, for example, graph convolutional networks (GCNs) and graph neural networks (GNNs), empower scientists to gain portrayals of natural organizations straightforwardly from information, catching progressive elements and complex connections inside organizations.

Additionally, network arrangement methods expect to coordinate natural organizations across various species or conditions by distinguishing saved subnetworks and adjusting relating hubs and edges between networks. By adjusting networks, scientists can move information and explanations across species or conditions, working with near examination and practical comment of natural substances.

Organic organization combination has various applications across different fields, including frameworks science, drug revelation, accuracy medication, and practical genomics. In frameworks science, network combination empowers scientists to demonstrate and mimic complex natural frameworks, distinguish key administrative hubs or pathways, and foresee framework ways of behaving under various circumstances. In drug revelation, network coordination works with the recognizable proof of medication targets, biomarkers, and medication reusing open doors by breaking down network irritations and communications. In accuracy medication, network reconciliation empowers the definition of patients in view of subatomic profiles and organization properties, directing customized treatment methodologies and remedial mediations.

Generally speaking, organic organization combination addresses a strong methodology for incorporating different natural information modalities into network-based portrayals, empowering specialists to unwind the intricacies of organic frameworks and gain bits of knowledge into health, sickness, and remedial intercessions. By utilizing progressed computational strategies and AI calculations, organic organization mix can possibly change biomedical exploration and medical care conveyance, prompting worked on tolerant results and customized medication.

Applications in Precision Medicine

Accuracy over medication arises as a conspicuous use of multimodal information combination, offering customized and custom-made medical care arrangements in light of individual patient qualities, including hereditary cosmetics, sub-atomic profiles, clinical information, and natural elements. Accuracy medication expects to streamline patient results by delineating people into unmistakable subgroups in light of their extraordinary subatomic marks, illness vulnerability, and treatment reactions.

Multimodal information combination assumes a critical part in accuracy medication by coordinating different datasets, including genomics, transcriptomics, proteomics, metabolomics, imaging information, and clinical records, to produce far-reaching patient profiles and illuminate customized treatment techniques. By utilizing progressed computational strategies, computerized reasoning calculations, and measurable models, multimodal information combination empowers analysts and clinicians to extricate significant bits of knowledge from heterogeneous datasets and tailor intercessions to individual patient necessities.

One vital utilization of multimodal information combination in accuracy medication is the ID of illness biomarkers and restorative targets. By incorporating omics information with clinical aggregates and treatment results, scientists can distinguish sub-atomic marks related with illness powerlessness, movement, and reaction to treatment. This empowers the advancement of biomarker boards for early recognition, visualization, and treatment checking, as well as the disclosure of novel remedial focuses for drug improvement and accuracy treatments.

In addition, multimodal information combination works with the improvement of prescient models and choice emotionally supportive networks for clinical direction. By incorporating multimodal patient information, including hereditary data, biomarker profiles, imaging information, and clinical records, scientists can foster prescient models to evaluate infection risk, anticipate treatment reactions, and streamline treatment regimens for individual patients. These models empower clinicians to pursue more educated choices, tailor mediations to individual patient attributes, and enhance patient results.

Besides, multimodal information combination empowers the definition of patient populaces into particular subgroups in view of sub-atomic profiles, clinical aggregates, and treatment reactions. By coordinating multimodal patient information, scientists can recognize atomic subtypes of sicknesses, portray patient heterogeneity, and design therapy systems to specific patient subgroups. This empowers the improvement of customized treatment conventions, versatile clinical preliminaries, and designated intercessions for patients with various sickness subtypes or therapy reactions.

By and large, accuracy medication addresses a promising use of multimodal information combination, offering customized and custom-made medical care arrangements in light of individual patient qualities. By coordinating assorted datasets and utilizing progressed computational methods, accuracy medication empowers specialists and clinicians to unwind the intricacies of illness science, advance treatment methodologies, and work on persistent results in the period of customized medication.

Computational Tools and Resources

A wide cluster of computational instruments and assets are fundamental for empowering multimodal information combination and progressing bioinformatics research. These apparatuses envelop different programming bundles, data sets, libraries, and stages intended to work with information incorporation, examination, perception, and understanding across assorted information modalities.

One class of computational devices centers around information mix and preprocessing, giving functionalities to combining, fitting, and normalizing heterogeneous datasets from various sources and modalities. Models incorporate instruments for information standardization, group impact adjustment, quality control, and information change, like Bioconductor, SciPy, and Orange.

One more class of apparatuses is devoted to factual investigation and AI, offering calculations and techniques for examining multimodal datasets, distinguishing examples, and getting experiences from coordinated information. These devices envelop a great many strategies, including relapse examination, grouping, order, dimensionality decrease, and organization examination, executed in libraries, for example, scikit-learn, TensorFlow, and PyTorch.

Besides, representation devices and stages assume a critical part in multimodal information combination, empowering specialists to investigate, imagine, and decipher coordinated datasets in a natural and intelligent way. These instruments include programming bundles for creating heatmaps, scatterplots, network outlines, and different perceptions to explain connections, examples, and designs inside coordinated information. Models incorporate apparatuses like Matplotlib, ggplot2, Cytoscape, and Gephi.

Furthermore, data sets and stores act as significant assets for getting to and sharing multimodal datasets, explanations, and metadata, working with information reuse, reproducibility, and joint effort in bioinformatics research. These assets envelop public data sets, stores, and information entryways facilitating many natural information, including genomics, transcriptomics, proteomics, metabolomics, imaging information, and clinical records. Models incorporate data sets like NCBI, ENSEMBL, GEO, TCGA, and UniProt.

In addition, arising stages and structures for multimodal information coordination and examination are ceaselessly being created, offering far-reaching answers for specialists to perform start-to-finish investigation pipelines, from information preprocessing to understanding. These stages influence distributed computing, dispersed registering, and superior execution processing foundations to empower versatile, proficient, and reproducible investigation of huge-scope multimodal datasets.

Generally, computational apparatuses and assets are fundamental for empowering multimodal information combination and progressing bioinformatics research, giving analysts the vital abilities to coordinate, investigate, and decipher heterogeneous datasets across assorted information modalities. By utilizing these apparatuses and assets, analysts can open the maximum capacity of multimodal information combination, prompting groundbreaking revelations and progressions in biomedical examination and medical services.

Future Directions and Challenges

A few future headings and difficulties lie ahead in the field of multimodal information combination for bioinformatics simulated intelligence reconciliation. These envelop arising patterns, possible progressions, and impediments that scientists might experience as they endeavour to saddle the maximum capacity of coordinating man-made intelligence philosophies with multimodal information combination methods in bioinformatics.

One future bearing is the improvement of further developed and modern simulated intelligence calculations custom fitted explicitly for multimodal information combination undertakings. This involves the plan and execution of novel profound learning structures, support learning draws near, and generative models fit for taking care of mind boggling, high-layered multimodal datasets and catching complex connections between different information modalities.

Besides, there is a developing requirement for interdisciplinary coordinated effort and combination across different spaces, including bioinformatics, software engineering, measurements, and space explicit fields like science and medication. By cultivating cooperation and information trade among specialists from assorted disciplines, analysts can use corresponding ability and viewpoints to address complex difficulties and drive advancement in multimodal information combination for bioinformatics and man-made intelligence mix.

Besides, tending to ethical, legal, and social implications (ELSI) is vital for guaranteeing capable and moral utilization of man-made reasoning–driven multimodal information combination advancements in bioinformatics. This includes creating rules, approaches, and systems for information the board, security, and moral direct, as well as advancing straightforwardness, reasonableness, and responsibility in artificial intelligence–driven examinations and dynamic cycles. Moreover, beating specialized difficulties related with information heterogeneity, interoperability, versatility, and interpretability stays a key center region for future examination.

Creating vigorous strategies and calculations for information preprocessing, mix, and examination, as well as resolving issues connected with information quality, predisposition, and reproducibility, are fundamental for guaranteeing the dependability and legitimacy of multimodal information reconciliation approaches in bioinformatics. Moreover, upgrading the openness and ease of use of computational devices, assets, and stages for multimodal information combination is basic for democratizing admittance to cutting-edge logical capacities and enabling analysts with assorted foundations and ability to use multimodal information coordination techniques in their examination.

By and large, the future of multimodal information combination for bioinformatics simulated intelligence reconciliation holds incredible commitment for propelling comprehension we might interpret complex natural frameworks, opening new experiences into infection components, and preparing for imaginative answers for pressing biomedical difficulties. By tending to arising patterns and difficulties, scientists can bridle the maximum capacity of artificial intelligence driven multimodal information combination to increase the speed of revelation and alter medical services conveyance in the time of accuracy medication.

Notwithstanding the previously mentioned future bearings and difficulties, a few different viewpoints warrant thought in the domain of multimodal information combination for bioinformatics artificial intelligence mix. One basic region for future investigation is the advancement of interpretable man-made intelligence models for multimodal information combination. As man-made intelligence strategies, especially deep learning models, become progressively perplexing and dark, there is a developing need to improve model interpretability and logic. Scientists are effectively exploring techniques for deciphering man-made intelligence driven examinations, removing significant experiences from complex models, and giving straightforward clarifications to demonstrate expectations, particularly in biomedical settings where interpretability is urgent for clinical direction and administrative consistence.

Moreover, the mix of multimodal information progressively or close constant settings addresses an arising outskirt in bioinformatics simulated intelligence combination. With the coming of wearable sensors, versatile well-being advances, and remote observing gadgets, there is a chance to catch multimodal information streams persistently and progressively, empowering customized medical care mediations, early illness recognition, and distant patient checking. Be that as it may, coordinating and dissecting streaming multimodal information continuously present critical computational and specialized difficulties, including information transmission, capacity, handling, and security, which should be addressed to understand the maximum capacity of constant multimodal information combination in bioinformatics man-made intelligence mix.

Also, the reception of multimodal information combination procedures in clinical practice and medical services settings requires thorough approval, assessment, and administrative endorsement. Clinical interpretation of simulated intelligence–driven multimodal information combination approaches requires vigorous proof exhibiting their clinical utility, adequacy, well-being, and dependability across assorted patient populaces and medical services settings. Laying out norms and rules for approving computer-based intelligence models, leading clinical preliminaries, and getting administrative endorsement for man-made intelligence–driven diagnostics, prognostics, and therapeutics is fundamental for encouraging trust, reception, and boundless spread of multimodal information combination advancements in clinical practice.

Finally, encouraging schooling, preparing, and labor force improvement in bioinformatics artificial intelligence reconciliation is significant for developing the up and coming age of analysts, clinicians, and information researchers furnished with the fundamental abilities and aptitude to tackle the force of multimodal information combination for progressing biomedical exploration and medical services. Drives, for example, interdisciplinary preparation programs, studios, hackathons, and open-access instructive assets can assist with overcoming any barrier between disciplines, encourage joint effort, and engage specialists to use multimodal information combination procedures in their exploration attempts.

By tending to these extra viewpoints and difficulties, specialists can additionally propel the field of multimodal information combination for bioinformatics man-made intelligence joining, driving development, disclosure, and groundbreaking changes in biomedical exploration and medical services.

Conclusion

All in all, this chapter shows the promising direction and complex difficulties intrinsic in the joining of man-made brainpower (man-made intelligence) systems with multimodal information combination methods in bioinformatics. Multimodal information combination offers a strong way to deal with coordinating different organic information modalities, including genomics, transcriptomics, proteomics, metabolomics, imaging information, and clinical records, empowering scientists to acquire a far-reaching comprehension of natural frameworks and drive developments in accuracy medication, customized medical care, and biomedical exploration.

As described throughout the chapter, the future of bioinformatics computer-based intelligence coordination holds enormous potential for interpreting complex organic cycles, unwinding illness components, and speeding up the improvement of novel diagnostics, therapeutics, and mediations. By utilizing progressed computational strategies, AI calculations, and measurable models, analysts can extricate significant experiences from heterogeneous datasets, reveal stowed away examples, and infer noteworthy information to direct clinical navigation and work on understanding results.

However, the acknowledgment of this potential is dependent upon tending to a horde of difficulties, including information heterogeneity, interoperability, versatility, interpretability, moral contemplations, and administrative consistency. Defeating these difficulties requires interdisciplinary cooperation, imaginative systemic turns of events, and deliberate endeavours to lay out principles, rules, and best practices for multimodal information combination in bioinformatics computer-based intelligence mix.

Looking forward, the coordination of computer-based intelligence approaches with multimodal information combination methods holds guarantee for changing biomedical examination and medical services conveyance in the time of accuracy medication. By embracing arising patterns, tending to key difficulties, and cultivating joint effort and development across disciplines, scientists can open the maximum capacity of bioinformatics computer-based intelligence incorporation to drive groundbreaking changes and work on human well-being and prosperity.

Fundamentally, the section highlights the significance of outfitting the cooperative energy among artificial intelligence and multimodal information combination in bioinformatics, making ready for momentous disclosures, creative arrangements, and customized ways to deal with medical care in the 21st century. Through aggregate endeavours and groundbreaking drives, what's in store holds limitless open doors for utilizing artificial intelligence driven multimodal information combination to address pressing biomedical difficulties and change the scene of medical services for a long time into the future.

References

1. Das, S., *et al.*, Multimodal Data Fusion: A Review of State-of-the-Art Methods. *Inf. Fusion*, 52, 44–60, 2019.
2. Liu, H., *et al.*, Deep Learning for Multi-Modal Medical Image Analysis. *Healthcare Inf. Res.*, 26, 3, 187–202, 2020.
3. Zhang, J., *et al.*, Multi-Modal Data Fusion: A Comprehensive Review. *IEEE Trans. Knowl. Data Eng.*, 33, 6, 2345–2363, 2021.
4. Burugadda, V.R., Jadhav, N., Vyas, N., Duggar, R., Exploring the Potential of Deep Reinforcement Learning for Autonomous Navigation in Complex Environments. *2023 7th International Conference on Computing, Communication, Control and Automation (ICCUBEA)*, Pune, India, pp. 1–6, 2023, doi: 10.1109/ICCUBEA58933.2023.10392109.
5. Rahmani, A., *et al.*, A Review of Multi-Modal Data Fusion Methods in Remote Sensing: State-of-the-Art and Future Perspectives. *ISPRS J. Photogramm. Remote Sens.*, 153, 166–177, 2019.
6. Yu, L., *et al.*, Multi-Modal Data Fusion for Improved Patient Diagnosis and Treatment: A Review. *J. Med. Syst.*, 43, 9, 1–14, 2019.
7. Wang, R., *et al.*, Recent Advances in Multi-Modal Data Fusion for Remote Sensing Applications: A Review. *Remote Sens.*, 12, 20, 1–27, 2020.
8. Kumar, A., Kumar, S.A., Dutt, V., Dubey, A.K., Narang, S., A Hybrid Secure Cloud Platform Maintenance Based on Improved Attribute-Based Encryption Strategies. *Int. J. Interact. Multimed. Artif. Intell.*, 8, 2, Universidad Internacional de La Rioja, 150, 2023, doi: 10.9781/ijimai.2021.11.004.
9. Kumar, S.A., Kumar, H., Dutt, V., Soni, H., Self-Health Analysis with Two Step Histogram based Procedure using Machine Learning. *2021 Third International Conference on Intelligent Communication Technologies and Virtual Mobile Networks (ICICV)*, Tirunelveli, India, pp. 794–799, 2021, doi: 10.1109/ICICV50876.2021.9388427.
10. Ji, S., Xu, W., Yang, M., Yu, K., 3D convolutional neural networks for human action recognition. *IEEE Trans. Pattern Anal. Mach. Intell.*, 35, 1, 221–231, 2017.
11. Punugoti, R., Dutt, V., Anand, A., Bhati, N., Exploring the Impact of Edge Intelligence and IoT on Healthcare: A Comprehensive Survey. *2023 International Conference on Sustainable Computing and Smart Systems (ICSCSS)*, Coimbatore, India, pp. 1108–1114, 2023, doi: 10.1109/ICSCSS57650.2023.10169733.
12. Peng, J., Xiang, S., Wang, Z., A review of multimodal data fusion for image-guided radiotherapy. *Engineering*, 4, 6, 841–848, 2018.
13. Rasmussen, C.E. and Williams, C.K.I., *Gaussian processes for machine learning*, MIT Press, 2006.
14. Burugadda, V.R., Pawar, P.S., Kumar, A., Bhati, N., Predicting Hospital Readmission Risk for Heart Failure Patients Using Machine Learning Techniques: A Comparative Study of Classification Algorithms. *2023 Second*

International Conference on Trends in Electrical, Electronics, and Computer Engineering (TEECCON), Bangalore, India, pp. 223–228, 2023, doi: 10.1109/TEECCON59234.2023.10335817.

15. Swarna, S.R., Kumar, A., Dixit, P., Sairam, T.V.M., Parkinson's Disease Prediction using Adaptive Quantum Computing. *2021 Third International Conference on Intelligent Communication Technologies and Virtual Mobile Networks (ICICV)*, Tirunelveli, India, pp. 1396–1401, 2021, doi: 10.1109/ICICV50876.2021.9388628.
16. Sasubilli, S.M., Kumar, A., Dutt, V., Improving Health Care by Help of Internet of Things and Bigdata Analytics and Cloud Computing. *2020 International Conference on Advances in Computing and Communication Engineering (ICACCE)*, Las Vegas, NV, USA, pp. 1–4, 2020, doi: 10.1109/ICACCE49060.2020.9155042.
17. Zhou, Z.H., A brief introduction to weakly supervised learning. *Natl. Sci. Rev.*, 5, 1, 44–53, 2017.

14

Emerging Technologies in IoM: AI, Blockchain and Beyond

Sumit Bansal[1*] **and Vandana Sindhi**[2]

[1]*Department of Computer Science and Engineering, Gurukul Kangri (DU), Haridwar, Uttarakhand, India*
[2]*Department of Computer Science, Punjabi University, Patiala, Punjab, India*

Abstract

In this chapter, the role of AI, blockchain, and emerging requirements will be analyzed as drivers of the revolutionary impact of emerging technologies for the Internet of Medicine (IoM). The chapter addresses the issue of the integration of these new technologies into the healthcare system, while at the same time trying to assess whether or not they are evidently efficient. This chapter offers various perspectives on how AI could transform healthcare administration, therapy personalization and diagnostics. Additionally, the essay investigates how the blockchain ledger can be innovatively exploited to protect medical data, maintain transparency and become a part of decentralized system of healthcare. The chapter studies other technologies that govern the Internet of Medical Management (IoMM) along with some enabling work of AI and Blockchain. It looks at their joint possibility as well as the moral issues emerging when they are used repeatedly. Researchers, practitioners, and policymakers aiming for a better understanding of how rapidly evolving technologies are transforming the healthcare sector may find this chapter to be a main source of information as the healthcare industry goes through a massive change.

***Keywords*:** Internet of medicine (IoM), emerging technologies, artificial intelligence (AI), blockchain in healthcare, healthcare transformation

**Corresponding author*: sumitbansal.cse@gkv.ac.in

Umesh Kumar Lilhore, Abhishek Kumar, Narayan Vyas, Sarita Simaiya and Vishal Dutt (eds.) Multimodal Data Fusion for Bioinformatics Artificial Intelligence, (305–322) © 2025 Scrivener Publishing LLC

14.1 Introduction

The Internet of Medicine (IoM) with its seamless use of digital technology along with the old conventional medical layout has become a force of disruption that has positive impacts in treatment and diagnosis [1]. AI and blockchain demonstrate the leading role in this process; these slabs create a perfect and secure foundation for the IoM ecosystem [2, 3].

Already, healthcare has greatly benefited from artificial intelligence thanks to the technology's ability to precisely diagnose medical conditions, customize treatment regimens, and foresee certain health outcomes. Machine learning algorithms that are part of artificial intelligence have demonstrated the ability to realise the entirety of crucial actions such as pattern-detecting, the course of diseases forecasting and better treatment methods like treatment plan improvement [4]. The enormous potential that AI has in processing and analyzing a broad range of medical data at a faster pace, AI is highly positioned to advance the quality of care and boost more effective and patient-centred healthcare systems [5].

However, it is important to note that the safety and integrity of confidential patient data should be the number one priority since IoMM relies on the exchange of this data among different networks. Known for the features of impenetrability and decentralization, the blockchain technology is the solution to many interoperabilityand data security problems. Blockchain restricts the possibility of data breaches and brings secure data sharing among authorised institutions, and this digital ledger makes the records more reliable by being immutable and transparent [6].

Blockchain and AI are two technologies that work better in unison than separately, so to speak. The role of blockchain in giving secure transactions along with data integrity perfectly matches the needs of AI in terms of having dependable dataset [7]. This partnership protects patient privacy and data authenticity while improving the accuracy of AI models and fostering a sense of confidence within the IoM ecosystem. Furthermore, because blockchain is decentralised, there is less chance of a single point of failure, which keeps Internet of Medical Things (IoMT) systems resilient and operational.

14.1.1 Importance of the Internet of Medicine

With respect to the IoM, AI integrated with blockchain is not only a technological trend; rather it is a model change with deep repercussions for all occupants of healthcare [8]. This chapter is geared towards demystifying this convergence and unpacking the potential of this integration to improve patient care, streamline administrative processes and facilitate joint research collaborations [9]. On our way through the realms of AI, blockchain, and beyond, the IoMT implications are enormous, turning the health care system into an intelligent, secured, and unprecedented innovatory sector full of revolutionary solutions.

14.2 Artificial Intelligence (AI) in Healthcare

AI in healthcare encompasses the utilization of sophisticated computational algorithms, machine learning and big data analysis tools to accelerate the discovery of new medicines, improve diagnosis accuracy, facilitate personalized treatment and streamline healthcare operations [10]. The introduction of AI into healthcare can revolutionize the entire industry, because it can help enhance productivity, decrease costs and improve patient outcomes. Figure 14.1 depicts where AI is likely to best complement different healthcare sectors.

14.2.1 Diagnostic Imaging and Radiology

The high precision with which AI systems diagnose medical images of CT, MRI, and X-ray scans is achieved by the AI systems. By providing a more detailed and accurate diagnosis, it allows early diagnosis of diseases like cancer [10].

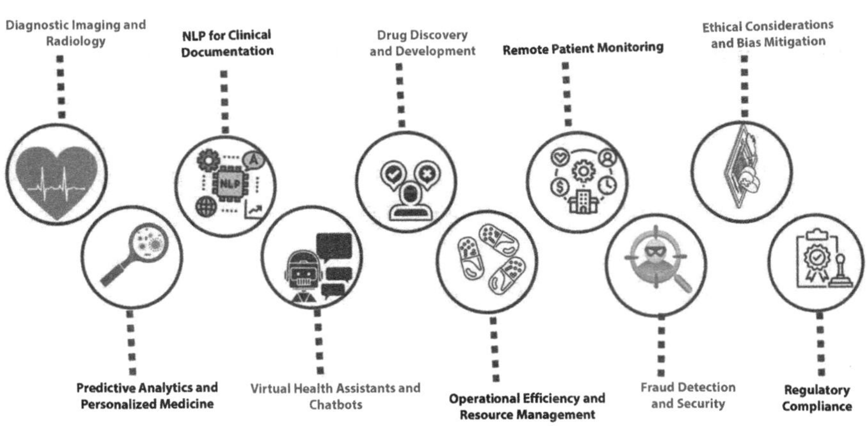

Figure 14.1 Artificial intelligence in healthcare.

14.2.2 Predictive Analytics and Personalized Medicine

AI systems, using patients' data, examine the probability of disease development. This creates a push to personalized medicine by allowing people to be proactive and adopt customized therapies to prevent, manage or heal illnesses [11].

14.2.3 Natural Language Processing (NLP) for Clinical Documentation

NLP is a tool that can help extract key information from clinical notes and other unstructured textual data that may be present in electronic health records. These are made more practical with the use of this data.

14.2.4 Virtual Health Assistants and Chatbots

The AI-enabled chatbots and virtual assistants can respond to queries, provide information, and in some cases help in monitoring a chronic illness [12]. This results in patient engagement, successful monitoring and supervision plans.

14.2.5 Drug Discovery and Development

AI accelerates the drug discovery process by evaluating the effectiveness of possible therapeutics through the analysis involving massive data sets. This reduces the resources and time necessary in bringing the new drugs to the market.

14.2.6 Operational Efficiency and Resource Management

AI spares clinics and hospitals from several non-essential operations by enhancing overall efficiency, putting resources to optimal use, and freeing humans from boring jobs. Thus it involves patient flow management, supply chain management and staff scheduling.

14.2.7 Remote Patient Monitoring

AI can be applied to devices with IoT and monitored patients with chronic illnesses remotely whenever necessary. This will enable healthcare providers to receive warning signals earlier in time and, hopefully, a visit to the hospital will be avoided [13].

14.2.8 Fraud Detection and Security

AI is an important feature of security in healthcare data as it is able to detect and prevent potential security breaches. It is also possible to detect coupon or insurance billing related fraud.

14.2.9 Ethical Considerations and Bias Mitigation

AI implementation should not forget about ethical issues. Fairness, openness, and the decrease of AI models prejudice towards patient outcomes and care are the main goals, according to [14].

14.2.10 Regulatory Compliance

The rules and regulations must be followed by AI systems in the field of healthcare as well. To keep the patient data private and secure legislation such as HIPAA needs to be fully complied with.

Even though the use of AI in healthcare carries a huge potential, there are some drawbacks, too, for example, data protection, complicated regulations and the need for professional interdisciplinary collaboration, which must be taken into consideration. It is important to draw a balance between creativity and the moralities involved in the employment of artificial intelligence in healthcare improvement.

14.3 Blockchain in the Medical Landscape

This technology, originally designed as the basis for the inception of cryptocurrencies like Bitcoin, has found application in various areas of the medical field [15]. Blockchain is being applied in the medical profession to overcome problems with security of data, interoperability, transparency, and trust [6].

14.3.1 Data Security and Integrity

The ability of blockchain to form a tamper-resistant and transparent book is one of the most important features of it. It achieves this objective of preventing data breaches and unauthorised access by making sure that medical records are impossible to hack in the healthcare industry.

14.3.2 Interoperability

Blockchain facilitates building a common and interoperable platform of patient records. This would allow the problems posed by incompatible EHR systems to be solved, thus enabling the automatic exchange of patient data amongst healthcare service providers.

14.3.3 Patient Empowerment

Nowadays, patients control and own their health data by blockchains. The patients can do this by allowing specific practitioners and researchers to have access to certain parts of their data [17].

14.3.4 Supply Chain Management

Blockchain makes the pharmaceutical supply chain transparent and traceable. Through the production, distribution, and intake monitoring, it reduces the chance of counterfeit medicines and enhances the safety of patients.

14.3.5 Clinical Trials and Research

Blockchain, by making the study findings transparent and immutable, helps to increase the validity of clinical trial data. It can also foster collaboration among researchers and increase others' trust in research results.

14.3.6 Smart Contracts

Healthcare operations can be automated through smart contracts, which are self-executing agreements where the terms of the agreement are coded directly into the code. It is composed of billing, adhering to the treatment plans, and processing the insurance claims.

14.3.7 Identity Management

Blockchain helps identity management by providing a distributed, secure method of keeping patient IDs. In healthcare, it can help ensure proper patient identification and reduce the case of identity theft.

14.3.8 Credentialing and Certification

Blockchain technology can be used to develop a distributed and immutable system for professional credentials [18]. This ensures that healthcare workers have valid and updated certifications at all times.

14.3.9 Data Sharing and Consent

Through blockchain technology, patients can either allow or deny access to specific information pieces, thus providing more precise control over their health data. The latter encourages patient trust and complies with privacy rules.

14.3.10 Cybersecurity

Better cybersecurity is the outcome of blockchain because of its decentralized structure [19]. The likelihood of a single point of failure or a significant data breach is minimized since the data is not stored in a central repository.

Despite any potential benefits, there are still barriers that need to be addressed for a wide popularity of blockchain in medicine. Such challenges comprise scalability issue, regulatory uncertainty, and the need to have standardization across the industry. Blockchain is capable of transforming the security, interoperability and transparency of data within healthcare by evolving the technology and adjusting the regulatory environments.

14.4 Benefits of Using Technologies in IoM

There are numerous advantages of the integration of technology in the Internet of Medicine (IoM) that transform patient outcomes, medical research and health care delivery in different aspects [20]. Figure 14.2 explains the various advantages associated with the implementation of the latest technology in the IoM.

14.4.1 Remote Monitoring and Telemedicine

Technological advances that allow the monitoring of patients' vital signs and health parameters in real-time are facilitating fast response time and omnipresent care by healthcare professionals. Due to telemedicine, remote

Figure 14.2 Benefits of using latest technologies in IoM.

consultations are fostered. Consequently, healthcare services accessibility is enhanced, including among the poor or remote areas [21].

14.4.2 Improved Diagnostics and Treatment

Big data can be processed through the process of AI to detect anomalies, forecast the disease path and ensure customized drug recommendations. This is likely to lead to more accurate, faster, and effective diagnosis, better treatment decisions and in general better results for patients.

14.4.3 Genomic Medicine and Data Analytics

These are just some examples of the technologies like data analytics and genomics which give patients more individualized treatment. Healthcare providers are able to enhance the effectiveness of treatment by tailoring medicines to suit individual genetics, as they can examine an individual's genetic makeup, as well as the history and data of their particular health.

14.4.4 Automation and Robotics

In surgical robotics and the automation of operations which are monotonous, productivity can rise, mistake rates can fall to zero and the period of recovery may be shortened. The cost may therefore be declining and the healthcare processes more effective.

14.4.5 Wearables and IoT Devices

Patients can get involved in their health management by the use of wearables and Internet of Things (IoT) devices as they can transform their lifestyle and get health updates in real time [22]. Such a strategy enhances a proactive approach to well-being and one's feeling of empowerment.

14.4.6 Virtual Reality (VR) and Augmented Reality (AR)

In conjunction with virtual reality and augmented reality technology, interactive simulations can teach medical personnel how to execute complicated tasks without the fear of failure. Furthermore, they also introduce the latest research procedures such as the visualization of complex structures.

14.4.7 Telehealth and Mobile Health (mHealth)

By using mobile apps and telehealth services, patients would be able to get information regarding their health and consult the physician remotely. Remote areas and the elderly particularly benefit from telemedicine which is available through the internet.

14.4.8 Blockchain for Healthcare Management

The supply chain management, insurance claim processing, and billing are the main administrative tasks which the blockchain can instantly expedite. With the effiency and transparancy offered by blockchain technology, these risks are kept at bay as well as administrative costs [23].

14.4.9 Data Analytics and AI in Research

The route to discovering and developing new drugs can be shortened due to the use of modern analytics together with AI algorithms to analyze vast data sets. Researchers will be able to pinpoint a wide range of possible medication candidates faster by using data-driven knowledge and predictive modelling.

14.4.10 Blockchain and Encryption

Blockchain, in its turn, reduces the possibility of a data breach by ensuring the safety and integrity of a patient's data. Encryption technologies that ensure the protection of sensitive data beyond reasonable doubt are also deployed, a measure that improves patient confidentiality and compliance with data privacy regulations.

Such inclusion not only improves the level of healthcare but also makes it accessible, accurate, and patient-oriented. Yet beyond the care of a specific patient, these benefits include the research that leads to better medicine, and the education that guides more efficient delivery of healthcare services.

14.5 Integration of Cutting-Edge Technologies

Blockchain reduces the opportunity of a data breach through verification of data safety and integrity. Sensitive data is additionally guarded by encryption tools, which in the first place provide patients with confidence in privacy and data security [24].

Technology integrations have become essential aspects of healthcare systems, increasing their accessibility, effectiveness and patient-centerness. However, care for one patient is not the only benefit; research, education, access, and the general streamlining of delivery systems will be improved too [25]. Through this strategic integration processes, performance and capabilities are highlighted because of the combining and inclusion of the latest and most advanced technology in the entirety of the system, process, or application. This thinking includes by all means the use of the latest innovations to produce a bigger impact that surpasses the potential of any individual technology. By establishing smooth interactions and interoperability across various cutting-edge technologies, the integration process seeks to promote an effective and comprehensive approach to problem-solving or optimisation in a variety of disciplines [26]. Emerging technologies like artificial intelligence (AI), the Internet of things (IoT), blockchain [27–29], augmented reality (AR), virtual reality (VR), and other cutting-edge solutions are frequently essential elements of this integration.

The goal is to utilize the synergies of these technologies to stimulate innovation, enhance the efficiency of procedures, and achieve better performance that surpasses all predecessors in various industries, including industry, health, and finance [30]. Thorough analysis, team member collaboration, and flexibility should be a priority so that these disruptive innovations can work harmoniously leading to this great revolution.

14.6 Beyond AI and Blockchain: Exploring Additional Technologies

It is an essential study of the electronic systems that lie beyond the areas of blockchain and artificial intelligence. This concept underlines the existence and need to innovate in discovering unique ways of dealing with issues and thus improving the sectors and fields [31]. This section presents a thorough investigation.

14.6.1 Internet of Things (IoT)

Data for the healthcare processes is gathered and made available to health systems through IoT devices. Examples of this group of machines are smart watches and smart medical equipment. This data set includes vital signs, such as heart rate, medication adherence and lifestyle measures. IoT is used to create smart care, preventive care is made real, and there is real-time monitoring when IoT is integrated with IoM.

14.6.2 3D Printing in Medicine

The ability to create customised implants, tissues, and even medical devices with the help of 3D printing technology is also feasible. Thus, it is now possible to design treatments which would suit each individual patient, improving favourable surgical outcomes and reducing probability of rejection.

14.6.3 Augmented Reality (AR) and Virtual Reality (VR)

Immersion of patients into educational categories, surgical planning and medical training can be enhanced with the help of AR and VR technologies. While VR serves the therapeutic interventions and mental health treatments, AR permits the surgeons to visualize the anatomy of their patients as they operate.

14.6.4 Genomic Medicine

By using the genetic analysis, in genomic medicine each patient's medical care can be tailored accordingly. What is remarkable is that developments in genetics allow diseases to be treated based on genetic predisposition, which as a result helps provide more personalised and targeted treatment plans.

14.6.5 Robotics in Surgery

Surgical robots perform minimally invasive procedures in accordance with the experienced surgeons' commands. Through higher precision, fewer invasive procedures, and even remote surgery, these robots essentially increase the accessibility to specialized cures.

14.6.6 Natural Language Processing (NLP) and Voice Assistants

With NLP, computers become able to understand and operate on human language. Voice assistants and NLP (natural language processing) can provide more accessible and user-friendly IoMT (Internet of Medical Things) by providing natural-language interaction between patients and the healthcare system.

14.6.7 Edge Computing

This means that the processing of data happens at the point of generation, thus reducing latency and improving medical data analysis in real time [32, 33]. This is one of the key aspects regarding the Internet of Medical Things applications that necessitate instantaneous decision making, like emergency response systems and remote patient monitoring.

These emergent technologies have the potential to integrate the Internet of Medicine and create a more interconnected, proficient, and patient-oriented healthcare system in return. These innovations can be expected to improve diagnostics accuracy, contribute to enhanced treatment outcomes, increase accessibility to healthcare services, and ultimately change how health-care is delivered and experienced.

14.7 Ethical Considerations in Implementing Emerging Technologies

Innovations in emerging technologies have their own set of ethical concerns that organizations and individuals are required to carefully consider. key ethical considerations in implementing emerging technologies are considered below.

14.7.1 Privacy Concerns

Emerging technologies frequently include data collection, retention, and analysis on an extreme scale. Adherence to privacy rules, transparent data practices and having proper user consent for data collection are mandatory for ethical implementation.

14.7.2 Data Security

There is a need to safeguard the data of a sensitive nature as the business world is becoming more dependent on data-driven technology. Implementors must bear in mind the various cyber risks, unauthorised accesses, and data breaches [34] in order to reduce them.

14.7.3 Bias and Fairness

The algorithms and models of evolving technologies may take unintended decisions that expose present biases from previous data. In AI apps, ethical issues arise, and we have to make a constant effort to eradicate the bias of the AI in order to enjoy impartial and equal outcomes.

14.7.4 Transparency and Explainability

The mechanisms by which emerging technologies come into action should be disclosed to users and all stakeholders. These implementers, necessarily, have to render explainability a top priority, so that a user may have the capability to understand the reasoning and decision-making process of these technologies.

14.7.5 Informed Consent

Those who use innovative AI applications must be committed to gaining the informed consent of all people who are affected by this and other developing technologies [16]. With this type of approach, an individual can realize what impact technologies may have on their life activities and ways in which data is used.

14.7.6 Accessibility

It is, however, significant that universal access to emerging technologies is guaranteed, no matter the physical constraint, socioeconomic background or other variables, for their utilization to be ethical. This means designing technology, which in turn doesn't compound on the pre-existing inequality.

14.7.7 Job Displacement and Employment Impact

AI and automation involve the risk of job losses at the workplace. Disclosure of the effects on employment, retraining of those affected, and a sensible adoption of new technology are all ethical issues.

14.7.8 Environmental Impact

With time, there is an increase in concern about sustainability. Technologies' environmental impact should be evaluated by people who implement the technologies. This would include factors such as the amount of waste generated, the resources consumed, and the energy consumed.

14.7.9 Dual-Use Concerns

Technologies designed for one goal can have secondary negative effects unintendedly and dangerously. Ethical issues reflect the assessment of possible dual-application bias effects and regulations to avoid misuse.

14.7.10 Accountability and Liability

Liability and accountability have to be pinned down. The assignment of responsibility of those responsible and the strategies to deal with and rectify these issues, which may arise as a result of the emergence of new technologies, causing unintended consequences or harm, is of utmost importance.

14.7.11 Regulatory Compliance

The application of ethics complies with the most recent laws and regulations. All implementers must make sure that they follow relevant legal regulations as well as ethical demands to guarantee their technologies have these parameters fulfilled.

14.7.12 Cultural Sensitivity

Technologies are somehow biased to certain cultures and viewpoints. This entails paying attention to the cultural environment in which technologies are used and ensuring that they are not turned into stereotypes of cultural norms.

14.7.13 Long-Term Impacts

Medium and long-term impact of technology on people, the economy and society as well as an ethical dimension are of equal importance. The assessor should determine the most probable outcomes and be visionary enough to tackle them in the long run.

The approach has to be not only active and multidisciplinary including engineers, ethicists, legislators and other stakeholders but also it has to be coordinated. With the use of novel technologies being able to promote sustainable innovation and to generate a positive social impact becomes possible, as long as ethics is given high priority.

14.8 Conclusion

To summarise, this part of the chapter outlines the extent to which the advanced technologies, among others, Artificial Intelligence (AI), blockchain, and other cutting-edge inventions have on the Internet of (IoM) medicine. It showcases the many ways these technologies can be integrated into the healthcare system, the benefits they bring, as well as the challenges that these technologies may face. This information, therefore, points out that AI is a huge game changer in the healthcare industry, where it helps in administration of healthcare, designing of personalised treatments, and improving diagnosis efforts. Furthermore, it examines blockchain's revolutionary potential in establishing decentralised healthcare systems and ensuring data security and openness. Studying other blockchain and artificial intelligence technologies beyond the leading edge brings the need for partnership and dilemmas to the light.

This chapter emerges as an invaluable aid during the renovation of the global healthcare system. It is a repository of invaluable information about the way healthcare tech is evolving and the parallel implications of it after a certain period of adoption.

References

1. Bradley, R., Harnett, J., Cooley, K., McIntyre, E., Goldenberg, J., Adams, J., Naturopathy as a model of prevention-oriented, patient-centered primary care: A disruptive innovation in health care. *Medicina*, *55*, 9, 603, 2019.
2. Malamas, V., Chantzis, F., Dasaklis, T.K., Stergiopoulos, G., Kotzanikolaou, P., Douligeris, C., Risk assessment methodologies for the internet of medical things: A survey and comparative appraisal. *IEEE Access*, *9*, 40049–40075, 2021.
3. Amponsah, A.A., Adebayo, F.A., Weyori, B.A., Blockchain in insurance: Exploratory analysis of prospects and threats. *Int. J. Adv. Comput. Sci. Appl.*, *12*, 1, 2021.
4. Kumar, S.A., Kumar, H., Dutt, V., Soni, H., Self-Health Analysis with Two Step Histogram based Procedure using Machine Learning. *2021 Third International Conference on Intelligent Communication Technologies and Virtual Mobile Networks (ICICV)*, Tirunelveli, India, pp. 794–799, 2021, doi: 10.1109/ICICV50876.2021.9388427.
5. Bjerring, J.C. and Busch, J., Artificial intelligence and patient-centered decision-making. *Philos. Technol.*, *34*, 349–371, 2021.
6. Yaqoob, I., Salah, K., Jayaraman, R., Al-Hammadi, Y., Blockchain for healthcare data management: opportunities, challenges, and future recommendations. *Neural Comput. Appl.*, 1–16, 2021.
7. Tyagi, A.K., Aswathy, S.U., Abraham, A., Integrating blockchain technology and artificial intelligence: Synergies perspectives challenges and research directions. *J. Inf. Assur. Secur.*, *15*, 5, 1554, 2020.
8. Allioui, H. and Mourdi, Y., Exploring the Full Potentials of IoT for Better Financial Growth and Stability: A Comprehensive Survey. *Sensors*, *23*, 19, 8015, 2023.
9. Johnson, K.B., Wei, W.Q., Weeraratne, D., Frisse, M.E., Misulis, K., Rhee, K., Zhao, J., Snowdon, J.L., Precision medicine, AI, and the future of personalized health care. *Clin. Transl. Sci.*, *14*, 1, 86–93, 2021.
10. Bi, W.L., Hosny, A., Schabath, M.B., Giger, M.L., Birkbak, N.J., Mehrtash, A., Allison, T., Arnaout, O., Abbosh, C., Dunn, I.F., Mak, R.H., Artificial intelligence in cancer imaging: clinical challenges and applications. *CA Cancer J. Clin.*, *69*, 2, 127–157, 2019.

11. Mathur, S. and Sutton, J., Personalized medicine could transform healthcare. *Biomed. Rep.*, *7*, 1, 3–5, 2017.
12. Sasubilli, S.M., Kumar, A., Dutt, V., Improving Health Care by Help of Internet of Things and Bigdata Analytics and Cloud Computing. *2020 International Conference on Advances in Computing and Communication Engineering (ICACCE)*, Las Vegas, NV, USA, pp. 1–4, 2020, doi: 10.1109/ICACCE49060.2020.9155042.
13. Punugoti, R., Dutt, V., Anand, A., Bhati, N., Exploring the Impact of Edge Intelligence and IoT on Healthcare: A Comprehensive Survey. *2023 International Conference on Sustainable Computing and Smart Systems (ICSCSS)*, Coimbatore, India, pp. 1108–1114, 2023, doi: 10.1109/ICSCSS57650.2023.10169733.
14. Norori, N., Hu, Q., Aellen, F.M., Faraci, F.D., Tzovara, A., Addressing bias in big data and AI for health care: A call for open science. *Patterns*, *2*, 10, 2021.
15. Siyal, A.A., Junejo, A.Z., Zawish, M., Ahmed, K., Khalil, A., Soursou, G., Applications of blockchain technology in medicine and healthcare: Challenges and future perspectives. *Cryptography*, *3*, 1, 3, 2019.
16. Felzmann, H., Villaronga, E.F., Lutz, C. and Tamò-Larrieux, A., Transparency you can trust: Transparency requirements for artificial intelligence between legal norms and contextual concerns. *Big Data Soc.*, 6, 1, 2053951719860542, 2019.
17. Chima, S.C., Evaluating the quality of informed consent and contemporary clinical practices by medical doctors in South Africa: An empirical study. *BMC Med. Ethics*, *14*, 1, 1–17, 2013.
18. Arenas, R. and Fernandez, P., CredenceLedger: a permissioned blockchain for verifiable academic credentials, in: *2018 IEEE International Conference on Engineering, Technology and Innovation (ICE/ITMC)*, IEEE, pp. 1–6, 2018, June.
19. Kshetri, N., Blockchain's roles in strengthening cybersecurity and protecting privacy. *Telecommun. Policy*, *41*, 10, 1027–1038, 2017.
20. Kumar, A., Kumar, S.A., Dutt, V., Dubey, A.K., Narang, S., A Hybrid Secure Cloud Platform Maintenance Based on Improved Attribute-Based Encryption Strategies. *Int. J. Interact. Multimed. Artif. Intell.*, 8, 2, Universidad Internacional de La Rioja, 150, 2023, doi: 10.9781/ijimai.2021.11.004.
21. Wilson, N.W., Couper, I.D., De Vries, E., Reid, S., Fish, T., Marais, B.J., A critical review of interventions to redress the inequitable distribution of healthcare professionals to rural and remote areas. *Rural Remote Health*, *9*, 2, 1–21, 2009.
22. Schüll, N.D., Data for life: Wearable technology and the design of self care. *BioSocieties*, *11*, 317–333, 2016.
23. Mak, K.K. and Pichika, M.R., Artificial intelligence in drug development: present status and future prospects. *Drug Discov. Today*, *24*, 3, 773–780, 2019.

24. Thapa, C. and Camtepe, S., Precision health data: Requirements, challenges and existing techniques for data security and privacy. *Comput. Biol. Med.*, *129*, 104130, 2021.
25. Mateo, J., Steuten, L., Aftimos, P., André, F., Davies, M., Garralda, E., Geissler, J., Husereau, D., Martinez-Lopez, I., Normanno, N., Reis-Filho, J.S., Delivering precision oncology to patients with cancer. *Nat. Med.*, *28*, 4, 658–665, 2022.
26. Wierenga, B. and Van Bruggen, G.H., The integration of marketing problem-solving modes and marketing management support systems. *J. Mark.*, *61*, 3, 21–37, 1997.
27. Sprung, R.C. and Jaroniec, S. (Eds.), *Translating into Success: Cutting-edge strategies for going multilingual in a global age*, vol. 11, John Benjamins Publishing, 2000.
28. Chatterjee, S., Chaudhuri, R., Kamble, S., Gupta, S., Sivarajah, U., Adoption of artificial intelligence and cutting-edge technologies for production system sustainability: A moderator-mediation analysis. *Inf. Syst. Front.*, 1–16, 2022.
29. Swarna, S.R., Kumar, A., Dixit, P., Sairam, T.V.M., Parkinson's Disease Prediction using Adaptive Quantum Computing. *2021 Third International Conference on Intelligent Communication Technologies and Virtual Mobile Networks (ICICV)*, Tirunelveli, India, pp. 1396–1401, 2021, doi: 10.1109/ICICV50876.2021.9388628.
30. Adikari, A., De Silva, D., Moraliyage, H., Alahakoon, D., Wong, J., Gancarz, M., Chackochan, S., Park, B., Heo, R., Leung, Y., Empathic conversational agents for real-time monitoring and co-facilitation of patient-centered healthcare. *Future Gener. Comput. Syst.*, *126*, 318–329, 2022.
31. Javed, A.R., Saadia, A., Mughal, H., Gadekallu, T.R., Rizwan, M., Maddikunta, P.K.R., Mahmud, M., Liyanage, M., Hussain, A., Artificial intelligence for cognitive health assessment: State-of-the-art, open challenges and future directions. *Cognit. Comput.*, 1–46, 2023.
32. Burugadda, V.R., Pawar, P.S., Kumar, A., Bhati, N., Predicting Hospital Readmission Risk for Heart Failure Patients Using Machine Learning Techniques: A Comparative Study of Classification Algorithms. *2023 Second International Conference on Trends in Electrical, Electronics, and Computer Engineering (TEECCON)*, Bangalore, India, pp. 223–228, 2023, doi: 10.1109/TEECCON59234.2023.10335817.
33. Bansal, S., Aggarwal, M., Aggarwal, H., Advancements and applications in fog computing, in: *Security Designs for the Cloud, IoT, and Social Networking*, pp. 207–240, 2019.
34. Burugadda, V.R., Jadhav, N., Vyas, N., Duggar, R., Exploring the Potential of Deep Reinforcement Learning for Autonomous Navigation in Complex Environments. *2023 7th International Conference on Computing, Communication, Control and Automation (ICCUBEA)*, Pune, India, pp. 1–6, 2023, doi: 10.1109/ICCUBEA58933.2023.10392109.

15

Natural Language Processing in Biomedical Literature

Molina Mukherjee[1], Prachi Punia[2], Adil Husain Rather[1] and Hardik Dhiman[3]*

[1]Department of CSE, UIE, Chandigarh University, Mohali, Punjab, India
[2]Faculty of Life Sciences and Biotechnology, South Asian University, New Delhi, India
[3]Department of Mechanical Engineering National Chung Cheng University, Minxiong, Chiayi, Taiwan

Abstract
In this research we have provided an overview of the use of Natural Language Processing (NLP) in analysing biomedical literature. We begin with describing what biomedical literature is and in what ways it is useful, then we move towards understanding the need of NLP in biomedical literature. To understand the context of NLP in biomedical text better, a brief note on the origin of this technology is covered here. Additionally, the fundamentals of NLP and the phases through which a piece of text goes through in order to draw useful insights from it, is briefly described. To understand the kind of data we'll be analysing better we've discussed the sources of diversity in biomedical literature. Further we have covered the conflicts and disagreements that must be taken into account to make improvements in the methodologies being used. This chapter also discusses the emerging trends and patterns in the field of NLP in biomedical literature and its useful applications. Overall, the chapter summarizes the usefulness, drawbacks and potential of using natural language processing to analyse biomedical text.

***Keywords*:** Natural language processing, biomedical literature, healthcare, research, analysis

**Corresponding author*: hardikdhiman29@gmail.com; ORCID: https://orcid.org/0009-0001-9985-5468
Molina Mukherjee: ORCID: https://orcid.org/0009-0006-0167-288X
Prachi Punia: ORCID: https://orcid.org/0009-0001-1385-9725
Adil Husain Rather: ORCID: https://orcid.org/0009-0004-7854-825X

Umesh Kumar Lilhore, Abhishek Kumar, Narayan Vyas, Sarita Simaiya and Vishal Dutt (eds.) Multimodal Data Fusion for Bioinformatics Artificial Intelligence, (323–340) © 2025 Scrivener Publishing LLC

15.1 Introduction

Biomedical literature is a collective noun used to refer to data from various research publications, clinical data gathered from different fields like anatomy, genetics, physiology, epidemiology, etc. It acts as a source of reference for people working in the healthcare industry. These kinds of manuscripts contain scientific findings, current advancements in the field of medicine and epidemiology trends and helps researchers and medical professionals to find information related to treatments, drug discovery and many such other things. Reviewing the existing literature is a major aspect in identification of gaps in current knowledge which can aid researchers in building hypotheses and design experiments for new discoveries (Burugadda, Pawar, Kumar, & Bhati, 2023). Biomedical literature is typically published in journals that are peer-reviewed; consequently, the published work has to undergo diligent evaluation procedures by experts of the field prior to its release. This ensures reliability and quality of the information presented in these publications. There are numerous academic libraries, online databases and scholarly publishing platforms through which these literature works can be accessed. The primary source of freely accessible textual data information in biomedicine and molecular biology is MEDLINE. It encompasses over 12,000,000 abstracts maintained by National Library of Medicine (NLM), accessible through the PubMed suite (Krallinger *et al.*, 2005). Protein information is majorly accessed through another database like SwissProt.

Retrieval and interpretation of biomedical literature poses significant hurdles for students, professionals or the general public. The boundless amount of literature that is already available can lead to information overload, resulting in difficulties in identification of relevant articles for any specific topic of interest or clinical question. The literature and the data keeps on increasing at a tremendous rate with each passing minute. It can be found in many different formats like reviews, articles, preprints, etc., and imposes challenges in prioritizing and navigating through the information. Technical terminology that is used in this literature is most of the time not intelligible for individuals who do not have a strong background in the field. To address many such challenges we need to devise efficient search strategies or employ advanced search tools and techniques that will make comprehension of the biomedical literature trouble-free.

Natural language processing (NLP) can significantly aid in comprehending biomedical literature by utilization of computational methods for extraction, analysis and interpretation of relevant information from the vast literature repository. NLP algorithms are employed to mine text data from biomedical literature available in the databases or the clinical notes. Using these algorithms, desired information can be extracted such as gene sequences, protein interactions, drug compounds, associations and treatments of diseases from unstructured data, thus aiding researchers in getting indispensable insights and knowledge.

One of the recently advancing branches of biomedical is proteomics. It involves protein analysis for understanding their roles in various biological pathways, cellular processes and disease mechanisms, and study of post translational modifications and investigation of protein-protein interactions (McArdle and Menikou, 2021). NLP algorithms are useful to mine text data related to proteins and aid in understanding of protein biology and its implications in health, treatments and drug discoveries.. They can extract critical information including amino acid sequences, different domains of proteins, structural motifs, and functional annotations (Krallinger *et al.*, 2005). By analysing this information, researchers can get a better understanding of structural characteristics of proteins, their folding patterns, and how they would interact with another protein or a target molecule or receptor in the biological system. The search of novel drug targets majorly relies on computational methods that aids in identifying the most suitable protein based on its properties. Which can then be followed up by laboratory procedures for confirmations.

The process of understanding the context of words or phrases within a text data and analysing relation between entities such as genes, proteins, drugs, symptoms and many other biomedical concepts is termed as semantic analysis and entity recognition (Krallinger *et al.*, 2005). NLP tools can aid in identification and categorization of the entities and structuring the information available. The information extracted is also used in recognizing relationships between the entities which can in turn be used for constructing knowledge graphs. This is particularly of assistance in understanding molecular pathways and disease mechanisms.

Lengthy biomedical texts can be easily summarized with the help of NLP tools that retrieve key information and offer concise overviews of research finding, treatment outcomes or clinical studies. This makes the information understandable as well as making the search convenient. Hence, navigation through large volumes of text can be performed more efficiently and in less time.

Another powerful tool of molecular biology is microarray. It is used to measure the expression levels of thousands of genes simultaneously (Lysov *et al.*, 2017). It enables scientists to study how the genes are turned on or off in different conditions and provide insight into gene regulations, identifying biomarkers of different diseases, and discovery of potential drug targets. Microarrays provide an extensive pool of data points which is too complex for human interpretation and analysis and hence requires computational methods or NLP for proper understanding and comprehension (Burugadda, Jadhav, Vyas, & Duggar, 2023).

NLP can be used for the retrieval of gene sequences and functions which can further be subjected to sequence alignment tools to figure out evolutionary relationships between numerous existing species as well as predicting sequences of the extinct species that no longer exist. Many different algorithms like ClustalW, MUSCLE and MAFFT are being used for DNA alignment or protein sequencing.

In conclusion, applying NLP in different biomedical fields improves knowledge discovery, retrieval of necessary information and interpretation of complex data, which in turn enhances clinical decision making and assists in reaching new milestones in biomedical research and healthcare practices worldwide.

15.2 History

The use of Natural Language Processing (NLP) in biomedical literature is a proof of the significance of computational linguistics and its usefulness in biomedical research and treatment. Various tools, softwares and methods have been invented and deployed to extract useful insights from biomedical texts.

NLP was first used in the field of biomedicine to analyse text and perform computer-assisted retrieval. In the 1960s, the idea of information retrieval systems was first talked of, when researchers looked at automatic indexing and searching of biomedical texts. The creation of MEDLINE database by National Library of Medicine (NLM) in 1964 was considered a revolutionary achievement, which was created with the intention of making indexing and abstraction of biological literature easy (Humphreys & Lindberg, 1993).

NLP techniques and algorithms have seen enormous growth during the 1970s and 1980s. Tasks like named entity recognition, syntactic parsing and categorization were performed using NLP during these years. NLP applications saw significant development with invention of text mining systems like LEMIMI and Protee.

The 1990s proved to be a time of great significance for the field of science with the growth of NLP and bioinformatics. With the introduction of internet the amount and availability of biomedical literature significantly increased. Many scientists started using Natural Language Processing techniques for knowledge discovery, information extraction from text and biomedical text summarization. Scientists collaborated a lot during this time with the introduction of initiatives like Protein Information Resource (PIR) and BioCreative project (Cohen, 2005).

During the last few years the combination of NLP with other interdisciplinary fields such as genomics, proteomics and clinical informatics has led to development of new applications and methodologies. These include the Clinical Text Analysis and Knowledge Extraction System (cTAKES) and OpenAI Bio platform, which have helped in demonstrating the usefulness of NLP in biomedical text normalization, drug discovery and phenotypic extraction.

Natural language processing (NLP) is of paramount importance in cases where scientists or researchers want to find hidden patterns and draw useful insights from biomedical texts. Apart from the benefits there are also some challenges in the use of NLP in biomedical literature like the need for annotated datasets, ontologies and domain specific language models. Interdisciplinary collaborations help to create robust NLP solutions specifically to analyse biomedical literature (Gupta and Kumar, 2018)

Over the years NLP has changed the way in which information is extracted from biomedical text. Interdisciplinary cooperation and the use of modern NLP techniques has allowed scholars to draw useful insights from the vast amounts of biomedical textual data, resulting in advancement in healthcare delivery, research and medicine discovery (Kumar, Kumar, Dutt, Dubey, & Narang, 2023).

15.3 Theoretical Foundation: Natural Language Processing in Scientific Writing

15.3.1 Natural Language Processing (NLP) Overview

Natural Language Processing is a interdisciplinary and one of the various subfields of Artificial Intelligence which in simple words enables computers to understand and generate human-like language using various algorithms.

15.3.2 Key Concepts in NLP

- **Tokenization:** It refers to dividing words into units or parts

- **Part-of-Speech (POS) Tagging:** Labelling of words according to their grammatical context
- **Named Entity Recognition (NER):** It refers to the extraction of information from unstructured literature and classifying it into different groups which can be proteins, patient categories, genes, etc.
- **Syntactic parsing:** Analysis of the structure of a sentence to understand the relation between the words and the way they are arranged.
- **Semantic analysis:** Interpreting the actual meaning of words by understanding the context of the sentence in which they appear.

15.3.3 Biomedical Text Analysis Using Natural Language Processing (NLP)

The steps below cover the journey of data from raw sources to processed output, that has been generated by going through various phases of natural language processing. Figure 15.1 visually represents this journey of transformation of raw data to insightful data using NLP.

15.3.3.1 Beginning Point: Unprocessed Biomedical Text Information

Data is collected from various sources such as research papers, clinical notes and electronic health records. This data is given as input to the next phase.

15.3.3.2 Data Preprocessing

- **Tokenization**: The data collected is divided into parts or tokens (Manning *et al.*, 2009).
- **Stopword Removal:** To concentrate on the important material, frequently used words that don't have much meaning—like "the," "and," and "of"—are eliminated.
- **Lemmatization/Stemming:** To minimise inflectional forms and variants, words are reduced to their base or root form.

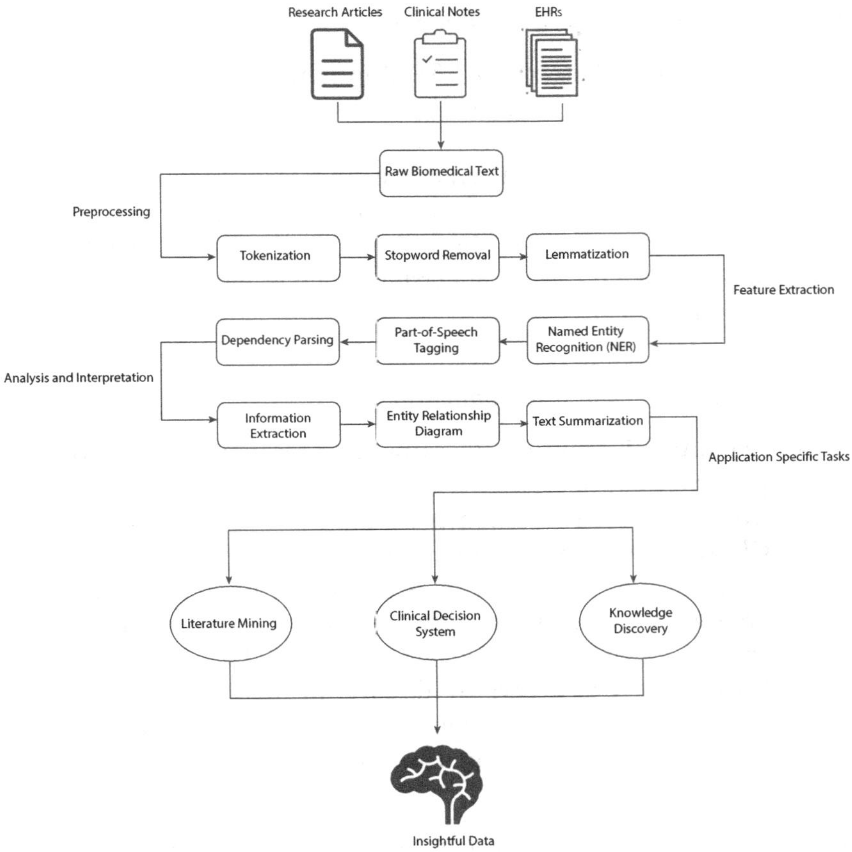

Figure 15.1 Biomedical text analysis using NLP.

15.3.3.3 *Feature Extraction*

- **Named Entity Recognition (NER):** NER performs the extraction of information from unstructured text and classification of it into different groups. In this case the entities can be proteins, patient categories, genes, etc. (Wei *et al.*, 2013).
- **Part-of-Speech (POS) Tagging:** The words in the text are divided into adjectives, verbs, and nouns and labelled.
- **Dependency Parsing:** To understand the connection between the words present in the text, the syntactic structure of the sentences is examined.

15.3.3.4 *Interpretation and Analysis*

- **Information Extraction:** Useful insights such as relationships, biological concepts, facts, discoveries are extracted from the text.
- **Entity Relationship Extraction:** This step interprets the associations between the words hidden within the text.
- **Text Summarization:** In order to enhance readability and to make it easy to understand the insights, the data is summarized.

15.3.3.5 *Specific Tasks for Applications*

- **Exploiting Literature:** The extracted information is used to perform trend analysis, clustering and knowledge discovery from biomedical text (Cohen, 2005).
- **Clinical Decision Support System:** The information obtained from medical texts is utilized to assist healthcare professionals in identifying diseases, suggesting treatments, and recognizing events (Chapman *et al.*, 2011).
- **Knowledge Discovery:** By discovering new correlations, trends, and patterns, insights from text analysis help to advance biomedical research and healthcare delivery.

15.3.3.6 *Final Product: Knowledge and Insights from Biomedical Text Data*

Using NLP for biomedical texts, useful information can be extracted from the text.

This information can be used in biomedical research and doctors can use this information in many applications to improve the medical industry (Punugoti, Dutt, Anand, & Bhati, 2023).

15.4 Sources of Diversity in Biomedical Literature's Natural Language Processing

The efficiency of Natural Language Processing (NLP) algorithms are subjected to a variety of sources of variation found in biomedical literature. In order to understand how these factors affect the NLP algorithms we'll now see the sources of variation.

15.4.1 Complexity of Linguistics

Linguistic complexity is one of the important sources of variance. The data is collected from various sources such as clinical notes, patient records, research articles. Each type of text has unique linguistic characteristic, writing style and terminology. Often NLP algorithms face difficulties in properly analysing text due to use of jargon, acronyms, etc. (Cohen and Hunter, 2008).

15.4.2 Heterogeneity of Data

As mentioned above, data in biomedical literature is collected from a variety of sources and is heterogeneous in nature. Each source holds a different characteristic, the analysis of multimodal data types, such as text, images and structured data (Zargar *et al.*, 2023).

15.4.3 Variability in Annotation

Annotation guidelines, expert opinions and subjective interpretation are few of the ways in which variability is introduced in the annotation process of biomedical text for NER and relation extraction. The dependability of annotated datasets used in the NLP model is based on annotator consistency and agreement. This can certainly affect the performance of Natural Language Processing algorithms (Khaki *et al.*, 2020).

15.4.4 Domain Specificity

Biomedical literature covers data from a wide range of fields like clinical medicine, pharmacology, and genetics. Each of these fields has a different set of vocabulary needs, concepts associated and methods to represent information (Kumar, Kumar, Dutt, & Soni, 2021). NLP algorithms that are trained on data containing normal or what we call vocabulary that can be understood by normal people may face difficulties in dealing with the jargon found in medical writings. To handle these domain-specific difficulties, domain-specific strategies and specialised resources are needed (Alsentzer *et al.*, 2019).

These sources of variance hinder the development of robust natural language processing algorithms that are used to analyse biomedical text. With the interdisciplinary cooperation, domain specific resources, standardised annotation processes and machine learning algorithms these issues can be handled.

15.5 Disagreement and Conflict

The use of Natural Language Processing in biomedical literature is a vast area of discussion and hence there are many conflicts and disagreements associated with it. Methodological discrepancies, data heterogeneity, and interpretation difficulties are a few of them.

It is often difficult to choose the perfect NLP technique and algorithm. Suppose if different teams are working on item recognition, relation extraction and text classification then there are chances that there will be differences in how different research groups interpret the result (Smith and Ceusters, 2010) The lack of standardization makes it difficult to conduct comparative analysis, which acts as a reason for disagreement between researchers (Ehrmann *et al.*, 2024).

NLP models that are trained on general datasets may find it difficult to interpret literature with medical jargon, linguistics patterns and complex writing style (Manning *et al.*, 2009). This can lead to lack of generalization and poor performance across various biomedical domains due to differences in the performance of NLP systems (CheshmehSohrabi and Mashhadi, 2023).

Usually NLP algorithms are considered highly accurate in extracting information from raw data but at times they may give rise to conflict in the way in which they are interpreted by NLP, since interpretation needs domain knowledge. Diverse interpretations and conclusions may lead to biases, subjective interpretation and disparities (Friedman and Hripcsak, 1999).

Hence, it can be concluded that data heterogeneity, diverse methodologies, and interpretation difficulties may cause disagreement about the efficiency of NLP to analyse biomedical texts. In order to overcome these issues interdisciplinary cooperation, transparent feedback system and robust testing methods should be employed.

15.6 Natural Language Processing Trends and Patterns in Biomedical Literature

Nowadays the use of NLP in mining biomedical text has significantly increased. This has opened ways to many scientific discoveries, healthcare services and research fields. Let's take a look at the emerging trends and patterns.

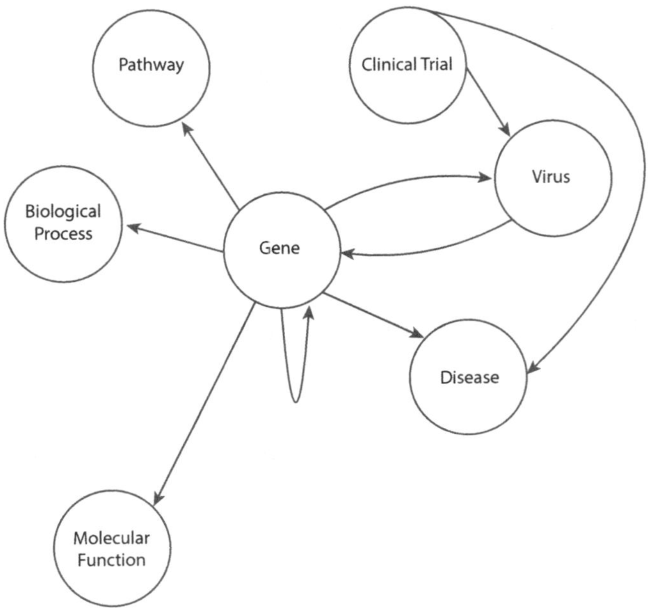

Figure 15.2 Biomedical knowledge graph.

15.6.1 Graphs of Biomedical Knowledge

Biomedical knowledge graphs give a pictorial representation of biological concepts, entities, the interaction between them and the facts linked to it. The data represented in knowledge graphs in this case is collected from electronic health records (EHRs), ontologies, literature databases, etc. Graph-based representation of entities makes semantic search easy and fast and therefore it is quite handy in NLP-based systems. Figure 15.2 is an example of a biomedical knowledge graph that represents how genes and gene products are referenced by the gene node.

15.6.2 In-Depth Learning Frameworks

Deep Learning is widely used in the field of biomedical natural language processing. Transformer based models like BERT (Bidirectional Encoder Representations from Transformers) and GPT (Generative Pre-trained Transformer) are two of the extensively used models and are pretrained on a large quantity of medical text. These models can perform relation extraction, entity recognition and document categorization. The efficiency of such models can be significantly increased by fine-tuning them using domain-specific data (Beltagy *et al.*, 2019; Swarna, Kumar, Dixit, & Sairam, 2021).

15.6.3 Multimodal Analysis of Biomedical Data

The nature of data collected from biomedical sources is heterogeneous in nature. Molecular sequences, clinical notes and medical photographs are some instances. This kind of data can be effectively analysed using NLP, computer vision and bioinformatics methods (Sasubilli, Kumar, & Dutt, 2020). This approach helps to interpret complex data and facilitate research, discovery and diagnosis.

15.6.4 Regulatory and Ethical Aspects

Privacy is one of the major concerns in this area, hence proper measures, legal frameworks and no-bias NLP algorithms should be taken into consideration. This can be made possible with cooperation between researchers, legislators, and industry stakeholders (Rajkomar *et al.*, 2018).

15.6.5 Results

These emerging trends in the field of biomedical literature have significantly contributed to the advancements in biomedical research, medical assistance and scientific discovery. Key areas of innovation and investigation in the discipline include multimodal data analysis, ethical considerations, deep learning architectures, and biomedical knowledge graphs. Through the utilisation of these patterns, scientists and medical practitioners can get fresh perspectives, quicken breakthroughs, and enhance patient results in the field of biomedicine.

15.7 Natural Language Processing's Useful Applications in Biomedical Literature

Natural language processing and literature mining makes the process of text mining extremely easy. By defining some sort of criteria, the keyword or fact search in an article can be automated. Professionals from the medical field can use this technology to find trends, patterns in biomedical text. Techniques like sentiment analysis, topic modelling and document clustering can be used to draw insights from the text (Wei *et al.*, 2013).

15.7.1 Annotated Text in Biomedicine

NLP technology helps to annotate text; it makes the annotation process extremely easy. Explanatory notes regarding the relationships, named entities and medical facts can be added (Zhou *et al.*, 2014).

15.7.2 Systems for Clinical Decision Support (CDSS)

CDSS systems are powered by NLP. As shown in Figure 15.3. These systems help medical professionals to draw insights from electronic health records (EHRs) and clinical notes. Natural language processing algorithms can be used to find and extract the hidden meaning from medical texts, which in turn assists medical professionals to find patterns, treatment recommendations and diagnosis of different diseases.

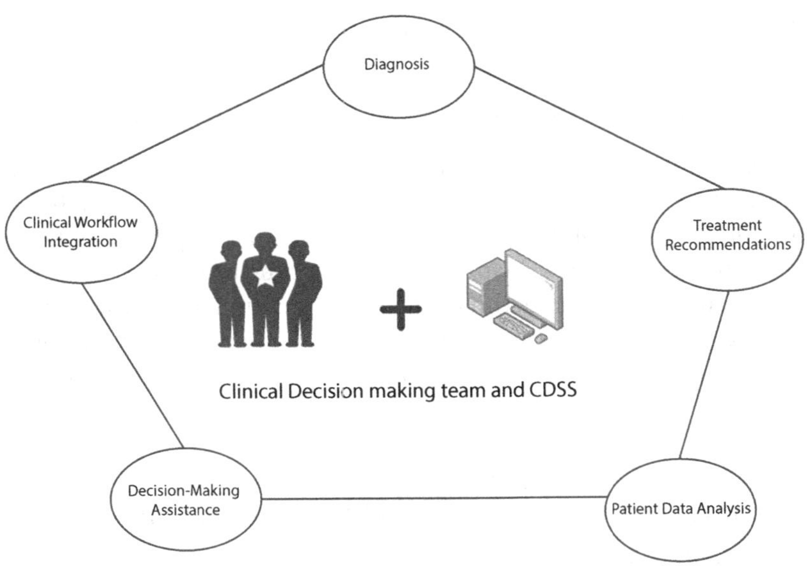

Figure 15.3 Clinical decision support systems.

15.7.3 Investigating Biomedical Information

Apart from just finding hidden patterns, this technology can help in discovering new information simply by identifying relationships, correlations and patterns in the data. This helps to contribute information to the world of biomedical science.

15.7.4 Biomedical Text Synopsis

The volume of medical texts present in the world is humongous, and it's not possible to extract knowledge from all of them manually. Hence, NLP tools help to easily summarize the text and allow users to get the essence of clinical notes, research papers, etc.

15.7.5 Information Retrieval and Semantic Search

NLP-based information retrieval tools help in understanding user queries and give results accordingly. This helps in fast retrieval of information. These systems use ontologies, sophisticated language models, and semantic indexing techniques to extract and deliver precise responses to queries.

15.7.6 Evaluation of Quality and Bias Identification

It's extremely important to check the text for biases in order to assess the quality and reliability of the literature. NLP tools can be used to analyse the methodology, design and reporting quality. Overall it helps in maintaining the integrity of the text and helps users to draw conclusions (Li *et al.*, 2023).

By utilising the above methods, medical practitioners, researchers and healthcare professionals can effectively utilize biomedical texts to obtain useful data which in turn will contribute to the advancements in medical science.

15.8 Future Prospects of NLP in Biomedical Literature

Driven by new research areas and rising trends, the field of natural language processing (NLP) in biomedical literature has enormous promise for revolutionary advances in the future. Future directions in this field aim to address obstacles, take use of technology improvements, and explore fresh applications in order to further boost scientific discovery, healthcare delivery, and biomedical research.

The invention and integration of efficient deep earning architectures can be used to analyse biomedical text and can open gates to many other inventions. Transformer-based models are considered very efficient. Two of the popular transformer-based models are GPT (Generative Pre-trained Transformer) and BERT (Bidirectional Encoder Representations from Transformers). These tools help in smooth analysis of biomedical texts (Beltagy *et al.*, 2019).

Data processed by NLP in this field is multimodal in nature; it can be images, text or any other structured or unstructured data. NLP users can analyse this heterogeneous data by using NLP and computer vision together. The tools developed can be used to facilitate medication development, predictive analysis, etc. (Li *et al.*, 2023).

Ethical practices are quite important in healthcare industries. Patient data privacy, security and vulnerability of algorithms to bias are a few of the ethical concerns (Rajkomar *et al.*, 2018).

While developing NLP solutions to analyse biomedical literature, developers should make sure to take care of ethical considerations, technical innovation and interdisciplinary collaboration. The information derived from these biomedical texts can be used by researchers to find emerging trends, new insights and overcome issues faced in the healthcare industry.

15.9 Conclusion

With the help of NLP, healthcare professionals and researchers can now analyse texts and draw conclusions much faster than traditional methods. In this chapter we have summarized the need, origin and fundamentals of NLP such as tokenization, part-of-speech tagging and named entity recognition. The use of NLP in biomedical texts has found to be of paramount significance in areas like biomedical research healthcare delivery, which is possible due to the effectiveness on NLP in information extraction, literature mining, clinical decision support and semantic search.

Apart from all the benefits, there are certain aspects that act as a hindrance, such as domain specificity, data heterogeneity, lingual complexity and variability in annotations. To cope with this issues it is important to include domain-specific resource, standardised annotation methods and cooperation between professionals from different fields of expertise. Taking these steps greatly contributes to the increase in robustness of NLP algorithms in the biomedical field.

Technical advancements in bioinformatics have resulted in introducing deep learning architectures, multimodal data analysis and biomedical knowledge graphs. With the help of these methods scientists and researchers can get quick breakthroughs and enhance patient results in the field of biomedicine.

Natural Language Processing in the biomedical field is a thriving field that has the potential to greatly influence the world of AI and medicine. By embracing cross-disciplinary collaboration, investing in emerging trends and addressing the challenges in this field, healthcare professionals can harness the power of NLP to improve biomedical research quality, healthcare delivery and contribute to the betterment of mankind.

References

Alsentzer, E., Murphy, J.R., Boag, W., Weng, W.-H., Jin, D., Naumann, T., McDermott, M.B.A., Publicly Available Clinical BERT Embeddings, 2019.

Beltagy, I., Lo, K., Cohan, A., SciBERT: A Pretrained Language Model for Scientific Text, 2019.

Burugadda, V.R., Jadhav, N., Vyas, N., Duggar, R., Exploring the potential of deep reinforcement learning for autonomous navigation in complex environments, in: *2023 7th International Conference On Computing, Communication, Control And Automation (ICCUBEA)*, Pune, India, pp. 1–6, 2023, https://doi.org/10.1109/ICCUBEA58933.2023.10392109.

Burugadda, V.R., Pawar, P.S., Kumar, A., Bhati, N., Predicting hospital readmission risk for heart failure patients using machine learning techniques: A comparative study of classification algorithms, in: *2023 Second International Conference on Trends in Electrical, Electronics, and Computer Engineering (TEECCON)*, Bangalore, India, pp. 223–228, 2023, https://doi.org/10.1109/TEECCON59234.2023.10335817.

Chapman, W.W., Nadkarni, P.M., Hirschman, L., D'Avolio, L.W., Savova, G.K., Uzuner, O., Overcoming barriers to NLP for clinical text: the role of shared tasks and the need for additional creative solutions. *J. Am. Med. Inform. Assoc.*, 18, 540–543, 2011, https://doi.org/10.1136/amiajnl-2011-000465.

CheshmehSohrabi, M. and Mashhadi, A., Using Data Mining, Text Mining, and Bibliometric Techniques to the Research Trends and Gaps in the Field of Language and Linguistics. *J. Psycholinguist Res.*, 52, 607–630, 2023, https://doi.org/10.1007/s10936-022-09911-6.

Cohen, A.M., A survey of current work in biomedical text mining. *Briefings Bioinf.*, 6, 57–71, 2005, https://doi.org/10.1093/bib/6.1.57.

Cohen, K.B. and Hunter, L., Getting Started in Text Mining. *PLoS Comput. Biol.*, 4, e20, 2008, https://doi.org/10.1371/journal.pcbi.0040020.

Ehrmann, M., Hamdi, A., Pontes, E.L., Romanello, M., Doucet, A., Named Entity Recognition and Classification on Historical Documents: A Survey. *ACM Comput. Surv.*, 56, 1–47, 2024, https://doi.org/10.1145/3604931.

Friedman, C. and Hripcsak, G., Natural language processing and its future in medicine. *Acad. Med.*, 74, 890–895, 1999, https://doi.org/10.1097/00001888-199908000-00012.

Gupta, K. and Kumar, A., Natural Language Processing and Unsupervised Learning: It's Significance on Biomedical Literature. *IJCRR*, 10, 9–15, 2018, https://doi.org/10.31782/IJCRR.2018.10143.

Humphreys, B.L. and Lindberg, D.A., The UMLS project: making the conceptual connection between users and the information they need. *Bull. Med. Libr. Assoc.*, 81, 170–177, 1993.

Khaki, S., Pham, H., Han, Y., Kuhl, A., Kent, W., Wang, L., Convolutional Neural Networks for Image-Based Corn Kernel Detection and Counting. *Sensors*, 20, 2721, 2020, https://doi.org/10.3390/s20092721.

Krallinger, M., Erhardt, R., Valencia, A., Text-mining approaches in molecular biology and biomedicine. *Drug Discov. Today*, 10, 439–445, 2005, https://doi.org/10.1016/S1359-6446(05)03376-3.

Kumar, A., Kumar, S.A., Dutt, V., Dubey, A.K., Narang, S., A hybrid secure cloud platform maintenance based on improved attribute-based encryption strategies. *Int. J. Interact. Multimed. Artif. Intell.*, 8, 2, 150, 2023, https://doi.org/10.9781/ijimai.2021.11.004.

Kumar, S.A., Kumar, H., Dutt, V., Soni, H., Self-health analysis with two step histogram based procedure using machine learning, in: *2021 Third International Conference on Intelligent Communication Technologies and Virtual Mobile Networks (ICICV)*, Tirunelveli, India, pp. 794–799, 2021, https://doi.org/10.1109/ICICV50876.2021.9388427.

Li, M., Yang, H., Liu, Y., Biomedical named entity recognition based on fusion multi-features embedding. *THC*, 31, 111–121, 2023, https://doi.org/10.3233/THC-236011.

Lysov, Y., Barsky, V., Urasov, D., Urasov, R., Cherepanov, A., Mamaev, D., Yegorov, Y., Chudinov, A., Surzhikov, S., Rubina, A., Smoldovskaya, O., Zasedatelev, A., Microarray analyzer based on wide field fluorescent microscopy with laser illumination and a device for speckle suppression. *Biomed. Opt. Express*, 8, 4798, 2017, https://doi.org/10.1364/BOE.8.004798.

Manning, C., Raghavan, P., Schuetze, H., *Introduction to Information Retrieval*, 2009.

McArdle, A.J. and Menikou, S., What is proteomics? *Arch. Dis. Child. Educ. Pract. Ed.*, 106, 178–181, 2021, https://doi.org/10.1136/archdischild-2019-317434.

Punugoti, R., Dutt, V., Anand, A., Bhati, N., Exploring the impact of edge intelligence and IoT on healthcare: A comprehensive survey, in: *2023 International Conference on Sustainable Computing and Smart Systems (ICSCSS)*, Coimbatore, India, pp. 1108–1114, 2023, https://doi.org/10.1109/ICSCSS57650.2023.10169733.

Rajkomar, A., Hardt, M., Howell, M.D., Corrado, G., Chin, M.H., Ensuring Fairness in Machine Learning to Advance Health Equity. *Ann. Intern. Med.*, 169, 866, 2018, https://doi.org/10.7326/M18-1990.

Sasubilli, S.M., Kumar, A., Dutt, V., Improving health care by help of internet of things and bigdata analytics and cloud computing, in: *2020 International Conference on Advances in Computing and Communication Engineering (ICACCE)*, Las Vegas, NV, USA, pp. 1–4, 2020, https://doi.org/10.1109/ICACCE49060.2020.9155042.

Smith, B. and Ceusters, W., Ontological realism: A methodology for coordinated evolution of scientific ontologies. *Appl. Ontol.*, 5, 139–188, 2010, https://doi.org/10.3233/AO-2010-0079.

Swarna, S.R., Kumar, A., Dixit, P., Sairam, T.V.M., Parkinson's disease prediction using adaptive quantum computing, in: *2021 Third International Conference on Intelligent Communication Technologies and Virtual Mobile Networks (ICICV)*, Tirunelveli, India, pp. 1396–1401, 2021, https://doi.org/10.1109/ICICV50876.2021.9388628.

Wei, C.-H., Kao, H.-Y., Lu, Z., PubTator: a web-based text mining tool for assisting biocuration. *Nucleic Acids Res.*, 41, W518–W522, 2013, https://doi.org/10.1093/nar/gkt441.

Zargar, H.H., Zargar, S.H., Mehri, R., Review of deep learning in healthcare, 2023.

Zhou, X., Menche, J., Barabási, A.-L., Sharma, A., Human symptoms–disease network. *Nat. Commun.*, 5, 4212, 2014, https://doi.org/10.1038/ncomms5212.

Zhu, Z., Weber, E., Strohsal, T., Serhan, D., Sustainable Border Control Policy in the COVID-19 Pandemic: A Math Modeling Study, 2021.

16

Biomedical Research Enrichment Through Sentiment Analysis in Patient Feedback: A Natural Language Processing Approach

Soumitra Saha[1], Umesh Kumar Lilhore[2*] and Sarita Simaiya[2]

[1]*Department of Computer Science and Engineering Chandigarh University Punjab, India*
[2]*Galgotias University, Greater Noida, UP, India*

Abstract
This chapter consults the trajectory committed by utilizing patient feedback (PF) in the wake of biomedical research through sentimental analysis (SA) in natural language processing (NLP). PF has been compared to a gold mine for the healthcare industry, delivering clinical efficacy, preserving quality, and overall insight into a disorder. Analyzing these patient responses is vastly more time-consuming and more likely to be subjective. However, employing SA can efficiently extract beneficial insights from this feedback by automating patients' positive, negative, or neutral sentiments. By systematically investigating thousands or millions of observations to identify familiar themes, distinct concerns, and patient satisfaction levels, researchers can employ these sentiments to understand disease status, improve patient care, and assist in making intelligent decisions by analyzing judgments. Miscellaneous traditional methods depend on surveys or structured questionnaires to accumulate PF that fails to deliver the preferred results in terms of sentiment. On the other hand, by studying sentiment data from mixed social media posts and electronic health records, SA can work with structured and unstructured data to furnish favorable results, allowing researchers to sweeten the grade of biomedical research. Eventually, this chapter discloses worthwhile wisdom to enrich biomedical research by employing PF through SA.

***Keywords*:** Biomedical research, natural language processing, healthcare, sentimental analysis, machine learning

---

**Corresponding author*: umeshlilhore@gmail.com

Umesh Kumar Lilhore, Abhishek Kumar, Narayan Vyas, Sarita Simaiya and Vishal Dutt (eds.) Multimodal Data Fusion for Bioinformatics Artificial Intelligence, (341–374) © 2025 Scrivener Publishing LLC

16.1 Introduction

The 21st century has witnessed numerous remarkable technological and expansion developments, and human civilization is now beginning to reap the benefits of this phenomenal technological breakthrough. This transformation continues, and the breakthrough will become even more widespread as the search for new technologies continues. When anyone speaks about the contribution in terms of this success of technology, then the most enormous contribution behind this success is the abundance of data. In order to solve various problems in different sectors, data are of different types depending on the problem. Observing the right problem makes it possible to achieve the best results for a particular problem by using appropriate data. The accuracy or performance of any classification can be enhanced if the number of training data is increased to solve a particular problem [1].

Along with this phenomenal improvement in technology, the amount of data worldwide has also increased to a large extent, and various types of data are constantly being generated for different problems. When only the relevant data can be used from the data collected from various sources, the irrelevant and relatively less critical data can be excluded, and the correct approach can be adopted to solve the problem. Achieving the desired results will therefore become much more manageable. The main reason for excluding irrelevant data is that it can increase the reaction time of the model, and the classification accuracy of a given model will be poor [2]. The use of data in any sector, including healthcare, education, transportation, agriculture, energy, manufacturing, and telecommunication, is undeniable, and using data in appropriate models is the primary tool to achieve the best results. *Artificial intelligence* (AI) is the tool through which the desired results can be easily achieved by solving any problem using appropriate data.

AI refers to creating a computer system that can presume like a human, make judgments like a human, and assist in achieving desired outcomes by solving problems in the best possible way out of existing solutions. The primary reason for using AI is to efficiently and accurately work on specific problems and find optimal results, which is much more time-consuming for a human. AI can be compared to the human brain, like intelligence, when considered the gold standard [3]. AI is a specific algorithm or program that assists a specific machine by using previous experience and consequently providing desired results by using new inputs to solve the most challenging problems that are almost unsolvable for a human being. Figure 16.1 illustrates the diverse subfields available in AI and the distinct applications in NLP.

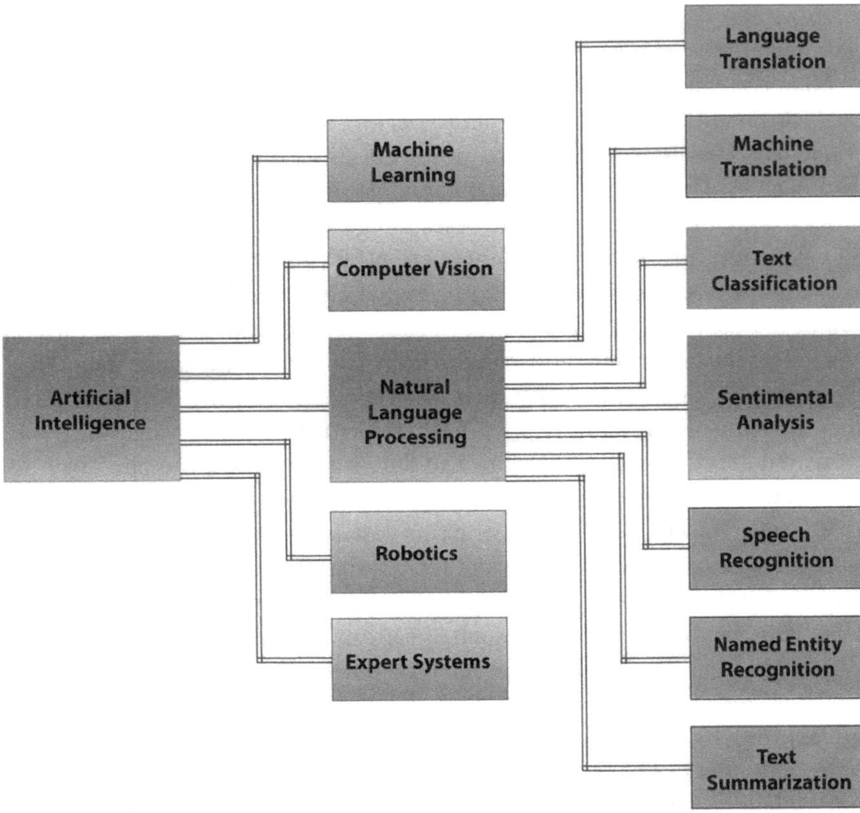

Figure 16.1 Subfields of artificial intelligence and applications of natural language processing.

AI systems operate by imitating human knowledge, whereby processing various types of data, they collect various necessary information from the existing data, play an essential role in making the model effective by eliminating unnecessary information, finding the existing patterns in the data, contradicting and helping to find interdependent data. They succeed in making appropriate decisions by using all these information and details [4]. AI is divided into two parts depending on the work variation. One is weak AI, mainly used to perform a specific task, and this system is used to solve relatively simple problems. On the other hand, the other is general AI that can consider all areas, is used to solve the most formidable problems, and behaves like human judgment when making decisions. AI has various sub-sections that are used in different tasks, and some of the main essential sections based on the scope of work are machine learning (ML), computer vision, robotics, expert systems, and NLP.

NLP is a subset of AI in which the various languages used in human civilization and computers interact to perform essential tasks [5]. Through efficient NLP algorithms, these applications can provide much better results in less time and with less power consumption. With the help of NLP, processing can provide effective results regarding a particular text based on relevance [6]. In terms of language, NLP's principal and only task is to try to understand, interpret, and provide good results from the various languages used by different human groups. Input data can be of various types: text, audio, video, and handwritten. To work with these data, NLP extensively uses unique techniques such as statistical methods, ML, and deep learning (DL) algorithms. These algorithms mainly work on enormous data sets, and as the size of the data set increases, the effectiveness and accuracy of these algorithms increase to a large extent. In the 21st century, large datasets are created using this vast amount of data. NLP plays an essential role by preprocessing data from a dataset containing a particular language and later extracting information from that processed data, which helps with various applications such as sentimental analysis (SA), machine translation, text classification, speech recognition, etc. NLP uses a variety of processes for a particular application, depending on the task type, importance, problem description, and expected results. The neurons in artificial neural networks (ANN) are interconnected, with thousands to millions of hidden layers in the connections. Hidden layers can perform tasks intelligently and quickly transfer significant results to the next layer. That is why DL and ANN are now widely used in all NLP activities, as they are correlated, and the advancement of DL is breathtaking in miscellaneous types of NLP applications [7]. How well the languages used can be processed depends on how well and cleanly a particular application can perform its functions. The type of algorithm that can be used depends mainly on the specific application and the task it will perform. These widely used and popular applications are now widely used in education, health, military intelligence, industry, and other vital sectors.

Different types of diseases, the presentation of different variants of a particular disease, health risks due to environmental changes, cross-breeding of different illnesses, and outbreaks of certain disorders have become very common. For this reason, NLP is now a different part of the medical field and is being used more than ever before. Big data in the contemporary technological world is now a trend as all NLP applications can now employ this, and SA or opinion mining is one of the utmost applications among them [8]. Almost all applications involving NLP are now used to treat the human body, and SA can be given particular importance among those applications. The principal reason for giving this more importance is to collect appropriate data evidence by reviewing a particular person's physical and mental condition by conducting sentiment analysis and taking action by making decisions based on it. The sentimental score plays an integral role in accelerating the research process of a particular person and increasing health awareness.

Biomedical research refers to the study of various biological processes and medical aspects of a living organism to conduct scientific investigations and collect relevant data to discover the problems related to health and miscellaneous diseases regarding the human body. The modern biomedical research field can deal with most of the interior points of the human body and also be able to provide anticipated solutions using computing technologies that are high-performance in nature [9]. Complete and adequate use of SA can be used for biomedical research on a large scale as the sentimental score can be surprising and successful in achieving the desired results in this investigation. Among the various disciplines involved in biomedical research, some of the most important disciplines are biology, medicine, genetics, pharmacology, and biochemistry, where in every field, biomedical research expansion enables the community to live a more satisfactory life [10]. Each mentioned branch is related to different diseases affecting the human body. If SA is used in all these branches practically, and if the method of SA can play a significant role in disease detection and the advancement of biomedical research, then it will be a very happy aspect for humankind. The first and foremost goal of conducting biomedical research in the context of these disciplines using SA is to explore the underlying causes of various incurable diseases in the human body and to find appropriate ways to use those diagnostic tools developed by the management to fix the diagnosis of newly emerging diseases. Designing innovative new medical systems and adequately using them ultimately plays a robust role in the overall progress of revolutionizing medical science. If it is possible to test and analyze various types of data on the human body through biomedical research and observe the essential functions of the human body, then improving health, increasing the immune system in the human body, and solving the most complex diseases in the human body by replacing the relationship with the environment will be very easy to find out.

This article is classified into the subsequent steps: Section 16.2 defines the distinct types of NLP applications widely employed today. Section 16.3 explains the background studies of SA, one of the most critical parts of NLP. Section 16.4 clarifies the methodology needed to conclude the SA task for a given dataset. Finally, Section 16.5 illustrates the conclusion and discussion about SA in biomedical research and the significance of the patient's feedback regarding SA.

16.2 Applications of NLP

NLP processing establishes relationships between machines and humans in different languages. Since there are many varieties of languages in the world and people from different environments use different languages to communicate, it is straightforward to connect people of different languages by substituting the appropriate relationship between humans and machines. Various applications of natural language processing are dealt with by relational substitution. Different processes are used for individual applications, and through execution, these applications play an essential role in the ultimate welfare of humankind. The more accessible and characteristic ways these applications are used, the more uncomplicated it is to collect data from any language to achieve practical and relevant results. The most widely used applications in Natural Language Processing are Machine Translation, Named Entity Recognition (NER), Chatbots and Virtual Assistants, Text Classification, Language Translation, Speech Recognition, Text Summarization, Sentiment Analysis, etc. Now, these applications of NLP are discussed below, and we can see how they can succeed significantly in various fields.

16.2.1 Machine Translation

Machine translation is a sub-field of NLP where the principal task is to help the algorithm and model used to solve a specific problem so that they can easily automatically convert one language into another language. Machine translation acts as a means of communication to facilitate information exchange and overcome linguistic problems between people who speak different languages. It can be done without human involvement, as only a computer system is utilized for optimization [11]. This application helps to determine how pairs of words are related in large data sets and how to create meaningful and inconsistent structures from those pairs of words. Translating from natural to sign language is a comparatively unexplored field in the NLP research area by which, with the help of a grammar-based machine translation system, sentences from one language to another can be decrypted effortlessly, like from the English language to the Sign Language of Pakistan [12].

This process uses three methods, each with advantages and disadvantages. Rule-based machine translation works based on predefined rules, generating new translations using the input data. Linguistic knowledge is fundamental to using this method. Statistical machine translation extracts information from data using statistical models and mapping functions. The main reason for using statistical methods is to determine probabilities for establishing relationships between input texts. A more popular and recently used method is the Newer Machine Translation. Deep learning techniques are used in this process to solve the most challenging problems, where it is possible to quickly achieve significant results by working with the most complex structures. Machine translation is now playing a role in making important decisions and delivering results in areas as diverse as business, education, the tourism industry, government operations, and social media.

16.2.2 Named Entity Recognition (NER)

Named entity recognition is one of the most critical applications of NLP, where entity selection is made based on predefined categories, and the selected entities are classified or extracted [13]. All the meaningful words used in a sentence are separate entities in an extensive data set or a small range. For example, an entity can be a person, an organization, a location or place name, day, date, time, amount, measurement, and many more. Its primary function is to separate the words used in the data set into different categories and to provide considerable flexibility to the algorithm by using data from the same category. Separating entities is vital as it easily converts from one language to another using entities of distinct categories. It is also beneficial in almost all circumstances such as fake news, which can be easily detected through a blend of NLP and named entity recognition, which is an essential and functional aspect of this application and can be conducted with the help of in-domain and cross-domain analysis [14].

Although several techniques are available, basically three techniques are used in this process. Rule-based techniques are where entities are identified using predefined rules or patterns. Mapping functions provide predictions where statistical methods are used and probabilities are calculated simultaneously. Different algorithms are used in neural networks (NNs) where layer architectures solve relatively tricky problems on large data sets. Ambiguities or variations in different languages often make implementation difficult. Domain-specific knowledge, context modeling, and multi-task learning can be used to overcome the issues by using Named Entity Recognition as a technique. Methods like Precision, Recall, and F-Score are used to measure the performance of these applications.

16.2.3 Chatbots and Virtual Assistants

Chatbots and virtual assistants are some of the most critical applications used in NLP, whose primary function is to substitute the relationship between the user and the natural language and by substituting the relationship to assist in achieving the desired results through the exchange of various performance information and collaboration. The use of this application is so weighty that 17% of the entire production in the United States of America is being contributed by chatbots and virtual assistants [15]. It is an AI-based system through which it becomes much easier to achieve desired results simply, in less time, with expected accuracy, and without external help. By simply typing text or listening to a specific language, the system can create a much more beautiful interaction with the user and consequently perform appropriate actions to provide effectual output in terms of input. Due to the widespread technology and the prevalence of different languages, the trend of using this system has increased a lot. As a result, almost all types of organizations now use this system to perform language-related tasks.

For example, students' inquiries during the discussion can be accumulated, and the structured data can be employed with the benefit of AI-based virtual assistants so that the college authority can control the placement activities relatively effortlessly [16]. This system only uses texts of different languages and can play a vital role in achieving the desired results by performing the required functions. By managing dialogues in different languages, it is easy to find out how a particular sentence is related to other sentences and how the words in the same sentence are related. This system also plays a vital role in improving performance using ML algorithms. Speech recognition is one of the central and vital parts of NLP, and this system can efficiently recognize speech and provide a response accordingly.

16.2.4 Text Classification

Text classification is an introductory task in NLP that separates heterogeneous text into categories based on content. The machine provides full support by extracting words from large amounts of text in large datasets so that those extraction techniques can be successfully used in the context of specific applications. Technology is blossoming, so some margins will increase the data transfer rate. For that, text classification in a proper way using NLP and ML is very beneficial [17]. From labeled data, interrelated data based on job type and the problem is segmented using different ML algorithms for easy access at the point of use. Supervised ML algorithms can distinguish similar words or phrases and are widely used in this task. The first step in this task is to preprocess the text and convert the processed text into a specific format.

These tasks include streaming, tokenization, and stop word removal, which results in an excellent dataset shape, mainly through dimensionality reduction. It is significant to find the essence of a particular word and prepare it to achieve the desired result by appropriately using it in a particular task, and this can be successfully done through feature extraction. Text classification is an essential aspect of any application related to NLP that can provide wished consequences as nicely and fluently as language-to-text classification is possible. For text classification, widely used ML algorithms such as Support Vector Machine, Decision Tree, Random Forest (RF), Naive Bayes Classifier, Regression mode, newly invented DL models like CNN, recurrent neural networks (RNNs), and transformers such as BERT are widely used as these algorithms can provide breathtaking influences to distinguish textual information from dissimilar languages [18]. In recent years, transfer learning methods have also been widely used for text classification tasks. Various evaluation metrics such as accuracy, precision, recall, and F-score are used to evaluate the model's performance in terms of text classification, and an attempt is made to maintain the balance between precision and recall, considering the specific application.

16.2.5 Language Translation

Different human races live in different places depending on the region and nature, and all have their own language to communicate with each other. However, that language will likely be helpful only to one's society or group. That is why language translation is so important for communicating with people who use other languages. To translate English sentences into Persian, a specific protocol-based system, namely quantum long short-term memory (Q-LSTM), was proposed by [19], where many quantum circuits sentences were used as input. Language translation is the automated process of NLP through which a particular language can be converted into another language, and consequently, a particular language is used as a communication medium. Translating languages can overcome linguistic barriers, establish global communication, and open up effective channels of information exchange. Translating a language does not only mean converting from one language to another by considering the grammatical aspects but also working with the emotions expressed in that language by reviewing the structure of a particular language. Suppose there is a moderate understanding of the structure of a particular language. In that case, enough knowledge can be gained about the words, nouns, pronouns, adjectives, verbs, adverbs, prepositions, and conjunctions used in that language. It is then possible to achieve the desired results after translating the language.

Every country has its own sign language; for the USA, it is American Sign Language (ASL); for the UK, it is British Sign Language (BSL); for Pakistan, it is Pakistan Sign Language (PSL), and so on and hence each sign languages has its structure of sentences and a big communication gap exists between these languages [12]. Different algorithms are used depending on different concerns in terms of translating languages. As chaos and diversity can be observed due to environmental characteristics among different languages, combining ML, DL, and neural networks (NN) can achieve significant success for better results. Among the various methods used, one of the most prominent and influential language translation methods used in NLP is Neural Machine Translation (NMT), where this technique uses a mapping function. Whereby a good correlation between the input used and the target language is substituted, resulting in specific and efficient results, as the NN can work with the most challenging patterns to produce optimal results.

16.2.6 Speech Recognition

Speech recognition, an essential application of NLP, refers to a technology through which a computer system extracts necessary information from a spoken language by observing and reviewing it. This conversion tool simultaneously works with the available features using computer science and computer systems, and signal processing in a particular language helps convert those words into new languages by using them thoroughly or finding out the underlying meaning of that language. Like many other day-to-day fields in the modern world, speech recognition is widely used in medical science and will acquire breathtaking results. A structured reporting (SR) system is strongly recommended in radiology diagnosis, as this system will provide free-text reporting (FTR), and the radiologists recommended it for better speech recognition [20]. If the speech recognition technology is automatic and robust enough in the working process, then the speed of the NLP procedure could be boosted to a greater extent in the diagnostic field [21]. The entire speech recognition process is divided into different parts, and the most important of these are processing the signal in terms of that particular speech, extracting features from the processed signal, and creating a model of the language to be converted. The collected signals are made into practical and usable input through signal processing; feature extraction separates the key components, such as sounds and syllables extracted from the signal from other less important features, and finds the underlying meaning in the context of the language to be converted. Words are then decoded to extract and form meaningful sentences. Two methods are mainly used to do this: statistical models and DL models. The HMM is traditionally considered the most efficient among the statistical models. However, since the discovery of DL models such as RNN and CNN, they have been widely used to increase performance and efficiency as they can automatically process complex patterns from audio data and provide good results. More specifically, some well-developed and well-established DL methods such as wav2vec2.0, Wav2vecU, WavBERT, and HuBERT are used extensively in the field of NLP because of their increased knowledge-capturing and better solution-providing skills [22]. Since the collected audio files can be in different languages and use different extensions, and the quality of the audio files can be both good and bad, it is elementary to find the most efficient algorithm and use it for the appropriate problem.

16.2.7 Text Summarization

Data has played the most crucial role in bringing about this unprecedented development of information technology in the 21st century. The abundance of data, the presence of various types of data for performing any task, the description of data characteristics, and the use of data in appropriate situations have taken a unique form. However, data collected from various sources is only sometimes valid for execution. Most of the time, there is less necessary and irrelevant data among those data, which hinders the performance and even reduces the model's performance. Text summarization is the method of NLP through which only necessary and effective words or phrases are found from the text used in a specific language in terms of specific performance, and unnecessary data is excluded from the dataset by summarizing. Due to the exclusion of noncontroversial data, the model's efficiency increases, and the desired results can be achieved by using relatively less time.

Text summarization is divided into two main parts based on methodological and work scope judgments: Extractive and Abstractive Summarization. An extractive summarization isolates a particular sentence or phrase from the original language and creates a new summary. This method isolates the most important, relevant, and influential sentences based on the relevance and significance of the problem statement. The method finds the most critical sentences using sentence scoring, graph-based ranking methods, and ML methods to determine the importance of a particular sentence. For example, video summarization is a process in which the video file is first converted into an audio file. After that, the audio file is converted into a text file, a high-quality text-based summary full of all critical information captured from the video file, and an extractive-video-summarizer process is proposed by [23] where the state-of-the-art ML models are used.

On the other hand, the abstractive summarization method creates new sentences whose summary is related to the original sentence, but the main sentence is no longer used in this summary. The main task of this method is to create new sentences based only on meaning, properties, nature, and type of function. To increase the significance of the text summary, abstractive text summarization plays an integral role, as with the use of the seq2seq concept from the TensorFlow Python library, DL-based data augmentation is used here and provides satisfying results which are evaluated with (BLEU) criterion [24]. This approach summarizes various advanced techniques because it is valuable and practical for solving relatively tricky problems.

16.2.8 Sentiment Analysis

SA, also known as sentiment or opinion mining, is considered one of NLP's most critical applications, considering the usage requirements and scope. The first and foremost important task of SA is to find out the sentiment existing in the text in terms of a particular language. The massive increase in information on the Internet, including reviews of various social media products, education, medicine, agriculture, and online discussions, has fueled the trend of researching SA in many areas. Different languages use different words and have different meanings. It is critical to review the different tones used in the language, evaluate them, extract the given meaning from a particular text through sentiment, and provide appropriate information through proper evaluation in its context. Through SA, these tasks are possible to do quite easily. Although the nature of language is diverse and there are many conventions of usage, sentiment is generally divided into three main categories: positive, negative, and neutral.

As sentiments are either positive, negative, or neutral, and on distinct scales, may be very bad, bad, favorable, sound, or very good, in these circumstances, the SA task can be treated as a classification task in the ML method where SA algorithms can be used to improve every type of customer services [25]. Words used in a language come under positive sentiment if they have a positive meaning, negative sentiment if they have a negative meaning, and neutral sentiment if that word can find neither positive nor negative meaning. The words are then divided and arranged according to the score. The conversion from one language to another can be done as beautifully as the words in any language can be incorporated into these three types of sentiments. The ambiguity of different languages used by different people is the main reason for working with SA. Due to this added complexity, as numerous languages are available worldwide, researchers emphasize using combinational systems where rule-based, ML, and DL systems work together to make the best effort for sentiment prediction and achieve the desired results.

16.3 Background Studies in Sentimental Analysis

Among the diverse applications operated in NLP, SA is one of the most critical applications, and it is much more comfortable to perform tasks and accomplish expected results in the context of a respective disease. Only by utilizing precise sentiments and effectively monitoring the feedback from the patient can we make appropriate decisions.

Sarcasm is a headache for the internet user, and its availability in any textual data is a significant threat to obtaining maximum efficiency in the SA task. In these circumstances, a DL with NLP-enabled SA (DLNLP-SA) techniques is being proposed by [26], where the authors perform with sarcasm classification by which one can effortlessly notice the occurrence of sarcasm in a given data and skillfully categorize them with the help of the input value. For performance evaluation of the DLNLP-SA model, the authors use the News Headlines Dataset, and the results demonstrate that the suggested method dominates the existing approaches. The COVID-19 Twitter dataset is used by [27], where the authors talked about dissimilar types of applications that are enormously used in SA in distinct business fields. As data is increasing with rapid growth, the authors focus on big data and how this data can improve the performance of SA in real-world scenarios from a business perspective. Expressing opinions during the COVID-19 pandemic on social media, such as Twitter, expanded significantly, enabling analysis of human psychology.

An optimization method, namely Marine Predator Optimization with NLP for Twitter SA (MPONLP-TSA), was proposed by [28], which is an SA process and MPO algorithm is used to do hyperparameter tuning optimally, and the tuning process sweetens the classification accuracy of the proposed model over the contemporary strategies. The mental health of a human being can be predicted with the help of the SA, and the author [29] proposed a model that uses the NLP techniques so that they can investigate different types of expressions and sentiments that are related to human manifestation. Detached ML techniques are used here to extract the feature set from the input data, and the extracted features are the key components to analyze mental health. Mental health also affected the PhD scholars by a considerable margin, as a survey says that at least 86% of PhD students in the UK encounter some unhappiness, anxiety, and nervousness, which is visible in their social media posts and hence the author [30] uses social media to build a dataset for the Pakistani PhD scholar. Among the 5,096 posts, 46.7% are anxiety-related, 12.6% are depression related, and 40.7% are mental health levels posts. For checking out the mental health status of the student, ML methods like SVM, ANN, and RF are used, and results show that 59.3% of students have health issues.

Turkish language and different ML techniques are used here, and an SA-based task is performed where the text data are collected from Twitter [31]. A dataset was constructed by using different types of tweets in the Turkish language regarding the COVID-19 pandemic, and the outcomes of the tweets were positive, negative, and neutral. The process obtained 87% accuracy in the test data, and simultaneously, for the sample dataset, the process obtained 4% accuracy. SA will also perform sufficiently in the Brazilian Portuguese language, where the author [32] operates a combination of five separate NLP tasks and three distinct ML classifiers for evaluating the SA in Portuguese text and the results illustrate that dissimilar combination will influence the predictive performance.

A novel ontology-based NLP method is presented by [33], using DL-oriented feature extraction and classification techniques. For the feature extraction process, sentiment-based text was utilized, and the extraction process was carried out with the help of the famous Markov model-based auto-feature encoder (MarMod-AuFeaEnCod). The authors are using Twitter and Facebook ontology-based SA datasets where the method accomplished 98% accuracy, 95% precision, 93% recall, 91% F-1 score, 88% RMSE, and 70.2% loss curve in the Twitter dataset. At the same time, the method performed 96% accuracy, 92% precision, 94% recall, 91% F-1 score, 77% RMSE, and 68.2% loss curve in the Facebook dataset. The term SA is now enormously used in social media as the number of internet users and the online activities of those users have increased favorably. People now often share their thoughts or opinions on social media like Facebook, Twitter, Instagram, etc., and the authors use the

Twitter dataset to conduct a study covering miscellaneous approaches in social media for SA [34].

Approaches like Naive Bayes Classification and Support Vector Classification (SVC) are used where the SVC method performs better than the other state-of-the-art classifiers. After surveying the social media and other related data, the authors [35] proposed a novel architecture for extracting the data and an identical model using the Lambda Architecture to predict the mental condition of a given user. The mental state or condition of a given user can help to maintain mental health and also can take additional focus on the secretiveness and the solitariness of the data. With the help of social media and e-commerce platforms reviews which the end user posts, a Heuristic-based SA system is proposed by [36]. Cross Similarity Score (CSS) and Joint Similarity Score (JSS) are used here to subtract the statistical features among dissimilar types of keywords. Figure 16.2 represents the investigation of SA-related research papers published between 2019 and 2024.

CNN with Bidirectional Long Short-Term Memory (BiLSTM) is employed here, which permits the generation of an enhanced Galactic Swarm Optimization (IGSO) algorithm, and the IGSO algorithm ultimately helps to improve a hybridized model. Diverse social media websites like Facebook, WhatsApp, Twitter, etc., are utilized to construct big data, and a novel method for SA on Twitter data for dissimilar types of cloth products is proposed by [37] with use of Simulated Annealing incorporated with the Multiclass SVM (SA-MSVM) approach. SA-MSVM is a particular type of

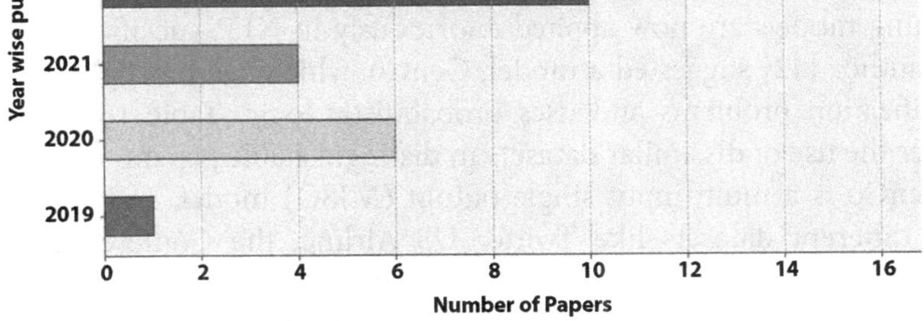

Figure 16.2 Breakdown of research papers between 2019 and 2024.

hybrid heuristic method that can select and, at the same time, classify text-based sentimental words. After implementing the SA-MSVM method in MATLAB, they show that it acquires 96.34% accuracy, which is better than the state-of-the-art SVM method.

A method for evaluating a person's facial expression when buying a product regarding a specific brand in a supermarket is proposed by [38]. That person's emotions bloomed in the face during the purchasing time after evaluating the product. Hence, after seeing the buyer's expression, the seller can provide feedback on the products and ensure the best-selling product requirement. SA recreates a crucial role in customer reviews as users' feedback or reviews will be very influential in determining whether the product is satisfactory, whether the quality is as expected or needs to be enhanced, and many more. Hence, a hybrid classifier was developed by [39], where they used two-stage LSTM and SVM for the training purposes of the sentimental classes among the dataset, and the method acquired 92% accuracy, which was more satisfactory than the state-of-the-art methods. Packaging plays a significant role in maintaining the quality of any product, and the author has proposed a new method to maintain the quality of packaging by considering customer reviews [40]. Any packaging has to undergo miscellaneous physical tests before it reaches the customer, and only after passing all the tests is the packaging used. SA is used here, and this task is carried out by considering the customers' positive and negative reviews. By using SA, it is possible to quickly understand how a particular packaging is performing, how long it lasts, and what can be done to improve the quality of the packaging.

Aspect-based SA is a process in NLP by which the input given from a dataset is broken into aspects that are nothing but the most essential features of the dataset. With the help of these aspects alongside the CNN architecture, a model is proposed for performing the SA tasks in Twitter data [41]. In contrast, CoRank, a graph-based ranking model, deducts unwanted or irrelevant data. The proposed model achieves 94.52% accuracy in the SA task and outperforms the other NN methods. Generative learning models are now applied enormously in NLP, specifically in SA. The author [42] suggested a model, GenCo, which can be applied to text classification problems and uses probabilistic logic. Table 16.1 demonstrates the use of dissimilar datasets in distinguishable papers.

GenCo is a multi-input single-output (MISO) model, and the model uses different datasets like Twitter US Airline, the Conference Paper, and the SMS Spam, where it achieved 98.40%, 89.90%, and 99.26% accuracy, respectively. Interactive SA is a scheme by which the sentiment changes between a conversation can be discovered, and the author [43]

Table 16.1 Comparison of distinguishable datasets utilized in distinct articles (**Y** denoted Yes and **N** denoted No).

Study	Year	News headlines dataset	Fake news detection datasets	LIAR dataset	SentimentSet (Balli 2021)	Ontology-based twitter dataset	Ontology-based Facebook dataset	Twitter dataset	COVID-19 twitter dataset	NLPCC2014 dataset	Weibo dataset	SMS spam dataset	Twitter US airline dataset	Conference paper dataset
C. M. Tsai [14]	2023	N	Y	Y	N	N	N	N	N	N	N	N	N	N
A. R. W. Sait & M. K. Ishak [26]	2023	Y	N	N	N	N	N	N	N	N	N	N	N	N
C. Balli *et al.* [31]	2022	N	N	N	Y	N	N	N	N	N	N	N	N	N
D. K. Jain *et al.* [33]	2024	N	N	N	N	Y	Y	N	N	N	N	N	N	N
V. Tandon & R. Mehra [34]	2023	N	N	N	N	N	N	Y	N	N	N	N	N	N
S. M. Srinivasan *et al.* [27]	2021	N	N	N	N	N	N	N	Y	N	N	N	N	N
M. Kanipriya *et al.* [41]	2020	N	N	N	N	N	N	Y	N	N	N	N	N	N
B. Zhang *et al.* [45]	2022	N	N	N	N	N	N	N	N	Y	Y	N	N	N
C. P. Thamil Selvi & R. PushpaLaksmi [37]	2023	N	N	N	N	N	N	Y	N	N	N	N	N	N
T. Vaiyapuri *et al.* [28]	2023	N	N	N	N	N	N	N	Y	N	N	N	N	N
Z. E. Ekolle & R. Kohno [42]	2023	N	N	N	N	N	N	N	N	N	N	Y	Y	Y

represents an informal database, ScenarioSA, which helps with interactive SA. Interactive SA is also functional in text sentiment classification as it produces the expected result. Hence, the author [44] presented a novel Interactive Dual Attention Network (IDAN) approach with contextual semantics and sentimental tendency knowledge from a given text.

A novel SA model was proposed by [45], the name of which is MoLeSy, where they use three NNs, and their output vectors are attached. The model employs the CNN model, long short-term memory (LSTM) networks, and fully connected dense NNs as grammatical channels. Widely exploited datasets like NLPCC2014, Douban movie reviews dataset, Weibo, and hotel are being utilized, and in these circumstances, the proposed MoLeSy method supplied the best interpretation regarding the state-of-the-art algorithms. Chatbots can support the user by which the user employs different types of inputs like voice or text, and after finishing the NLP process, the demanded response is generated. Finding the end users' requirements at the time of digital conversion is the most formidable task in Chatbots.

Hence, the author [46] suggests a model that can respond immediately using Bi-directional RNN with a Fuzzy Naïve Bayes classifier (BRNN-FNB). As this system is an SA-based system that performs with AI's help, it can interact accurately with the end user and achieve 93% accuracy using the Seq-to-Seq technique and 92% accuracy without using the Seq-to-Seq technique. Data is only sometimes clean as it is almost always noisy. A generalized SA-based model is proposed by [47], where they handle the noisy data out of Vocabulary Words (OOV) and work in the sentimental loss available in the reviews data. The Bi-directional Encoder Representation from Transformers (BERT) based Convolution Bi-directional RNN (CBRNN) model can work with the syntactic and semantic information from a given text, and the contextual vectors are departed in the NN.

Music is part and parcel of modern life, and the author [48] represents a model that is a music recommendation system that operates the SA process to recommend music with the usefulness of the NLP. The method uses dissimilar AI tools like Word2Vec for word vectorization and NLP for recognizing sentimental information, achieving 80% overall accuracy. In the field of NLP, SA also plays a vital role in the movie industry by providing public opinion in positive, negative, and neutral sentiments. An SA process regarding the movie review is presented by [49], where an ML model was built with the help of different classifiers like Naïve Bayes, Logistic Regression (LR), and SVM. After evaluating dissimilar evaluation metrics like accuracy, precision, recall, and F1-score, the result shows that SVM performs better at 73% accuracy.

16.4 Processes Needed for Sentimental Analysis

NLP is a breakthrough invention for dealing with linguistic problems and replacing conversational communication between people of different languages. There are different types of applications in NLP, and each application follows specific rules for executing and collecting results. How a particular application will work, what kind of data it will work with, what kind of results can be expected in terms of what data, and how effective methods can be used to replace communication after gathering the desired results depends on the nature and design characteristics of that particular application. The ability to process accurately is critical for all applications of NLP, including sentiment analysis.

Processes are different methods or techniques that achieve natural language data understanding capabilities and will be very influential for the implication of sentiment analysis. Different processes are used in different contexts to achieve understanding, to cut out "unnecessary" data from the data set, to find less critical data, and to extract accurate and actionable information from the data. It is almost impossible to achieve the desired results if the process cannot use the data correctly and effectively in the context of a particular application. So, observing which methods a particular process can perform and which give the best results is essential. Consequently, the processes to use as an SA application and how to use them are discussed below.

16.4.1 Tokenization

The process of dividing an existing text into more minor elements or parts is called tokenization, and each part obtained after splitting is called a token. The primary purpose of creating tokens using tokenization within a given text is to find the different phrases used in different languages and to make them useful for later use by finding responses. The more well-defined and well-planned it is possible to separate tokens from a given text, the better it is to translate that language into the desired result. A token is a sequence of characters with a particular meaning that will be applicable in translating different languages. Figure 16.3 defines the distinctive working flow of the sentimental analysis procedure in NLP.

Tokens are the most crucial information for the system, and they will directly connect to the model's performance when assessing SA.

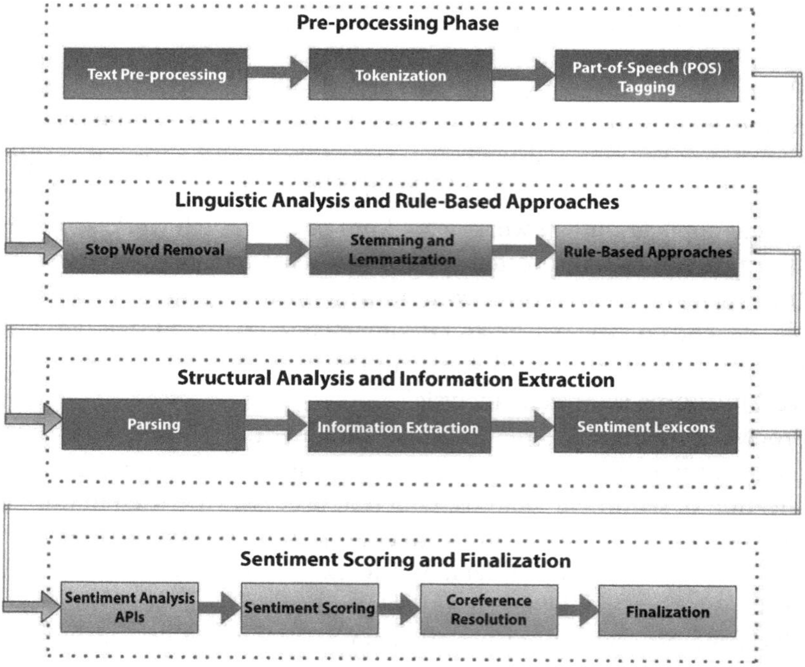

Figure 16.3 Typical working flow of sentimental analysis process.

Examples of tokens can be a word, a punctuation mark, a symbol, a comma, a semicolon, or anything. In the first step of tokenization, "unnecessary" or extraneous tokens are pruned and discarded. Individual tokens are then extracted from the text, and different algorithms have been developed for this task based on the output and input text. Better results can be easily achieved if the algorithm collects only the most essential tokens while discarding irrelevant and less important ones. The essential tokenizations among many are word tokenization, sentence tokenization, and subword tokenization. The critical points of tokenization are as follows:

- Segmentation of text into miniature units, which can be anything.
- Constructing the vocabulary in the text so that the meaning of the language will be fruitful.
- Handle the ambiguity issues between the texts if they arise.

16.4.2 Part-of-Speech (POS) Tagging

Part-of-speech tagging is a process used in NLP to categorize the data contained in a text. Due to linguistic differences and variations, different text types are encountered when performing NLP tasks. Because of the variety and diversity of texts, texts are distinguished using appropriate and significant conventions when working in different linguistic contexts. The principal reason for proper segregation is that every small part can be used correctly, and the desired result can be achieved. Each piece of data has to be leveled based on similar parts of speech, such as nouns, pronouns, adjectives, verbs, adverbs, conjunctions, interactions, etc. When used in a well-organized way to perform their tasks, each component can produce meaningful results in any language and application.

Different models are being used for part-of-speech tagging, and depending on the variety of languages and types of tasks, these models can provide better results in terms of problem and language-specific performance. Speech tagging can be done using rule best models, statistical models, or a combination of both. Each model has its rules, and only in terms of those rules can the models provide the most acceptable results. The most widely used parts of speech tagging, among many, are the Hidden Markov Model (HMM) and neural network base models, such as Recurrent Neural Networks (RNNs) and Convolutional Neural Networks (CNNs). Among the various critical points of parts of speech tagging, the most important ones are:

- Need to understand the syntax and the structure of a given text properly.
- Extraction of the features is unavoidable for every NLP application.
- Provide exact guidelines to understand the semantic understanding of the text.

16.4.3 Stemming and Lemmatization

Due to the variety of languages, it is more difficult to understand the types of words used in a particular sentence. Different types of words refer to which words are original and which words are derived from other words to form sentences. Finding only the keywords from a sentence using a proper and well-planned method is possible. In that case, it is possible to achieve good results in applications for any language with very little expenditure of time and energy. Stemming and lemmatization are two well-known processes that reduce a word to its base form, that is, to convert a modified word into a central word. This technology is used to retrieve specific information from a sentence or to increase the effectiveness or acceptability of a sentence. Only the base words can be found from the various parts of speech used, or the original words can replace the transformed words by following some rules and regulations; then, it is easy to get a good idea about the main content of the sentences by collecting data from the existing sentences. Stemming does its job by using prefixes and suffixes.

On the other hand, the lamination work depends on the basis and characteristics of the original word. Both approaches have pros and cons depending on the wording of the sentence and the targeted outcome. Nevertheless, in terms of time and energy, the lamination process is relatively expensive because it uses a whole dataset to perform the task. Key points regarding the stemming and lemmatization are:

- Try to normalize the text into words from every sentence.
- Reduce the computational complexity and boost the processing speed.
- Because of the preferred information retrieval, the model's simplicity is gained.

16.4.4 Parsing

One of the easiest ways to gain adequate knowledge of a particular language is to review relationships through a close observation of the structure of sentences produced by that language. Understanding the structure of a particular sentence and the interrelationship of the words within it is essential to understanding why a sentence is formed, how it is formed, what is meant by that sentence, and how the previous and subsequent sentences relate to that sentence. *Parsing* is a process, which is also called syntactic analysis, a method of NLP that analyses a particular sentence's structure and how the sentence's elements are related.

Once structural features and relationships are found, they can be easily usable in future research. Different types of parsing are used to perform different tasks, considering sentence structure, interrelationships, types of words in the sentence, and the relevance of sentence meaning. However, parsing is primarily divided into two categories, namely constituency parsing and dependency parsing. Phrases like nouns, pronouns, prepositions, etc., are built by the breakdown of a sentence in constituency parsing.

Nevertheless, a directed graph is present where the nodes and edges are in a relationship in the dependency parsing. Although parsing plays a vital role for almost all types of languages in terms of desired results, at the same time, parsing sometimes fails to provide the desired consequences due to linguistic issues and variations between languages and sometimes increases the complexity of the model to a large extent to provide the expected outcomes which ultimately ends the process without giving good impacts. The essential factors regarding parsing are:

- Find out the grammatical structure of a given sentence.
- Use the grammatical rules and construct a syntax tree for better representation.
- After extracting information from sentences, try to find specific pieces from there.

16.4.5 Stop Word Removal

Due to linguistic multiplicity, different types of words are used in different languages to form a particular sentence, which requires different types of words that make the sentence meaningful and help to express ideas correctly by connecting with other sentences. All these sentences contain enough unnecessary or less necessary and irrelevant words, and these prevent the substitution process of another language or deal with a particular application of a particular language. So effectively, if all these unnecessary words can be removed from the sentence, then the model's performance can be increased to a great extent. At the same time, the desired result can be achieved in less time and less energy waste. Stop word removal is a vital, well-known, and necessary process in NLP. By using this process, words that have little or no importance in the context of a sentence are eliminated. For example, prepositions, conjunctions, and pronouns are used in sentences to express a sentence correctly.

However, they do not carry important information for language processing, but they provide proper help in sentence formation and conveying the whole meaning of a sentence. The algorithm can provide better results because it is unnecessary and can cause irrelevant problems. At the same time, eliminating such confusing words efficiently reduces the algorithm's ambiguity and can quickly return results without creating complex relationships. Examples of some common stop words used in English sentences are the, and, or, but, a, an, in, of, etc. The NLTK stop word list is the most common method for stopping word removal. The primary reasons for using the stop word are as follows:

- Increase efficiency by preprocessing the text and realizing unnecessary words in a sentence.
- In SA, interpretation of the text will be influenced to a great extent.
- It is very beneficial for customization purposes in domain-specific analysis.

16.4.6 Rule-Based Approaches

Working with different varieties and mixtures of language requires specific rules and regulations to be followed to achieve the desired results, as different languages have different formation processes, and different words are used in different formations to construct sentences. Using those developed rules correctly is essential when creating and researching any language. The rules for researching a particular language are fixed through scrutiny. If the rules are correct and well-organized, converting one language into another is facilitated. Rule-based approaches are specialized analysis processes in NLP that consist of pre-defined grammatical and syntactical rules to analyze the data, diagnose it, and act on it by using it. It can contribute significantly to any text analysis due to different patterns in existing rules. Linguists and NLP experts set these rules where syntax and grammar are used as needed. Since the formation process differs from language to language and different words have different meanings in the context of a particular language depending on the presentation, those rules are more important and work better in finding results for any particular language. For example, if rules are created to find named entities, then the process can easily classify names based on the names of people, place names, and organization names. These rules will work similarly for any entity other than name. However, due to linguistic differences, a particular named entity only applies to the rules used in that language. It will only be applicable in some cases for other languages. These rules often also use ML algorithms to find effective patterns if necessary. The foremost reason for using the Rule-based approach despite linguistic differences is as follows:

- Interpretability and transparency for any language and any applications will be increased.
- Explainability plays the most vital role.
- Because of its explainable nature, the complexity will be diminished hugely.

16.4.7 Coreference Resolution

For any language, several types of entities exist within a given text, including Person, Organization, Location, Date, Time, Percentage, Money, Quantity, Product, Event, and others. The first step in working with a text is identifying the relationships between similar entities by distinguishing them and discussing the next working step by substituting the relationships. If heterogeneous entities are present simultaneously, the model faces incredible difficulties in decision-making, which results in the model giving unexpected results. Coreference Resolution is an essential part of NLP through which the same entities or similar data in a text are linked by distinguishing them. The primary function of this process is to create coherence through correlation, communication skills, and consistency between corresponding data.

Correlated data is simultaneously positioned and prepared for the necessary operations and used in the next step in the fitting environment. A score is assigned to the correlated data by providing a threshold value, and pairs are created with the highest-scoring data. Again, this task can be done by identifying all existing entities in the data set and creating clusters of homogeneous data from those entries. The primary purpose of using a cluster is to bring similar data into a specific partition so that all the data can be used together for a specific task. Which method to use depends significantly on the existing data in the data set and the type of problem to be solved. Different prototypes are used depending on the type of problem and language, and the optimal model is found using considerable models. Coreference Resolution is employed for:

- It plays an integral role in summarizing text.
- Often, the text contains different types of ambiguous references, and it is used to deduct the ambiguity.
- Because of its scalable nature, the model's efficiency is also increased.

16.4.8 Sentiment Lexicons

The sentiment lexicon is an integral part of the NLP task that acts as a dictionary or database, and the words in it carry their polarity scores. This polarity score is mainly used to indicate the sentiment of the words, and the polarity score is divided into three types: positive, negative, and neutral. This polarity score is determined by using words in a sentence considering different contexts. SA is much more challenging because the same word has different meanings for a given language in different contexts. Hence, one has to be very careful while determining the polarity score. A manual process is followed while setting the sentimental lexicon for a particular word with the help of the researcher, and providing a score for each word using ML algorithms is another process.

A particular model can produce results as elegantly as expected if the score can deliver proper feedback for appropriate methods. Scoring the right way means figuring out which word is most important to a sentence and how best to express the sentiment score given that importance. Since the words can be sorted in terms of scoring and word variation, it is straightforward to find words based on these scores during any task. As a result, the time complexity is much less, and the complexity of the model can be reduced to numerous aspects. SentiWordNet is a widely used sentiment lexicon that assigns a sentiment score to the words in the WordNet and uses a numerical representation to assign this score. The most important findings from using the sentiment lexicon are:

- Sentimental labels help separate different types of words, such as positive, negative, or neutral.
- Extraction of the features for the SA model has taken place.
- Calculate the polarity of the words and provide information about the strength of the words for a given task.

16.4.9 Text Pre-Processing

Text processing plays a significant role in working with any NLP application and achieving the expected results in terms of functional text. Data is collected from different sources for performance and can be of different types depending on the source. Differences can be observed between data extracted from nature and generated data. As the source of data collection may be different, the nature of the data may be different, and the results achieved in terms of a particular application by using the extracted data are also different, so using the appropriate data and text by processing in a reasonable way will increase the performance of the model. Data used while working in a particular language may contain unknown text, relatively less important or irrelevant text, missing values, and multiple types of data in a particular dataset, which increases the complexity of the model and, consequently, the desired results may face obstacles.

Finding only the practical and most important words is essential for performing and achieving the desired function. Representing all words in use only with lowercase letters, splitting words into smaller units using tokenization, making the dataset usable by finding and removing different types of punctuation, finding and eliminating different types of Stop words, which increases the complexity of the model, creating appropriate tokens by converting numeric values, selecting correct words by spell checking so that it does not cause any problems later, removing various types of HTML tags used, etc., are the everyday preprocessing tasks in NLP. The most critical tasks considered in NLP preprocessing are:

- Dividing words into smaller units through tokenization.
- Remove Stop words and find the principal words from different categories of words.
- Convert existing numeric values to text by manipulating them.

16.4.10 Information Extraction

Text or data collected from any medium is only partially usable. As a result, important information needs to be monitored by following specific rules to obtain appropriate results from the existing data in the dataset. Information extraction (IE) is a technique used in NLP to automatically find organized information from unevenly distributed data. Finding correlated data with structured information is critical to achieving expected results with less energy and time wasted. Suppose correlated data can be randomly extracted from a dataset and partitioned set-wise by entity through IE. In that case, it becomes much easier to use them and observe changes and improvements in the results accordingly. IE can vary and yield results by adopting specific techniques based on the task and situation. For example, name entity recognition refers to extracting information in terms of a person's name, organization name, or place name, and name entity extraction does this by extracting information in terms of name.

Similarly, relationship extraction means substituting relations between related entities that carry the same or similar meaning. Coreference resolution is used when different expressions are considered the same entity. Event extraction refers to extracting information about various events, considering the actions of the individuals participating in the event, and reviewing their contributions to specific actions. The rule-based techniques and ML approaches are prevalent among the extraction techniques used. Different approaches are adopted depending on the problem type, nature, desired results, and surrounding environmental conditions. IE is more important than ever since there is no specific source from which to extract the data, and the abundance of data has increased the complexity of existing datasets. Hence, the principal reasons to use IEs are:

- Aiding performance by providing an organized structure to the dataset.
- Substitution of functional relationships provides greater flexibility and consequently eases implementation.
- Splitting words in terms of names is more important than other entities for almost all languages.

16.4.11 Sentiment Analysis APIs

The Sentiment Analysis API in the NLP process is a particular type of API used to collect and process sentiments used in different languages and automatically provide interpretations. The most significant function of this API is to detect emotional tone from text using various ML algorithms and distinguish positive, negative, or neutral tone section-wise by performance. This API works primarily by using supervised ML algorithms where large datasets are utilized to find underlying relationships and determine sentiment based on those relationships.

The easier it is to establish relationships between entries using the API, the more accessible and more elegant the subsequent steps to achieve the desired results will be. Even though the range of knowledge related to NLP is not much, just by using this API, it is straightforward to link the application considering the sentiment of a particular language, and the conversion task to another language becomes easy. Considering the type of problem and scope of work, some of the most widely used APIs are Google Cloud NLP API, Microsoft Azure Text Analytics API, and IBM Watson NLP API. The most important aspect of using these APIs is that less time is spent on thorough trial analysis, and fewer errors are made in achieving the expected consequences. Some of the indescribable benefits of using SA API are:

- It plays a vital role in increasing the performance and efficiency of the model.
- Data confidentiality is necessary in this growing technological world.
- Multilingual support allows working on different problems simultaneously to accomplish desired results in less time and with minor errors.

16.4.12 Sentiment Scoring

Many languages are used worldwide, and each language has some rules for sentence formation and expression of thoughts. The same word can have different meanings for different sentences and circumstances, and if certain words have different meanings, then using them correctly is one of the most critical steps to achieve the desired result. Sentiment score is significant for determining how a word is used, why, what meaning it carries, and how that particular meaning replaces the relationship with other words used in the sentence. Concerning scoring types, three types of sentiment scores are used to filter and differentiate words: positive, negative, and neutral. The words with the highest scores, i.e., those with the highest positive, negative, or neutral meaning, are at the top, and the lower-scored words are at the bottom in order.

By doing this, it is straightforward to understand how effective the words used in a sentence are for making decisions or expressing thoughts. Different methods are used to calculate the score using sentiment in terms of words, and the most important ones are rule-based systems, ML systems, and hybrid systems. In rule-based systems, scores are calculated by following specific keywords or patterns. ML systems mainly use supervised algorithms such as SVM, Naive Bayes, and different types of neural networks. Hybrid systems are a combination of these two systems. Since there is no dearth of languages used in the world, there is much variation within each language, and even the same language is used in different ways in different places, so appropriately using a sentiment score means making the conversion from one particular language to another easier, and a step forward in achieving desired results by using less energy. Some of the most important factors are:

- Scores derived from text data play an influential role in decision-making.
- Support automated task management for segmenting text data.
- Considering the context of e-commerce gives a better understanding of customer response and experience.

16.5 Conclusion

This tremendous advancement in technology has given unimaginable dimensions to various fields of AI, and NLP has played one of the leading roles in accomplishing this incredible success of AI. One of the principal justifications for the exponential increase in NLP is its incredible success, straightforward and well-organized use of data, and conducting the desired results with less energy consumption through proper usefulness in the workplace. This article reviews how the diverse applications of NLP can be valuable in different fields, specifically regarding what kind of breakthroughs can be achieved in the medical field using SA. Biomedical research is now one of the paramount parts of medical science, and the discussion here is predominantly about how well biomedical research can be performed if it is possible to work by observing and reviewing various types of feedback from patients and using the correct and effective methods of SA.

The mixture of sentiments from the patient, which primarily depends on the patient's physical condition, constitution, lifestyle, diet, and environmental characteristics, can significantly reduce the illness if proper action planning is done and the sentiments are divided into the correct categories and used for appropriate action. In time, any additional significant problem can be solved flexibly by wasting less energy, which can be crucial in achieving incredible achievements for biometric research and human civilization employing SA. As feedback from different people varies across environments, regions, lifestyles, and ethnicities, collecting patient feedback accurately and efficiently to develop appropriate algorithms for correct problem-solving is now the most crucial task, which is somewhat complicated but possible.

Acknowledgment

I wish to thank Dr. Umesh Kumar Lilhore, my advisor, for providing the best suggestions to assist me with this work. His knowledge and practical suggestions supported me in preparing this study material and finalizing the article. I also thank Chandigarh University for collaborating with Dr. Umesh Kumar. Finally, I am happy to share the working results of the above subject, which communicates the review with a large audience.

References

1. Saha, S., Sarker, P.S., al Saud, A., Shatabda, S., Hakim Newton, M.A., Cluster-oriented instance selection for classification problems. *Inf. Sci.*, 602, 2022. doi: 10.1016/j.ins.2022.04.036.

2. Brighton, H. and Mellish, C., Advances in instance selection for instance-based learning algorithms. *Data Min. Knowl. Discov.*, 6, 2, 2002. doi: 10.1023/A:1014043630878.
3. Korteling, J.E.(H)., van de Boer-Visschedijk, G.C., Blankendaal, R.A.M., Boonekamp, R.C., Eikelboom, A.R., Human- versus Artificial Intelligence. *Front. Artif. Intell.*, 4, 2021. doi: 10.3389/frai.2021.622364.
4. Haenlein, M. and Kaplan, A., A brief history of artificial intelligence: On the past, present, and future of artificial intelligence. *Calif. Manage. Rev.*, 61, 4, 2019. doi: 10.1177/0008125619864925.
5. Khurana, D., Koli, A., Khatter, K., Singh, S., Natural language processing: state of the art, current trends and challenges. *Multimed. Tools Appl.*, 82, 3, 2023. doi: 10.1007/s11042-022-13428-4.
6. Galassi, A., Lippi, M., Torroni, P., Attention in Natural Language Processing. *IEEE Trans. Neural Netw. Learn. Syst.*, 32, 10, 2021. doi: 10.1109/TNNLS.2020.3019893.
7. Lauriola, I., Lavelli, A., Aiolli, F., An introduction to Deep Learning in Natural Language Processing: Models, techniques, and tools. *Neurocomputing*, 470, 2022. doi: 10.1016/j.neucom.2021.05.103.
8. Yadav, M. and Panvel, P.N.E.W., Data Analysis & Sentiment Analysis for Unstructured Data. *Int. J. Adv. Res. Comput. Sci. Software Eng.*, 2, 7, 2014.
9. Pribec, I., *et al.*, Efficient and Reliable Data Management for Biomedical Applications. *Methods Mol. Biol. (Clifton N.J.)*, 2716, 2024. doi: 10.1007/978-1-0716-3449-3_18.
10. Tom, T., *et al.*, Additive manufacturing in the biomedical field-recent research developments. *Results Eng.*, 16, 2022. doi: 10.1016/j.rineng.2022.100661.
11. Rishita, M.V.S., Raju, M.A., Harris, T.A., Machine translation using natural language processing. *MATEC Web Conferences*, 277, 2019. doi: 10.1051/matecconf/201927702004.
12. Khan, N.S., Abid, A., Abid, K., A Novel Natural Language Processing (NLP)–Based Machine Translation Model for English to Pakistan Sign Language Translation. *Cognit. Comput.*, 12, 4, 2020. doi: 10.1007/s12559-020-09731-7.
13. Xu, Y., Zhou, Z.Q., Zhang, X., Wang, J., Jiang, M., Metamorphic testing of named entity recognition systems: A case study. *IET Software*, 16, 4, 2022. doi: 10.1049/sfw2.12058.
14. Tsai, C.M., Stylometric Fake News Detection Based on Natural Language Processing Using Named Entity Recognition: In-Domain and Cross-Domain Analysis. *Electron. (Switzerland)*, 12, 17, 2023. doi: 10.3390/electronics12173676.
15. Agarwal, S., Agarwal, B., Gupta, R., Chatbots and virtual assistants: a bibliometric analysis. *Lib. Hi Tech.*, 40, 4, 2022. doi: 10.1108/LHT-09-2021-0330.
16. Ranavare, S.S. and Kamath, R.S., Artificial Intelligence based Chatbot for Placement Activity at College Using DialogFlow. *Our Heritage*, 68, 30, 2020.
17. Li, H. and Li, Z., Text Classification Based on Machine Learning and Natural Language Processing Algorithms. *Wireless Commun. Mobile Comput.*, 2022, 2022. doi: 10.1155/2022/3915491.

18. Kosiv, Y.A. and Yakovyna, V.S., Three language political leaning text classification using natural language processing methods. *Appl. Aspects Inf. Technol.*, 5, 4, 2022. doi: 10.15276/aait.05.2022.24.
19. Abbaszade, M., Salari, V., Mousavi, S.S., Zomorodi, M., Zhou, X., Application of Quantum Natural Language Processing for Language Translation. *IEEE Access*, 9, 2021. doi: 10.1109/ACCESS.2021.3108768.
20. Jorg, T., *et al.*, Efficient structured reporting in radiology using an intelligent dialogue system based on speech recognition and natural language processing. *Insights into Imaging*, 14, 1, 2023. doi: 10.1186/s13244-023-01392-y.
21. Ciampelli, S., Voppel, A.E., de Boer, J.N., Koops, S., Sommer, I.E.C., Combining automatic speech recognition with semantic natural language processing in schizophrenia. *Psychiatry Res.*, 325, 2023. doi: 10.1016/j.psychres.2023.115252.
22. Ahmed, S., ASER: Arabic Speech Emotion Recognition Employing Wav2vec2.0 and HuBERT Based on BAVED Dataset. *Trans. Mach. Learn. Artif. Intell.*, 9, 6, 2021. doi: 10.14738/tmlai.96.11039.
23. Mishra, P., Garg, K., Rathi, N., Video-to-Text Summarization using Natural Language Processing. *Int. J. Adv. Res. Science Commun. Technol.*, 2023. doi: 10.48175/ijarsct-9160.
24. Ilango, B., A machine translation model for abstractive text summarization based on natural language processing. *Sci. Temper*, 14, 03, 2023. doi: 10.58414/scientifictemper.2023.14.3.20.
25. Maradithaya, S. and Katti, A., Sentimental analysis of audio based customer reviews without textual conversion. *Int. J. Electr. Comput. Eng.*, 14, 1, 653–661, 2024. doi: 10.11591/ijece.v14i1.
26. Sait, A.R.W. and Ishak, M.K., Deep Learning with Natural Language Processing Enabled Sentimental Analysis on Sarcasm Classification. *Comput. Syst. Sci. Eng.*, 44, 3, 2023. doi: 10.32604/csse.2023.029603.
27. Srinivasan, S.M., Shah, P., Surendra, S.S., An approach to enhance business intelligence and operations by sentimental analysis. *J. Syst. Manage. Sci.*, 11, 3, 2021. doi: 10.33168/JSMS.2021.0302.
28. Vaiyapuri, T., *et al.*, Sustainable Artificial Intelligence-Based Twitter Sentiment Analysis on COVID-19 Pandemic. *Sustainability (Switzerland)*, 15, 8, 2023. doi: 10.3390/su15086404.
29. Verma, R., Nipun, Rana, N., Arora, R.K., Mental Health Prediction using Sentimental Analysis. *Int. J. Res. Appl. Sci. Eng. Technol.*, 11, 12, 2023. doi: 10.22214/ijraset.2023.57534.
30. Noreen, R., *et al.*, Unraveling the inner world of PhD scholars with sentiment analysis for mental health prognosis. *Behav. Inf. Technol.*, 2023. doi: 10.1080/0144929X.2023.2289057.
31. Balli, C., Guzel, M.S., Bostanci, E., Mishra, A., Sentimental Analysis of Twitter Users from Turkish Content with Natural Language Processing. *Comput. Intell. Neurosci.*, 2022, 2022. doi: 10.1155/2022/2455160.

32. de Oliveira, D.N. and Merschmann, L.H.C., Joint evaluation of preprocessing tasks with classifiers for sentiment analysis in Brazilian Portuguese language. *Multimedia Tools Appl.*, 80, 10, 2021. doi: 10.1007/s11042-020-10323-8.
33. Jain, D.K., Qamar, S., Sangwan, S.R., Ding, W., Kulkarni, A.J., Ontology-Based Natural Language Processing for Sentimental Knowledge Analysis Using Deep Learning Architectures. *ACM Trans. Asian Low-Resour. Lang. Inf. Process.*, 23, 1, 2024. doi: 10.1145/3624012.
34. Tandon, V. and Mehra, R., An Integrated Approach for Analysing Sentiments on Social Media. *Informatica (Slovenia)*, 47, 2, 2023. doi: 10.31449/inf.v47i2.4390.
35. Shah, A., Shah, R., Desai, P., Desai, C., Mental Health Monitoring using Sentiment Analysis. *Int. Res. J. Eng. Technol.*, 2020.
36. Ramshankar, N. and Joe Prathap, P.M., Automated sentimental analysis using heuristic-based CNN-BiLSTM for E-commerce dataset. *Data Knowl. Eng.*, 146, 2023. doi: 10.1016/j.datak.2023.102194.
37. Thamil Selvi, C.P. and PushpaLaksmi, R., SA-MSVM: Hybrid Heuristic Algorithm-based Feature Selection for Sentiment Analysis in Twitter. *Comput. Syst. Sci. Eng.*, 44, 3, 2023. doi: 10.32604/csse.2023.029254.
38. Bera, C., Adhav, P., Amati, S., Singhaniya, N., Product Review Based on Facial Expression Detection. *ITM Web Conferences*, 44, 2022. doi: 10.1051/itmconf/20224403061.
39. Londhe, A. and Rao, P. V. R. D. P., Incremental Learning based Optimized Sentiment Classification using Hybrid Two-Stage LSTM-SVM Classifier. *Int. J. Adv. Comput. Sci. Appl.*, 13, 6, 2022. doi: 10.14569/IJACSA.2022.0130674.
40. Esfahanian, S. and Lee, E., A novel packaging evaluation method using sentiment analysis of customer reviews. *Packag. Technol. Sci.*, 35, 12, 2022. doi: 10.1002/pts.2686.
41. Kanipriya, M., Krishnaveni, R., Bairavel, S., Krishnamurthy, M., Aspect based sentiment analysis from tweets using convolutional neural network model. *J. Adv. Res. Dyn. Control Syst.*, 12, 4, 2020. doi: 10.5373/JARDCS/V12I4/20201423.
42. Ekolle, Z.E. and Kohno, R., GenCo: A Generative Learning Model for Heterogeneous Text Classification Based on Collaborative Partial Classifications. *Appl. Sci. (Switzerland)*, 13, 14, 2023. doi: 10.3390/app13148211.
43. Zhang, Y., Zhao, Z., Wang, P., Li, X., Rong, L., Song, D., ScenarioSA: A Dyadic Conversational Database for Interactive Sentiment Analysis. *IEEE Access*, 8, 2020. doi: 10.1109/ACCESS.2020.2994147.
44. Zhu, Y., Zheng, W., Tang, H., Interactive Dual Attention Network for Text Sentiment Classification. *Comput. Intell. Neurosci.*, 2020, 2020. doi: 10.1155/2020/8858717.
45. Zhang, B., Zhang, H., Shang, J., Cai, J., An Augmented Neural Network for Sentiment Analysis Using Grammar. *Front. Neurorob.*, 16, 2022. doi: 10.3389/fnbot.2022.897402.

46. Dongbo, M., Miniaoui, S., Fen, L., Althubiti, S.A., Alsenani, T.R., Intelligent chatbot interaction system capable for sentimental analysis using hybrid machine learning algorithms. *Inf. Process. Manage.*, 60, 5, 2023. doi: 10.1016/j.ipm.2023.103440.
47. Tabinda Kokab, S., Asghar, S., Naz, S., Transformer-based deep learning models for the sentiment analysis of social media data. *Array*, 14, 2022. doi: 10.1016/j.array.2022.100157.
48. Medina, A.L.S., Leon, R.S., Calderón-Vilca, H.D., Music Recommender System based on Sentiment Analysis Enhanced with Natural Language Processing Technics. *Computacion y Sistemas*, 27, 1, 2023. doi: 10.13053/CyS-27-1-4006.
49. Sharma, H., Pangaonkar, S., Gunjan, R., Rokade, P., Sentimental Analysis of Movie Reviews Using Machine Learning. *ITM Web Conferences*, vol. 53, 2023. doi: 10.1051/itmconf/20235302006.

About the Editors

Umesh Kumar, PhD is a postdoctoral research fellow at the University of Louisiana Lafayette, United States with more than 19 years of teaching experience and eight years of research experience. He has published many articles in reputed, peer-reviewed national and international Scopus journals and conferences. Additionally, he has served as a keynote speaker and resource person for several workshops and webinars conducted in India.

Abhishek Kumar, PhD is an assistant director and associate professor in the Computer Science and Engineering Department at Chandigarh University, Punjab, India with more than 11 years of teaching experience. He has over 100 publications in reputed, peer-reviewed national and international journals, books and conferences and has authored/coauthored six books and edited 25 books published internationally. He has been a session chair and keynote speaker at many international conferences and webinars in India and abroad and is a member of various national and international professional societies in the field of engineering and research.

Narayan Vyas is a Technical Trainer for Research at Chandigarh University, India where he is actively involved in research and development in computer science and engineering. He has published many articles in reputed, peer-reviewed national and international Scopus journals and conferences. Additionally, he has served as a keynote speaker and resource person for several workshops and webinars conducted in India. He recently presented one article at the 2023 7th International Conference on Computing Methodologies and Communication and two articles at the 2023 International Conference on Artificial Intelligence and Smart Communication.

Sarita Simaiya, PhD is an associate professor at the Apex Institute of Technology, Department of Computer Science and Engineering, Chandigarh University, India. She has over 15 years of academic teaching experience and has published over 80 papers, presentations, and book chapters. Her research includes digital transformation technologies such as Cloud Computing, Health care, Artificial Intelligence (AI), Quantum Computing, Internet of Things (IoT), and Modal Learning.

Vishal Dutt is an accomplished principal research consultant at AVN Innovations with extensive experience in academia and industry. He is a renowned freelance trainer for Android and Google Cloud with over seven years of academic teaching experience. He has authored over 50 publications in well-known and peer-reviewed national and international journals, SCI and Scopus journals, conferences, and book chapters. He has contributed to the editorial process of two books and is currently working on three more. Vishal has been a keynote speaker and a valuable resource for many workshops and webinars across India.

Index

Also of Interest

Check out these related titles from Scrivener Publishing

Artificial Intelligence-Based System Models in Healthcare, Edited by A. Jose Anand, K. Kalaiselvi and Jyotir Moy Chatterjee, ISBN: 9781394242498. Artificial Intelligence-Based System Models in Healthcare provides a comprehensive and insightful guide to the transformative applications of AI in the healthcare system.

EXPLAINABLE MACHINE LEARNING MODELS AND ARCHITECTURES: Real-Time System Implementation, Edited by Suman Lata Tripathi and Mufti Mahmud, ISBN: 9781394185849.
This cutting-edge new volume covers the hardware architecture implementation, the software implementation approach, and the efficient hardware of machine learning applications.

Natural Language Processing for Software Engineering, Edited by Rajesh Kumar Chakrawarti, Ranjana Sikarwar, Sanjaya Kumar Sarangi, Samson Arun Raj Albert Raj, Shweta Gupta, Krishnan Sakthidasan Sankaran, and Romil Rawat, ISBN: 9781394272433. Discover how Natural Language Processing for Software Engineering can transform your understanding of agile development, equipping you with essential tools and insights to enhance software quality and responsiveness in todays rapidly changing technological landscape.

MACHINE LEARNING TECHNIQUES FOR VLSI CHIP DESIGN, Edited by Abhishek Kumar, Suman Lata Tripathi, and K. Srinivasa Rao, ISBN: 9781119910398. This cutting-edge new volume covers the hardware architecture implementation, the software implementation approach, and the efficient hardware of machine learning applications with FPGA or CMOS circuits, and many other aspects and applications of machine learning techniques for VLSI chip design.

Intelligent Green Technologies for Smart Cities, Edited by Suman Lata Tripathi, Souvik Ganguli, Abhishek Kumar, and Tengiz Magradze, ISBN: 9781119816065. Presenting the concepts and fundamentals of smart cities and developing "green" technologies, this volume, written and edited by a global team of experts, also goes into the practical applications that can be utilized across multiple disciplines and industries, for both the engineer and the student.

Hybrid Intelligent Optimization Approaches for Smart Energy: A Practical Approach, Edited by Senthilkumar Mohan, A. John, Sanjeevikumar Padmanaban, and Yasir Hamid, ISBN: 9781119821243. Written and edited by a group of experts in the field, this is a comprehensive and up-to-date description of current energy optimization techniques, such as artificial intelligence techniques, machine learning, deep learning, and IoT techniques and their future trends.

NANODEVICES FOR INTEGRATED CIRCUIT DESIGN, Edited by Suman Lata Tripathi, Abhishek Kumar, K. Srinivasa Rao, and Prasantha R. Mudimela, ISBN: 9781394185788. Written and edited by a team of experts in the field, this important new volume broadly covers the design of nano-devices and their integrated applications in digital and analog integrated circuits (IC) design.

DESIGN AND DEVELOPMENT OF EFFICIENT ENERGY SYSTEMS, Edited by Suman Lata Tripathi, Dushyant Kumar Singh, Sanjeevikumar Padmanaban, and P. Raja, ISBN 9781119761631. Covering the concepts and fundamentals of efficient energy systems, this volume, written and edited by a global team of experts, also goes into the practical applications that can be utilized across multiple industries, for both the engineer and the student.

Electrical and Electronic Devices, Circuits, and Materials: Technical Challenges and Solutions, Edited by Suman Lata Tripathi, Parvej Ahmad Alvi, and Umashankar Subramaniam, ISBN 9781119750369. Covering every aspect of the design and improvement needed for solid-state electronic devices and circuit and their reliability issues, this new volume also includes overall system design for all kinds of analog and digital applications and developments in power systems.

MODELING AND OPTIMIZATION OF OPTICAL COMMUNICATION NETWORKS, Edited by Chandra Singh, Rathishchandra R Gatti, K.V.S.S.S.S. Sairam, and Ashish Singh, ISBN: 9781119839200. *Modeling and Optimization of Optical Communication Networks* is a comprehensive and authoritative book that delves into the optical networks, principles, technologies, and practical applications of optical networks, equipping readers with the knowledge needed to design, implement, and optimize optical networks for various applications, from telecommunications to scientific research. With its comprehensive coverage and up-to-date insights, this book serves as an essential reference in the field of optical networks.

WIRELESS COMMUNICATION SECURITY: Mobile and Network Security Protocols, Edited by Manju Khari, Manisha Bharti, and M. Niranjanamurthy, ISBN: 9781119777144. Presenting the concepts and advances of wireless communication security, this volume, written and edited by a global team of experts, also goes into the practical applications for the engineer, student, and other industry professionals.

ADVANCES IN DATA SCIENCE AND ANALYTICS, Edited by M. Niranjanamurthy, Hemant Kumar Gianey, and Amir H. Gandomi, ISBN: 9781119791881. Presenting the concepts and advances of data science and analytics, this volume, written and edited by a global team of experts, also goes into the practical applications that can be utilized across multiple disciplines and industries, for both the engineer and the student, focusing on machining learning, big data, business intelligence, and analytics.

ARTIFICIAL INTELLIGENCE AND DATA MINING IN SECURITY FRAMEWORKS, Edited by Neeraj Bhargava, Ritu Bhargava, Pramod Singh Rathore, and Rashmi Agrawal, ISBN 9781119760405. Written and edited by a team of experts in the field, this outstanding new volume offers solutions to the problems of security, outlining the concepts behind allowing computers to learn from experience and understand the world in terms of a hierarchy of concepts.

MACHINE LEARNING AND DATA SCIENCE: Fundamentals and Applications, Edited by Prateek Agrawal, Charu Gupta, Anand Sharma, Vishu Madaan, and Nisheeth Joshi, ISBN: 9781119775614. Written and edited by a team of experts in the field, this collection of papers reflects the most up-to-date and comprehensive current state of machine learning and data science for industry, government, and academia.

MEDICAL IMAGING, Edited by H. S. Sanjay, and M. Niranjanamurthy, ISBN: 9781119785392. Written and edited by a team of experts in the field, this is the most comprehensive and up-to-date study of and reference for the practical applications of medical imaging for engineers, scientists, students, and medical professionals.

SECURITY ISSUES AND PRIVACY CONCERNS IN INDUSTRY 4.0 APPLICATIONS, Edited by Shibin David, R. S. Anand, V. Jeyakrishnan, and M. Niranjanamurthy, ISBN: 9781119775621. Written and edited by a team of international experts, this is the most comprehensive and up-to-date coverage of the security and privacy issues surrounding Industry 4.0 applications, a must-have for any library.

CYBER SECURITY AND DIGITAL FORENSICS: Challenges and Future Trends, Edited by Mangesh M. Ghonge, Sabyasachi Pramanik, Ramchandra Mangrulkar, and Dac-Nhuong Le, ISBN: 9781119795636. Written and edited by a team of world renowned experts in the field, this groundbreaking new volume covers key technical topics and gives readers a comprehensive understanding of the latest research findings in cyber security and digital forensics.

DEEP LEARNING APPROACHES TO CLOUD SECURITY, Edited by Pramod Singh Rathore, Vishal Dutt, Rashmi Agrawal, Satya Murthy Sasubilli, and Srinivasa Rao Swarna, ISBN 9781119760528. Covering one of the most important subjects to our society today, this editorial team delves into solutions taken from evolving deep learning approaches, solutions allow computers to learn from experience and understand the world in terms of a hierarchy of concepts.

MACHINE LEARNING TECHNIQUES AND ANALYTICS FOR CLOUD SECURITY, Edited by Rajdeep Chakraborty, Anupam Ghosh and Jyotsna Kumar Mandal, ISBN: 9781119762256. This book covers new methods, surveys, case studies, and policy with almost all machine learning techniques and analytics for cloud security solutions.

SECURITY DESIGNS FOR THE CLOUD, IOT AND SOCIAL NETWORKING, Edited by Dac-Nhuong Le, Chintin Bhatt and Mani Madhukar, ISBN: 9781119592266. The book provides cutting-edge research that delivers insights into the tools, opportunities, novel strategies, techniques, and challenges for handling security issues in cloud computing, Internet of Things and social networking.

DESIGN AND ANALYSIS OF SECURITY PROTOCOLS FOR COMMUNICATION, Edited by Dinesh Goyal, S. Balamurugan, Sheng-Lung Peng and O.P. Verma, ISBN: 9781119555643. The book combines analysis and comparison of various security protocols such as HTTP, SMTP, RTP, RTCP, FTP, UDP for mobile or multimedia streaming security protocol.

SMART GRIDS FOR SMART CITIES VOLUME 2: Real-Time Applications in Smart Cities, Edited by O.V. Gnana Swathika, K. Karthikeyan, and Sanjeevikumar Padmanaban, ISBN: 9781394215874. Written and edited by a team of experts in the field, this second volume in a two-volume set focuses on an interdisciplinary perspective on the financial, environmental, and other benefits of smart grid technologies and solutions for smart cities.

SMART GRIDS AND INTERNET OF THINGS, Edited by Sanjeevikumar Padmanaban, Jens Bo Holm-Nielsen, Rajesh Kumar Dhanaraj, Malathy Sathyamoorthy, and Balamurugan Balusamy, ISBN: 9781119812449. Written and edited by a team of international professionals, this groundbreaking new volume covers the latest technologies in automation, tracking, energy distribution and consumption of Internet of Things (IoT) devices with smart grids.

Printed in the USA/Agawam, MA
September 16, 2026

910661.128